The publisher gratefully acknowledges the generous support
of the Music Endowment Fund of the University
of California Press Foundation.

Funky Nassau ·

MUSIC OF THE AFRICAN DIASPORA

Guthrie P. Ramsey, Jr., Editor
Samuel A. Floyd, Jr., Editor Emeritus

Funky Nassau

*Roots, Routes, and Representation
in Bahamian Popular Music*

Timothy Rommen

UNIVERSITY OF CALIFORNIA PRESS
Berkeley   Los Angeles   London

CENTER FOR BLACK MUSIC RESEARCH
Columbia College Chicago

Parts of chapters 1 and 3 originally appeared in "'Come Back Home': Regional Travels, Global Encounters, and Local Nostalgias in Bahamian Popular Musics," by Timothy Rommen, from *Latin American Music Review* 20, no. 2 (2009): 159–83. Copyright © 2009 by the University of Texas Press. All rights reserved. Parts of chapters 4 and 6 originally appeared in Timothy Rommen, "Home Sweet Home: Junkanoo as National Discourse in the Bahamas," in *Black Music Research Journal* 19, no. 1 (1999): 71–92.

University of California Press, one of the most distinguished university presses in the United States, enriches lives around the world by advancing scholarship in the humanities, social sciences, and natural sciences. Its activities are supported by the UC Press Foundation and by philanthropic contributions from individuals and institutions. For more information, visit www.ucpress.edu.

University of California Press
Berkeley and Los Angeles, California

University of California Press, Ltd.
London, England

Center for Black Music Research
Columbia College Chicago

© 2011 by The Regents of the University of California

Library of Congress Cataloging-in-Publication Data

Rommen, Timothy.
    Funky Nassau : roots, routes, and representation in Bahamian popular music / Timothy Rommen. — 1st ed.
        p.   cm. — (Music of the African diaspora ; 15)
    Includes bibliographical references and index.
    ISBN 978-0-520-26568-4 (cloth : alk. paper) — ISBN 978-0-520-26569-1 (pbk. : alk. paper)
    1. Popular music—Bahamas—History and criticism.   I. Title.
    ML3486.B34R66   2011
    781.64097296—dc22   2010041702

Manufactured in the United States of America

20 19 18 17 16 15 14 13 12 11
10 9 8 7 6 5 4 3 2 1

For my parents

CONTENTS

ILLUSTRATIONS

FIGURES

MUSIC EXAMPLES

TABLES

It's about 10 AM on June 27, 2007. I'm sitting in a small Nassau restaurant with Fred Ferguson and Ronnie Butler, and we are discussing the current state of affairs for musicians in the Bahamas. Fred, my good friend, guitarist, producer, and a former member of the Baha Men, has arranged for this breakfast with Ronnie, who is often called the godfather of Bahamian entertainers. He no longer entertains large crowds at local nightclubs each week as he did back in the 1960s and '70s. In fact, the closest he gets to really performing these days is through invitations to participate in one-off shows. Live entertainment itself has largely become a thing of the past for Bahamian musicians, and Ronnie (along with many other musicians) has resigned himself to singing over tracks (i.e., without a live band) for small crowds at restaurants like this one. He blames the Bahamian government. "My government done fuck me. Print that! The government ain't worth shit since Stafford Sands" (Ronnie Butler, interview with the author, June 27, 2007).

Fred is laughing hysterically, fully agreeing with Ronnie, and I'm trying to figure out how to make sense of the comment. Sir Stafford Sands, after all, was a member of the (in)famous Bay Street Boys, the elite, predominantly white oligarchy that monopolized business and politics in the Bahamas until majority rule was won in 1967. The road to independence ran, quite literally, through the Bay Street Boys, and Sands was a powerful member of that political establishment. In other words, this politician was invested in retaining power, ideologically and financially committed to maintaining the status quo. And yet it is Sands who, perhaps more than anyone else, is responsible for growing the tourism industry, for offering opportunities to Bahamian musicians, and for recognizing the value of entertainment to the economy throughout the 1950s and '60s. To suggest, as Ronnie just has, however, that the Afro-Bahamian majority governments that succeeded the Bay Street Boys have failed to protect or promote local music and musicians—that it was better when Stafford Sands was in charge—is not exactly uncontroversial.

This is not the first I've heard of this line of reasoning. Ronald Simms and Fred Munnings Jr., the proprietors of Da Island Club (formerly the Rum Keg Room) at the Nassau Beach Hotel, agree.[1] Ronald, himself a trumpet player for and former bandleader of the Soulful Groovers, distinctly remembers a conversation between then prime minister Lynden O. Pindling and several representatives of the Bahamas Musicians and Entertainers Union (Ronald was serving as the union's secretary) in 1973. The issue of the day revolved around asking the government to enforce rules that required cruise ships to close down all shipboard entertainment while in port. The government was reticent to take that kind of action, knowing that ships could simply call on other ports where no such rules were in place. The government's inaction on this matter certainly damaged the Bahamian entertainment sector, but a reduction in ship traffic would have hurt another (and larger) constituency even more directly. The rationale was simple—pragmatic even: "There are more straw vendors than there are musicians" (Ronald Simms, interview with the author, June 5, 2006). While Pindling undoubtedly saw this decision as a compromise and even as a painful means of improving the quality of life for the greatest number of Bahamians (and perhaps also as an electoral equation that would serve his long-term interests), Ronald understood this turn of events as the surest sign that entertainment was in serious trouble in the newly independent nation. Looking back on that decision, Ronald still feels strongly that this was the beginning of the end for live music in the Bahamas.

An even more broadly drawn indictment of government policy with regard to musicians and entertainment comes in the form of a joke related to me by Ed Moxey, former minister of parliament for the Coconut Grove constituency. The setting for the joke is the Mona, Jamaica, campus of the University of the West Indies. "Every so often when a group of Bahamian youngsters was sitting down at a table, some Jamaican would pass and say, 'Name the country who blow up the culture!' And everybody in the place used to say, 'the Bahamas!'" (Moxey, interview with the author, August 11, 2007). According to Moxey, this was a standard joke during the months that followed a widely publicized event in Bahamian national life—the demolition of Jumbey Village, accomplished with the help of explosives in 1987. The cultural center called Jumbey Village was built between 1971 and 1973, yet shortly after independence in 1973, the government decided that it was no longer going to fund Jumbey Village, leading Moxey to openly protest that budget cut in parliament and eventually to resign from the

Progressive Liberal Party (PLP) in 1976. Jumbey Village, for its part, was left to languish and deteriorate until it was finally demolished in order to clear ground for a new national insurance building.

The story of Jumbey Village underscores both the sentiment expressed by Ronnie Butler and the rationale embedded in Pindling's remarks to Ronald Simms. Put somewhat bluntly, the government has repeatedly made decisions that relegate culture, the arts, musicians, and entertainers to a rather low position on the nation's list of priorities. But the struggle over Jumbey Village also stands as a marker of the real challenges faced by the newly independent Bahamas in the cultural realm, and this especially in an economic environment increasingly dependent upon tourism for its health. The funding for Jumbey Village was not merely pulled, but rather redirected toward funding a tourist attraction called Goombay Summer. The government was optimistic that Goombay Summer would provide for the continued development of the Bahamian economy while also promoting Bahamian culture. Pindling was convinced of this, arguing that Goombay Summer "would not only foster Bahamian cultural expression, but showcase its unique qualities to the wider world" (Craton 2002, 226).

Each of these recollections focuses on a set of themes that inform this book. For starters, they each foreground the challenging move from Crown Colony to postcolony, one of the central and defining moments in the life of the modern Bahamas. Music and musicians have, of course, both contributed to and been deeply affected by this journey to nationhood, and this book is, in large part, concerned with tracing the various roles that music has come to play in the Bahamian national imaginary throughout the second half of the twentieth century and into the present millennium. Second, economic factors also play a major role here, not least because each of these interactions traces along the seams of the tourist economy, highlighting those rough edges ordinarily silenced in favor of press releases celebrating, say, the completion of yet another phase of Atlantis, the massive resort hotel complex on Paradise Island.[2]

A final theme, made explicit in Ed Moxey's account but silently present in both other accounts, concerns the geographic and sociocultural interposition of the Bahamas between the United States and the rest of the Caribbean. This theme, configured in Moxey's recollection as an intentionally humiliating joke directed against Bahamians by other Caribbean nationals, indicates some of the antipathy that has historically marked the relationship between the Bahamas and its regional (especially its Anglophone Caribbean) neighbors. Ronnie Butler and Ronald Simms, moreover, have each experienced the joys and frustrations of living in a place where the popularity of North American and Caribbean musicians and musical styles, the local listening habits established through Caribbean and North American media flows, and the influx of deejay technologies and practices—also flowing from both directions—have profoundly affected in both positive and decidedly negative ways their creative horizons and livelihoods. The Bahamas' interpolation within the region takes physical, political, sociocultural, and economic shapes and stretches throughout the history of the archipelago, shaping Bahamian social imaginaries and Bahamian music in the process. All three themes, moreover, suggest that musicians have a unique perspective to contribute to any discussion of the political and economic aspects of Bahamian life—a perspective steeped in long contemplation of Bahamian culture and seasoned by the need to confront questions of representation in and through their artistic choices.

It is against this backdrop that I explore the musical articulations of Bahamianness offered by rake-n-scrape, goombay, and Junkanoo musicians, focusing attention on the ways these musical articulations (from the 1950s on) trace across, intersect with, and nuance the overarching themes introduced so poignantly in the conversations above. This book, then, is concerned with the insights music offers into places, politics, and economics (and vice versa) in the Bahamas. It is also about thinking through these issues with the musicians and entertainers who have each uniquely represented the Bahamas to the world and, more importantly, to Bahamians themselves.

Ronnie Butler and I sat down again a day after he had blasted away at the Bahamian government. During this conversation he told the story of his life in music and voiced many other concerns about the current state of entertainment in the Bahamas, among which the following lament stood out with special clarity: "I just think that after giving pretty much fifty years to my profession I feel I have a lot to say in terms of what I have seen, what it was as compared to what it is. They don't want to know it" (Ronnie Butler, interview with the author, June 28, 2007). Though Ronnie will undoubtedly find room to disagree with some of the conclusions I reach in the pages that follow, and though his voice is joined here by many others, this book reflects my deep desire to understand who sings the nation and how—to understand the musical practices that helped to shape and continue to inform Bahamian understandings of both self and nation (Butler and Spivak 2007). This much is certain: Ronnie has sung the nation.

ACKNOWLEDGMENTS

This book has developed in large part through the generosity and kindnesses extended to me by Bahamian entertainers, many of whom I have come to count as "true-true" friends during the years I have spent encountering the roots and routes of Bahamian music. Tinkle and Melody Hanna, in particular, welcomed me into their home during my first fieldwork trip to the Bahamas back in 1997. They introduced me around and encouraged me to consider a long-term research project in addition to the single article I was working on at the time (Rommen 1999). As it turned out, I would not return to the Bahamas until the winter of 2004, by which time I was ready to begin just the kind of project that Tinkle and Melody had envisioned some seven years earlier. Since 2004, I have stayed at the Hannas' home on numerous occasions while conducting fieldwork in Nassau, and I am deeply grateful to both of them for their friendship, for their enthusiasm, and for encouraging me to entertain the possibility of this book in the first place.

In the years since 2004—the years during which I have researched and written this book—I have come to count many other Bahamian musicians and entertainers as collaborators and friends. Foremost among them are Fred Ferguson, Ronald Simms, Ronnie Butler, Raphael Munnings, Ed Moxey, Isaiah Taylor, Obie Pindling, Charles Carter, Ancient Man, Nicolette Bethel, and Chris and Yonell Justilien. Many thanks go out to each of them for sharing with me their time and their stories, their insights, and their concerns. This book is, in large part, an attempt to do at least some measure of justice to representing the multiple and richly nuanced ways of understanding Bahamian music that emerge out of their collective experiences. Special thanks, however, are due to Fred and Ronald.

Their consistent and far-reaching assistance, along with their deep, personal engagement with the project, have enriched this book immeasurably. Their friendship, moreover, has enriched my life in ways for which I am truly thankful.

This project could not have emerged without the generous support of several institutions. The Center for Black Music Research awarded me a Rockefeller Resident Fellowship during 2004–5, which provided me with research leave and afforded me the opportunity to begin the fieldwork for this project. During 2006–7, a Mellon Faculty Research Grant at the Penn Humanities Forum provided an ideal intellectual atmosphere within which to continue thinking about and begin writing this book. In addition, the University of Pennsylvania awarded me a University Research Grant in 2007–8, which enabled me to purchase recording equipment and cover my continuing fieldwork expenses. I am grateful to all of these institutions, for without the generous financial and intellectual assistance I received from these sources, I would not have been able to complete this project.

Friends and colleagues have, of course, made writing this book a thoroughly enjoyable experience, and several deserve special thanks. I am deeply grateful to Ken Bilby for the many hours he spent in conversation with me during the process of researching and writing this book. His insights and suggestions have been invaluable to me over the years. I also thank Phil Bohlman, Gage Averill, Jocelyne Guilbault, Michael Largey, Mark Butler, Guy Ramsey, Mimi Sheller, and Rich Jankowsky for the various ways they have each contributed to making this a better book. I have benefited throughout this process from the expertise and care with which Mary Francis handles her editorial responsibilities at the University of California Press. I thank her for her dedication to this project, and I am grateful to Eric Schmidt, Jacqueline Volin, and the entire production staff at the press for their careful attention to the project. Many thanks also to copy editor Mary Ray Worley and indexer Jessamyn Doan.

I am the beneficiary of the loving attentions of three daughters, who have all had to make sacrifices over the past several years as I researched and wrote this book. But my daughters have also, each in her own way, gently ensured that I remained engaged in the regular rhythms of family life. Natalia, Arianna, and Anika, thanks for living in the moment and insisting that I live in the moment too. My wife, Kim, has been my constant companion and partner on this journey, and I continue to encounter her anew with each new itinerary we create together.

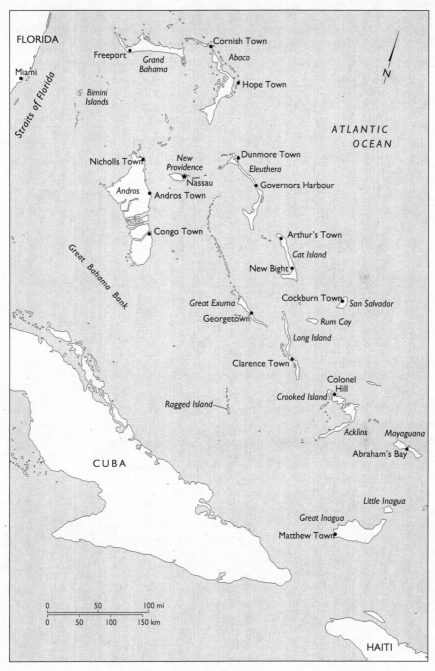

The Bahamas

Nassau's Gone Funky

Sounding Some Themes in Bahamian Music

Just last week, a few Caribbean nationals joked that The Bahamas is the 51st state of the United States of America. As you can imagine, I was not amused and jumped to the defensive in true Bahamian fashion. Although I would never admit it to my regional brethren, I must reluctantly confess that there was a bit of truth to their satirical claims. For someone who loves The Bahamas and our culture (or what remains of it) like myself, there is nothing that hurts more than the truth.

—ANDREW EDWARDS, *NASSAU GUARDIAN WEEKENDER*, MAY 19, 2006

It's rake-n-scrape. It's rhyming, the way we Bahamians do it. It's rushing, both in the streets, and around our churches. It's the double-rack, the heel-and-toe, the anthem, the story-song that we use to keep one another enter-tained. It's that real Bahamian guitar riff, it's the way the stomach jumps when a real bass rhythm is played. It's the rescuing of trash, the conversion of ordinary, undervalued objects like cardboard and paper into works of art. It's the way we laugh when the cowbells start, the way we dance when we hear the beat. What "the world" wants is stuff that's raw, that isn't over-processed. What "the world" wants is something that makes "the world" remember its own humanity. And what "the world" wants we have. . . . We must listen to our music, not just to the people who are popular now, but to our fathers and grandfathers and their fathers, to draw upon all the rich-ness that is ours. And then we must take what we learn from both, and create—and package to sell—our own.

—NICOLETTE BETHEL, BAHAMIAN DIRECTOR OF CULTURE,
   IN THE *NASSAU GUARDIAN*, MAY 20, 2004

From the Arawaks right down to the Bahamians of the present, Bahamian culture and literature [have] been produced under a situation of dependency, in the sense that the needs and hopes of the Bahamian people to chart and direct our own economic and political destinies, to create societies which

*responded to our way of being and developed according to our own ideas . . .
have constantly been sidetracked by the imposition on Bahamians of the
ideas, plans, and needs of forces that have come from outside the area.*
—ANTHONY DAHL, *LITERATURE OF THE BAHAMAS, 1724–1992*, 2

The epigraphs opening this chapter combine to paint a picture of several pressures
facing the Bahamas—pressures that continue to shape dilemmas and challenges
for which solutions have not been readily forthcoming. The first of these epigraphs succinctly illustrates the interposition of the Bahamas between the United
States and the rest of the Caribbean, a space in-between that serves to highlight
and intensify questions of cultural identity, raising the specter of the nation—and
of nationalism in particular—in the process. Nicolette Bethel, a former director of
culture for the Bahamas, transposes these questions of cultural identity neatly onto
the "national" product that the Bahamas presents and sells to the world. According
to Bethel, however, that export product stands in need of a bit of an overhaul, one
that can be realized by understanding that the power of cultural identity and cultural production rests in the past to be recovered for use in the present. The comments of Anthony Dahl, for their part, suggest that the nation's colonial and postcolonial histories have powerfully affected and continue to affect the conditions of
possibility for pursuing the project that Nicolette Bethel proposes.[1]

Throughout this book, I suggest that Bahamian musical life has been deeply
influenced and shaped by three separate but deeply interrelated themes embedded
in these epigraphs: the physical interposition of the Bahamas between the United
States and the rest of the Caribbean, tourism, and the nation's colonial and postcolonial histories. These geographic, economic, and political influences, moreover, are unthinkable without considering the ways that travel is implicated in
each of them—that is, the centrifugal and centripetal routes that are taken
through them. For travel operates at several registers in the Bahamian context,
including human itineraries, musical migrations and media flows, and journeys
related to time and nostalgia.

The physical travels I explore in the chapters that follow include the journeys
of Bahamians within and outside the nation; the influx of Caribbean migrants
from places such as Haiti, Trinidad, and Jamaica; and the itineraries of tourists
who flock to places like Paradise Island and Freeport, enjoying (or consuming)
the sun, sea, and sand of the Caribbean (Sheller 2003). The musical migrations
and media flows I trace here, moreover, highlight the internal center-periphery
migrations attendant to Bahamian music (Nassau/Freeport–Family Islands)
while also illustrating the long-standing and intimate relationships instantiated

between Bahamian musics and the musics of the islands' Caribbean neighbors (Trinidad, Jamaica, Cuba, and Haiti in particular). In addition, Florida-based radio stations, and more recently cable television, have instantiated other networks of musical and cultural relationships—other journeys that continue to powerfully affect musical production and reception in the Bahamas.

Leading up to and in the wake of independence in 1973, Bahamians increasingly found themselves considering what it sounds, looks, and feels like to be Bahamian, resulting in a concerted attempt by those concerned with cultural politics to explore the riches of the Bahamian past for answers to these questions. The narratives that emerge from these constructions of Bahamianness, from the process of what Svetlana Boym (2002) has called "prospective nostalgia," have resulted in a dynamic by virtue of which the "Real Bahamas" is (re)located in the past to be recovered in the present.[2] These journeys of memory, time, and nostalgia, then, constitute the third register of travel with which I think about Bahamian musics throughout the book.

These registers of travel, furthermore, are all complicated exponentially by the geopolitical structure of the Bahamas itself, not least because the geography of the archipelago marks the center-periphery relationships always attendant to the nation-state in the starkest of terms. Citizens who live on New Providence or Grand Bahama are located in the center. Those who do not are separated from the center not only in terms of the diminished resources and infrastructure available to them but also by virtue of their being physically isolated from the everyday political life of the nation. Regardless of the power relationships forged between various locations within the nation, though, the Bahamas as a whole remains peripheral within the larger context of the Caribbean.[3] The centrifugal and centripetal flows that inform the musical travels I explore thus operate both with respect to the internal shape of the nation itself and in relation to the place of the nation within the region.

Following the work of James Clifford (1997), I conceptualize place as an active point of engagement in order to think of location as an "itinerary" rather than as a bounded site—as a series of "encounters" and translations. Clifford's theorization of location is productively aligned with the more recent work of Mimi Sheller and John Urry (2004), who use the dynamic framework of play to explore places themselves as sites that are "in play"—a concept that has particular advantages for thinking more creatively about places ordinarily understood as tourist destinations. I am also influenced throughout this book by the work of Claudio Minca and Tim Oakes, who posit that performance of place cannot be reduced to physical infrastructure or to discourses about that place:

> Places are intertwined with people through various systems that generate and reproduce performances in and of that place (and by comparison with other

places). . . . Moreover, in such performances there is no simple and unmediated relationship of subject to object, presence and absence. There is a hauntingness of place, through voices, memories, gestures, and narratives that can inhabit a place for locals and for visitors, although this distinction too becomes increasingly difficult to sustain. These ghostly presences of place are in between subject and object, presence and absence. This "atmosphere" of place is irreducible either to physical or material infrastructures or to discourses of representation. (Minca and Oakes 2006, vii–viii)

These various approaches to place combine to allow for more nuanced readings of, say, Bay Street, or Nassau, or the Family Islands in relation to the routes that lead to and from those particular places. They allow for an archaeology of many different kinds of presences, and they invite readings of place that privilege analysis of all the registers that make a place *particular:* the people (both resident and visiting), the homes (of both residents and visitors), the sounds (both local and nonlocal), the histories (local, regional, personal, national), the various networks (travel agencies, governmental institutions, media flows, personal and business relationships, etc.) that are combined, recombined, and put "in play" in that fluid process. Music, moreover, provides a particularly appropriate and useful means of interrogating—reading—the "ghostly presences of place" described by Minca and Oakes. The following journey through landscapes of the pre-nation and across spaces within the postcolony, then, provides a context within which to situate the musical explorations I examine in this book.

BAHAMIAN ROUTES I:
OF LANDFALLS AND ARCHIPELAGOS

The Bahamas is a place in between—the first and best example of an itinerary in the New World. The images commonly associated with the Bahamas illustrate this quite well: the Bahamas is a collection of places that have served as a gateway for Columbus; a refuge for pirates; a hot spot for wrecking (salvage work); a way station for blockade runners; a staging area for rumrunners; and, more recently, a resort playground for tourists.[4] Significantly, even these crude characterizations of Bahamian participation in regional history indicate how firmly the Bahamas came to be interpolated between the Caribbean and the United States, between the New World and the Old.[5]

Part of this betweenness is directly related to the geography and geology of the archipelago itself. Comprising some seven hundred islands and cays and spread across about fifty-five hundred square miles at the juncture of the Atlantic Ocean and Caribbean Sea, the Bahamas has historically struggled with the fragmented nature of its own physical layout while simultaneously serving as a gateway to the Caribbean and the Gulf of Mexico. Very few mineral resources and a general lack of freshwater and arable land (there is only one river in the Bahamas, and the soil, where it can be found in the mostly rocky limestone islands, is very thin) made the Bahamas far less attractive to colonial powers than were, say, Hispaniola or Cuba. The Bahamas, then as now, was not an ideal location for what Antonio Benítez-Rojo (1996) has called "Columbus's machine"—the plantation.

The Bahamas nevertheless supported an estimated twenty thousand Lucayans (the islands' native people) by the time those living on the island they called Guanahani first encountered Christopher Columbus (October 12, 1492). Columbus quickly claimed all that he could see for the Spanish crown, christening the island San Salvador, and having failed to find sufficient quantities of gold, compelling seven Lucayans to board his ship and guide it deeper into the archipelago. The callous disposition toward the Lucayans at evidence in his log entry for October 14, 1492, is perhaps a harbinger of things to come for the Bahamas: "These people are very unskilled in arms, as Your Highness will see from the seven that I caused to be taken to carry them off to learn our language and return; unless Your Highness should order them all to be taken to Castile or held captive in the same island, for with 50 men they could all be subjected and made to do all that one wished" (quoted in Morison 1963, 68). The violence of this encounter, both in symbolic and physical terms, often overshadows the strategic deflection accomplished by the Lucayans that October. The Bahamas was not what Columbus was looking for, and the Lucayans underscored that by pointing him in the direction of the gold (or perhaps more pragmatically, away from the Bahamas).

This initial encounter was, however, only the first of many, and the initial deflection to other locations in the Caribbean seems only to have focused the colonial gaze on other possibilities. Accordingly, subsequent encounters were much more devastating, for the Bahamas came to be mined for the only resource useful to the colonial effort: the Lucayans themselves. Systematically relocated to the mines of Hispaniola and, a bit later, to the pearl beds off Cubagua, the Lucayans were soon living and dying in slavery far from home. As Michael Craton and Gail Saunders point out, "Ponce de León as early as 1513 came to the conclusion that the islands were completely empty of people" (Craton and Saunders 1992, 55). This genocidal exploitation of Lucayans, accomplished in a staggeringly short space of twenty-some years, illustrates the role of the Bahamas within Columbus's machine. The people, not the place, could be exploited.

The ensuing century witnessed the Bahamian archipelago standing essentially empty at the front door of the Caribbean. Because the Bahamas was virtually ignored by Spain and experienced only unsuccessful claims to settlement by the French (primarily a failed twin settlement in Abaco, founded in 1565), it was the English who first managed to establish permanent settlement in the Bahamas starting in 1648, when the Eleutheran Adventurers (a group of religious independents led by William Sayle) made landfall from Bermuda and laid claim to the territory. Some 150 years after Columbus's first landfall, however, little had changed. The archipelago, which had thus far proved next to useless to the colonial project, in fact provided very little from which the Eleutheran Adventurers would be able to craft a significant livelihood or move into the mainstream of exchange.[6] The new inhabitants were, from the beginning, placed at a distinct disadvantage simply by virtue of their chosen location, as Craton and Saunders point out: "The Bahamas presents a particularly awkward and atypical picture: playing no part in the general [colonial] process before the mid-seventeenth century, first peopled by a thin trickle of settlers from Bermuda . . . gradually reinforced by heterogeneous recruits from all points of the compass, and seeking a livelihood without plantations that when not actually parasitic (during the age of piracy), was peripheral to Antilles and mainland alike. From the beginning of English settlement, therefore, the Bahamian people were a people apart" (Craton and Saunders 1992, 63).

These observations illustrate the dual nature of the Bahamas' interpolation within the region. The archipelago itself stands between the Caribbean and colonial Europe. This in-betweenness thus extends to the people who began to settle there starting in 1648, providing them with a home in-between the mainland and the Caribbean. By 1666, the makings of a settlement on New Providence had taken shape, with perhaps as many as a thousand people living in small settlements on Eleuthera, its surrounding cays, and New Providence. But it would be another sixty years before the Bahamas started to stabilize as a colony (1720s), and that long again before the makings of the modern Bahamas were in place both demographically and politically (1780s).

Beginning in 1670, the Bahamas came under the rule of a proprietary government, and the absentee proprietors did little but hope that a series of governors—John Wentworth, Charles Chillingworth, Robert Clark, Robert Lilburne, Thomas Bridges, and Nicholas Trott, among others—would be able to turn profits from privateering and manage to weather the intermittent but inevitable conflicts with the Spanish and French that those ventures engendered. Though the city of Nassau was born during Trott's governorship, indicating a significant increase in the size of the population, the Bahamas was not destined to offer a rich return on any investments other than those associated with intermittent wrecking to recover goods from shipwrecks throughout the archipelago. It was, moreover, predictable that the inhabitants of Eleuthera, Harbour Island, and New Providence were not particularly inclined to offer their full cooperation to a governor claiming authority granted by absentee proprietors. Governing the Bahamas was thus an exercise in frustration, not least because of unrealistic economic mandates but also because of the archipelago's relative isolation and prevailing sociopolitical environment.[7]

The proprietors thus largely ignored the Bahamas in favor of their other interests, especially in the Carolinas, thereby making matters infinitely worse for their governors in the Bahamas and leading the British crown to begin reasserting its control over the islands, in part by installing a vice-admiralty court (with judge, registrar, and marshal) in Nassau (1697). Even this measure, though, did little to instill stability or law and order. In fact, the Bahamas were at that very moment embroiled in an era of piracy, much of which has been mythologized, but the realities of which nevertheless kept the young colony from establishing a real political presence in the region or sufficient social stability to attract any significant influx of settlers between the 1690s and the 1720s.[8]

Suffice it to say here that pirates were often aided by the proprietary governors and, later, by crown-appointed governors, and that pirates, for a time at least, effectively controlled the Bahamas. This state of affairs had serious consequences for the fledgling city of Nassau, leading John Graves, the colonial secretary in the Bahamas, to remark in 1706 that the inhabitants of New Providence "lived scatteringly in little huts, ready upon any assault to secure themselves in the woods." Graves wrote that he had left on the island a mere twenty-seven families, no more than four to five hundred persons in all, dispersed within a two-hundred-mile radius of the capital (quoted in Craton 1986, 88). John Oldmixon, another witness to conditions in Nassau during this time, goes so far as to dismiss the Bahamas out of hand: "This Island [New Providence] is chief of those called the Bahama Islands, and notwithstanding that Character is so inconsiderable in itself, that it had been well if it had never been discovered; for all the Advantage the Inhabitants can pretend it is to England or the other Colonies is, that it lies convenient for Wrecks. . . . And it being some Hundreds of Miles out of any Ship's regular Course, to or from any of our Colonies and England, it is certain we had never lost any Thing by it had it never been heard of" (Oldmixon 1949, 11).

According to Craton and Saunders, however, the era of piracy was a moment of signal ambiguity for the inhabitants of the Bahamas. "A pragmatic middle ground was sought between profiting from the pirates and being taken over by them, though such a position proved increasingly difficult [to maintain]" (1992, 106). For the purposes of the present study, this early moment in Bahamian life is significant because, though the circumstances have changed in the course of subsequent encounters, the substance of the principal dilemma facing Bahamians seems to have continued to involve just these kinds of ambivalences and compromises, even up to the present—and this with respect to both regional politics and local economics. Dahl's words regarding outside influences on Bahamian culture thus ring true.

The first quarter of the eighteenth century, then, was characterized by attempts to live with the pirates, preemptive attacks and reprisals from nations repeatedly victimized by pirates based in the Bahamas (especially Spain), ineffective governors, and poverty, relieved on occasion through salvage work and maintaining manageable (if not always comfortable) relationships with the pirates themselves.

TABLE 1 Bahamian census data, 1731

Island	Men	Women	Children	Blacks	Total
New Providence	190	135	308	409	1,042
Harbour Island/Eleuthera	66	55	181	44	346
Total	256	190	489	453	1,388

SOURCE: Adapted from Craton and Saunders 1992, 120.

And yet, toward the end of this era and under the direction of the royal governors Woodes Rogers and George Phenney, several significant markers of change took place: the proprietors surrendered the civil and military government of the Bahamas to the British crown (1717); the pirates were gradually expelled; the first censuses of the Bahamas were conducted (1722, 1731, and 1734); the first substantial number of slaves were imported to the colony (295 people in 1721, by Woodes Rogers himself), followed rapidly by the issuance of the first slave laws for the Bahamas (1723); the establishment of the first Anglican church in Nassau (1723); and the replacement of the old representative system of colonial government rule by governor-in-council (1729) (Craton 1986). The census results of 1731, compiled under Governor Rogers, are worth reproducing here, because they provide a marker against which the dramatic demographic changes toward the end of the century can be interrogated and understood (see Table 1).

According to the 1731 census data, fully 75 percent of the population lived on New Providence, and 32 percent of the population was black (that proportion stood at 40 percent for New Providence). These demographics indicate that the dominant role of New Providence in Bahamian life was, by this time, clearly established in terms of both population and political importance. They also point to the very slow population growth for the Bahamas between 1670 and 1731, attesting to the difficult circumstances of those years.. But these population figures, even in isolation, also provide evidence of just how "apart" the Bahamas were within the New World. By way of comparison, in 1700 there were an estimated 134,000 African slaves in Barbados, and slaves outnumbered whites by four to one (Curtin 1969). Or to take another example, by the middle third of the eighteenth century Havana was home to at least thirty thousand people and was the third-largest city in the hemisphere (trailing only Mexico City and Lima).[9] That the first substantial shipment of slaves was not imported to the Bahamas until 1721, moreover, speaks to the diminutive size of the population, the lack of a viable plantation economy, and the relative dearth of interest in the archipelago on the part of colonial powers. This state of affairs was to change toward the end of the century, but the middle years of the eighteenth century did—by comparison to the early decades of that century, at least—carry with them some measure of political and social stability.

BAHAMIAN ROUTES II: OF PEOPLE AND POLITICS

By the time of the American Revolutionary War, the Bahamas had changed considerably. The census taken in 1773 found Bahamians living on New Providence, Eleuthera, Harbor Island, Spanish Wells, Exuma, and Cat Island. It also indicated that slaves and free blacks had assumed a slight majority in the colony. By this time, a series of slave laws had been enacted (including those passed in 1729, 1734, and 1767), but although blacks now outnumbered whites on New Providence, the assembly did not rush to more tightly control the free black population. In fact, according to Whittington Johnson, "instead of regimenting the lives of blacks, the assembly concluded that free blacks and persons of color had the same obligation to defend the colony as did whites. Hence, all whites, free blacks, and free persons of color between the ages of sixteen and sixty were required to serve in the militia" (Whittington B. Johnson 2000, xviii). It is owing to this obligation that one of the earliest references to music in the Bahamas was recorded, for when the American Navy briefly occupied Nassau in 1776, black militia sentinels sounded the warning call—with drums (Pascoe 1901).[10] Johnson is interested in this warning call and wonders about it: "The signal to assemble in Fort Nassau and repel the invaders was the drumbeat. Was this the usual manner of sounding the alarm, or was the drumbeat used to summon blacks, perhaps even slaves?" (Whittington B. Johnson 2000, xix). Though answers to these questions are not readily forthcoming, it is nevertheless significant that drums were used for this purpose, not least because the narrative provides one of the earliest accounts of musical instruments in the Bahamas.

It was the influx of loyalist planters, their families, and their slaves, as well as free black loyalists in the wake of the Revolutionary War (between 1783 and 1788) that provided the most dramatic changes within the Bahamas in the late eighteenth century. That migration tripled the population, shifted the proportion of blacks from just over 50 percent to fully 75 percent, led to the effective settlement of several additional islands (including Abaco, Andros, Long Island, San Salvador, Rum Cay, Crooked Island, and Acklins Island), and installed the plantation system more pervasively throughout the Bahamas (see Table 2).

This influx of loyalist migrants set the stage for the making of the modern Bahamas. All told, some sixteen hundred whites and fifty-seven hundred slaves and free blacks made landfall in the Bahamas and presented no small threat to the established Bahamian elite (Craton and Saunders 1992). One of the strategies adopted to mitigate this threat was to actively encourage the loyalists to settle the "Out Islands," but even this marginalizing strategy could not prevent the newcomers from rapidly consolidating their power in the local political scene. Michael Craton, for example, points out that already, "by the end of 1784, provision had been made for the admission of Members from five new Out Island constituencies" (1986, 150).

TABLE 2 Population figures by island, 1773–1807

Island	1773			1786			1807		
	Blacks	Whites	Total	Blacks	Whites	Total	Blacks	Whites	Tota
New Providence	1,800	1,024	2,824	4,019	1,572	5,591	4,315	1,720	6,03
Harbour Island, Spanish Wells	90	410	500	149	365	514	460	650	1,11
Eleuthera	237	509	746	315	486	801	1,210	575	1,78
Exumas	24	6	30	638	66	704	1,130	50	1,18
Cat Island	40	3	43	305	59	364	750	30	78
Abaco	—	—	—	384	282	666	17	250	26
Long Island	—	—	—	99	41	140	800	140	94
Andros	—	—	—	59	2	61	185	10	19
San Salvador, Rum Cay	—	—	—	—	—	—	386	20	40
Crooked, Acklins Islands	—	—	—	—	—	—	900	20	92
Total	2,191	1,952	4,143	5,968	2,873	8,841	10,153	3,465	13,6

SOURCES: Data for 1773 and 1807 from Craton and Saunders (1992); data for 1786 from Craton (1986).

That said, it is interesting to consider the term *Out Islands* here, a formulation used to distinguish New Providence (and later Grand Bahama) from every other inhabited island in the archipelago, thereby marking periphery from center in common parlance as well as economically and politically.

Although several additional islands were settled during this period, New Providence retained its position at the political and economic center of the colony, though the ruling elites were nonetheless forced to allow for new voices in government. Somewhat paradoxically, the very process of the loyalist migration to and settlement of other islands in the archipelago served to more thoroughly define the geography of the colony's periphery. And though a great deal of attention is paid to the political and economic effects of the loyalist influx (read white), according to Craton and Saunders, "it was probably the slave and free black majority of newcomers who most indelibly shaped the social history of the Bahamas" (1992, 178).[11]

Perhaps not coincidentally, this is the very moment at which a bit of commentary about music enters the written record in connection with the Bahamas. One of the earliest accounts of musical life in the Bahamas comes from Johann David Schoepf, a German who had assisted the British in the Revolutionary War and who wrote a travelogue titled *Travels in the Confederacy* (1788). During his travels, he journeyed to Nassau, noting, "In the town itself, at this time [1784], no quarters were to be had because all the houses were filled with refugies [sic] escaped from North America" (Schoepf [1788] 1911, 264). His comments on musical entertainment were actually made while en route to the Bahamas, not in Nassau, but they describe a very interesting set of practices that were to become part and parcel of Bahamian musical life during the nineteenth century, and they are thus worth quoting at length.

> Another sort of amusement was furnished us by several among the negroes on board, native Africans. One of them would often be entertaining his comrades with the music and songs of their country. The instrument which he used for the purposes he called Gambee; a notched bar of wood, one end of which he placed against an empty cask, or some other hollow, reverberant body, and the other against his breast. In his right hand he held a small stick of wood, split lengthwise into several clappers (something after the fashion of a harlequin's mace); in his left hand also a small thin wooden stick, unsplit. Beating and rubbing both of these, vigorously and in time, over the notches of the first stick, he produced a hollow rattling noise, accompanied by a song in the Guinea tongue. At the first, his gestures and voice were altogether quiet, soft, and low; but gradually he raised his voice, and began to grin and make wry faces, ending in such a glowing enthusiasm that his mouth foamed and his eyes rolled wildly about.
>
> Another musical instrument of the true negroe is the Banjah. Over a hollow calabash (*Cucurb lagenaria L.*) is stretched a sheep-skin, the instrument lengthened with a neck, strung with 4 strings, and made accordant. It gives out a rude sound; usually there is some one besides to give an accompaniment with the drum, or an iron pan, or empty cask, whatever may be at hand. In America and on the islands they make use of this instrument greatly for the dance. Their melodies are almost always the same, with little variation. The dancers, the musicians, and often even the spectators, sing alternately. Their national dances consist of wonderful leaps and a riotous bending and twisting of the body. (Schoepf [1788] 1911, 260–62)

The instruments Schoepf describes here are probably the *gimbe* (often a two-piece hardwood scraper, though here the performer used two different tools in order to rake out his rhythms on the scraper) and the banjo. The singing and dancing he witnessed, moreover, bear strong resemblance to the ring dances that came to be called jumping dances in the Bahamas.[12] The moment of loyalist migration was also a formative musical migration that bears serious inquiry. I will explore these ideas in greater detail in chapter 2.

The loyalist migration into the Bahamas came to an end in 1788, by which time the Bahamas was actively attempting to develop its fledgling plantation economy (a project ultimately destined for failure). Like Trinidad, the Bahamas entered into the plantation economy very late—generating a substantial quantity of export products (cotton) only starting in the 1780s (1790s for Trinidad)—and came to depend on that economic model within a colonial context already moving toward abolition.[13] This led to inevitable tension between the ruling elites in the Bahamas and the British crown, which was, by this time, increasingly committed to abolition.[14] The political events in neighboring St. Domingue and the alarm that the Revolution caused among Bahamian elites led to local reactions that did not mirror prevailing sentiments in the Colonial Office—reactions that led, for example, to the passing of the first Consolidated Slave Act for the Bahamas in 1797 at the very moment that the Colonial Office was seriously beginning to debate abolishing the slave trade.

In 1807, the British crown did decide to ban the slave trade, a measure that did not affect the Bahamas too dramatically, not least because the plantation system was already failing as a large-scale enterprise, thereby obviating the need for augmenting the labor force through ready access to slave labor. Some of the other policies introduced by the British, however, were cause for serious protest in the Bahamas. The most contentious of these was the decision to garrison black troops from the West India Regiments in Nassau starting in 1801. The idea of armed blacks was, to say the least, an unsettling one to Nassau's elites, especially given the revolutionary events taking place in neighboring St. Domingue at the time.

The amelioration period (1824–34) was ushered in uneasily; evidence of that unease can be found in the new slave act of 1824, which, for the first time, included "specific prohibitions against riotous and unlawful assemblies of slaves. Owners or those in charge of slaves were to be penalized if they allowed more than twelve 'strange' slaves 'to assemble together, or beat their drums or blow their horns or shells'" (Craton and Saunders 1992, 229). This is, then, the first legal response to serious concern among elite Bahamians over the potential consequences of allowing blacks to assemble too freely or, even—and perhaps especially—to engage in musical performances together.

And it is an interesting coincidence that one of the earliest descriptions of the kinds of celebrations that occurred during the customary three-day Christmas holiday antecedent to later Junkanoo celebrations was penned during the Christmas of 1823. The author, a Dr. Townsend, who was visiting from New York, observed in his diary: "Being Christmas, our ears were assailed with the noise of the black & white boys playing on the green before our house. We should not have noticed ten times as much sound in Newyork but in this still town it seemed quite grating. We were also regaled last night at Christmas eve until 3 or 4 in the morning with some bad music on hoarse cracked drums & fifes by groupes of negroes parading the streets" (Townsend [1823–24] 1968, 20).[15]

Townsend's diary also includes a passage that describes the dances of the white Bahamian elite. In an entry dated January 1, 1824, Townsend reports: "After coffee, tea, cake, etc, danced a succession of tedious and laborious country dances till 4 next morning, allowing a short time for supper about 1 o'clock. The music was very good, two fifes (black) from the garrison, 2 or 3 fiddles, tambourine & drum. . . . The Floors were very tastily chalked with devices appropriate to the occasion & commencement of the year" ([1823–24] 1969, 22). It is worth noting the presence of the black fife players in this description, for events such as these were, almost certainly, one of the primary influences (both musically and choreographically) on the quadrille dancing that became a major component of black social dance in the Bahamas during the nineteenth century (Bilby and Neely 2009). I will return to these musical currents in later chapters.

By the time emancipation was announced on August 1, 1834 (a date that was followed by four more years of apprenticeship, meaning that the ex-slaves were, in reality, not totally free until August 1, 1838), the local elites had accomplished the feat of legally manumitting a significant portion of the slave population such that a class of free blacks stood as a buffer class between them and those slaves who were at that moment being freed. That legislative move, which was part of the penultimate slave act signed into law in the Bahamas in 1826, attempted to ensure that only a certain kind of slave was able to obtain freedom. According to Craton and Saunders, the law was structured so that "in practice . . . only those slaves whom masters deemed worthy of freedom and who had sufficient means and incentive to enter the intermediate class of the black petty bourgeoisie were given their freedom" (1992, 231).

After emancipation, the white oligarchy maintained control through subtler means. These strategies included calculated efforts such as manipulating the standards for voting eligibility so that they favored white electors, bribing Out Island communities for votes in order to install white representatives in the assembly, and instituting mechanisms of virtually ensured poverty such as the truck system.[16] It was in this highly discriminatory atmosphere that free blacks, liberated Africans, and recently freed ex-slaves first banded together to form officially sanctioned friendly societies.[17] The Grant's Town Friendly Society, for instance, was inaugurated and incorporated in 1835, and many other friendly societies and lodges were to follow its model. Participation in friendly societies and lodges has, in fact, been one of the consolidating and distinctive aspects of Afro-Bahamian culture and social organization since that time (Craton and Saunders 1998).

The middle years of the nineteenth century found the Bahamas continuing to operate outside of the international mainstream and witnessed the local center—New Providence—further distancing itself from its own interior other, the Out Islands. Boom-and-bust economics continued, in this case revolving around blockade running, which during the American Civil War provided for a measure of economic boom. But the boom years were, upon the resolution of that conflict, quickly followed by a long period of recession.[18] "So severe and prolonged was the depression," writes Michael Craton, "that most Bahamians came to wish that they had never enjoyed the brief interlude of garish prosperity during the war" (1986, 225). He continues: "Some men made fortunes from the blockade; but they were mostly foreigners, commercial agents, captains, pilots, who had flocked to Nassau for the duration and began to leave as soon as Wilmington fell. Very few Bahamians profited from the war and they were the worst sufferers from the inflation that followed the flood of Confederate money into Nassau. . . . Once emptied of cotton and war supplies, the new warehouses lay empty for fifty years" (Craton 1986, 225).

The one industry that seemed to promise long-term stability for at least the merchant class in the Bahamas was sponging. And yet even this market was destined to fail. Though the market for sponges expanded steadily from the 1860s through the early twentieth century, a fungus destroyed almost all of the Bahamian sponges in 1938, leaving this sector of the economy in ruins. The human toll of the sponging industry, moreover, was extraordinarily high. The merchants who served as the wholesalers at the Nassau Sponge Exchange generally pushed their contractors into perpetual debt through the truck system, and it was through these exploitative means and by carefully controlling access to capital that the Bay Street Merchants continued to consolidate their hold on the economy and on the politics of the colony throughout the nineteenth century (Craton 1986; Craton and Saunders 1992).[19]

BAHAMIAN ROUTES III:
OF TOURISTS AND INDEPENDENCE

In spite of the entrenched boom-and-bust economic cycle that continued to affect Bahamians during the nineteenth century, the last third of that century brought about the first taste of the possibilities related to tourism. Steam was beginning to replace sail, and thanks in large part to this new advance in marine technology, regular services began to open up, especially between the mainland United States and Nassau.[20] The Cunard Line, for instance, "promised a voyage of as little as three days from New York, compared with at least a week by sailing ship" when it added Nassau as a stopover on its New York–to–Havana route in 1859 (Craton and Saunders 1998, 75). The potential of attracting an increasing number of visitors thanks to these developments in transportation prompted the decision to build the Royal Victoria Hotel.[21] Construction on the ninety-room hotel commenced in the summer of 1860, and the building was complete by the end of the 1860–61 winter season.

And yet, growing transnational connections and hotel construction notwithstanding, the Bahamas was still entrenched at the margins of the region. Once the bust following the Civil War settled in, for instance, the Royal Victoria Hotel sat next to vacant, up for sale and without any potential buyers (Craton 1986, 225). In 1888, L. D. Powles, who wrote a memoir about his time as a circuit magistrate in the Bahamas, penned the following:

The day before I corrected the last proof of this work a prominent West Indian Merchant said to me, "Why do you waste your time writing about the Bahama Islands? We in the West Indies know no more about the Bahamas than we do about an Irish village." No doubt he said no more than the truth, for though included in the list of her Majesty's West Indian possessions, the Bahamas have so little in common with the other islands that I believe a man might spend his life traveling about the rest of the West Indies without ever hearing their name, and I am sure he might pass his days in the Bahamas and have no more idea of the mode of life or condition of the people in the rest of the West Indies than if he had never been beyond the limits of an English county. What can be more noteworthy than the fact that Mr. Froude, in his recently published work, never even mentions the Bahama Islands? . . . [This] goes far to prove how little they come within the range of thought or observation of the ordinary West Indian tourist. (Powles 1888, v–vi)

The Mr. Froude of whom Powles writes is none other than James Anthony Froude, author of the notoriously racist *The English in the West Indies; or, The Bow of Ulysses* (1888).[22] Apart from reinforcing the peripheral position of the Bahamas within the Caribbean, this passage is also interesting in that it offers a sense of the growing tourism industry—the "ordinary West Indian tourist" was at this time beginning to emerge as an identifiable character, and according to Powles, the Bahamas was not, as of yet, able to attract much attention from that tourist.

Other kinds of tourists were beginning to notice the Bahamas, however, for the majority of the winter residents and the lion's share of interest in visiting the Bahamas came not from the colonial metropole, but rather from the United States. In fact, the Bahamas was, even as early as Peter Henry Bruce's visit (1741–45), touted as a health resort, and by the time Powles was in residence there, the idea of Nassau as a destination for health tourism had caught on.[23] Doctors had been actively sending patients to the Bahamas for some time; individual travelers, especially from the northeastern United States, sought out the warmth on their own; and the Royal Victoria had been designed with a view toward housing just these kinds of visitors. Take, for instance, the journey of the New England–based lawyer Charles Ives in 1879–80, who, "influenced mainly by sanitary considerations, fled from frost to the islands of unending summer" (Ives 1880, 14), stayed in the Royal Victoria Hotel while in the Bahamas, and subsequently published a travelogue about his experiences. The book is filled with idealized, paternalistic, and overly rhapsodic passages about the climate, people, and economy of the Bahamas, but it does indicate that the fledgling tourist economy was active, perhaps even more active than Powles realized.[24]

The increasingly close ties to the United States, created both thanks to tourist visits and through transportation contracts and networks, served to further solidify the interpolation of the Bahamas between the rest of the Caribbean and the

United States. In fact, in 1898, only a few short years after Powles wrote his memoir, a wealthy Florida-based businessman, Henry M. Flagler, arranged to create regular steamship connections between Nassau and Miami, purchased the Royal Victoria Hotel, and built the Hotel Colonial (which opened in 1900) to accommodate the anticipated tourist volume of the early twentieth century.[25] According to Craton and Saunders, though, "Nassau's summer and winter visitors were still counted in tens and hundreds in 1900, and a sense of the resort's isolation outweighed its antique charm" (1998, 82). It would, in fact, take several more decades to realize Flagler's dream of a bourgeoning tourist economy in the Bahamas (1930s), and the wait for the Out Islands would be roughly twice as long (1960s).

In addition to the gradually increasing tourist activity and the growing infrastructural projects that grew alongside these economic shifts, the fin de siècle also provides a set of written records illustrating interest in the folktales and music of the Bahamas. Charles Ives offered some notes on the sacred songs of Afro-Bahamians in his memoir, including a few texts to hymns and anthems that were sung for them by young Bahamians.[26] More useful are the recollections of L. D. Powles, who affords several valuable glimpses into the musical lives of Bahamians and, significantly, of Out Island musical practices, describing the songs and dances that he observed during his journeys around the Bahamas as a magistrate. So, for instance, he describes Junkanoo here, some fifty years after the first local references to it. Significantly, his account also offers some early confirmation of the active nightclub scene in Nassau.

> About Christmas time they seem to march about day and night, with lanterns and bands of music, and they fire off crackers everywhere. This is a terrible nuisance, but the custom has the sanction of antiquity, though no doubt it would have been put down long ago if the white young gentlemen had not exhibited a taste for the same amusement. They are very fond of dancing, and I am afraid no amount of preaching or singing hymns will ever be able to put down the dancehouses, which are terrible thorns in the side of both magistrate and inspector of police. (Powles 1888, 147)

The first scholarly account of musical practices and the oratory arts was undertaken by Charles Edwards, who wrote *Bahama Songs and Stories: A Contribution to Folk-Lore* for the American Folk-Lore Society in 1885. Although he focuses most carefully on sacred musical practices and the storytelling tradition, which was at that time still quite active, there are also included here glimpses of social dance music:

> The evening is the playtime of the negroes. The children gather in some clump of bushes or on the seashore and sing their songs, the young men form a group for a dance in some hut, and the old people gossip. The dance is full of uncultured grace; and to the barbaric music of a clarionet, accompanied by tambourines and triangles, some expert dancer "steps off" his specialty in a challenging way, while vari-

ous individuals in the crowd keep time by beating their feet upon the rough floor and slapping their hands against their legs. All applaud as the dancer finishes; but before he fairly reaches a place in the circle a rival catches step to the music, and all eyes are again turned toward the centre of attraction. Thus goes the dance into the night. (Charles Edwards [1895] 1942, 17)

Passages such as these do not go very far toward painting a detailed picture of what was going on musically in the Bahamas, but they do provide an interesting commentary, and not least because some of the practices that were inaugurated at the turn of the previous century had, by this time, clearly taken hold. These descriptions also chronicle the gradual creolization of these practices, illustrating the incorporation of European instruments (in this case a clarinet) into the social dances of Afro-Bahamians and the tentative adoption of Afro-Bahamian dance and festival practices by younger white Bahamians (Junkanoo). I will return to these ideas in chapters 2 and 4.

Several other infrastructural and technological changes important to the continued growth of tourism occurred in the years of the late nineteenth and early twentieth centuries. A telegraph cable was laid between Cable Beach, New Providence, and Jupiter, Florida, in 1892, opening direct and rapid communication with the mainland United States and England (Storr 2000). Cars were first imported to the Bahamas in 1905, the telephone was inaugurated in 1907, sewer services began to be implemented around this time, and electricity was brought to Nassau in 1909. These technologies, it must be reiterated, affected only New Providence. The Out Islands remained without access to any of these advantages, and the true scale of the disenfranchisement inflicted on Out Islanders is cast into particularly sharp relief when the population statistics for the turn of the twentieth century are considered. For in 1901, more than 75 percent of Bahamians still lived in the Out Islands; the benefits of steam, electricity, and communications technology thus effectively benefited only one out of every four Bahamians.[27] These center-periphery inequities notwithstanding, in 1914 the Development Board was authorized and charged to "promote tourism, negotiate with carriers, and coordinate matters related to tourism" (Cleare 2007, 68). Trickle-down benefits would eventually also reach the Out Islands, but the board's primary focus was developing New Providence's tourist infrastructure.

The Bahamian economy was to experience one more boom-and-bust cycle before settling into steady growth based on tourism. The boom came thanks to the Prohibition era in the United States (1920–33), and the short-term wealth it generated aided the efforts of the Development Board to lay the groundwork for a sustainable tourist economy. Bootleggers and rumrunners based their operations out of Nassau and realized immense profits from the illegal trade. The increased activity in Nassau contributed to an influx of people and generated additional construction and technological advances. For instance, the Montagu Hotel (later renamed the Fort Montagu Beach Hotel) was built in 1926, partially in response to the great demand for lodging during the Prohibition era. In addition, Nassau Harbor was deepened, the Prince George Wharf was built, and Pan American World Airways inaugurated scheduled flights between Miami and Nassau, all in 1929.[28] This was also the moment at which major nightclubs began springing up in Nassau. Two of the earliest include Dirty Dicks (ca. 1930) on Bay Street and, a bit later, the Chez Paul Meeres (1939) at Fleming Street, Over-the-Hill.[29]

The concomitant rise of the first wave of Afro-Bahamian professional musicians found bands performing at places like the Nassau Yacht Club and the Royal Victoria Hotel during the Prohibition era. Groups with names like the Cambridge Orchestra and the Chocolate Dandies vied with imported musicians from the United States for chances to perform, but they performed for white audiences at these venues because the Bay Street hotels remained segregated.[30] The American-owned Hotel Colonial, for instance, was so strongly committed to this racist policy that it "attempted to exclude blacks from all but the most menial work, employing Cubans or other Latin Americans in the absence of suitable and willing local whites" (Craton and Saunders 1998, 245). I will return to explore these issues and trends in much greater detail in chapter 3.

The bust following the repeal of Prohibition was sustained and intense, a severe economic depression (matched worldwide, in this case) lasting from 1933 until the beginning of World War II, after which tourism finally came to occupy the central place in the Bahamian economy toward which it had been moving since the late nineteenth century. The years between 1949 and the present constitute the primary historical period under consideration in the chapters that follow. Chapters 2 and 4 explore this period as a whole in order to offer a larger context for considering rake-n-scrape and Junkanoo, respectively. Chapters 3 and 5 explore the years leading up to independence in 1973—considered the golden years of entertainment in the Bahamas—and those that followed, respectively. Chapter 6 considers the 1990s as well as the most recent developments in Bahamian musical life. For this reason, I offer only the briefest of comments here, designed to outline the overarching context for thinking about the Bahamas from midcentury to the new millennium. This context necessarily includes the progressive and highly successful development of the year-round tourism industry after 1949, the architects of which were the predominantly white merchant-political oligarchy known as the Bay Street Boys. A summary of the staggeringly rapid growth of tourism through the middle decades of the twentieth century offers perhaps the quickest measure of the Bay Street Boys' success (see Table 3).

It should come as no surprise that these developments in the tourism sector demanded a much larger labor force, especially in Nassau and, a bit later, in Freeport. As a result, a concomitant and equally rapid internal migration from the

TABLE 3 Tourist visits,
1950–1970

Year	Total Visitors
1950	45,371
1955	132,434
1960	341,977
1965	720,420
1970	1,298,344

SOURCE: Data from Cleare 2007,
pp. 148, 162–63, 244.

TABLE 4 Bahamian population statistics, 1901–1970

Census Year	New Providence and Grand Bahama		Out Islands		Total Population
	Population	Percent of Total	Population	Percent of Total	
1901	13,803	26	39,932	74	53,735
1911	15,378	27	40,566	73	55,944
1921	14,670	28	38,361	72	53,031
1931	21,997	37	37,831	63	59,828
1943	31,724	46	37,122	54	68,846
1953	50,220	59	34,621	41	84,841
1963	89,137	68	41,083	32	130,220
1970	127,362	75	41,450	25	168,812

SOURCE: Data from Craton and Saunders 1998, p. 200.

Out Islands to New Providence and Grand Bahama shifted the majority of the population of the Bahamas, which had to that point been concentrated in the Out Islands, decidedly toward Nassau and Freeport.[31] Between 1931 and 1953, for example, the population of Nassau more than doubled, while that of the Out Islands fell slightly. So, while the periphery/center ratio was effectively inverted over the course of the first seventy years of the twentieth century, the trend accelerated dramatically after World War II (especially in the late 1940s). The end result was that by 1970 three out of every four Bahamians were living in Nassau and Freeport (see Table 4).

These demographic shifts were accompanied by steady West Indian migration to the Bahamas, as well as by the often illegal migration into the Bahamas from Haiti of individuals seeking new political and economic horizons, especially from the 1950s on (see Tinker 1998 and Marshall 1979). These decades of rapid demographic changes also witnessed the burgeoning Bahamian labor movement, which included the Burma Road Riots of 1942 and the formation of the Bahamas Musicians and Entertainers Union in 1949 (see Alexander 2004 and Horne 2007). Increasing dissatisfaction over the realities of minority rule, moreover, led to the eventual formation of the first Afro-Bahamian political party, called the Progressive Liberal Party, to a successful transition to majority rule in 1967, and to national independence in 1973.

Throughout the two-decade period between 1945 and 1965, the nightclubs, restaurants, and taxi drivers of Nassau were doing booming business. By the end of the 1960s, however, many of the Over-the-Hill nightclubs were beginning to struggle and fail, and by the middle of the 1970s it was clear that the foundation for sustaining live entertainment was on the decline throughout the Bahamas. My own fieldwork, beginning in 1997 and continuing to 2010, provided ample evidence for the difficult circumstances under which contemporary musicians labor to secure any kind of performance opportunities at all. Today there are only two clubs that feature live bands in anything resembling regular appearances (Da Tambrin Tree, since 2010 closed for relocation, and the Backyard Club), though a few do feature individual artists singing to tracks when they are not employing deejays to spin entertainment. Hotels employ only a very few local musicians to perform in public areas, and the best concerts are high-priced affairs at the hotels for which major international artists such as Barbara Streisand are contracted. The chapters that follow, then, engage with these trends in the musical life of the Bahamas while interrogating them against the broader context of the geographic, economic, and political themes I have addressed throughout this brief introduction to the archipelago. At this point, however, I turn my attention to the musical practices that animate the remainder of this book.

BAHAMIAN ROOTS:
RAKE-N-SCRAPE, GOOMBAY, AND JUNKANOO

The following section briefly introduces the three principal musical styles that sound out across the remainder of this book—rake-n-scrape, goombay, and Junkanoo. The genres are not as easily separated from one another as these labels suggest, however, intersecting with one another and overlapping in multiple ways. Ed Moxey, born on Ragged Island in 1933, for instance, has a particularly strong sense of the common source of Bahamian music. He is convinced that "rake-n-scrape is not really rake-n-scrape, it is really goombay music, an African sound . . . the music for Junkanoo is not 'Junkanoo music' but 'goombay music at the Junkanoo festival.' It's all just a variation of goombay music. . . . The cowbells and whistles are complementing the basic beat" (quoted in Lomer 2002, 125–27).

Moxey's perspective on Bahamian music is not that dissimilar from the opinion of Basil Hedrick and Jeanette Stephens, who make an even more overarching, comparative statement in their study of Bahamian folk music, *In the Days of Yesterday and in the Days of Today*. Gathering together not only the three styles under discussion here but also the sacred musical traditions they encountered during their research in the Bahamas, they write: "The same rhythmic patterns occur in secular as in religious music (and in recent vs. traditional music); however, lyrics and performance styles vary considerably" (Hedrick and Stephens 1976, 6).

Although I am interested in the first portion of this statement (and in Moxey's assertions), and while I will be careful to explore the overlaps and intersections that emerge in the course of the analyses that follow, I am primarily interested in Hedrick and Stephens's final point. The lyrics and performance styles do, indeed, "vary considerably," not least because rake-n-scrape, goombay, and Junkanoo have come to occupy quite different spaces within the Bahamas—spaces that find musical style used in very different ways and accruing radically different meanings, for Bahamians and visitors alike. It is toward these performative spaces, toward that "hauntingness of place, through voices, memories, gestures, and narratives that can inhabit a [musical] place for locals and for visitors" described by Minca and Oakes (2006, viii) that I turn in the chapters that follow. The stylistic sketches below are thus offered primarily in order to provide some measure of heuristic differentiation—to provide a point of departure, as it were.

Rake-n-Scrape

The musical style today called rake-n-scrape is a traditional music that originally accompanied social dancing like quadrilles and jumping dances. Rake-n-scrape, however, has not always been known by that name. In fact, until well into the 1960s, it was commonly called goombay music (Moxey 2007). In 1969, Charles Carter, prominent radio host and cultural advocate in the Bahamas, was regularly hosting a radio show called *Young Bahamians* on ZNS-1. This program was designed to showcase the talents of Bahamians, and according to Ed Moxey, Charles Carter recorded a band playing goombay music and subsequently interviewed band members about their style of music, coining the term *rake-n-scrape* in the course of their on-air conversation. Carter, though, does not take credit for coining this term, leaving the origins of the label shrouded in myth (Carter 2007).[32]

What can be said for certain here is that the term *rake-n-scrape* emerged right around the time the Bahamas was pushing for national independence (1969), right around the time the Out Islands became the Family Islands in the national imagination (1971), and right around the time that a new term was needed for the traditional music of the Bahamas (much more on this in chapters 2 and 3). The term *goombay*, like its later update—*rake-n-scrape*—then, tended to designate the drumming as well as the whole range of music that generally accompanied social dancing from the nineteenth century to the 1960s.

FIGURE 1. Ophie and the Websites. Photograph by Timothy Rommen, 2006.

Though the instrumentation of the ensemble has in recent decades come to be standardized around accordion, saw, and goat-skinned drum, the ensembles that were used on the occasion of these social dances throughout most of the nineteenth and well into the twentieth century were generally highly flexible, consisting of whatever instruments happened to be at hand (see Figure 1).

Clement E. Bethel has described the hybrid nature of this music and of the ensembles themselves: "Wooden barrels . . . were converted into drums; cowbells substituted for African bells; scraped saws, bottles, washboards, and animal jawbones replaced the scraped instruments of Africa; and gourds, calabashes and coconut shells filled with dried seeds were excellent surrogates for the shaken rattles of Africa. For playing the melody line, the slaves used anything they could lay their hands on. Sometimes it was a banjo, guitar or fiddle, sometimes a fife, accordion or concertina" (Bethel 1983, 85). It is not insignificant that this fluid ensemble, generally accompanying a wide range of social dances, including both European and African derived forms, appears and reappears in various guises and under different names throughout the Eastern Caribbean. The rhythm, altered a bit here and there and played on different instruments, such as shakers, washboards, squashes (a kind of guiro), and triangles, is called by other names depending on where you happen to be. So in the Turks and Caicos Islands, it is called rip-saw; in the U.S. Virgin Islands, the rhythm is central to scratch bands; in the British Virgin Islands, it is known as fungi; and in Dominica, it is called jing ping.

In the Bahamas, the central rhythm that carries across dance genres and drumming styles and that might even have been performed on the "gambee," or *gimbé*, observed by Johann David Schoepf in 1784, finds its modern Bahamian expression on the saw. According to Ed Moxey, "When we couldn't find the hardwood for the gimbe, we substituted the saw" (quoted in Lomer 2002, 126). Clement E. Bethel offers an excellent description of the techniques used by saw players: "It's an ordinary carpenter's saw, but in the hands of an expert player it becomes a musical instrument of great eloquence. With the handle firmly lodged in his left armpit and the blade gripped in his left hand, the player produces a steady, hypnotic rhythm by scraping the notched edge with a screwdriver held in his right hand. From time to time, the instrument moans eerily as the player flexes the blade to and fro in his left hand while continuing to scrape away with his right" (Bethel 1983, 82).

An alternate technique that players use in order to perform on the saw involves placing the blade end on the ground in front of them and securing it with a foot, but this is only practical when performing in a seated position (see Figure 1). The characteristic saw rhythm consists of a continuous sixteenth-note pattern with accents on the offbeats of one and two in 2/4 meter (see Example 1). This characteristic rhythm is then placed into a context including the goat-skinned drum and a melody instrument—today, usually the accordion.

Rake-n-scrape music—and here the rhythms associated with rake-n-scrape are perhaps most important—has occupied a series of spaces within the Bahamian musical landscape. That said, the primary space assigned to rake-n-scrape in the Bahamas is configured along axes generally considered rural and traditional. In chapter 2, I explore the journeys that have witnessed rake-n-scrape's move into the urban spaces of Nassau and Freeport as popular music (from 1950 to the 1970s) and that have, later still, found this musical style reappropriated as roots music (beginning in the late 1990s). The sociocultural tensions that rake-n-scrape comes to mediate as it moves back and forth between ostensibly provincial and rural Family Island practice and those spaces in Nassau and Freeport constructed as their cosmopolitan and urban antithesis, and the questions of identity that arise and are negotiated as rake-n-scrape participates in reconfiguring the relationship of center to periphery—these are the journeys that inform the analyses offered in chapter 2.

Goombay

Although *goombay* was originally the term used to designate the musical styles discussed in the preceding pages, the label took on a new meaning within the

EXAMPLE 1. Characteristic saw rhythms in rake-n-scrape.

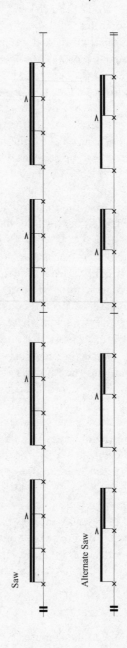

entertainment industry in Nassau beginning in the 1940s. By the 1950s, the term *goombay* had come to be used in order to distinguish the musical style of local popular musicians and nightclub entertainers from the sounds of calypso. This was not merely an arbitrary shift in meaning, however, and this becomes especially clear when considered against the backdrop of the rapidly increasing tourist presence in Nassau and the parallel rise in the popularity of calypso throughout the Caribbean, but especially in the United States.[33] The musicians in Nassau now found themselves in need of a product, and that product needed to represent a pan-Caribbean feel without losing its Bahamian specificity. Goombay was the perfect solution to this dilemma, both in terms of terminology and with regard to the stylistic and rhythmic possibilities it afforded entertainers.

Goombay thus came to represent Bahamian popular music for tourists, not only in name, but also symbolically (through exoticization), and sonically (in and through musical style). That said, this representation was made possible in large part through a recognition that goombay was traditional Bahamian music and through the simultaneous distancing of that traditional practice from the modern spaces of Nassau's nightclubs. As such, the goat-skinned drum, often called the goombay drum by Nassauvians, came to stand in for authentic Bahamian culture in an environment where the claim itself was more important than the practices that were being invoked. Many bands, for example, didn't use the goat-skinned drum per se, choosing the more efficient (and more cosmopolitan) conga drums instead.[34] The bands that played goombay music, moreover, made an increasingly clear distinction between the inspiration they drew from the drum (history/memory) and the music they now played (modern/metropolitan). Rake-n-scrape's characteristic rhythms thus made rather subtle appearances in the goombay music performed in Nassau's nightclubs, usually through transfer to other instruments. The saw rhythm, for instance, was often played on maracas, and the rhythms usually played on the goat-skinned drum were generally (but not always) translated in some fashion to the conga.

I will focus much more on this in chapter 3, but suffice it to say here that this strategic use of the term *goombay* and the highly selective use of its associated instruments and rhythms had the effect of relegating traditional practice to the more exoticized selections in any given evening's program, and even then it was not always a welcome part of the show. Musical selections that were designed to showcase native folkways, then, provided moments during which the goat-skinned drum could be incorporated as one of the featured accompanimental instruments. The fire dances and limbo dances that came to be a part of the local nightclub floor shows of the 1950s and '60s, for instance, were often held to the beating of the "goombay" drum, though even in these performances the goat-skinned drum was often replaced with a conga drum.

Another significant factor during the goombay years is that there were two distinct nightclub scenes. The first of these was the exclusive Bay Street club scene. This scene included all of the major hotels of the day, most of which operated several rooms where live music could be heard and all of which welcomed only white clientele. Another group of nightclubs, known collectively as the Over-the-Hill scene, was the home of entertainment by and for Bahamians. This scene was a part of the so-called chitlin' circuit, and as a result Bahamians had the chance to see many of the major African American entertainers of the day come through nightclubs like the Cat and Fiddle Club during the 1950s and '60s. Importantly, both tourists and local Afro-Bahamian clients were welcome at these clubs, and it is significant that the exoticized floor show routines so popular in the Bay Street clubs also played well in the Over-the-Hill clubs.

The negotiations through which local goombay artists found themselves able to craft their representations of themselves and the Bahamas to tourists in ways calculated simultaneously to garner warm reception by other Bahamians, the ironies embedded in the gradual destruction of the Over-the-Hill scene during the very moment that the Bahamas came under majority rule and attained national independence, and the move away from the umbrella of goombay and toward other modes of representation in the 1970s and '80s are explored at length in chapter 3.

Junkanoo

Bahamian Junkanoo is a celebration—including masquerade, dance, music, and art—rooted in West African spirituality and sharing some connection to similar traditions in Jamaica, Belize, North Carolina, St. Kitts and Nevis, and Bermuda. Unlike pre-Lenten Carnival celebrations in places such as Trinidad, New Orleans, and Brazil, Junkanoo is a yuletide festival, traditionally celebrated on or around Christmas, Boxing Day, and New Year's Day. Today Junkanoo is the primary marker of Bahamian national identity. It is sponsored by the state and is touted as a space within which all Bahamians can come together in equality. As such, it is a civic—that is, a "secular"—festival (Rommen 1999). Junkanoo, though, also exists as a popular music that draws its legitimacy in part from the festival itself. Although these two types of Junkanoo are intimately connected to each other, they also facilitate separate and quite different discursive spaces within which the nation is imagined and narrated. In this sense, Junkanoo is much like goombay—split, that is, into two spheres of music making and musical meaning that nonetheless overlap with and are informed by each other across very different performance contexts.

Ken Bilby (2008), working to trace the archaeology of Junkanoo in the circum-Caribbean, notes that it was likely a well-established practice in Jamaica as early as the late seventeenth century. The first written accounts of Junkanoo in the Caribbean date from the early eighteenth century (1707), but there is, by contrast, no record of Junkanoo in the Bahamas until well after the loyalists settled there. The first accounts of Afro-Bahamian yuletide celebrations in the Bahamas date from just before emancipation (1823 and 1831), but they do not unambiguously describe Junkanoo. Although these accounts describe celebrations held during the customary release from their duties granted to slaves in the early morning hours of Boxing Day (December 26), a time when they were permitted to congregate and enjoy the holiday with family and friends, it would take another decade before similar accounts highlighted celebrations that clearly map onto Junkanoo practice (the 1840s).

After emancipation in 1838, these yuletide celebrations are increasingly recognizable as Junkanoo, yet, like Carnival elsewhere in the Caribbean, they were highly stigmatized by the establishment.[35] The African roots of the music, combined with the violence and disorder that occasionally accompanied the celebration, caused widespread concern among the middle and upper classes. As in the early steel band movement in Trinidad, rival groups would "rush" the streets during the celebration and compete with each other in an attempt to defeat the other groups through music, costumes, and, on occasion, violence. The government attempted to stop the celebration on several occasions and, when that failed, passed laws limiting it in various ways.[36] Thus, while Junkanoo continued to be celebrated, political pressure, in conjunction with middle- and upper-class resistance to the practice, kept it from gaining broad acceptance during the nineteenth century. Gradually, however, the celebration became less controversial, and by the middle of the twentieth century, Junkanoo was a reasonably well-accepted Bahamian cultural marker.

Because Junkanoo is a nighttime festival and is not a pre-Lenten celebration but a Christmas one, it is distinct from Mardi Gras and Carnival in other parts of the circum-Caribbean. Ironically, one of the most dramatic influences on Junkanoo in the twentieth century after World War II was tourism. As a result of visitors' interest, in the early fifties enterprising merchants on Bay Street began to sponsor Junkanoo and organized the celebration into a formal parade with rules for competition and prize money, progressively transforming Junkanoo into a spatially fixed event.

While smaller celebrations do take place throughout the Bahamas (and always have), the primary location of Junkanoo is Bay Street in Nassau, so much so that Junkanoo has disappeared in some of the Family Islands. Cat Island, for instance, witnessed the disappearance of Junkanoo during the middle years of the twentieth century.[37] By the time the Bahamas gained independence, the popularity of Junkanoo was such that it was recognized as a politically and nationally powerful symbol. While the festival is open to tourists, and many visit each year, the festival is for and about Bahamians and has become an embodied experience that locates the Bahamas in a very specific and bounded way, distinguishing it from other nations and offering a musical event through which Bahamians can participate in the nation.

Postindependence efforts by the state contributed a great deal to this perception of Junkanoo. They focused on creating a unifying and universalizing approach to Junkanoo, an agenda exemplified by the government's absorption of the privately administered Masquerade Committee into its Ministry of Tourism. In addition, the nation's first prime minister, Lynden O. Pindling, participated in the festival each year. Maureen "Bahama Mama" DuValier, one of the most famous Junkanoo women, has noted that this top-down participation in the festival contributed to a sense of community pride.

Tinkle Hanna (1999b) claims that "Junkanoo is, above all else, a rhythm." This rhythm is constructed by combining various layers of drums and percussion instruments. The drums are divided into three groups (first, second, and bass) and are complemented by cowbells, foghorns, and whistles. Each instrument contributes an independent line to the composite rhythm, and the performers are afforded a high degree of improvisatory freedom (see Example 2). The pattern played by the second bell players in this transcription is known as kalik and represents what until recently was the most common bell pattern. Since about 1976, the tempo of Junkanoo music has increased, prompting the bell players to raise the rhythmic intensity of their line as well (see Example 2, bells 1). The first and second drummers combine in any number of ways, although the first, or lead drummers usually play a more complex line than that of the second drummers. The bass drummers carry the pulse of the music, and the most common rhythm is transcribed in Example 2.

During the 1970s and 1980s, this rhythmic field and the sonic markers attendant to the festival were increasingly translated into popular music by way of a drum kit and additional percussion instruments. Unlike the negotiations that saw traditional goombay reinvented as popular music—negotiations that distanced the instruments and practices while recontextualizing the rhythms—festival Junkanoo was translated more directly into the repertory and instrumental shape of Bahamian dance bands. It was not uncommon, for example, to incorporate small-scale Junkanoo rushes into concerts (Dr. Offfff was particularly known for this), and bands found it easy to incorporate the cowbells, whistles, and bass drums of festival Junkanoo into their compositions and recordings, thereby marking and marketing their music quite explicitly as Junkanoo. The Baha Men, for example, titled their first major label release *Junkanoo!*, appeared on the cover dressed in Junkanoo costumes, and deliberately saturated most of the album with the sounds of festival Junkanoo instruments.

EXAMPLE 2. Junkanoo rhythms (Wood 1995).

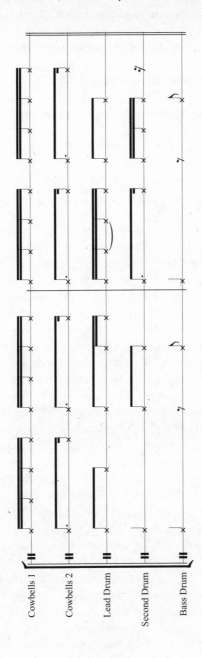

Popular Junkanoo must also be understood as heir to the musical life of Nassau, as the music that replaced goombay music in nightclubs and hotels during the 1970s and '80s. In order to adequately address the role of Junkanoo in the Bahamas, I explore the festival itself in chapter 4 and the popular music in chapters 5 and 6. The increasing connection of Junkanoo to the nation-building project, the nostalgia embedded in the rhetoric about festival Junkanoo and in the lyrics of popular Junkanoo, and the spaces that these practices thereby open for thinking about Bahamian histories and futures form the core of the inquiries I pursue in these chapters.

"BACK TO THE ISLAND":
MUSIC AND THE POETICS OF REPRESENTATION

The historical narratives traced in the first section of this chapter offer a sense of the Bahamas' inexorable move toward tourism as the most viable and, indeed, the best option for long-term economic growth. They illustrate the gradual and contested journey from Crown Colony to independent nation and the concomitant shift from minority to majority rule within the Bahamas. They also provide a clear sense of not only the interposition of the Bahamas between the United States and the rest of the Caribbean, but also the internal center/periphery negotiations attendant to Bahamian life.

The musical styles introduced in the second section of this chapter, for their part, already begin to complicate these histories, not least because the journeys they instantiate are always already moving both centrifugally and centripetally—looking inward while simultaneously reaching outward to specify meaning. In so doing, rake-n-scrape, goombay, and Junkanoo provide particularly powerful lenses through which to think about the Bahamas. The chapters that follow, thus, read these histories—these various forms of travel—against these musical articulations of Bahamianness, focusing attention on the ways these musical practices and the discourses they engendered (from 1949 on) offer insights into the contested and complex poetics of representation at play in the Bahamas. This poetics of representation finds expression both in the process of negotiating internal representations of the Bahamas (i.e., relationships between the Family Islands and Freeport/Nassau) and with respect to the regional representations with which Bahamian musicians have at times necessarily aligned themselves and which have at other times provided a foil against which musicians were able to construct specifically Bahamian images and sounds.

The chorus to the song "Funky Nassau," recorded in 1970 by the Beginning of the End, offers a fitting segue into the chapters that follow, for it illustrates the historical and musical complexities introduced in this chapter in the starkest of terms:

Nassau's gone funky,
Nassau's gone soul.
And we've got a doggone beat now,
We're gonna call our very own.

The lyrics illustrate the influence of North American musical style and language on the Bahamas. However, they simultaneously construct a sense of place and local identity, not least because the changes described are happening in Nassau, where Bahamians have a beat that they "call their very own." The beat to which the song refers, and which the Beginning of the End uses in this song, combines rake-n-scrape and Junkanoo rhythms within an arrangement that privileges funk-driven horns and guitars.

I will have much more to say about this song in chapter 5, but suffice it to say here that the recording opens a window onto the complex context within which Bahamian popular music was and continues to be produced. Media flowing from North America and the Caribbean, along with tourist visitors intimately familiar with archetypal regional representations (the sun, sea, and sand of the Caribbean) as well as North American popular musics, created an atmosphere within which local musicians were called upon to create partial alignments with these genres and regional images while simultaneously constructing in and through their musical choices a case for distinctively Bahamian practices.

That local distinctiveness, however, needed to be carefully constructed so as to present the Bahamas as a modern, cosmopolitan space. The Family Islands are thus often relegated to a background or secondary role, appearing as heritage, inspiration, and folklore, or as a premodern foil for contemporary Nassauvian musical life, when they are not actually silenced (as they are in the song). The Beginning of the End accomplished these multiple negotiations both musically and lyrically in "Funky Nassau," and the chapters that follow aim to better understand the representational dynamics that were at play before that song was created as well as the challenges that continue to inform musicians' choices. I begin by turning to the musical style that has come to be called rake-n-scrape.

2

"Muddy da Water"

Provincializing the Center, or Recentering the Periphery through Rake-n-Scrape

It's about 9:30 in the morning on Saturday, August 11, 2007, and I am sitting at a picnic table in Ed Moxey's backyard. Ed, a former minister of parliament (Coconut Grove), an accomplished organist, and a rake-n-scrape performer, was born in 1933 on Ragged Island but has lived in Nassau for much of his adult life. He settles right into relaying some of his memories about the musical dimensions of his childhood: "When I was a boy, going to the well for water, we used to have a habit of beating the bucket. And my great-grandmother—if she was living she would be over a hundred and fifty year—but she used to say to us, 'Edmund, stop beating that goombay music on that drum before you beat hole in it.' All right?" (Edmund Moxey, interview with the author, August 11, 2007). He launches directly into a few of his thoughts about goombay as a Bahamian musical practice:

> So, every Family Island where there was slaves, and that includes all the Family Islands, because if you go to Abaco, they had, ah—what do you call it in those days?— the plantations. Each, ah, you would find those structures in all the Family Islands where there were black people of African descent. Now what happened was, when the missionary came, you see, when the missionary came, goombay music—gyrating and dancing, whatnot—that was taboo. God don't like that, you see, cause there ain't no goombay music in heaven [laughs]. That's the message that the missionary brought to the Bahamas. Now you will find that, from island to island where there was that religious influence, the indigenous stuff took backstage, from island to island. All right? Until in some islands [trails off]. When I was elected to parliament in 1967, ah, there were no indigenous music in Abaco, there were none in Eleuthera, there were very little in Andros, all the major islands. But at one stage or another

they all had the same basic goombay music, quadrille, jumping dance, fire dance."
(Edmund Moxey, interview with the author, August 11, 2007)

These recollections provide a conceptual frame for this chapter because they offer a glimpse at the terminological slippage at play in speaking of rake-n-scrape, a genre that was known as goombay music until about 1968–69, and because they attempt to bring into view the long and complex history of this constellation of musical practices in the Bahamas. In a similar fashion to quadrille—itself only one of several social dances for which rake-n-scrape performers provided the musical engine and which is coming increasingly to be understood as a highly variegated set of social dance conventions on a theme—rake-n-scrape is best understood as a multivalent performance practice which admits to a great range of variations on its principal musical characteristics (Bilby and Neely 2009).

Ed's recollections concerning the ubiquity and subsequent decline of rake-n-scrape practice throughout the Bahamas, furthermore, offer a window onto another set of issues I explore in this chapter. Though missionary attitudes toward secular music and dance practices undoubtedly contributed significantly to the gradual decline of rake-n-scrape in the Bahamas and to the concomitant prevalence of sacred anthems and rhyming spirituals, the prevailing center/periphery dynamic (thoroughly entrenched by the middle of the nineteenth century) also began to exert a tremendous amount of pressure on Family Islanders—and this was particularly the case during the twentieth century.[1] Internal migration to Nassau (the center), and even extended stays abroad in order to take advantage of labor contracts in the United States, severely disrupted the social context in which rake-n-scrape had previously functioned. It is no coincidence, therefore, that rake-n-scrape, along with the social dances it accompanied, was rapidly falling out of use by the time Ed Moxey was elected to parliament in 1967. The move toward independence, moreover, brought a particularly nationalist ideology to bear on cultural forms that could fruitfully be mobilized in service of Bahamian identity. It comes as no surprise, then, that rake-n-scrape was considered particularly useful in constructing in centripetal fashion narratives of heritage and folklore (Boym 2002).

Rake-n-scrape, the genre label used to circumscribe this variegated and multivalent set of Bahamian musical practices, then, attempts to hold in view a great many threads: the long history of goombay music; the more recent developments in rake-n-scrape practices, accomplished largely without recourse to the grounding that social dance forms erstwhile provided; the centripetal and centrifugal flows that contribute to the ongoing interactions between periphery and center—that contribute to the provincialization of the center or, perhaps more accurately, to the recentering of the periphery (depending on which space is being inhabited); and the roots-driven nostalgia currently propelling the ongoing musical experiments with the genre in the early twenty-first century.

In this chapter, I trace some of the trajectories of rake-n-scrape, focusing particular attention on several moments at which the changing sounds of this style offer poignant insights into these forms of travel. Through exploring the various shapes of traditional goombay music during the nineteenth and early twentieth centuries, by analyzing the incorporation of characteristic rhythms and aesthetic ideas adapted from traditional goombay into the popular music performed in Nassau during the middle of the twentieth century, and through interrogating the recent roots explosion for which rake-n-scrape serves as both ideological inspiration and musical template, this chapter illustrates the complex spaces that rake-n-scrape inhabits within Bahamian musical life, thereby contributing a (counter) narrative that, in the spirit of Dipesh Chakrabarty (2000), refuses one register of address in favor of multiple, competing, partial, and intersecting registers emanating concomitantly from both center and periphery.

RAKE-N-SCRAPE? GOOMBAY AND THE POLITICS OF MUSICAL LABELING

I begin in the middle, which is to say that I choose as my point of entry into this music the moment at which goombay music came to be called rake-n-scrape. In order to situate this a bit, it is helpful to quote at length from a conversation that Ed Moxey and I had regarding rake-n-scrape:

> In 1967, when I came on the scene, I thought to go into a venture to, first of all, research, promote, and cultivate the indigenous music and culture of the Bahamas. And it happened so that the day I went, the trip I made to Cat Island, I couldn't get nobody on Cat Island to play rake-n-scrape music. All right? They were all drawing back and saying "Uhh-uhh-uhh" [shaking his head]. I found one man in New Bight, Cat Island—Chippie was his name—and he had a drum. And I heard this man beating this drum, but I couldn't get nobody to—I couldn't find nobody who wanted to dance the quadrille and whatnot. All right? At the end of the day, because Charles Carter was on one of those shows [*Young Bahamians*], and he was on Cat Island, and what I did were, I took a drummer from here [New Providence/Nassau]—and he wasn't even a goatskin drummer, he was a conga drummer, bongos and conga, Nattie Small—I took Nattie Small from here up to Cat Island with me, said, "Nattie, come, let's go see what's happening on Cat Island," just like that, you know. And when we couldn't find nobody to, right? This is in 1969–1970 in Cat Island.
>
> Now, at the end of the day, the hotel that we were living in, Charles and myself sitting down to the bar, and I said, "Man, Charles," and Charles said he couldn't find anything to take back for his *Young Bahamians* show. So I said, "Man, you can't go empty-handed." I said, "Now let us make some music." And we sat down and he taped us at a resort called Cutlass Bay, and he taped myself, and Nattie Small, and another fellow from Nassau, one of Nattie's neighbor. And he brought that down and, ah, put it on the radio, and said it was Cat Island music [laughs]. It

was my music. And he was all praises to this good music and whatnot, and whatnot, and whatnot.

Two weeks later I went to Cat Island, because I was having the Cultural Festival (the Jumbey Festival, that is, where the Jumbey Village and everything), so, two weeks later I was having this festival and one man said, "Moxey, go back to Cat Island. Something there." I went back to Cat Island. When I got back to Cat Island, we had a meeting in Old Bight, Cat Island. . . . The people: "We didn't know you all appreciate that music, you know? We didn't know people in Nassau appreciate that kind of music." I said, "Appreciate?" I said, "I tell you what, I want to take a whole quadrille cast down to Nassau with me for the festival." And they said, "Yes, we will go."

I brought twenty-three Cat Islanders down to that festival, and they danced, and they danced, and danced, and danced, and that rhythm, that Cat Island rhythm. It was there, but it wasn't dead. The difference is, it was already gone, I mean it was gone in many of the Family Islands. But it was there in Cat Island, and they were afraid to let people really play it. Not afraid, I wouldn't say afraid, but there were questions. You see? That's devil music. (Edmund Moxey, interview with the author, August 11, 2007)

Moxey's narrative brings into view several conversations that were taking place in the Bahamas during the years following the move to majority rule (1967) and leading up to independence (1973). Most of these conversations revolved around the increasing desire to identify practices that could serve as links to a uniquely Bahamian heritage, and around a growing recognition that cultural markers needed to be actively mobilized in order to shape and then promote a national identity in the wake of colonialism. In his capacity as a minister of parliament, Moxey was heavily invested in these conversations and strongly believed that the Out Islands—not coincidentally renamed the Family Islands in 1971 (Craton and Saunders 1998, 359)—held several keys to constructing narratives that draw their authority from structural nostalgia (Herzfeld 1997).

The creation of the cultural festival, and, later, of the cultural center called Jumbey Village in Nassau to which Ed referred in our conversation, was part of Moxey's practical contribution to these conversations (as were his journeys around the Family Islands in the late 1960s), and he was, in this sense, only one of many politicians and cultural activists who were turning their sights to the past in order to recover a Bahamian present equipped to withstand the challenging move from colony to postcolony (Mbembe 2001). This shared heritage was also hitched to explicitly genealogical, familial rhetoric in imagining the independent nation. A case in point can be found in remarks made by Lynden O. Pindling during the drive toward independence:

What does it take to be a Bahamian? Loyalty to our Bahamas over and above all others; zeal for our Bahamas unmatched by any other; concern for other Bahamians above all others. . . . Our Bahamian Nation is unfolding before our very eyes as we ring down the final curtain on this great family drama in which all of us have played star roles. . . . You have come to refresh your memories about the past; you have come to examine the present; and you have come to plan the future. . . . Living as we are on these Islands we are children of the sea. Living on these Family Islands, we are one Family. (quoted in Craton 2002, 198–99)[2]

I will devote much more attention to Jumbey Village and to the rhetoric of local politics in chapter 5, but it is important to note here Moxey's importation of a Cat Island quadrille cast into the context of his cultural festival and to emphasize that the space of the Bahamian "family" in the present still revolved unequivocally around Nassau. In other words, the center (Nassau and Freeport) operated in the contemporary moment, whereas heritage was imported to the center from the periphery. What interests me most about Moxey's account, then, is the imagined location of the past within the almost-independent Bahamas, for the past is here connected with and directly related to the periphery—to the lifeways and musical practices of Family Islanders.

This habitual reading of the Family Islands as the antithesis of the cosmopolitan, modern Bahamas was progressively entrenched during the nineteenth century and remained a liability for Family Islanders well into the 1960s. In fact, it was only during the late 1960s that attitudes began to shift, and then only insofar as these antimodern spaces came to be seen as potentially useful to the project of identifying cultural content that could productively be translated into the postcolony. Cat Islanders' reticence to perform traditional musics and dances—while certainly related to changes in the Family Islands themselves—was thus influenced in part by their desire not to reinforce among the inhabitants of Nassau and Freeport attitudes and perceptions of Family Islanders as rural and provincial. And they had good reason to be wary of these center-periphery dynamics. About a decade earlier, for instance, Samuel Charters and Ann Danberg spent the best part of the summer living and working on Andros. Stopping over in Nassau on their return journey to the United States, they encountered the very attitudes that Ed Moxey, in his official capacity, no doubt embodied for Family Islanders a decade later.

Wondering what they would say about the music we had traveled to Andros to find we brought the tape recorder back downstairs, set it up on a table, and played some of the songs from Fresh Creek. The owner, again in one of his white shirts and dark trousers, listened and nodded his head. "That's the old way, that's the old way when I grew up." It seemed to be completely natural to him that some of the people on Andros were still singing like that. What was still a little confusing to all of them was that Ann and I were so excited by it. He didn't seem to be concerned about any of the music as part of a tradition that he shared with the Andros people. One of the men called out from another table. "Those boys a little behind." The owner smiled indulgently. "They know how to do it. We have to give them that. They know how to do it." (Charters 1999, 167)

Ed Moxey, for his part, was indeed genuinely interested in rake-n-scrape music and jumping dance and quadrille in 1969, for he saw what these practices could offer to the nationalist agenda promulgated by the majority-rule Progressive Liberal Party government. Family Islanders, however, were wary of that interest and initially adopted a conservative, even defensive approach in response to his requests. It was only after they heard some of the sounds of goombay on the radio (emanating from the center, that is) that Cat Islanders chose to participate in Moxey's project. That symbolic link between heritage and the Family Islands, enacted in and through the performances of the Cat Island quadrille cast at the cultural festival, however, was still mobilized in service of center/periphery political ends and, as such, represented only a shift in emphasis, not a move toward rethinking the periphery. Put otherwise, the move from being considered provincial and "a little behind" to being touted as culture-bearers and traditional practitioners does not, in fact, entail a move beyond the provincial stereotype attached to Family Islanders, but simply recasts those very stereotypes in terms that can be appropriated and made useful in service of the center.

By the late 1960s, then, rake-n-scrape came to be chained into Bahamian nationalist discourse (read as centripetal and internal) and, importantly, also set in motion a folklorizing trajectory for the practice. But there was a second space within Bahamian life, already several decades in the making by this point, within which rake-n-scrape was called upon to serve in a manner that contrasts dramatically with the nationalist space I have been describing here. That other space was located in the explicitly public and extranational popular music industry of Nassau (read as centrifugal and produced for consumption). This space, which rake-n-scrape inhabited in predominantly discursive as opposed to actual (musical) fashion, relied on the same archaeology of Bahamian heritage, but did so in order to craft a product that was both regional (Caribbean) and grounded in local practice (Bahamas). Before exploring these trajectories of rake-n-scrape, however, it remains for me to explore the earlier instantiations of goombay music that informed the music and dance from the nineteenth century on and shaped the practices that Moxey remembers from his childhood and sought out in Cat Island. What was Moxey after? What did he expect to find when he traveled to the Family Islands?

THE BALLROOM COMPLEX AND RING DANCES: GOOMBAY MUSIC AND SOCIAL DANCE IN THE BAHAMAS

Any discussion of nineteenth- and early twentieth-century musical practices in the Bahamas must, unfortunately, be prefaced by an explicit acknowledgment that very little documentation exists for this period of Afro-Bahamian musical life.[3] Further complicating matters, there is very little evidence for a generalized practice throughout the Bahamas. Put otherwise, it is much more likely that each of the Bahamian Islands developed its own approaches to social dance forms and quadrille figures than that a shared practice emerged throughout the archipelago. That said, however, several important aspects of the early history of social dance in the Bahamas need to be introduced and interrogated here.

For starters, quadrille was only one among a range of dances within what might be called the Continental ballroom complex. According to Kenneth Bilby and Daniel Neely,

> Throughout the nineteenth century, a range of social dances originally associated with the European ballroom found favor in the colonies and became the basis for subaltern adaptations. These included round dances such as the polka, mazurka, polka-mazurka, varsovienne, two-step and gallop; circle dances like maypole; longways dances like the contradance and country dance; solo dances like jigs and clogs; and square dances like the cotillion, quadrille, and lancers. Many of these included steps that functioned as interchangeable parts of dance suites; others, such as particular longways and square dances, were themselves suites that included as few as four (but generally more) individual "figures." On the continent, individual and figure dances were highly prescribed affairs, characterized in their original forms by a lack of physical intimacy, though this eventually changed, particularly through the international popularity of the waltz. In the colonies, not only did these dances become the basis for local and sometimes idiosyncratic choreographic interpretation, but they were sometimes reconfigured, recontextualized, and resignified to such an extent that the only obvious remaining connection to their Continental forebears was their name. (Bilby and Neely 2009, 232)

Upon its arrival in the Caribbean in the early decades of the nineteenth century, the quadrille seems to have relatively rapidly found itself coming unmoored from its prescribed, Continental format. That format generally cycled through five figures, including *le pantalon, l'été, la poule, la pastourelle,* and *finale.* Another figure, called *la trenise,* sometimes replaced the *pastourelle* but could also be added to the end of the suite (as happened in Viennese practice, for instance). In a discussion of the rise of the quadrille to a position of prominence within the Paris ballroom scene, Maribeth Clark points out the general musical shape that people came to expect from this dance:

> The structural regularity of the quadrille contributed to its popularity while it detracted from its value as music. Unlike dance suites of the 17th and 18th centuries, all quadrilles were designed so that they might accompany dance. Contrast between the phrases or figures could never be introduced through dramatic changes of movement, such as that between an allemande, a courante, and a gigue. Rather, the composer or arranger created musical interest through contrasting melodies, surprising harmonic gestures, or rhythmic play within the 2/4 or 6/8 meter. Aside from the potential rhythmic, melodic, and harmonic interest an arranger might

introduce, the genre experienced a predictable uniformity of pulse, phrasing, and form, its five movements or *airs de danse* written to match the physical dimensions of the figures they accompanied. The movement accompanying each figure was generally composed of four- or eight-measure melodic phrases with a simple chordal accompaniment, its 32 or 24 measures providing just enough music for the active pair of dancers to complete the required figure. . . . The identity of the quadrille was linked more with the figures and the formal construction of five movements than with a strict metrical emphasis. (Clark 2002, 504–5)

Clark's description of the musical character of quadrille, at least in terms of its meter, brevity, and function, continued to operate within colonial contexts throughout the Caribbean, but as many scholars have observed, naming conventions, actual formal structures like the number of figures, the order of figures, and the content of figures, and even the dance steps associated with all of these were subject to great variation across the circum-Caribbean. John Szwed and Morton Marks, for instance, observe: "A European dance name may refer to an entirely different dance; or a native New World term may disguise a well-known European form; and the European name for a step may label a complex dance in its own right" (Szwed and Marks 1988, 29). In Carriacou, for instance, the six figures that constitute a full quadrille performance came to be known simply as figure 1, figure 2, and so on. "The first four figures of the Carriacou English quadrille remain the same from performance to performance. The fifth figure is typically upbeat, and the sixth figure takes the form of either a waltz quadrille, a *cacian,* or the 'heel and toe' polka" (Miller 2007, 68).

The same general principal was operative on Cat Island, where Cleophas "Ophie" Webb and Pumpey "Bo Hog" Johnson both talk about quadrille figures as being called out as "one time" (first figure), "two time" (second figure), and so forth. But in an interview with Ken Bilby, Bo Hog describes a quadrille that has seven figures, including four quadrille sets, a round dance, a heel-and-toe polka, and a waltz. He goes on to add, however, that the lead dancer had control of the exact number of quadrilles that would be danced. So, for example, after the first quadrille, the dancer could call out "five time," meaning that the musicians should play the round dance next, thereby skipping over the other three quadrille sets (Ken Bilby, personal communication with the author, June 2008). An illustration of the fluid nature of quadrille performance from island to island in the Bahamas presents itself when we consider that Ed Moxey adds a ring dance to the end of the litany of dances offered by Bo Hog. But rather than talking about eight sets, he speaks in terms of five, eliminating all but the first quadrille set from his count. Suffice it to say here, then, that the Bahamian quadrille participated in the same processes that Bilby and Neely and Marks and Szwed identify as characteristic of the fluid nature of social dance during the nineteenth century in the Caribbean.

The progressive adaptation to Caribbean contexts of the ballroom complex, however, was not only a matter of rethinking music and dance in at times highly idiosyncratic ways, for these practices were also freighted with particularly strong class associations. They arrived, that is, ready to be utilized in service of a Eurocentric sociocultural agenda. Interestingly, the quadrille in particular was to undergo a bit of a class-adjustment in the process of its translation into Caribbean contexts. Maribeth Clark makes a compelling assertion that during the 1820s and 1830s the quadrille came to be read within the Parisian scene as an encroachment of bourgeois mediocrity on spaces reserved for aristocratic civility (Clark 1995). Elsewhere she observes: "In almost every way, the genre fits squarely into Carl Dahlhaus's nether region of trivial music" (Clark 2002, 505). The quadrille experienced a similar, if slightly later, shift from elite to popular spaces in England. Rebecca Miller points out that by the 1830s the quadrille was "firmly established as the foremost ceremonial court dance" (Miller 2007, 78). She goes on to note that by the middle of the nineteenth century quadrilles "became less of an elite pursuit, and, like many expressive genres, moved into the culture of the European lower classes. . . . Because Britain and France were key imperialist world powers during these centuries, quadrille and its variants spread prolifically throughout the English and French colonies worldwide" (Miller 2007, 79).

These class associations notwithstanding, upon its arrival in the Caribbean, the quadrille was read in quite different terms. Jocelyne Guilbault, for instance, reminds us that for colonial elites one of the important aspects of Continental dances such as the quadrille was their capacity to illustrate in and through their very performance the contrasts envisioned to exist between European- and African-derived cultural models—a fact that, in one deft move, reconstituted the quadrille as an elite dance in its own right. A dialectic turning on superiority, mastery, order, knowledge, and cultivation on the one hand and inferiority, subordination, chaos, ignorance, and barbarousness on the other, informed the class associations that accrued to ballroom (high-class) and folk (low-class) dances (Guilbault 1985, 34). In a rather ironic reversal of fortunes, then, the quadrille came to be read in the Caribbean as the epitome of refinement and civility.

A prime illustration of this idea can be seen in any number of newspaper reviews of balls in the Bahamas during the middle of the nineteenth century. I offer two representative examples here in order to illustrate the extent to which taste, refinement, class, respectability, and dance became part and parcel of upper-class affairs in this Bahamian context.

> The Ball given at the Mess House by Major Clarke and the Officers of the Garrison last evening, in honor of Her Majesty's Birth-day, passed off most agreeably. The company began to assemble at 8 o'clock, and on the arrival of His Excellency the Governor and Mrs. Gregory at half-past 8, dancing commenced, Major Clarke and Mrs. Gregory

opening the ball. The room was very tastefully decorated, flags overhanging each window in graceful festoons, while two of ample folds were placed at the head and foot, under which hung full-length portraits of Her Majesty and Prince Albert. The nicely-chalked floor exhibited appropriate devices, the Crown and Royal Initials "V.R." occupying a prominent position in the centre. "1st West India Regiment" being encircled above and the Ordnance Arms, with the motto "Sua tela tenant," standing out in bold relief below. A star of bayonets glittered on the northern wall, under which were the seats appropriated for the Governor and his Lady. Chinese lanterns, covered with the most laughable and grotesque figures, were suspended from the eastern windows, and the whole *coup d'eil* was exceedingly animated and pleasing. . . . Dancing was kept up with great spirit till past 12—quadrille, waltz, polka, and schottische following in quick succession—when "The Roast Beef of Old England" from the musicians, announced that the time had arrived for retiring to the supper table, which was filled with every delicacy of the season. . . . After supper dancing was resumed with the same spirit with which it commenced and concluded with "Sir Roger de Covetley" at 3 o'clock in the morning. (*Nassau Guardian*, May 28, 1851)

Though the following example does not specifically enumerate the types of dances enjoyed by the previous evening's guests, it does offer a further glimpse into the kinds of dress, decoration, social company, and cuisine that, when combined with ballroom dancing, served to create the superiority, mastery, order, knowledge, and cultivation associated with the elite.

Seldom have we had an opportunity of recording a Ball so elaborately got up as that which took place at Government House last evening in honor of the marriage of H. R. H. the Prince of Wales with H. R. H. Princess Alexandra of Denmark. That happy event, as our readers are aware, was celebrated at Windsor on Tuesday last and to commemorate it in this loyal isle, His Excellency Governor Bayley, C.B., and his universally beloved partner spared neither pains nor expenses. The guests, which numbered about 160, comprised the Members of the Legislature and their wives, the Officers of the Garrison and 2nd W. I. Regiment, the Officers of H. M. S. *Barracouta*, the new U.S. Consul and many other Americans, besides most of our leading citizens. They began to assemble at 9 o'clock and in about half an hour dancing commenced. The ladies were elegantly dressed, white trimmed with pink predominating. . . . The numerous and appropriate motives emblazoned on beautiful and diversified scrolls in characters of the Fourteenth century, met with deserved admiration. . . . After the first eleven dances the company repaired to the supper room, which, it is needless to state, was laid out with every delicacy that could be procured. . . . Dancing was resumed after supper and continued with spirit till 4 o'clock this morning. The Band of the 2nd W.I. Regiment was stationed on a platform erected close to the southern piazza and played admirably. (*Nassau Guardian*, March 14, 1862)

L. D. Powles, who had occasion to spend eight months in the Bahamas during 1886–87, offers a somewhat less enthusiastic appraisal of dancing among the upper crust of Nassau:

Their favourite amusement is dancing, and their devotion to Terpsichore is positively abnormal, considering the heat of the climate, which renders physical exertion more or less trying at the best of times. In fact the upper crust rarely unbend except at a dance. Then dignity is laid aside for the nonce, and Governor, Commander-in-Chief, Privy Councillors, Nobles, and Commoners, mingle with reckless youngsters in one wild and giddy whirl. Proh Sudor! There is not much of the poetry of motion about their dancing but unquestionably there is a great deal of go. But they are wedded to their own style, and when an English lady, who was particularly graceful in her movements, ventured to suggest one or two improvements, she was not thanked. (Powles 1888, 131–32)

Powles offers valuable (if rather sarcastic) perspective on the social dance scene in Nassau, not least because he points out the idiosyncratic style that had, by the end of the nineteenth century, come to define Bahamian ballroom dancing. But Powles was residing in the Bahamas because he was an appointed stipendiary and circuit justice, which means that in addition to hearing cases in Nassau he also toured the Out Islands twice during his term of service. In the course of his circuit travels throughout the archipelago, he made a point of documenting some of the dancing he witnessed, thereby offering one of the early accounts of social dancing among Afro-Bahamians. It should come as no surprise that Afro-Bahamians had learned the music and dance conventions of the ballroom scene and adapted them to their own communal use.[4] By the middle of the nineteenth century, then, these dances were integral to Afro-Bahamian community gatherings and celebrations in New Providence as well as throughout the Family Islands. The following passage, in which Powles describes celebrations attendant to a wedding on Fortunate Island (near Acklins and Long Cay) is particularly important in that it illustrates practices that had become conventional by the late nineteenth century:

It took a long time to start the dancing, as everyone was shy of beginning, but when once it did start it soon waxed fast and furious. A dance called the "Marengo," imported from Cuba, seemed to be the favourite, and a great many quadrilles were danced with elaborate figures and a great deal of bowing and scraping. The dancers moved with much grace and brought every muscle of their bodies into play. The music consisted of a fife, a large accordeon, and two tambourines which had to be continually taken out and warmed at a large fire in the yard to keep them going. About midnight a bevy of old ladies in their working-dresses appeared and danced jigs for an hour with all the energy of their first youth. One of them, the bride-groom's mother, was fearfully and wonderfully fat, but she hopped about like a bird. The jigs the darkies dance are ordinary Irish jigs, and they seem to consider them quite as much their national dance as the Irishman does. (Powles 1888, 257)

In addition to a clear illustration of the ubiquity of the quadrille, the passage also sheds light on the musical influence of the Bahamas' large neighbors to the west and south, Cuba and Haiti. According to Clement Bethel, the "Marengo" would gradually come to be known in its transplanted Bahamian context as a dance called skullin' (Bethel 1978). It is important to consider these intraregional flows of musical style and dance because these flows dramatically shaped practices throughout the region, providing other options and suggesting new possibilities for communities struggling to negotiate points of intersection between elite, European-derived musical practices and local, African-derived inheritances. "Marengo," or skullin', thus forms an oblique deflection, useful in the Bahamas precisely because of its distance from the local context within which the ballroom complex was being translated into Afro-Bahamian social dance. These intraregional flows can fruitfully be read in terms of a dynamic which I have elsewhere called the negotiation of proximity (Rommen 2007), and I will have occasion in later chapters to return to this idea. For now, however, I continue illustrating the range of social dancing prevalent among Afro-Bahamians during Powles's tenure in the archipelago.

I have thus far focused attention primarily on the ballroom complex, but the full scope of social dance among Afro-Bahamians also included fire dance, jumping dance (or jump-in dance), and ring plays.

A form of open-air dancing has also a great hold upon them. It is called a "fire-dance" and is, no doubt, a relic of savage life. I had heard so much about these fire-dances that I arranged with the sergeant of police to have one got up for my especial benefit, and I went to see it in company with a Russian gentleman who happened to be staying at the hotel. The people formed a circle, and a fire was lighted in their midst. The music consisted of two drums that would not work unless frequently warmed at the fire. The company clapped their hands without ceasing all through the dance, chanting all the while in a sort of dreary monotone, "Oh kindoiah! kindoiah! Mary come along!" When the dance was about half through, the refrain was suddenly changed to "Come down, come down," repeated over and over again in the same dreary monotone. Every now and then a man or a woman, or a couple together would rush into the centre of the circle and dance wildly about. There appeared to be no step or idea of figure about the performance, the aim and object of the dancers, as far as one could make it out, being to execute as many extravagant capers in and over, and around, and about the fire as they could without burning themselves. (Powles 1888, 148)

This passage offers an important window onto the types of dances that stood alongside the ballroom dance complex in Afro-Bahamian experience during the late nineteenth century. The drums Powles noted are undoubtedly goat-skinned drums (even well-crafted drums need to be "fired" every thirty to forty minutes in order to keep the head taught enough for performance). The ring dance format itself is important in that it suggests strong links to African-derived practices, and we have already encountered the ring dance in the context of Ed Moxey's quadrille sets (Floyd 1996). In a passage concerned with fire dances, penned in 1930, Zora Neale Hurston offers a more detailed description tracing along the same outlines offered by Powles some forty years earlier. Her account, moreover, offers much more information about the music that accompanied the social dances. Interestingly, Hurston suggests that the jumping dance and the ring play are best understood as two "types" of fire dancing. I offer Hurston's description at length:

> There are two kinds of the dance, the jumping dance, and the ring play, which is merely a more elaborate form of the jumping dance. The dances are purely social.
>
> In either form of this dancing, the players form a ring, with the bonfire to one side. The drummer usually takes his place near the fire. The drum is held over the blaze until the skin tightens to the right tone. There is a flourish signifying that the drummer is all set. The players begin to clap with their hands. The drummer cries, "Gimbay!" (a corruption of the African word *gumbay,* a large drum) and begins the song. He does not always select the song. The players more often call out what they want played. One player is inside the ring. He or she does his preliminary flourish, which comes on the first line of the song, does his dance on the second line, and chooses his successor on the third line and takes his place in the circle. The chosen dancer takes his place and the dance goes on until the drum gets cold. What they really mean by that is, that the skin of the head has relaxed until it is no longer in tune. The drummer goes to the fire and tunes it again. This always changes the song.
>
> As an example we may take Bimini Gal. A player has just been chosen. The whole assembly is singing in concert.
>
> "Bim'ni gal is a hell of a trouble." Player makes his flourish while yet in the circle.
>
> "Never get a licking till you go down to Bim'ni." Player dances out to center of the ring.
>
> "Eh, lemme go down to Bim'ni." He does his own particular step, which is varied according to the skill of the dancer.
>
> "Never get a licking till you go down to Bim'ni." He dances up to the one he chooses and takes his place back in the circle, as the next dancer winds up for her flourish. Men usually choose women and vice versa. The children play too, and with the adults.
>
> In the ring play, it is to be noted that the songs are longer, as befits a more elaborate dance. The procedure is the same, except that the dancer in the ring does not retire immediately upon selecting his successor. The one chosen enters the ring with him and the two dance a sensuous duet for a full minute or so, then the retiring dancer is swung to his place.
>
> This dancing is universal in the Bahamas, the educated Negroes excepted. It resembles the Cuban *rumba* and the dances held in New Orleans after the great migration of Haitian and Santo Dominican Negroes after the success of L'Ouverture. Every dry night the drums can be heard throbbing, no matter how hard the dancers have worked that day, or must work the next. (Hurston 1930, 294–95)

Like Powles, Hurston offers a real sense of the multiple registers at which Afro-Bahamians were negotiating musical practice, in her case invoking connections to music and dance in Cuba and New Orleans in order to illustrate the performances she observed in the Bahamas. And she was right to point to these flows of sound and practice, for they provided an important space within which Afro-Bahamians continued to balance their interactions with and translations of the ballroom complex against those practices that had more direct genealogical ties to African models. These interactions had tangible consequences, such as the adaptation of the clave, called cleavers by Bahamians, into their musical practice. That said, however, the clave did not function as a means of communicating time line as it does in rumba, for instance, but rather as a percussion instrument that could contribute another rhythmic layer to a performance. I will explore the role of the clave in greater detail in chapter 3.

Unlike Hurston, however, Clement Bethel maintains that there were three distinct types of ring dances in the Bahamas during the nineteenth century—the fire dance, the jumping dance, and the ring-play (Bethel 1978). Gail Saunders, drawing on Bethel's ideas, maintains that the dances were all "held upon the formation of a ring where the participants stood in a circle around one or more dancers. There was always some type of rhythmic accompaniment, either singing, chanting, clapping, drum rhythms, or a combination of these. Solo dancing took place at some point in the proceedings. The sequence of events in all three dances was similar. To begin, a solo dancer would perform in the center of the ring and start the dance. After dancing for a short time, he would choose some person of the opposite sex from the circle to replace him. The succeeding dancer imitated this sequence until each person had danced in the ring" (Saunders 1985, 163).

So, in addition to the various dances adapted from the ballroom complex, at least three types of ring dances as well as a more informal type of dance, eventually called skullin', seem to have been popular among Afro-Bahamians beginning in the nineteenth and continuing into the twentieth century. The fire dance came to be reinterpreted in the nightclub scene of Nassau as an exotic "native" dance, finding expression alongside limbo dance and other novelty acts in a professional environment quite far removed from the community-based atmosphere that had animated the ring dances in the nineteenth and early twentieth centuries. Basil Hedrick and Jeanette Stephens, for example, observed: "The ubiquitous 'fire dances' and 'limbo' viewed in awe and amusement by tourists and Bahamians alike are not Bahamian in origin and have never been performed as popular couple dances, being primarily reserved for showmanship in a solo performance situation" (Hedrick and Stephens 1976, 32). I will return to explore these strategic aspects of Nassauvian floor shows in chapter 3.

With the exception of the various ring dances, which were generally accompanied only by drums (sometimes in pairs), then, all of these forms of social dancing were accompanied by goat-skinned drum and some combination of additional percussion and melody instruments (recall, for example, the ensemble that Powles observed, which included "fife, a large accordeon, and two tambourines"). Banjo, guitar, fife, and washtub bass were all regular participants in these dance bands, but the goat-skinned drum was the constant ground upon which these ensembles were built. While this flexibility in terms of instrumentation remained a hallmark of goombay music through the first half of the twentieth century, the use of saw and accordion in conjunction with the drum came to be relatively normative by the mid-twentieth century, and this trio of instruments has since that time come sonically to mark traditional goombay (rake-n-scrape) music.[5]

GOOMBAY MUSIC AS FOLKLORE? THE RECORDINGS
OF LOMAX, STEARNS, AND CHARTERS

Before returning to the late 1960s, when Ed Moxey was working to uncover signs of the quadrille in Cat Island, it is important to consider the scholarship that was being conducted in the Bahamas during the first half of the twentieth century. In particular, it is worth exploring the recordings made by several folklorists who spent time collecting music in the Bahamas and Key West between 1935 and 1959. These scholars invested themselves in documenting folk music and folkways in the Bahamas, but they may also have (unintentionally) contributed to chronicling what, in retrospect, can be understood as the gradual folklorization of goombay music in the Bahamas. I suggest that the relative lack of goombay music in their catalogs reflects this trajectory and helps to indicate the place (or lack thereof) of goombay music in the lives and representational strategies of Bahamians between 1935 and 1964.

A large percentage of the recordings made by scholars like Alan Lomax, Marshall Stearns, and Samuel Charters document sacred musical practices like anthems and rhyming spirituals. Another group of recordings focuses attention on sea chanteys and work songs. A few tracks point to the goombay tradition, but these performances are, by far, in the minority across these collections. In 1935, when Alan Lomax first recorded performers in the Bahamas, the shape of what was then still called goombay music looked very much like it had a half-century before, when Powles was making his "circuits." And yet the recordings Lomax made do not include any songs identified as quadrilles, focusing instead on round dances and ring plays. This absence raises some very interesting questions about what quadrille practice actually looked like by the interwar period. Was it already on the verge of passing out of active practice? If so, why did Lomax and others neglect to record it? Recorded on Andros and Cat Island, the majority of his material is made up of work songs, chanteys, and anthems, as opposed to social dance music stemming from the ballroom complex, perhaps indirectly confirming Ed Moxey's assertion that missionary attitudes toward these secular dance forms informed choices in terms of what kinds of music should be supported (at least in front of microphones held by researchers).

Lomax went on to release two albums, both currently available from Rounder Records: *Deep River of Song: Bahamas 1935, Chanteys and Anthems from Andros and Cat Island* and *Deep River of Song: Bahamas 1935, Vol. 2, Ring Games and Round Dances.* The work songs and anthems are collected under one cover, while the ring games and round dances, both of which fall into the category of play and social dance, are gathered under separate cover. In setting up a dichotomy cutting across serious/frivolous, work/play, sacred-vocational/secular-recreational, Lomax's Rounder releases in fact offer a good indication of the spaces that these musical pursuits filled in Bahamian life. And yet it is interesting to note that in Lomax's work the secular and recreational side of this dichotomy is filled with performances that do not address the ballroom complex in any sustained way. Granted, round dances found their way into the quadrille in the Bahamas, but Lomax seems to have been much more interested in recording ring plays and story songs than he was in addressing himself to creolized set dances. His field notes (very scant), as well as his recording log (again, quite minimal in terms of information), do not offer any insights along these lines either. Given that Lomax was not reticent to record creolized practices elsewhere in the Caribbean, it seems reasonable to suggest that he was either more interested in the ring games or that he never had occasion to record performances of quadrille, waltz, and the like.[6] If the latter was the case, then the absence may constitute evidence that the quadrille and the entire ballroom complex were already falling out of active practice in the archipelago.

Marshall Stearns, who recorded the performances released on *Religious Songs and Drums in the Bahamas* (Folkways 4440) in 1953, chose a strategy similar to that of Lomax, recording primarily sacred songs and contrasting these with drumming. In this case, Stearns includes a fire dance, a jumping dance, a track he calls a jook dance, and a ring play. The track that stands out in the midst of these selections as connected to the ballroom complex is a track simply called "Heel and Toe Polka." Of this track, Stearns writes in the liner notes only that "it is social rather than religious." His recordings of Bahamian music in Key West, Florida, released in 1964 under the title *Junkanoo Band—Key West* (Folkways 4492) offer a good sense of the connection between goombay music and Junkanoo celebrations in general, but very little sense of the range of musical possibilities and social dancing that was then still categorized as goombay music. Again, the ballroom complex was essentially inaudible.

Samuel Charters recorded a great deal of music during his fieldwork on Andros in 1958. In addition to an album featuring the music of guitarist Joseph Spence, he released two other albums, both in 1959: *Music of the Bahamas: Anthems, Work Songs, and Ballads from the Bahamas Islands* (Folkways 3845) and *Music of the Bahamas: Instrumental Music of the Bahamas* (Folkways 3846). The presence of the ballroom complex, however, is once again quite limited, including only one waltz, a polka, and a quadrille (these are the last three selections on the instrumental album). Charters briefly discusses the lively performance style of the band that played these dance songs (the Daniel Saunders Brass Band), and in the very last sentence of the album's liner notes, he asserts: "The three dances, the polka, the waltz, and the quadrille are still the most popular dances of the older settlements on Andros." The quadrille performance itself fades into silence at the end of the record, and Charters's assertion is, in similar fashion, left hanging in the air, as it were. Considering the quite small proportion of the recordings that are quadrilles, waltzes, and polkas seems to suggest otherwise.

It is perhaps fitting that the last track on Charters's album of instrumental recordings is a quadrille and that it ends with a fade-out, not least because the ballroom complex was by this time in very obvious decline. This is when most of the performers now active in rake-n-scrape circles grew up, and they all mark this as the moment during which social dancing in the Bahamas took a turn away from the ballroom and toward the radio, away from jumping dance and toward soul and funk. In 1976, folklorists Basil Hedrick and Jeanette Stephens wrote:

> Several European folk dances are, or at one time were, found in the Bahamas. These include the quadrille, polka, mazurka, lancer, and waltz. Of particular popularity was and, to a limited degree, is the quadrille, the dance composed of five separate parts, which was developed in France, brought to England and later introduced into the Bahamas. It spread widely among the local populace. Musical accompaniment for the quadrille and other European dances is provided by the ensemble of an accordion, saw, and goatskin drum. The accordion plays the melody, the saw provides the basic steady rhythm, and the drum introduces rhythmical intensification and variation. Around the turn of the century, singing voices, rather than the accordion, often provided the melody. Sadly, perhaps—at least to the traditionalist—it is far more common today to see the dances done throughout much of the Western Hemisphere, such as the Boogie, Merengue, the Bump, the Hustle, etc. (Hedrick and Stephens 1976, 32–33)

Because dancers increasingly gravitated toward the more cosmopolitan sounds emanating from their radios, and because the communal function of social dancing continued to erode because of out-migration and the emergence of alternative entertainment possibilities (like radio), the very function of goombay music was being called into question. In this climate of uncertainty, the sonic shape of goombay music, nevertheless, remains quite clear. The real question, it seems to me, was whether the music could stand to lose its close connection to dance. Ed Moxey, himself steeped in goombay music, thus came to Cat Island in the late 1960s in order to see performances of this wide range of dances—dances that were no longer prevalent in New Providence, and as it turns out, were passing out of active practice in Cat Island as well—and to hear the goat-skinned drum–driven music that accompanied these dances. He expected to find communities still actively playing goombay and dancing as part of the fabric of their lives. He anticipated encountering a set of practices that could be mobilized in service of the nation. What he found instead was a tradition of music making and social dance falling out of active use and experiencing in devastating fashion the pressures of out-migration.

Hedrick and Stephens seem to have read the musical geography of the Bahamas accurately (as did Lomax, Stearns, and Charters before them). The antecedents that contributed to the shape of social dance music—and in particular the dances—have indeed, by and large, fallen out of active practice in the Bahamas since the 1950s (a process that began perhaps as early as the 1930s). Today, only a very few specialists still know how to dance the quadrille, and beyond staged performances at events such as the Cat Island Rake-n-Scrape Festival or Junkanoo in June in Nassau, the dance no longer holds a place in the day-to-day lives of Bahamians. But the music that accompanied these social dances has found other contexts within which to sound out across the archipelago. It is not insignificant that goombay music's new label—rake-n-scrape—was articulated at precisely the moment when the music was (necessarily) shedding its accompanimental role and staking out ground as musical entertainment in its own right. With this historical context as backdrop, I turn now to an exploration of some of the ways that rake-n-scrape has traveled into new social and performative spaces throughout the second half of the twentieth century.

"RAKE-N-SCRAPE PARTY":
FROM BUSH TO BACKYARD AND BACK AGAIN

The sounds of what is today called rake-n-scrape music configure themselves along very specific axes of Bahamian life—along axes that include, in particular, the rural and the peripheral and that for many Bahamians reference spaces at the margins (both geographically and socially) of the nation's political and economic life. Traditional rake-n-scrape bands such as Bo Hog and the Rooters, Thomas Cartwright and the Boys, and Ophie and the Websites, for instance—are performing music that is most thoroughly associated with places like Cat Island and Long Island, the two Family Islands where rake-n-scrape has maintained the strongest presence. Rake-n-scrape is, of course, also present in places like Crooked Island, Exuma, and Andros, but Cat Island and Long Island have long fostered a strong rivalry and, as such, are well known for their rake-n-scrape performers. That said, Ophie and the Websites in particular cleverly announce through their band name (a pun on Ophie's surname—Webb) deep connections to modernity, technology, and the center, thereby suggesting that there are other ways of reading the sounds of rake-n-scrape, other possibilities that find rake-n-scrape occupying (claiming) quite different spaces within the Bahamian social imaginary.

In the following sections, I illustrate the centrifugal and centripetal flows that have animated the creation and reception of rake-n-scrape and do so through an exploration of three spaces that the genre has come to occupy within the Bahamas since the 1950s. Rake-n-scrape has followed a trajectory from peripheral, traditional music; to popular, urban soundtrack; and, more recently, to roots music.

"Muddy da Water": Rake-n-Scrape as Traditional Practice

Traditional rake-n-scrape today is usually played on accordion (commonly on a two-row button accordion), saw (literally a carpenter's saw), and goat-skinned drum. Before 1969, the year that rake-n-scrape began to be called by that name, rake-n-scrape was performed in a variety of instrumental configurations (banjos, guitars, washtub bass, and ensembles including only drum and saw were all possibilities) that nevertheless participated in a larger practice unified in and through the presence of the goat-skinned drum and the rhythms "scratched" out on the saw, and by their functional role in facilitating social dances (Bethel 1983).

Excursus: Performing Quadrille, Learning a Repertory. The tune called "Times Table" illustrates the types of musical sounds and structures that characterize rake-n-scrape in the Bahamas. Three short eight-measure sections, each comprising two four-measure phrases, combine to create the overall structure of this particular quadrille, in this case an A-B-A form (see Example 3). The drummer generally reinforces the form, executing a single low-pitched stroke on the *and* of the second beat of the second and fourth measures (antecedent) and performing an extended fill starting in the fifth or sixth measure (depending on improvisatory gestures) that eventually culminates *on* the second beat of the eighth measure (consequent), thereby rhythmically emphasizing the end of each section. This gesture of rhythmic emphasis is called "hitting the bar" by Dodger Webb, who plays the goombay drum for both the Websites and the Rooters. Hitting the bar is the element least likely to be subjected to the stylistic and improvisatory preferences of drummers, for it is grounded in the social dances that songs like "Times Table" used to accompany. While one drummer may or may not play the offbeats as prominently as another, both will drive toward and then "hit" the bar at the end of each section. The saw player meanwhile performs a sixteenth-note rhythm that accents the *and* of each beat (one *and* two *and,* in 2/4 meter), subtly bending and releasing the saw in order to get different timbral effects.

"Times Table" does have lyrics, though they are incidental to the performance. The lyrics for songs in the rake-n-scrape repertory are generally quite short, focus on pedagogical or values-oriented messages, sometimes grow out of actual events, and can be extemporized or extended as the situation warrants. That said, however, many performances of "Times Table," for example, are completed without ever singing the words. Individuals who have grown up with this repertory know the lyrics, but what matters most is being able to recognize the rhythms and then to respond with the appropriate dance steps and figures. In this particular case,

EXAMPLE 3. "Times Table." Transcription used with the permission of Fred Ferguson.

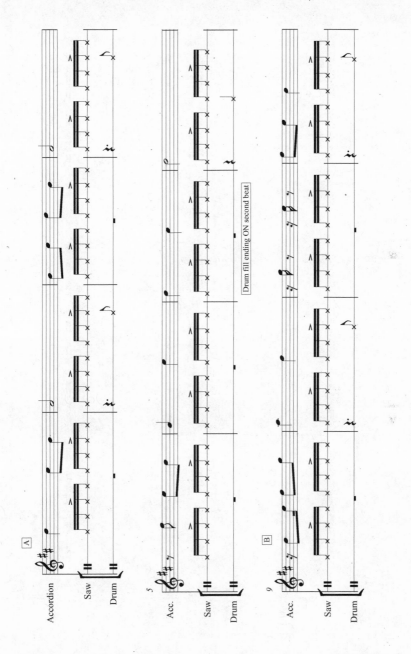

(continued)

EXAMPLE 3. *continued*

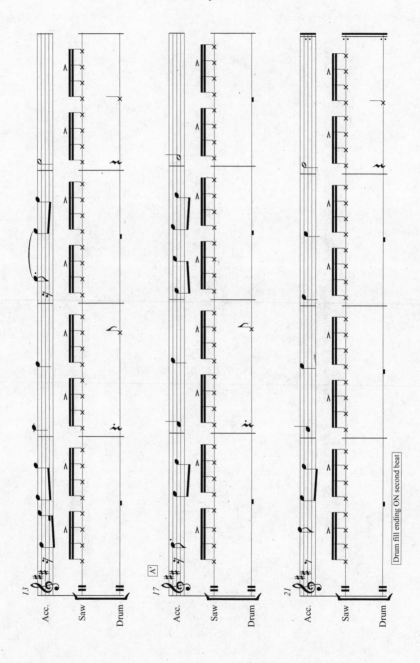

the lyrics are as educational as the title implies: "Twice one are two, twice two's a four," and so on up to twelve.

"Times Table" is called a quadrille by Bahamian rake-n-scrape musicians, a label that indicates not only its connection to the quadrille dance, but also its position as the first in a series of five figures included in a full-fledged quadrille dance. According to Ed Moxey, the remaining figures include the round (or moon) dance, the heel-and-toe polka, the waltz, and the ring dance. That said, however, it is very difficult to make any strong assertions about standardized quadrille formats in the Bahamas, as each of the Family Islands seems to have developed idiosyncratic variations on that overarching theme. So, for instance, in Pumpey "Bo Hog" Johnson's opinion, the quadrille, when performed in its entirety, includes four quadrille figures followed by a round dance, a heel-and-toe polka, and a waltz, but no ring dance, making for a total of eight figures, not five. Complicating matters further is the fact that lead dancers can skip figures of the quadrille at their discretion in order to move into the round dance more expeditiously.[7]

Each drummer, moreover, interacts with the repertory in idiosyncratic fashion. This is the case especially today, when drummers are no longer held strictly to their former function as the rhythmic leaders of the dance. Now that rake-n-scrape is performed outside of the context of social dancing, drummers no longer feel as bound to mark the bar or to offer dancing cues in the precise ways that were formerly required of them. It is also the case that the quadrille no longer tends to be performed as a set of figures; rather, individual songs are played and selected with a view toward their fit within a given performance as opposed to their fit within the quadrille proper. The following analysis is thus intended only to illustrate the four figures that current performers tend to agree on as part of the quadrille and to offer an introduction to the range of repertory that is expected of performers. In so doing, I am, of course, also sketching out the general shape of the current repertory which traditional rake-n-scrape artists still draw from in shaping their performances.

The song "When Ya Mama Send You to School" is a representative example of the round dance. The lyrics are, again, quite short: "When ya mama send you to school, why you don't go?" This song, like "Times Table," explores the importance of the offbeat *and-of-two* drum stroke, but adds significantly to the overall accent pattern vis-à-vis the quadrille. Whereas the quadrille focuses attention and accent on the offbeat until the last measure of each section, at which point the second beat of the last measure is played *on* the beat, the round dance emphasizes the downbeat of every other measure through a pattern that privileges both offbeats in the preceding measure, followed by the downbeat itself (see Example 4). The accented strokes on the offbeats counterbalance the weight of the downbeat, not least because most drummers play the downbeat stroke much more quietly and pitch it somewhat lower. Because rake-n-scrape performers habitually stomp their

EXAMPLE 4. "When Ya Mama Send You to School."
Transcription used with the permission of Fred Ferguson.

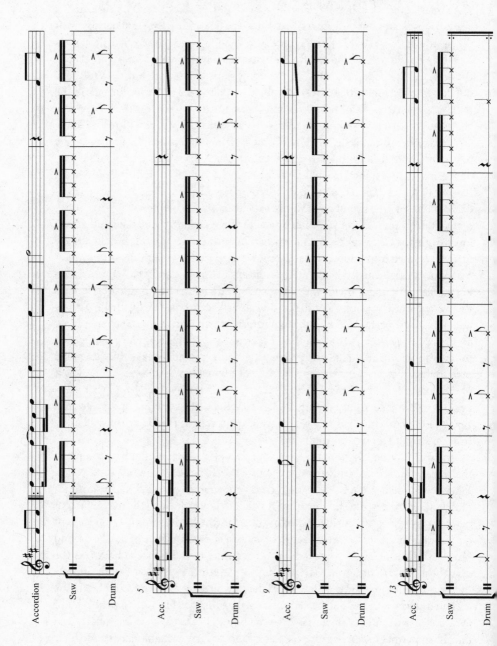

feet on the first and second beat of each measure, the understated downbeat stroke blends in with that texture, allowing the offbeat accented strokes in the preceding measure to stand out more sharply. Not every drummer plays the round dance in this fashion, however. Unlike Ed Moxey's drummer, who chooses to make this distinction between the quadrille and the round dance clear in his playing, Dodger Webb chooses to play a pattern much closer to the quadrille, working mostly to emphasize the offbeat *and-of-two* and only occasionally incorporating the offbeat *and-of-one* into the texture. That said, however, Dodger does not hit the bar nearly as sharply in round dances as he does in quadrilles, reflecting in this performative gesture his understanding of the erstwhile needs of dancers—put otherwise, a clearly articulated bar is necessary in quadrilles but not in round dances.

The heel-and-toe polka operates within a different rhythmic context than do the quadrille and the round dance, in spite of their shared 2/4 meter. A representative example of the heel-and-toe polka is a song entitled "Big Belly Man Polka," and the lyrics here consist only of one repeating line: "Big belly man, come muddy da water." In contrast to both the quadrille and the round dance, the drummer plays the downbeat of the first measure, returns to play a stroke on the downbeat of the third measure, and then brings the first four measures to a close by playing strokes on *and-two* of the fourth measure (see Example 5). What strikes me as particularly interesting here is the movement, however slight, toward placing stronger emphasis on the downbeats of the polka than on the offbeats (as is the case in the quadrille and round dance). The accent pattern now really privileges the downbeat of measure one and three and combines that strong emphasis with an emphasis on the second beat of measure four.

Waltzes such as "Nobody's Darling but Mine" (see Example 6), "My Bonnie Lies Over the Ocean," and "Irene Goodnight" are all triple-meter dance songs, and the saw and drum assume complementary roles in order to emphasize this metric change within the quadrille set. The goat-skinned drum accents the first beat of each measure while reserving the second and third beats for light, generally higher-pitched strokes and occasional improvisatory flourishes. The saw accents the second and third beats of each measure while maintaining its customary (in this case eighth-note) pace. Because the saw produces a sound not nearly as powerful as a firmly struck drum head, the balance created by the two instruments retains a solid accent on the first beat of each measure. Generally the accordion player will play through the chord changes by intoning the root of the chord on the downbeat and then offering the upper chord tones on the second and third beats of the measure.

The last movement in a quadrille cycle is the ring dance, which is performed by the drummer and saw player without accordion. The rhythms utilized for the ring dance very closely mirror those of festival Junkanoo, a fact that offers support for Ed Moxey's assertion that both rake-n-scrape and Junkanoo are variations and

EXAMPLE 5. "Big Belly Man Polka (Muddy Da Water)."
Transcription used with the permission of Edmund Moxey.

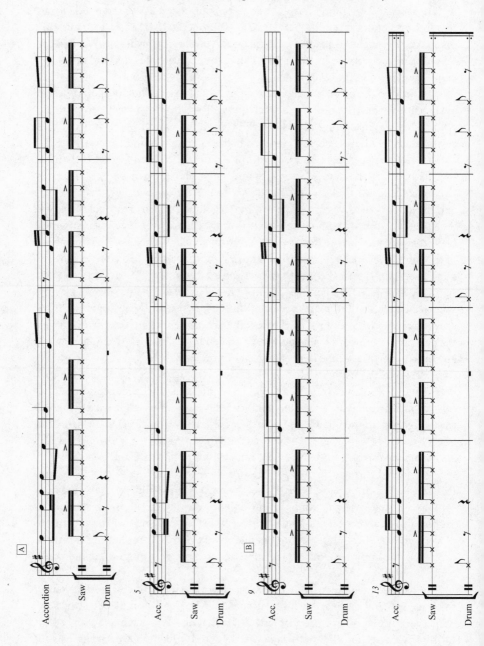

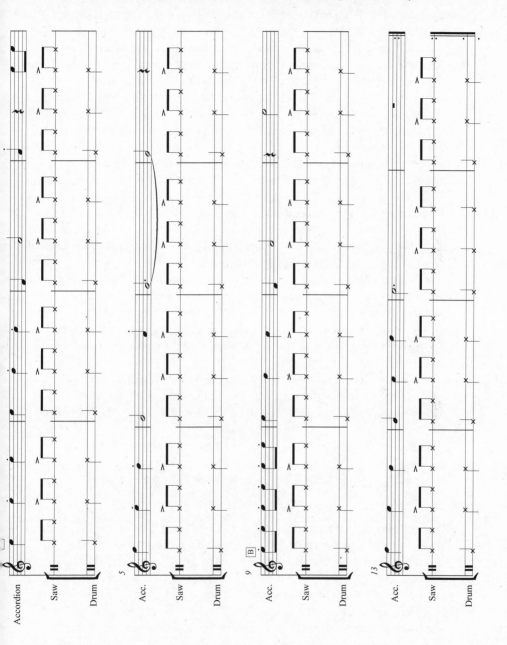

EXAMPLE 6. "Nobody's Darling but Mine."
Transcription used with the permission of Thomas Cartwright and the Boys.

adaptations of goombay rhythms (Moxey, quoted in Lomer 2002, 125–27). I will return to explore the ring dance in more detail in chapter 4.

I conclude this analysis with a brief reflection on the rhythmic trajectory that emerges when the first four figures of the quadrille are performed in order. A schematic rendering of the central rhythmic accents at play as musicians move through these figures illustrates the movement toward increasingly on-beat- and downbeat-oriented rhythms (see Example 7). When read from top down, with the saw playing a constant role, the following developments become apparent: (1) The quadrille emphasizes the offbeat of the second beat and, only at the end of each eight-measure phrase, the second beat itself. No downbeats are accented, and if the drummer plays on the first beat of a measure, it is in unaccented, light strokes. (2) The round dance, for its part, finds the drummer beginning to mark the downbeat in a more assertive fashion. This emphasis on the first beat of the measure is juxtaposed with an intervening measure emphasizing the offbeats of both one and two. (3) The heel-and-toe polka takes this trajectory and moves it more definitively into a pattern emphasizing on-beat accents. The downbeat is treated in a fashion similar to the round dance, but the alternating measures set up an accent *on* the second beat by strokes on the offbeat of one and the on-beat of two. Beats one and two are thus privileged in alternating fashion throughout a performance of a heel-and-toe polka. (4) The waltz moves this trajectory to a pattern repeated every measure, a pattern that heavily emphasizes the downbeat and then places secondary accents on the second and third beats of each measure. The saw player reinforces the secondary accents, shifting the accent pattern to on-beats for the first time in the cycle.

I must reiterate at this point that the very act of positing this analysis as in any way normative for the archipelago would be to unduly reify the highly idiosyncratic nature of quadrille performance throughout the Bahamas. For this reason, I clarify again that I am merely offering some comments on the rhythmic relationships that emerge out of this particular configuration of quadrille—a configuration that Bo Hog, Ed Moxey, and Ophie Webb consider central to quadrille, but which is, in no sense, meant to stand in for all of Bahamian practice.

This ballroom dance complex and its associated musical styles, so popular a few generations ago and performed widely though not exclusively in the Family Islands—that is, away from the bigger cities like Nassau and Freeport—have been dramatically affected by successive waves of emigration (Boswell and Chibwa 1981). Many inhabitants of places like Cat Island and Long Island, for instance, have been making the journey, first to Nassau or Freeport, and then to London, Miami, and New York, and these itineraries are most often initiated in search of better employment and educational opportunities (Craton and Saunders 1998;

EXAMPLE 7. Schematic comparison of accents in Bahamian
quadrilles, round dances, and heel-and-toe polkas.

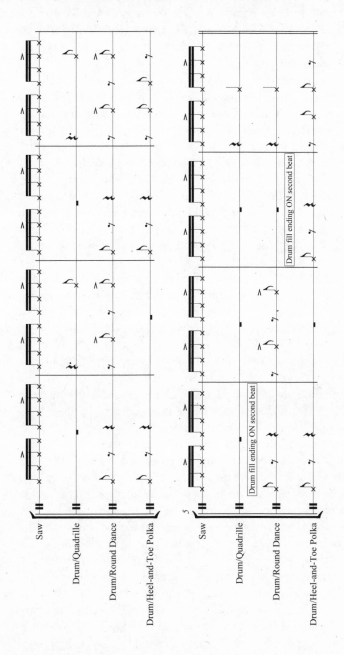

Howard Johnson 1991). Ophie himself works in the service industry in Freeport, traveling to Cat Island only when his holiday schedule affords him that luxury. Unlike Ophie, however, many others have never returned. This process started in earnest at the beginning of the twentieth century, intensified during World War II (because of contract labor offered in the United Sates), and again in the wake of independence during the 1970s.

By the 1970s, a dramatic redistribution of people across the Bahamas had taken place. In 1900, some 75 percent of Bahamians lived in the Family Islands. By 1970, however, that ratio had been inverted, with 75 percent of all Bahamians living in New Providence and Grand Bahama. This trajectory toward the center and away from places like Cat Island continues, a state of affairs well illustrated in government census data since the 1970s (see Table 5). The population of New Providence, Grand Bahama, and Abaco roughly doubled in size between 1970 and 2000, while the populations of the other islands declined (eight of the sixteen), remained essentially static (five of the sixteen), or grew only very moderately (three of the sixteen). This continuing trend has translated into an even more center-weighted distribution:, some 85 percent of the Bahamian population now live on New Providence and Grand Bahama.

It should come as no surprise that this centripetal pattern (understood as a centrifugal one from the perspective of those Family Islanders who have remained behind) effectively disrupted traditional systems of tutelage and made it exceedingly difficult to pass on either social dances or rake-n-scrape music in the Family Islands. Ophie, for instance, described the change between the 1950s and the 1970s: "In the 1950s we used to have big dances in the school house on weekends and holidays. . . . But people moved, people died, and by the 1970s we didn't maintain the quadrille dance. No one learned how to dance it. It was like dead. Everyone wanted to dance like James Brown" (Ophie Webb, interview with the author, June 3, 2006). As a result, rake-n-scrape has come to be played in new contexts and for different reasons. The social dances it used to accompany— including circle dances like jumping dance and ring plays in addition to the quadrille—fell out of active use, necessitating a new role for rake-n-scrape. No longer simply functional, rake-n-scrape needed an explicitly musical justification.

Returning to that critical juncture in the late 1960s addressed by Ed Moxey, I suggest that a new process was beginning to shape the music that was by then being called rake-n-scrape, for it was acquiring a new function in Bahamian life. The process of separating the music from its primary social context—resituating it as entertainment for its own sake—continued through the 1970s, eventually causing rake-n-scrape to stand out in sharp relief as a traditional practice in its own right. As late as the 1980s, however, traditional rake-n-scrape bands were still not particularly popular among Bahamians, and this was especially the case in places like Freeport and Nassau (the center). Ophie, for example, remembers viv-

TABLE 5 Bahamian population statistics, 1970–2000

Island	1970	1980	1990	2000
New Providence	101,503	135,437	172,196	210,832
Grand Bahama	25,859	33,102	40,898	46,994
Abaco	6,501	7,271	10,003	13,170
Acklins	936	618	405	428
Andros	8,845	8,307	8,177	7,686
Berry Islands	443	509	628	709
Bimini	1,503	1,411	1,639	1,717
Cat Island	2,657	2,215	1,698	1,647
Crooked Island	715	562	412	350
Eleuthera	6,247	8,331	7,993	7,999
Exuma and Cays	3,767	3,670	3,556	3,571
Harbour Island	2,238	1,133	1,219	1,639
Inagua	1,109	924	985	969
Long Island	3,861	3,404	2,949	2,992
Mayaguana	581	464	312	259
Ragged Island	208	164	89	72
Rum Cay	80	78	53	80
San Salvador	776	747	465	970
Spanish Wells	983	1,167	1,372	1,527

SOURCE: The Commonwealth of the Bahamas, Official Website of the Government of the Bahamas, http://www.bahamas.gov.bs.

idly that when he first arrived on Grand Bahama in the mid-1980s, Freeport audiences booed him every time he played rake-n-scrape (Webb 2007).

Nevertheless, the rhythms and sounds of rake-n-scrape have journeyed to the center—to Nassau and Freeport, that is. This journey, though, has not unfolded in any unified or straightforward manner. Rather, rake-n-scrape has traveled in fits and starts—a rhythmic marker here, some instrumental roles there— gradually moving from traditional spaces to popular practice in the process. Moreover, these rhythms and sounds have been adapted to their new, more urban settings and adjusted to fit tourist desires. Another way of thinking about this journey to the center is that rake-n-scrape has been reread and then translated into a version that foregrounds certain musical registers in dynamic fashion and in response to other musical influences—not once but multiple times over the course of the last several decades. Allow me to illustrate this idea by backing up a bit and turning to a brief exploration of Nassau's nightclub scene in the 1950s and '60s.

"Bahamian Thing": Rake-n-Scrape as Popular Music

During the 1940s and 1950s, migration from the Family Islands to Nassau was accelerating, keeping pace with the rapid growth of tourism. Playing a style called goombay in Nassau's many nightclubs, musicians needed to present their music as uniquely Bahamian but engaged with current popular music in the United Sates and throughout the Caribbean.[8] By the mid-1950s, musicians like George Symonette, Eloise Lewis, and King Eric Gibson had crafted a sound that, while drawing on calypso as a general, regional model, also incorporated Cuban, North American, and specifically Bahamian sounds, thereby localizing the style while retaining its panregional accessibility for tourists. I will return to both the nightclub scene and goombay in greater detail in chapter 3, but for now I will briefly examine the basic translation of actual rake-n-scrape sounds into that scene.

"I Kissed Her Hand," a song recorded by George Symonette and his Goombay Sextet in 1955, illustrates how rake-n-scrape was incorporated into the representation strategies of artists during the 1950s (see Figure 2). Some of the rhythmic and sonic markers in this piece reflect and amplify the context within which the music was recorded. The rake-n-scrape content incorporated into the goombay sound is evident in the rhythmic figures performed on the maracas and through the presence of the goat-skinned "goombay" drum. In this context, the maracas assume the rhythmic responsibilities performed by the saw in traditional ensembles. The goombay drum, for its part, affords a double identification with rake-n-scrape. It constitutes a visual symbol of traditional practice, physically representing Bahamian musical traditions. But it also offers its sonic footprint to the recording, not least because the drummer emphasizes the *and* of two throughout, thereby referencing a prominent feature of traditional rake-n-scrape performance (quadrille). Symonette's recording nevertheless also incorporates other musical markers, including the clave, a sound referencing Cuban models that had found a prominent place in Caribbean and North American musics starting in the 1920s. Piano and upright bass, along with an electric guitar—instruments that were staples of North American jazz and pop—round out the ensemble's sound (see Example 8).

The song itself is modeled on popular verse-chorus structure, thereby moving away from the short forms and economical lyrical content of traditional rake-n-scrape songs. The lyrics, for their part, participate in the double entendre so common to calypsos of the day, a strategy well illustrated by the song's catchy chorus: "I kissed her hand, I kissed her lips, and I left her [pause] behind for you." At any rate, what George managed to do—what most Goombay musicians during the 1950s managed to do—is to fuse Bahamian sounds and rhythms with musical models more readily accessible to tourists, appealing to tourists by giving them mostly what they expected to hear, but carefully infusing the sound with their own specific and localized rhythms and instruments.

The incorporation of only a select few ideas and sounds from traditional rake-n-scrape is significant here. The saw rhythm is transferred to the maracas—by then already a very regional sound—and the goat-skinned drum manages to ap-

FIGURE 2. George Symonette. Promotional photo from
Da Island Club archive. Used with permission.

proximate some of the *two-and* feel of rake-n-scrape but simultaneously to imbue
the drum lines with a conga feel (indeed many performers preferred congas to
goat-skinned drums because they could stand up while performing and didn't
need to heat the drum between sets). The saw rhythm and the goat-skinned drum,
placed into what amounts to a jazz combo context, were the only registers of traditional rake-n-scrape that were translated into the nightclubs of the 1950s. Importantly, however, the rhetoric surrounding goombay—what sold it to tourists—
was that it was uniquely Bahamian, and the goat-skinned drum provided some
measure of tangible and visible (if not always aural) evidence for that claim.[9]

EXAMPLE 8. "I Kissed Her Hand."

I suggest that the goat-skinned drum drew its power to project Bahamianness precisely from the fact that musicians could point to traditional rake-n-scrape and the drum's central role in those ensembles without having to incorporate the other sights and sounds of those ensembles into the nightclub scene. That the genre was called goombay is itself a testament to this more symbolic than musical role. Fred Ferguson, a veteran Bahamian musician and producer, has characterized the dynamic between the center and its internal other as follows: "The saw and the accordion were visibly and sonically connected to the Family Islands. So they were considered old-fashioned and even embarrassing. You can imagine that that image didn't fit in the clubs, spaces where slick, totally cutting-edge material was the only thing that would work" (Ferguson, interview with the author, March 5, 2007). Nightclub musicians thus translated only those pieces that could be dissociated from the Family Islands into their performances while simultaneously crediting the Bahamian characteristics of their music to inspiration drawn from the Family Islands—those peripheral spaces where accordions and saws lived. And yet the centripetal move to identify specifically Bahamian sounds and practices is crucially important to the poetics of representation attendant to the nightclub scene during the 1950s.

I will explore this dynamic in much greater detail in chapter 3, but this brief introduction to the translation of traditional rake-n-scrape (goombay, as it was then called) into the popular nightclub scene is important in that it illustrates the extent to which these negotiations increasingly provided musicians with a template of possibilities. This negotiation eventually led to another shift in the relationship between traditional rake-n-scrape and the nightclubs of Nassau—a shift that further illustrates some of the nuances involved in these translations. In the late 1960s, Ronnie Butler introduced and then codified a combination of sounds that more directly translated rake-n-scrape into the nightclub scene in Nassau (see Figure 3). By this time a full electric dance band sound was becoming the order of the day, unlike the acoustic-driven goombay sound of the 1950s. Performers in the 1960s increasingly needed a core group of instruments that included drum kit, electric guitars, keyboard, and electric bass in order to get gigs in Nassau. With that instrumentation as a sonic template, Ronnie Butler proceeded to explicitly map rake-n-scrape rhythms onto the ensemble.

Over the course of several months' experimentation, he moved the saw rhythm to the hi-hat of the drum kit, effectively replacing the maracas; created a new focus for the rhythm guitar, which now reinforced the saw rhythm (a technique that is today called the yuk); translated the rhythmic emphases of the goombay drum to the bass guitar by writing bass lines that emphasize the *two-and* of each measure; and had the kick drum play *on* the first and second beats of each measure, carefully placing it well into the background of the mix in order to imitate the foot stomping so prevalent among rake-n-scrape artists. Alternatively, he

FIGURE 3. Ronnie Butler. Promotional photo courtesy of the Bahamas Musicians and Entertainers Union archives. Used with permission.

would "lock" the kick drum with the bass, arranging it so that both instruments performed a *two-and* pattern.

The rake-n-scrape sound was thus shifted more emphatically from a traditional ensemble to a popular dance band context. Unlike the goombay bands of the 1940s and '50s, however, there were no traditional instruments in sight (or in earshot)—only their rhythmic roles are translated. But this was Ronnie's goal. In a discussion about the process through which he accomplished these translations, Ronnie remembered: "I always felt that rhythm was the key" (personal communication with the author, August 2007). Ronnie's rake-n-scrape music, which many have emulated over the years, is well illustrated in a song called "Crow Calypso," recorded in 1969 (see Example 9).[10]

When compared to the lyrics typical of goombay during the 1950s, which often present themselves like advertising slogans for the Bahamas ("Island in the Sun," "Bahama Lullaby," "Nassau by the Sea") or relate humorous stories like the one in "I Kissed Her Hand," Ronnie's lyrics often accomplish something else entirely. Consider the lyrics of "Crow Calypso":

> Woke up early one morning, kiss my mama goodbye.
> Going back to the Island, I say, don't worry mama, don't cry.
> I'll be leaving on the Alice Mabel [a mail boat],
> I sure hope that she's still able.
> This evening round five o'clock,
> I'll stand on her bow and see the dock.
> Out in the field from dawn till dusk,
> Swimming in the blue hole is a must.
> Oh that Island where I was born,
> The first thing I'll do is grow some corn.
>
> I'll be cooking outside in the iron pot,
> Though young when I learned I haven't forgot,
> How to catch them black crab as they walking,
> Old folks smoking pipe and talking.
> Saturday night they gonna dance and sway,
> Shake my belly and do the goombay.
> Oh my people don't you understand,
> I'll live like a king and be a happy man.

"Crow Calypso" explicitly references things like mail boats, cooking in an iron pot, growing some corn, catching black crabs, and swimming in the blue hole. All of these images reference ways of living and interacting with the environment that constitute part of the way people in Nassau thought about the inhabitants of the Family Islands—that is, as people locked in time, still living as they did generations ago, and thus preserving a germ of Bahamianness long since lost to those living in the more cosmopolitan center.

In other words, stereotype and nostalgia meet and mingle in Ronnie's creation of the Bahamian nation (Boym 2002). According to Ronnie, he's "going back to the Island," which in this case refers to an unnamed Family Island. Reading a bit under the surface, it is also possible to understand these lyrics as engendering a bit of time travel. Put otherwise, the island to which Ronnie is proposing to journey is, in fact, located in the past. In a more recent song, "Bahamian Thing" (2001), Ronnie takes this imagery and embeds it in an explicitly nostalgic remembrance of childhood.[11]

> Early in the morning, as the sun is dawning,
> I go to the well to get my water to bathe.

EXAMPLE 9. "Crow Calypso." Transcription used with the permission of Ronnie Butler.

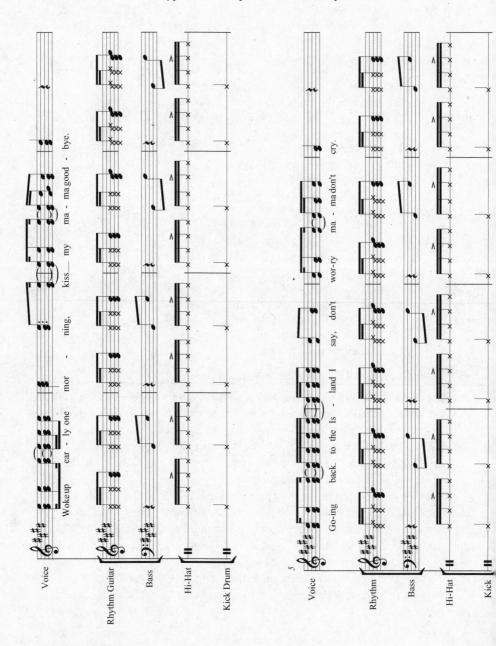

EXAMPLE 9. *continued*

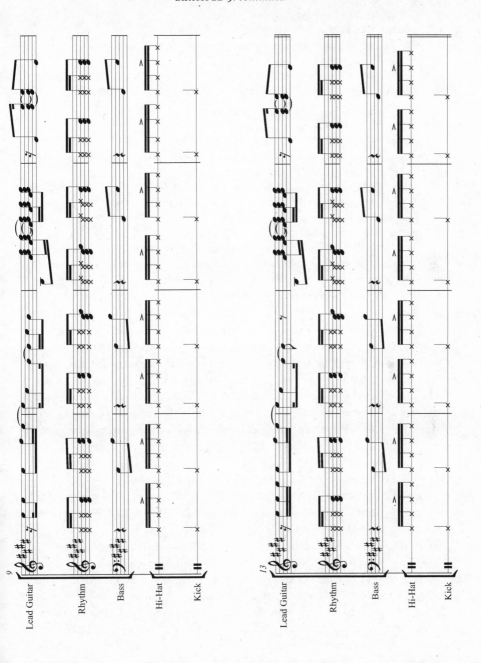

Get my wood from the bush to make my tea,
And eat my bread to fill my belly,
And get ready to go outside and play.
Get my friends from next door, to run with me to the store,
To get some salt beef and flour for mama to cook.
We pick some limes from the tree and we pick some sapodilly,
Then we make some switcher to drink to wash down the food.

My Bahamian thing, growing up on the Island.
Catching my fish with my bait and my line.
(Growing up on the Island) sitting on the rock everything is fine.
(Growing up on the Island) planting my corn and my peas and my sweet potato.
Nothing sweeter than Bahamian thing.
I remember when, things were better back then,
You didn't have to worry at all about locking your door.
Everyone was like your neighbor, take care of your son and daughter,
We had no bed so we had to sleep on the floor.
Go to church on Sunday (Hallelujah), get ready for school on Monday,
Study homework with a lantern till late at night.
Telling them old time stories like B' Bouky and B' Rabby,
And sleep to your heart's content till morning light.

References to lifeways that are no longer present in the same way in the Family Islands and the contrast drawn between the (implied) contemporary social situation and the days when "everyone was like your neighbor" invoke a Bahamas nostalgically remembered as "better" and, in one sense, also as lost. That the old-time stories like B' Bouky and B' Rabby and the storytelling tradition itself are also falling out of practice only serves to buttress the sense of a "real" Bahamas lost to modern, cosmopolitan Bahamians and accessed now only through nostalgic remembrances.[12] (I will explore this mobilization of nostalgia in greater detail in chapter 6.) Referencing these lifeways lyrically is qualitatively different from bringing those lifeways into the ensemble itself by actually utilizing accordions, saws, and goat-skinned drums. Rake-n-scrape thus traveled from the periphery to the center, from traditional to popular form, and then became a vehicle through which a temporal reevaluation—a nostalgic reenvisioning—of what the Bahamas could be (or, more pessimistically, what the Bahamas could never be again) was made possible.[13]

It is significant that this nostalgic nation-building impulse did not include the sounds of traditional rake-n-scrape per se. I suggest that in order for rake-n-scrape to function as a powerful and nostalgic symbol, it needed to remain in place (at least for the moment)—that is, it needed to maintain its reputation as rural, peripheral, and effectively folklorized. But what gets missed in the course of constructing a target for nostalgia is that the mid- to late 1960s were a time of profound change in places like Cat Island and Long Island, just as they were for

Nassau and Freeport. So, for example, Ophie and Dodger Webb were at that very moment experimenting with very different sounds than Ronnie and the Ramblers and Nassau-bound tourists would have expected, for they were appearing all over Cat Island in a band called Eddie and the Educators—a band that specialized in performing funk, rock, and R&B. While Ronnie was busy appropriating rake-n-scrape, Ophie was absorbing the Billboard charts—a better illustration of the routes that sound traveled in and through the Bahamas during the 1960s would be difficult to imagine.

"Call de Fire Engine": Rake-n-Scrape as Roots Revival

A brief final exploration concerns a rethinking of rake-n-scrape, accomplished in the last fifteen years. Although clearly building on and extending Ronnie Butler's project of the 1960s and '70s, this recent development nevertheless locates rake-n-scrape in an entirely different space. Whereas Ronnie was seeking to recuperate rake-n-scrape for the modern urban nightclub scene, artists like Ancient Man, Elon Moxey, and the Lassido Boys are seeking to create what amounts to roots music (see Figure 4).

To varying degrees, these artists are all reintroducing traditional rake-n-scrape instruments into their dance bands. They are clearing space for the goat-skinned drum and the saw by reducing the role of the drum kit primarily to intoning the kick drum on one and two (though elements from Ronnie Butler's popular rake-n-scrape drumming—most notably the hi-hat rhythm—are also invoked depending on the artist and the song). These roots artists are also reinstating the accordion as the primary instrument instead of guitars. Guitars remain part of their sound, but the accordion is now (again) central to the sound, with the guitars handling the yuk and some lead lines. This ensemble sound provides the background for tunes that remain structured in a popular verse-chorus idiom, and with the Family Islands finally welcomed to the performance, the nostalgic lyrics so common in Ronnie Butler's repertory are no longer necessary. "I Ain't Askin' fa Much," a song by Ancient Man, is a great example of this take on rake-n-scrape (see Example 10).

Particularly interesting here is the extent to which artists are recovering traditional rake-n-scrape instruments. This recovery can be read as an attempt to provide a bridge to a practice and sounds that are no longer readily available to Bahamians (as active practice, that is). As Ophie mentioned, by the 1970s quadrille dancing (and rake-n-scrape along with it) was in severe decline (Ophie Webb, interview with the author, June 3, 2006). Thirty intervening years of relative inactivity and continued migration have accomplished what Ronnie Butler and many of his contemporaries inadvertently heralded—namely, the gradual folklorization of rake-n-scrape. Just by way of example, since 1999 there has been an annual government-sponsored rake-n-scrape festival in Arthur's Town, Cat

FIGURE 4. Ancient Man in concert at the Cat Island Rake-n-Scrape Festival, 2006.
Photograph by Timothy Rommen.

Island. When considered in this light, rake-n-scrape can be understood as an endangered music project, fostered by the government as an example of Bahamian heritage (Kirshenblatt-Gimblett 1998).

And yet Ed Moxey sees this folklorization as a step in the right direction, for it is, at least according to him, an active and useful exercise. In a conversation about the recent revival of interest in rake-n-scrape, he singled out the increased presence of rake-n-scrape on the radio (on Island FM) as one of the principal factors. "It was not until two, three years ago, especially when Charles Carter radio came on, that we began promoting indigenous music. And right now, everything is go. People are into the rake-n-scrape music now. And they now appreciate it, and they are ready to tee off on it" (Moxey, interview with the author, August 11, 2007). One of the corollaries of this broad interest in the sounds of roots-oriented rake-n-scrape is that it is heavily represented on the annual compilation of Bahamian artists' singles, called *Best of the Best* for the year 2006. Of the fifteen tracks included, fourteen employ rake-n-scrape rhythms and instruments (all but one utilize saw, most use goat-skinned drum, and several include accordion). Tracks with titles like "Blame It on Rake-n-Scrape," "Das Rake-n-Scrape," and "Rake-

EXAMPLE 10. "I Ain't Askin' fa Much."
Transcription used with the permission of Ancient Man.

(continued)

EXAMPLE 10. *continued*

EXAMPLE 10. *continued*

(continued)

EXAMPLE 10. *continued*

n-Scrape Party" are only the most explicit in terms of lyrical connections to the sounds employed. This represents the culmination of a trajectory away from Junkanoo rhythms and toward rake-n-scrape—a trend that was almost a decade in the making—and it can be attributed to the great popularity of roots-oriented rake-n-scrape artists since about 1998.

Getting back to the efforts of artists like Ancient Man, then, we might read the incorporation of accordion, saw, and goat-skinned drum into urban dance bands as the sonic analogue to Ronnie Butler's nostalgic lyrical exhortations. In other words, the calls to cook in an iron pot, grow some corn, and swim in the blue pool—activities that were essentially obsolete in the Family Islands even during the 1960s but referenced in important ways a shared cultural heritage— are being refocused on rake-n-scrape as a musical practice, and this by a diverse group of artists, radio entrepreneurs, and government-sponsored festivals. Today essentially the preserve of only a handful of artists, the traditional rake-n-scrape sound is still a very potent marker of Bahamianness, and artists like Ancient Man, himself a Cat Islander living in Nassau, are tapping into this sentiment in and through their performances.

What emerges here is a very interesting relationship between the centrifugal and centripetal movements of rake-n-scrape. Although saw, accordion, and goat-skinned drum are now traveling in ways not possible even twenty years ago, rake-n-scrape as a traditional practice has been disciplined and institutional-ized, fixed in place at center stage during festivals dedicated to its preservation, packaged for radio play, and reduced to those components which are most read-ily useful in entertainment (as opposed to dance) spaces.

"COME BACK HOME":
TIME AND PLACE IN THE BAHAMAS

This brief sketch has illustrated some of the ways that the sounds of rake-n-scrape, the instruments that are most closely associated with these sounds, and the social contexts within which rake-n-scrape finds expression have been read, reread, and translated for new audiences and purposes, generating new mean-ings, trajectories, and sounds in the process. In recent years, the Bahamas have moved away from the immediacy of independence, and the nation-building im-pulse has accordingly dissipated considerably. What has not changed appreciably is the continued difficulty that musicians are facing with respect to securing live performance venues. The nightclub scene is essentially nonexistent, and the ho-tels and resorts are hiring only a few union musicians to perform in selected ar-eas of their resorts. The character of tourist travel; the continued media influx from North America and the Caribbean; the partial, centripetal, though far from practi-cal reimagining of the Family Islands as part of the center; and the continued travel abroad for educational and employment opportunities all remain serious challenges to local musical production and to local conceptions of Bahamian sound. Audiences are simply much more likely to gather in Nassau to hear a Beenie Man performance or to travel to Miami to hear a reggaeton show than they are to flock to a rake-n-scrape festival on Cat Island. Tourists, for their part, are much more likely to pay a high ticket price at their resort casino to hear Neil Diamond or Barbara Streisand than they are to venture out and pay a small cover charge to hear a Bahamian band at the Fish Fry (if they can even find a local band playing live to start with).

Travel, of both people and sounds—and not just travel but also the mode of conveyance and the relationships between travel and place—continues to deeply affect the kinds of sounds Bahamian musicians hear and produce and the types of venues in which they are able to perform. Rake-n-scrape has moved from the periphery of the nation to the center, from traditional music to popular music, and is now being reimagined as roots music. Goombay musicians of the 1950s blended and carefully mixed together local, regional, and North American sounds in order to represent themselves to each other and to the tourists who flocked to their performances. Ronnie Butler translated the rhythmic relationships of rake-n-scrape into the context of an electric dance band with drum kit, privileging the idea if not the reality of the Family Islands in the process. The roots musicians of the last few years have turned to the instruments as well as the rhythms of traditional rake-n-scrape in order to tap into sounds that have, in the last decade, been institutionalized as heritage, and this primarily through recourse to festivals.

Travel will undoubtedly continue to inform Bahamian music and musicians, even as these musicians further shape the soundscapes within which and into which both Bahamians and visitors continue to travel. And rake-n-scrape will continue to form the basis for new translations and fresh interpretations of Bahamian music, just as each of the moments traced in this chapter can be understood as efforts toward translating the demands of various forms of travel into the everyday life of the nation. In the following chapter, I trace in greater detail the dynamics at play during what are called the "goombay years," a period of unprecedented growth in the tourist industry and the moment at which rake-n-scrape came to figure in the nightclub scene throughout Nassau. The negotiations I so briefly addressed in this chapter with regard to the choices that goombay artists like George Symonette made are explored with regard to the demands of the tourist industry and in light of the poetics of representation that these demands necessarily engendered in the performances of goombay artists.

3

"Calypso Island"

Exporting the Local, Particularizing the Region, and Developing the Sounds of Goombay

The Caribbean has been repeatedly imagined and narrated as a tropical paradise in which the land, plants, resources, bodies, and cultures of its inhabitants are open to be invaded, occupied, bought, moved, used, viewed, and consumed in various ways. . . . The Caribbean has been re-naturalized as a virgin paradise in ways that continue to inform its contemporary desirability as the ultimate "place to play." . . . It is brought to the consumer in texts, images, and signs, and is fantastically consumed by tourists who draw on existing visual and sensuous performances to make certain kinds of movements in and through the Caribbean viable.

—MIMI SHELLER, "DEMOBILIZING AND REMOBILIZING CARIBBEAN
    PARADISE," IN SHELLER AND URRY, *TOURISM MOBILITIES*, 13

But in our tourist brochures the Caribbean is a blue pool into which the republic dangles the extended foot of Florida as inflated rubber islands bob and drinks with umbrellas float toward her on a raft. This is how the islands from the shame of necessity sell themselves; this is the seasonal erosion of their identity, that high-pitched repetition of the same images of service that cannot distinguish one island from the other. . . . What is the earthly paradise for our visitors? Two weeks without rain and a mahogany tan, and, at sunset, local troubadours . . . beating . . . "Banana Boat Song" to death.

—DEREK WALCOTT, *THE ANTILLES*

In 1961, an LP titled *Bahamas Treasure Chest* (Carib LP-2016) was released for the tourist market in the Bahamas. It is an example of the "existing visual and sensuous performances" to which Mimi Sheller points in the first epigraph above. The album's cover offers all of the images of drinks with umbrellas and tropical paradise to which Derek Walcott alludes in the second epigraph—leisurely consumption, luxury, and play at the edge of that fantastic "blue pool." In short, the cover participates in selling the images that tourists would have been inclined to desire or expect from a visit to the Bahamas: A wooden chest is centered on sand strewn with coins; its cover is flung open to reveal its treasure, which in this case is represented by an inset photograph of Paradise Beach—a beach populated exclusively by white bathers and made more inviting by virtue of calm, turquoise waters and cool, shade-giving palm leaf shelters.[1]

The liner notes, rendered in the form of a striking full-color photo essay, describe and illustrate the various sights, tastes, and sounds that a tourist might be likely to experience and consume in Nassau, including the landscape itself, the boating and fishing, and the local foods, as well as such spectacles as limbo dancing, fire dancing, and, of course, Junkanoo.[2] Elaborating a bit on opportunities for entertainment, the liner notes proclaim: "Nassau's nightlife is one of the Island's chief attractions. The native rhythms and the native gift for music that is part of the Bahamian's heritage produce entertainment that will both fascinate and amuse you. You can go to an 'over-the-hill' night-spot or see a show at a club in town. Wherever you go, you'll hear the invitation: 'Limbo, limbo come limbo with me!' and you'd better be sure your muscles are in top condition before you accept" (8).

Released a decade or so after the tourist industry became the dominant force within and the principal engine of the Bahamian economy (starting in earnest around 1949), *Bahamas Treasure Chest* affords a particularly interesting glimpse into the heyday of the Bahamian nightclub scene at its zenith. It clearly illustrates the strategic negotiation of tourist expectations, but more importantly, it also opens a window onto the politics and poetics of representation that accompanied the staggering growth of tourism during the middle decades of the twentieth century. The liner notes point to this idea by suggesting that tourists can avail themselves of the opportunity to see limbo in "an 'over-the-hill' night-spot" or "at a club in town" and that they can expect to witness it performed in a similar fashion in both venues.

These two spheres or scenes, however, were radically different from each other. The hotel clubs in town traded exclusively on tourist clientele, whereas the clubs located in the Afro-Bahamian section of Nassau known as Over-the-Hill catered to both local and tourist audiences. One was a space into which Afro-Bahamians were not permitted to enter as guests; instead, they were afforded entry only in order to perform certain services (ranging from housecleaning to entertainment). In stark contrast to these highly segregated venues, the Over-the-Hill clubs were expressly designed to provide for the entertainment needs of an Afro-Bahamian clientele—and tourists as well as white Bahamians were welcome to participate.

That the entertainment in both spaces traced along similar lines suggests that Bahamian entertainers like Roy Shurland, King Eric Gibson, Peanuts Taylor, Richie Delamore, Kasavubu, and John Chipman—all of whom are featured on *Bahamas Treasure Chest*—were carefully crafting their self-representations within at least two registers; they were representing themselves to their fellow Bahamians and concomitantly representing the Bahamas to tourists. The fact that the limbo dance was accepted by audiences variously attuned to one or the other of these registers of address is particularly interesting and forms one of the principal areas of inquiry in this chapter.

Bahamas Treasure Chest, nevertheless, also serves as a high-water mark against which the subsequent decline of the nightclub scene can be more fully understood. A decade or so after that "treasure" had found its way into tourist suitcases, the nightclub scene had fallen on very hard times. Indeed, most of the Afro-Bahamian-owned clubs had already failed or were on the verge of closing by the mid-1970s (a process that began in earnest in the late 1960s), and this crisis within the nightclub scene was exacerbated by the increasingly tight grasp on the local entertainment industry that the foreign-owned Bay Street hotels (the "clubs in town") were at that very moment consolidating for themselves. All of this, moreover, was played out against the sociopolitical backdrop of the push toward majority rule in 1967 and the subsequent celebration of national independence in 1973.

This chapter explores the musical dimensions of the goombay years—the twenty-five-year period between World War II and national independence—fondly remembered (memorialized) as the golden age of Bahamian entertainers. It does so by taking seriously the concerns raised by Mimi Sheller's epigraph over tourist expectations in places like the Bahamas and by privileging her concomitant realization that local bodies, sounds, and institutions participate in what made the Bahamas a "place to play" and a "place in play" during these years. Like Frank Manning's study of black clubs in Bermuda (1973)—aptly subtitled *Ethnography of a Play World*—this chapter attempts to nuance and complicate the relationships between tourists and hosts, between cosmopolitanism and provinciality, and between the various forms of double consciousness and "twoness" (to borrow from W. E. B. DuBois) that these relationships engender for local musicians. Manning sees club culture in Bermuda as essentially for and about local Bermudians: "Club play is not an imitation of the tourist ethos. Rather, it borrows forms and styles from the tourist environment and associates them with customs and concepts stemming either from the indigenous tradition or from external but decidedly nontourist influences. The result is the emergence of symbols consistent with the glamour of the holiday-maker's surroundings but representing an alternative set of meanings relevant to Bermudian social experience" (Manning 1973, 256).[3]

This chapter extends the basic outlines of Manning's reading into Bahamian spaces but, in order to adequately account for the particularities of the Bahamian context, makes the further point that "club play" simultaneously negotiates both Afro-Bahamian identity and tourist expectations, making the relationships between the forms and styles of the tourist environment and those "indigenous" aspects of the performative moment a much more contested arena of representation. In so doing, I place the musical dimensions of Bahamian life during the goombay years in productive dialogue with Walcott's sense that tourism represents the "seasonal erosion of their identity, that high-pitched repetition of the same images of service that cannot distinguish one island from the other" (Walcott 1992, n.p.).

Many of the songs included on *Bahamas Treasure Chest* were fixtures in the repertories of performers throughout the goombay years, and there is a sense in which they all participate in the very processes that so concern Walcott.[4] A closer interrogation of the nightclub scenes in Nassau, however, suggests that musicians were constantly addressing themselves to those concerns, creatively reframing them along the way. In order to trace the musical manifestations of these negotiations, I turn to an analysis of several versions of one of the songs included on *Bahamas Treasure Chest*—"Calypso Island."

"Calypso Island," referring in its very title to a musical genre associated most closely with Trinidad, was composed by a native New Yorker named Alice Simms, a frequent winter resident in the Bahamas. This song, performed by most artists active in the goombay years and recorded by many, illustrates the complexities and slippages attendant to musical life in the Bahamas during the 1950s and 1960s.[5] For starters, the lyrics, directed as they are toward the exoticizing expectations of tourists, open a window onto the economic framework within which Bahamian musicians were working at the time.

> Calypso island is calling, calypso island is calling.
> Beat the drum again, drink the rum again,
> Having fun again, everyone.
> Do, do, do, do, do, do, do, do, do, do,
> Like the natives do.
>
> Palm trees swaying, calypso playing
> Your love is waiting there just for you.
> Do, do, do, do, do, do, do, do, do, do,
> Like the natives do.
>
> Calypso island is just for lovers,
> Romantic lovers, there are no others.
> Calypso island, enchanted island,
> It makes you do, do,
> Like the natives do.

Don't resist it, you know you miss it.
A million thrills waiting just for you.
Do, do, do, do, do, do, do, do, do, do,
Like the natives do

These lyrics amply illustrate what Mimi Sheller has called the renaturaliza-tion of Caribbean bodies within a naturalized Caribbean. Put otherwise, the ro-mance and freedom ostensibly accruing to those visitors willing to "do like the natives do" was generated in and through the "objectification of Caribbean peo-ple as part of the natural landscape; the equation of that landscape (and hence those who people it) with sexuality and corruption; and finally, the marketing of the Caribbean via imagined geographies of tropical enticement and sexual avail-ability. . . . Thus a sexuality drawing on the colonial past and its racial and gender hierarchies is coded into the representation of Caribbean landscapes and the tourist pleasures to be found there" (Sheller and Urry 2004, 17–18).[6]

Moreover, the melody, harmonic structure, and rhythmic context that pro-vide the vehicle for "Calypso Island" participate in the promotion of a vision of generically recognizable pan-Caribbean sounds—any island will do. The song taken as a whole seems sonically designed to reinforce Walcott's concerns over "repetition of the same images [in this case sounds] of service that cannot dis-tinguish one island from the other." That said, however, the actual performances of "Calypso Island" within the Bahamian nightclub scene shifted dramatically from the mid-1950s to the 1960s, suggesting that the artists involved in putting these sounds on record and paid to perform them on stage were actively and strategically engaged in the process of shaping the meanings and identities that accrued to those sounds—deeply engaged in the poetics of representation.

I am interested in tracing these shifts in performance, for they illustrate the complex negotiations that were required of musicians during the goombay years as they made the Bahamas a "place to play" and (especially as the 1960s wore on) attempted to keep it alive as a "place in play." I do so by offering several parallel narratives: one concerns "Calypso Island" itself; another explores the club spaces within which goombay music was performed during those years; yet another explores the shifting terrain within which musicians were crafting their sounds (economics/technology/media); and a final narrative concerns the increasingly urgent call for majority rule and independence that accompanied the goombay years in the political realm. These accounts combine to provide a framework for thinking about the movement of people and sounds into and out of Nassau's nightclubs—a dynamic I began to outline in chapter 2—in order to consider the centripetal and centrifugal aspects of entertainment in the Bahamas and explore how those travels shaped the performances of Bahamianness offered by artists in the middle decades of the twentieth century.

TREASURED VISITORS:
BECOMING A PLACE TO PLAY IN THE 1950s

The goombay years were made possible in large part through the growth of mass tourism in the Bahamas in the wake of World War II. During the late 1940s and early 1950s, government officials, after reviewing the successful off-season promotional campaign utilized by Florida to attract visitors, began to aggressively target tourism as a means of economic growth (Cleare 2007, 110). Stafford Sands, one of the Bay Street Boys—the small group of local elites who monopolized politics in the colony—was put in charge of the Development Board in 1949, and he was largely responsible for shaping policy that effected a rapid transformation of the tourism sector.[7] As I indicated in chapter 1, the boom experienced during the Prohibition era was followed by a lengthy depression and then by World War II. As a result, very little infrastructural planning or development had taken place between about 1930 and 1949.[8] The 1950s were, by contrast, a moment of rapid expansion both infrastructurally and economically. In an article celebrating the growth of tourism during the 1950s, Sands put the decade in perspective and offered his optimistic assessment of the importance of tourism and capital investment for the continued health of the Bahamian economy:

> In the post–World War II years of the late 1940's, Nassau tourist influx was stabilized at just over 30,000 visitors each year. This trickle of tourism, based on a winter visitor season of 60 to 90 days, was not enough to provide the Colony's fast-growing population with sufficient employment and income for a sound economy. The past decade has seen the Bahamas' tourist industry rise from a 30,000-a-year sideline or adjunct to the economy to a healthy, prosperous business which now produces more than 200,000 visitors annually. This is an increase of about 700 per cent in 10 years. Tourism has become the *builder* of these islands with capital investment as the *provider* of facilities for modernization and expansion. (Sands 1960, 177–78)

The Development Board's promotional plan involved heavy investment in overseas print advertising, establishment of sales offices in major cities throughout the United States, and a heavy emphasis on public relations. In short, the Development Board actively promoted the Bahamas as a "place to play."[9] Although there was some initial resistance to these expenditures within the Bahamas, government spending on these efforts was met with staggering growth in the tourism sector—a clear sign that travelers and vacationers were willing to participate in creating ("building," as Sands would put it) Nassau as a "place to play."

And there was certainly a great deal of construction happening in the 1950s. At least seven new hotels, resorts, and residential clubs (some very exclusive indeed) opened during this decade, including the Emerald Beach Hotel (1953), the Dolphin Hotel (1956), the Mayfair Hotel (1957), the Nassau Beach Hotel (1959), the Pilot

TABLE 6 Development Board expenditures and colony revenues in pounds sterling, 1949–1958

Year	Expenditures of the Development Board	Total Visitors	Colony Revenue
1949	94,031	32,018	1,329,967
1950	156,150	45,371	1,579,748
1951	199,474	68,502	2,044,385
1952	292,247	84,718	2,397,097
1953	311,490	90,485	2,610,678
1954	340,386	109,605	3,095,541
1955	413,326	132,434	3,507,953
1956	475,242	155,003	4,078,921
1957	556,813	194,618	4,938,958
1958	658,482	177,867	5,198,975

SOURCE: Excerpted from *Bahamas Handbook,* 1960, pp. 183–85.

House Club (1950), the Coral Harbour Club (1956), and the Lyford Cay Club (1959) (Cleare 2007). Stafford Sands tabulated the relationship between Development Board spending, tourist arrivals, and government revenues from tourism and confidently proclaimed that the 1950s had only just begun to tap the real potential of the Bahamas "money tree" (see Table 6). It was a moment of sustained—and ostensibly sustainable—growth in the Bahamas, and the benefits of this boom did not fail to positively impact the prospects for local musicians and entertainers.[10]

Not surprisingly, then, this was the decade during which musicians began to think of themselves as goombay artists and to sell their music as such. This moment, moreover, had a particular sound. By the 1950s, New Providence had indeed become a "Calypso Island," and before tracing the growth of tourism and the bourgeoning nightclub scene that accompanied it in greater detail, I turn to a brief analysis of two versions of that song, recorded by two of the most prominent musicians working Nassau at the time—George Symonette and Eloise Lewis.

Excursus I: "Calypso Island," 1959

Recorded at the British Colonial Hotel in 1959 by George Symonette, "Calypso Island" was included on his album *Goombay Rhythms of Nassau* (Bahama Records-28). Symonette (1912–1988), at this time at the height of his fame, had been a member of the Chocolate Dandies (founded in 1935 and one of the first professional Bahamian orchestras) and had performed at the Chez Paul Meeres and the Spider Web during the 1940s. He would remain a fixture on the scene into the mid-1960s. During the 1950s, he had several standing gigs, including engagements at the Imperial Hotel Garden, the Waterside Club (formerly the Spider Web, later called the Junkanoo Club), the Royal Victoria Hotel, and Blackbeard's Tavern. Although it was recorded rather late in the 1950s and at a time when other artists were beginning to experiment with different sounds, this song nevertheless illustrates Symonette's continuation of a formula that had worked well for him over the years. By the time he made this recording, he was known as the king of goombay and was a household name among Bahamians and tourists alike. In chapter 2 I briefly discussed the musical characteristics of goombay music by pointing out the negotiations attendant to the incorporation of some traditional rake-n-scrape sounds into the spaces occupied by nightclubs, and I extend that introductory treatment in the analyses that follow.

George Symonette's version of "Calypso Island" is performed in what I call a goombay aesthetic. The recording incorporates traces of rake-n-scrape rhythms in the goombay drums, thanks to their very presence within the ensemble and also the drummer's emphasis on the *and* of the second beat of each measure. That said, the rake-n-scrape rhythms are smoothed out by the two sixteenth notes being played on the *and* of two instead of the single eighth note that characterizes rake-n-scrape drumming (quadrille). This gesture, however, is also central to the son conga rhythm, so popular in Cuban dance band contexts, and its inclusion within the sonic texture leaves the audience to parse between the two.

A similar nod to rake-n-scrape, accompanied by a simultaneous obscuring of that musical connection, is present in the part played on the maracas. In this case, the saw pattern is hinted at, though the characteristic accent pattern is evened out so as to obscure the distinctive rake-n-scrape rhythm. This ambiguity is reinforced by the much more explicit reference to the characteristic Bahamian Junkanoo rhythm, called kalik, a rhythm embedded in the scraper part emphasizing different portions of each measure vis-à-vis the saw rhythm (see Example 11). This combination of the saw and kalik rhythms serves to wash out both characteristic rhythms into a basic, four-square accent pattern (with accents evenly spaced on each eighth note), effectively allowing for their mutual incorporation but virtually canceling out their sonic impact. The use of these rhythmic ideas, then, operates primarily at a symbolic level. They are being performed, to be sure, but only those listeners able to distinguish them one from another and to isolate their sources of inspiration would be able to point to Bahamian roots here.

Finally, the performance, clipping along at approximately 86 beats per minute (in 2/4) and complete with 3/2 clave—a pervasive borrowing around the region referencing Cuban models—is quite typical of the panregional calypso sound cultivated in Nassau during the 1950s. George's sextet, complete with piano, guitar, bass, and three percussionists, then, excelled at adapting and hybridizing local and regional sounds and rhythmic markers—mixing and merging sounds both cosmopolitan and provincial—thereby highlighting the tensions inherent in attempting to provide a recognizable (i.e., familiar) sound while simultaneously creating a unique product that referenced the Bahamas. This sonic negotiation of places lies at the heart of what I am calling a goombay aesthetic.

EXAMPLE 11. Accent patterns in the kalik (Junkanoo)
and saw (rake-n-scrape) rhythms.

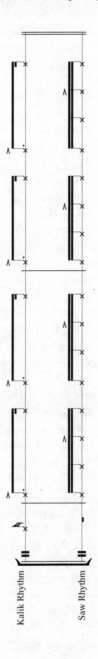

Kalik Rhythm

Saw Rhythm

Excursus II: "Calypso Island," 1960

One of George Symonette's contemporaries, the Florida-born Eloise Lewis (1927–1984), also recorded "Calypso Island" (see Figure 5). The first Bahamian artist to record for Decca records, Eloise Lewis became famous for her abilities as a guitarist and vocalist, and she included the song on her 1960 album *The Eloise Trio* (DL 8983). She recorded the song with her trio, which included George Wilson on upright bass and "Barbalou" on maracas, but she performed with a wide range of bands and ensembles throughout Nassau and Freeport during her career.

Eloise Lewis's version of the song takes a somewhat different approach than Symonette's. She slows her performance to the point that it becomes better to think of it in 4/8 time as opposed to the more characteristic 2/4 time used by Symonette. As such, the song unfolds at a more stately 108 beats per minute (in 2/4 the tempo would be 54 beats per minute compared to George's 86). Eloise's arrangement, moreover, suggests her familiarity with the Cuban bolero.[11] The bass line is characterized by long-short-short rhythmic cells, and her guitar work includes an arpeggiated strum (a sixteenth note triplet followed by an eighth note) on the second beat of each measure.[12] In addition, the trio sings the chorus in close harmony, whereas Symonette handled all the vocal duties by himself. The maracas are caught between accenting the bolero-like performance on guitar and bass and a rake-n-scrape saw rhythm. The central rhythmic cell, played out over the course of two measures in 4/8, unfolds as four eighth notes followed by four sixteenth notes and two more eighth notes. The maracas, then, support the guitar and bass parts but do not offer a distinct reference to rake-n-scrape or Junkanoo rhythms (as did the maracas in Symonette's recording).

No goat-skinned drum is present in this recording, negating some of the possible symbolic associations of the instrument itself within the ensemble's sound, but Eloise invokes the Bahamas (and the region) through her pronunciation and juxtaposition of particular words. For instance, she pronounces the word *island* with a very sharply delivered "ailaan," but this West Indian–inflected pronunciation is counterbalanced by a very North American rendering of the word *calling* as "cahwling." This juxtaposition, oscillating between the Caribbean and the (eastern) United States, contributes yet another layer of ambiguity to the sonic texture of Eloise's recording. That fewer instruments are available to Eloise than are present in George's recording causes the vocals to take on heightened significance here. And yet, in spite of the limitations imposed by the diminutive size of the ensemble, Eloise's recording also participates, albeit by way of different artistic choices, in casting "Calypso Island" within a framework best described as a goombay aesthetic.

The goombay aesthetic is particularly significant, moreover, when considered in relationship to the lyrics of the song itself, which posit a panregional, ambiguous locale. This "Calypso Island" could really be anywhere in the region, the

FIGURE 5. Eloise Lewis, ca. 1960. Promotional photograph courtesy of the
Bahamas Musicians and Entertainers Union Library.

perfect match for the generic regional identity promoted by development boards
throughout the region (and in the Bahamas) and cultivated by travel agencies.
Perhaps best summarized as "sun, sea, and sand," this generic panregional identity was part and parcel of the goombay aesthetic. It is almost calypso, yet not
quite. It hints at the Bahamas but makes that aspect of its sonic presence a subtle
element throughout the performance, especially as it is embedded in a dialogue
with what were understood as Cuban musical ideas.

This regional sound—the expectations that artists like George and Eloise were
managing—was partly driven by the explosion of calypso onto the North American scene during the 1950s. And this trajectory had roots in the 1920s, when Trini-
dadians first began traveling to New York in order to record calypsos for the

export market. By the 1950s, a series of hits by artists based in the United States (including "Rum and Coca-Cola," recorded by the Andrews Sisters in 1945, and the "Banana Boat Song," recorded by Harry Belafonte in 1956) had propelled calypso into the public imagination. Thanks in part to the recordings of artists like Harry Belafonte, calypso became associated not with Trinidad per se, but with the Caribbean in general. It is not coincidental, then, that Jamaican mento, Antillean string band music, and the goombay music of the Bahamas traded on these sounds, for the musicians needed to connect their local musical materials to a sound world that their visitors would be predisposed to understand and accept.

The same can be said for the pervasive use of Cuban musical materials, which had also risen to prominence within the United States (both on television shows like *I Love Lucy* [CBS, 1951–1960], and in dance band and jazz recordings).[13] The "Calypso Island" of which George and Eloise sing, then, is reinforced through the musical strategies employed in their arrangements and calculated to resonate with tourists without entirely losing a Bahamian grounding. Many of their contemporaries performed songs operating in this generic vein as well: "Caribbean Sea," "Island Woman," and "Island in the Sun" are only a few representative examples that match musical approach with lyrics to achieve this effect.

Place, then, operates at several levels in these two performances, marking both the region and a specific locale (the Bahamas and then only the center [Nassau, that is]), yet blurring these together while at the same time implicitly acknowledging the multiple spaces that exist in Nassau itself, not least because the "natives" themselves needed to be comfortable with and at least somewhat supportive of the way George and Eloise represented what they "do, do, do." These recordings, then, can be understood as embedded in spaces both regional and local, in spaces within which both tourists and Bahamians participated, and it is this doubleness (negotiating self and other in centripetal as well as centrifugal fashion) that I find so powerfully present in the goombay music of the 1950s.

I have thus far described the 1950s as a time when Nassau had a particular sound, a sound I have broadly outlined as a goombay aesthetic. But the kinds of ensembles and artists that traded on this aesthetic were varied indeed, and it is necessary to think carefully about the presence of the dance band orchestras in the 1950s as well as to interrogate the performances of smaller combos led by performers like George Symonette and Eloise Lewis in order to draw out the multiple ways that the goombay aesthetic was put into play.

Three types of entertainers—two kinds of musical groups as well as specialty acts (i.e., fire dancers, Junkanoos, and limbo dancers)—were active in Nassau during these years. On the one hand, there were orchestras which, when they did manage to play in the hotels and clubs of Bay Street, tended to play as local alternatives to artists imported from the United States and England. These orchestras were generally smaller, seven- to nine-piece ensembles, but in contrast to the smaller ensembles led by musicians like George and Eloise, the orchestras included horns and often a violinist. Although Bahamian orchestras had been around since the 1920s, it was during the 1930s and '40s—before the days of mass tourism, that is—that they gained momentum and became established as a fixture on the local scene. Several famous orchestras emerged out of this era, including the Cambridge Orchestra, led by Bert Cambridge (formed in 1923); the Chocolate Dandies, led by Leonard White (formed in 1935); the Rudy Williams Orchestra (formed in the late 1930s); and the Lou Adams Orchestra (formed during the late 1930s and still active in 2008).[14]

Most of those orchestras modeled their sound on the big band arrangements and recordings emanating from the United States and the conjunto sounds emerging from Cuba. The discriminatory policies of the hotels and clubs during the 1930s and '40s, however, sidelined these bands, causing them to play by the pools or in other spaces clearly not considered top tier. Gail Saunders notes: "If coloured musicians, such as Maxwell Thompson who played saxophone and clarinet in the Cambridge Orchestras [sic], wished to hear a foreign orchestra, they had to seek permission to enter the outside premises and were allowed to listen at the windows" (Saunders 2006, n.p.).

The headlining spaces, generally located in the dining rooms of the Bay Street Hotels, were dominated by foreign artists and orchestras, though "the Bert Cambridge Orchestra . . . played periodically in the off-season, to the exclusive Porcupine Club and at some of the hotels" (Saunders 2006, n.p.). The Chocolate Dandies were also able to play shows in venues like the Nassau Yacht Club, but such orchestras tended more often to play not on Bay Street but in Over-the-Hill clubs. In an essay about performing in the Bahamas during the 1930s and '40s, Chris Justilien, referencing an interview with Lou Adams, writes: "Make no mistake, Bahamian bands could play by the pool areas and maybe the bars, but the dining halls were off limits to local artists. These dining rooms would have Broadway shows that would change each week when the cruise ships arrived at the seaport in Nassau" (Christian Justilien 2004, n.p.).[15] These early orchestras, nevertheless, made some sporadic inroads into the hotels, inroads made more substantive and permanent once the Bahamas Musicians and Entertainers Union formed in 1949, not least because the union mounted a sustained lobby for more local representation in the hotels and clubs. By the mid-1950s, moreover, there was a highly public and very controversial antidiscrimination movement in the legislature, and this moved Bay Street merchants and hoteliers toward more inclusive practices, though it would take another decade to realize them in a broadly equitable fashion.

The successes (limited though they were) of these early orchestras also paved the way for what during the 1950s and throughout the 1960s became the most famous—and the most accomplished—of the local orchestras. This orchestra was

led by Freddie Munnings Sr. (1921–1995). He began his professional career by joining the Rudy Williams Orchestra (trumpet and vocals) in 1939. The orchestra initially performed at the Spider Web (which later became the Waterside Club and
the Junkanoo Club), but by 1940 it had moved to the Silver Slipper. During the
ensuing decade Munnings (known as F.M.) "became the most talked-about member of the band, for by this time he was vocalist, first trumpeter, and MC" (Moxey
1964, 3). He also learned to play clarinet and saxophone during those years, and in
the late 1940s, when Rudy Williams left the Bahamas for New York, Munnings
stepped in, inaugurating the Freddie Munnings Orchestra.[16]

After briefly pursuing formal study at the New England Conservatory (1954–
1955), Munnings returned to Nassau, moved his band from the Silver Slipper to
the Zanzibar for a time, and eventually opened the Cat and Fiddle Club in 1955
(Ronnie Armbrister, interview with the author, June 2006).[17] The orchestra's repertory included Latin jazz, big band standards, Broadway tunes, popular ballads,
calypso, and goombay music. Munnings's reputation as an arranger, bandleader,
performer, and impresario was cemented early and reinforced often during the
next two decades, and I will return to both Freddie Munnings Sr. and the Cat and
Fiddle club later in this chapter.

On the other hand were entertainers, often called troubadours, like Blind
Blake (Alphonso Higgs), Charlie Adamson, André Toussaint (Haitian), Maureen
"Bahama Mama" Duvalier, George Symonette, and Eloise Lewis.[18] These musicians were backed by small ensembles—trios, quartets, sextets—and the ensembles were very flexible in terms of instrumentation, such that they were fronted by
banjos (Blake), guitars (Adamson, Toussaint, and Lewis), piano (Symonette), and
vocalists (Duvalier). Just like their orchestra counterparts, however, the troubadours found themselves excluded from the main stages in the Bay Street venues.
Not only were Bahamian musicians subject to blatant discrimination, but they
were also exoticized in the very process of entertaining as hosts. Put otherwise,
the presence of Bahamian entertainers in these spaces was predicated on the appeal of their otherness. Their repertory and their image thus had to meet the expectations of their almost exclusively tourist clientele. And these venues remained
segregated spaces within the Bahamas until well into the 1960s.

And yet the musicians capitalized on the opportunities afforded them to sell
records to their "guests." As I illustrated with reference to *Bahamas Treasure Chest*,
the liner notes accompanying these export-ready records often served to index the
exoticized and othered role that these performers played on the Bay Street scene.
A typical example of this kind of writing comes from the back jacket of one of
George Symonette's early albums:

> Strolling troubadours have long been one of the romantic features of the Nassau back-
> ground, which especially appeals to the visitor and temporary resident in the Baha-

mas. The untutored, inbred talent of these rhythm-conscious "natives" expresses it-self, much like the old folk-songs, in lyrics with local appeal and native dialect, usually sung to the accompaniment of guitars. Little children pick up these songs and run behind carriages singing for the tourists to throw coins to them. . . . Even the most exclusive resort hotels have come to recognize the special appeal which this native calypso music has for its patrons. (Liner notes ALP-10, 1954, George Symonette)

The specialty (or novelty) acts that were interspersed between sets of music were, if possible, even more exoticized than were the "strolling troubadours." Limbo dancers, fire dancers, and Junkanoos commonly performed floor shows in order to keep the evening's entertainment flowing and varied. Their costumes and routines were designed to showcase "native" (i.e., primitive, though not al-ways particularly Bahamian) folkways. In some cases, the performers invented their own "native" traditions more or less on the spot. For instance, Naomi Tay-lor (known as the "Jungle Queen") and Becky Chipman have long been credited with developing the nightclub version of the fire dance (see Figure 6). Naomi started the trend and tells it as follows in a 1969 interview:

One night back in the.'50s . . . I was asked to entertain a large party, maybe forty or fifty people. I wanted to do something different. So I asked the maid to get me a tray, some candles, alcohol, absorbent cotton and half a glass of brandy. With these, I made a bed of fire. Then, I danced on it. That first time I couldn't stay in the flames more than a few seconds. The guests wanted more. But I couldn't do it again because I didn't have any more equipment. After that, I practiced at home. Later I was able to dance in the flames for ten minutes. (Naomi Taylor 1969, 43)

Becky Chipman added another dimension to the dance: "I was brought up on An-dros Island . . . and I can remember as a little girl the grownups would build bon-fires on the beaches at night and dance. The flames and moon lit up their moving bodies and made long shadows in the sand. It was called the Jumping Dance. Later I watched Naomi dance and learned everything I could, then I started developing one of my own. I created the fire dance as it is danced today" (Naomi Taylor 1969, 45).

Chris Rojek and John Urry have reflected on this dynamic between tourist ex-pectations and local performances by invoking Foucault, stating with a bit of flair that "living in a tourist honeypot is akin to being a prisoner in the panopticon" (Rojek and Urry 1997, 7). But their notion, while focusing attention on the con-stant visibility to which locals are subjected, does little to recognize the agency of locals in tourist "honeypots" like the Bahamas. Furthermore, it does not ade-quately address the fact that only certain local performances are considered worth "seeing."[19] Polly Patullo, quoting Gavan Titley, makes the point that "locals are not allowed, as it were, to be a part of global society. Lives which are concerned with daily chores—jobs, banks, cars and so on—which preoccupy many people in the Caribbean as much as in the developed North, are not seen as appropriate for

FIGURE 6. Naomi Taylor, mid-1950s, unidentified club.
Photo courtesy of Da Island Club collection.

the tourists' gaze. Thus local ('native') peoples are, it is argued, 'twice fetishised': first as objects of discovery, and then 'as being so close to nature that their dispositions are derived directly from the climate'" (Patullo 2005, 174).

How then did these artists and entertainers manage to maintain their desire to perform in an environment where an increasing ambivalence toward their own self-representations and their concomitant objectification and visibility must have been part and parcel of their experience? In order to begin answering this question, I explore some of the venues—some of the spaces—within which George and Eloise, along with Freddie and Naomi, would have had occasion to play. The following passage was printed in the *Nassau Magazine* in 1956. I quote it at length not only because it offers a glimpse into the strategies employed by the hotels vis-à-vis local entertainment, but also because it gives an excellent sense of the performers who were active during the mid-1950s.

The tribal tone beats of Africa, handed down through a half dozen generations, mingle here with the sophisticated rhythms of Broadway and the London Music Halls as Nassau tunes up for another record season. The hotels large and small, the Bay Street "hot spots" and the native "over-the-hill" emporiums of goombay and calypso have tuned pianos and tightened skinheads of bongo drums to entertain what the travel world has predicted will be the biggest invasion yet of music-hungry, fun-seeking vacationers. Biggest news is that the nimble fingers of Kurt Maier return to Nassau after two years of success at the Little Club in New York to take over the grand piano in the Prince George Hotel.... With Berkeley "Peanuts" Taylor at his side with the bongo drum, George will head the Junkanoo Club bill in a show that also includes Eloise [Lewis] and her string trio. George's appearances will come before and after his 10 to 2 open air stint at the Imperial Hotel Garden.... It will be music of the British Isles and of the Continent at the British Colonial Hotel, where Maestro H. Jefferson Jones and an all-British orchestra will hold forth in the new Cage aux Rossenyol (Cage of the Nightingale) Room.... Charles Carey and his Royal Victorians extend a long engagement on the Starlight Terrace of the famous old Royal Victoria Hotel, with Lois Cancino's piano filling in the intermissions. Out on the Old Vic's cocktail patio another old-timer, Blind Blake, strums his guitar and sings calypso numbers in a gravel throated baritone. Mystery still shrouds the plans of the Fort Montagu Beach Hotel, but an imported orchestra and one from Nassau will share the musical chores in the Coral Room and the Jungle Club, with a show of both native and imported talent.... A variety of visiting acts, doubled up on Saturday nights, will lean on the musical talents of Beacham Coakley and his dance band at the Emerald Beach Hotel. The show will be headed by Frank Gallagher as soloist and master of ceremonies.... Cruise ship visitors to Bay Street will continue to head for Dirty-Dick's, where Delbon Johnson and his goombay orchestra penetrate the eardrums. But the "over-the-hill" native places continue to attract the devotee of music hot and loud. There's plenty of it in Nassau. The old Paul Meeres' Place [Chez Paul Meeres] has been reopened as the Club Tropicana with a hot goombay orchestra and a show headed by Jonathan Kemp. Featured performers are Naomi "Jungle Queen" Taylor, David and Frenchie and soloist Kenneth Stubbs. Tojo leads the drum section, which sometimes expands to eight bongos. At the Silver Slipper Freddie Munnings makes with the music, boasting one of the best trained dance bands in town. When show time rolls around Freddie tops the bill as a soloist. Variety is the spice of life at the Confidential Room in Ardastra Gardens. Chippie Chipman, drummer extraordinary, has a brash group of instrumentalists ... backgrounding a show which changes from week to week but includes some of the best talent in the islands. (*Nassau Magazine* 9/2 [Winter 1956–57], 29–31)

This breathless review of the promising upcoming entertainment season in 1957 reinforces several of the themes already presented (i.e., foreign artists were headliners, and local musicians were exoticized), but it also introduces perhaps the most significant aspect of the live music scene in 1950s Nassau—the fact that visitors to Nassau would have had access to two very distinct nightclub scenes in Nassau during the goombay years. One of these, as I have already indicated, was firmly entrenched in the hotels along Bay Street. Places like the Jungle Club at the Montagu Beach Hotel, the Playhouse at the British Colonial, and the Rum Keg Room at the Nassau Beach Hotel were prime venues. Blackbeard's Tavern and Dirty Dick's were also part of the Bay Street scene.

In the 1940s and throughout the 1950s, most of the Bay Street clubs (and all of the hotel clubs) closed by about 11 PM or midnight. But this was not necessarily the end of the night for those tourists who wished to continue their evening's entertainment. Visitors who wished to get a sense of what was "really" happening in Bahamian music thus often found their way to the Over-the-Hill nightclubs. Ronnie Armbrister recalls: "Normally what would happen is the waiters, the waitresses, and the busboys, whoever worked at hotels, taxi drivers, these were the people responsible for bringing the tourists over the hill to various nightclubs. After you get off you'd cart the tourists over to one of these various spots and have a lot of fun" (Ronnie Armbrister, interview with the author, June 8, 2006).

Over-the-Hill nightclubs with names like the Silver Slipper, the Zanzibar, the Conch Shell, the Native Club, and the Skylark Club catered to the entertainment needs of Bahamians as well as to those tourists who, as Michael Craton and Gail Saunders put it, were possessed of "the condescending will to slum among picturesque natives" (1998, 265). And theirs is, in some sense, an accurate assessment in that, as noted earlier, many of these nightclubs put on floor shows that included fire dancing, limbo, staged mini-Junkanoo parades, and rake-n-scrape performances. In short, they were designed to showcase "native" (and not-so-native, but spectacular) folkways.

Craton and Saunders (1998) point out that during the 1930s and '40s, when these Over-the-Hill nightclubs began to open for business, they tended to formalize the rather more occasional interaction between locals and tourists that had been part of Nassau life since at least the end of the nineteenth century. Those tourists who in the past would have gone out of their way to watch a jumping dance in Fox Hill—individuals like J. D. Powles, for instance, who was inclined to experience the Bahamas beyond Bay Street—could now see Bahamians performing for Bahamians but be part of the scene, as it were. In one sense this was about a search for authenticity, but the change in venue most certainly created a different hierarchy of power and visibility, if not a major shift in repertory.

Musicians and entertainers (both local and visiting), as well as their clientele (again both local and visiting), were visible in multiple ways in these clubs, a fact that enabled the Over-the-Hill clubs to become, in Craton and Saunders's words, "important social crossing places, not just for tourists but for different levels of local society" (1998, 265). According to Charles Carter, the clubs had a very loyal and enthusiastic local following that should not be underestimated, because the Bahamian audience was part of what made the clientele at the Over-the-Hill clubs so diverse (Charles Carter, interview with the author, November 30, 2005). Saunders reinforces this idea:

> Two outstanding nightclubs, the Silver Slipper and the Zanzibar were built in Grant's Town in the 30s. Established first, early in the decade, was the Silver Slipper on East Street. Owned by a Jew, David Rashaw alias Davis, who operated a dry goods store on Bay and Deveaux Streets, it soon became popular for tourists and locals, white and black alike. So did the Zanzibar nightclub, built on Bailliou Hill Road, near Weary Willies, a local dance hall and drinking house. Co-owned by black entrepreneurs Milo Butler, Bert Gibson, Preston Moss, and Felix Johnson (who managed it), the Zanzibar attracted a varied clientele. Patrons attended in parties, usually fraternising only with those at their own tables. Liquor ordered by the bottle, was mixed with Coca-Cola or another brand of soft drink, at the table. The groups thus segregated their seating. On the dance floor, however, one was likely to rub shoulders with almost anyone. (Saunders 2006, n.p.)

The fluid spaces of the Over-the-Hill nightclubs contributed to a great deal of musical exchange. Lou Adams recalls that many of the foreign musicians would head there to jam once they finished their own sets at the hotels (quoted in Christian Justilien 2004, n.p.). As such, these clubs were sites of musical collaboration that could not be found anywhere else in Nassau, and certainly not at the hotels or in the Bay Street clubs. Ronald Simms, a trumpeter and longtime band leader for the Soulful Groovers, remembers being a kid of around eleven or twelve years old and climbing the tree that stood outside the Cat and Fiddle Club at his own peril (sometimes sitting on the roof) just to get a glimpse of the action: "People would dress up and go to the club, and I would get run out of that tree two, three, sometimes four times during the night. But I kept coming back because the music was so tight and the place was jumpin'. The Freddie Munnings Orchestra [the Cat and Fiddle's house band] was where most Bahamian musicians really learned to play" (Ronald Simms, interview with the author, August 8, 2007).[20]

Raphael Munnings, one of Freddie's sons, recalls the striking physical characteristics of the Cat and Fiddle as follows:

> The thing that I remember most, of course, was that it was an outdoor club, meaning it was just a perimeter of walls. The walls were maybe ten feet tall. And then around the perimeter, let's say like three-quarters of the club itself, there was an extension . . . like roof in case it rained or something that extended out about twenty feet going all around that perimeter there. And across the top it had chicken coop wire, so, sometimes the neighbors, they couldn't get in or what, they would throw stones or, you know, you didn't want anyone to be sitting in there and get hit in the head with bottles or something just to be malicious, [trails off]. . . . And the

other thing was that there were a lot of big trees all around, so it was like a really tropical setting . . . fruit trees that would bear sapodilly, sea grape, you know, ah, and of course some big rubber tree plant—very, very shady, so even though there was no roof . . . and then at the entrance was a big bar where pool tables [trails off] . . . and you had a ticket booth. So there was a ticket booth as you'd come in, you know, I'm walking in and to the right was a big bar, and to the left was a kitchen where they'd sell sandwiches and snacks and stuff. And then as you walked into the club itself . . . trees started in that area, and you walked farther back to-ward the stage. . . . Actually they could seat two thousand people in that place sit-ting down at tables. (Raphael Munnings, interview with the author, June 10, 2006)

On a typical night, hundreds of people would come to hear local and interna-tional artists perform. Indeed, performers like Nat King Cole, the Mighty Spar-row, Sam Cooke, Perez Prado, Harry Belafonte, James Brown, Duke Ellington, Brook Benton, Count Basie, and Byron Lee all found their way to Nassau begin-ning in the late 1950s and into the 1960s.

These Over-the-Hill clubs, then, were important musical and artistic cross-roads as well as social spaces. The more or less consistent interaction between musicians from the Caribbean and North America, combined with the increas-ing demands of the tourist industry—an industry that was then growing from a seasonal enterprise into a year-round industry—created an atmosphere in which Bahamian artists were perforce well attuned to current musical trends in the United States and the Caribbean.[21]

Artists in the 1950s thus generally performed for both tourists and Bahamians, and they did so in spaces that catered to Bahamian audiences as well as in venues that exoticized and marginalized their performances for the tourist industry. Many had standing engagements during the dinner hour in a Bay Street club and would then head "over the hill" in time to play the second set (usually starting around 12:30 to 1 AM) at the Zanzibar or Silver Slipper. Peanuts Taylor, for instance, juggled a very busy performing schedule during the mid-1950s. "I worked three jobs: I worked at Buena Vista from seven to ten; I worked at the Imperial Hotel Garden with George from ten o'clock until two o'clock, and then I went and worked with Paul Meeres Jr. over at the Paul Meeres until five o'clock in the morn-ing. So work was not a problem for musicians and entertainers in this country back in those days" (Charles Carter, *Bahamians*, radio program aired May 3, 2003).

Caricatured on the one hand and beloved on the other, artists carefully negoti-ated both local and tourist tastes throughout their careers. They were engaged in a double process of representing Bahamian identity at once to themselves (and to Bahamians) and to others (tourists)—both centripetally and centrifugally. In so do-ing, they managed to create music that fused elements of calypso and other regional styles with local Bahamian sounds and later the crooning of artists like Nat King Cole with Bahamian idioms; they managed to create a goombay aesthetic.

And this creative fusion was, according to Count Bernadino, a conscious and calculated activity and one that was bound up in a dialogue with other Bahamians. He recalls that "before we would perform a song on Bay Street or in the rooms out at Cable Beach—and definitely before we'd record it—we would try it out over the hill. If they liked it, it would be a hit. If not, it wasn't worth playing anywhere" (Count Bernadino, interview with the author, August 9, 2007). This statement, perhaps containing a bit of hyperbole, nonetheless points to the multiple layers of representation that musicians needed to internalize as performers.

To illustrate how these representations were negotiated, and as a means of introducing the concerns that came to be central to Bahamian musicians in the 1960s, I turn now to two additional versions of "Calypso Island" that point to some further reflections on the centripetal and centrifugal dynamics attendant to Nassauvian musical life. Recorded in 1961 and 1964, respectively, these recordings seem separated from each other by much more than a mere three years, illustrating in dramatic fashion the changing musical landscape within the nightclub scene. Shaped in part by the rapid growth of tourism, the increasing desire for independence from Great Britain, and the presence, especially during this period, of a wide range of entertainers in Nassau's Cat and Fiddle Club, these versions of "Calypso Island" trace the tensions accompanying the almost-independent nation through the 1950s and 60s.

Excursus III: "Calypso Island," 1961

The recording of "Calypso Island" included on *Bahamas Treasure Chest* was performed by King Eric and His Knights, led by Eric Gibson. The band (which, incidentally, included a young Ronnie Butler on percussion and occasionally on vocals) played a standing gig at a club called the Ba-Ma Room (part of the supper club at the Windsor Inne). The recording is notable for its move away from the goombay aesthetic that so characterized both George's and Eloise's versions. And yet it stands as somewhat of a transitional recording, for while it moves beyond Eloise's recording in several respects, the arrangement nevertheless covers similar sonic ground.

The similarities between King Eric's recording and Eloise's performance include a slowed 4/4-based tempo of about 106 beats per minute; a reliance on a bolero bass line; and a strong vocal arrangement that takes advantage of backing vocals. Interestingly, the similarities seem to provide a foundation from which a move away from the goombay aesthetic is easily accomplished. As such, King Eric uses a guitar strumming pattern that arpeggiates the harmonic progression with eighth notes, a technique that drastically limits the rhythmic role of the guitar; a rhythm on the maracas that minimizes offbeat accents and, with the exception of a sixteenth-note triplet on the "and" of the first beat, unfolds in a straight eighth-note pattern; and a vocal delivery that more than either of the earlier recordings emphasizes the vocalist's skill as a singer and, equally important, minimizes West Indian pronunciation patterns.

This recording is about the vocals to an extent that neither of the earlier versions pretends to be. It is also decidedly not about exploring the rhythmic possibilities afforded by references to traditional rake-n-scrape (or Junkanoo), as was George's version. King Eric has arranged "Calypso Island" as a ballad and performed it in a laid-back and rhythmically innocuous fashion designed to offer an island feel more through the content of the lyrics than through reference to the musical materials that offer a vehicle for the lyrics. This marks a significant shift away from the goombay aesthetic I traced earlier, and as such, King Eric's recording signals a trend that would become a hallmark of the 1960s.

Excursus IV: "Calypso Island," 1964

Almost a decade after playing the goombay drums in George Symonette's sextet—and for George's recording of "Calypso Island" discussed above—Peanuts Taylor, now playing conga drums instead of goat-skinned goombay drums, was a leading nightclub owner and bandleader in his own right (see Figure 7). Presiding over the newly opened Drumbeat Club (1964), he now led a band that recorded "Calypso Island" in a very different style. Imbued with references to jazz and then current pop idioms, his recording makes prominent use of vibraphone, a much more developed harmonic language, and crooner stylings in the vocals, sung by Peanuts himself.

The smooth vocal delivery, offered in a particularly North American vein, contrasts sharply with Symonette's choppy, energized interpretation and with Eloise's U.S./West Indian juxtapositions, extending the logic underlying King Eric's recording (i.e., that it is a ballad). The entire arrangement, moreover, points to a shifting aesthetic within the Nassau nightclub scene much more directly than did King Eric's version. The heavy use of reverb, more pronounced in the initial moments of the song and then focusing in as the first verse gains momentum, vocally suggests motion toward an island, shrouded from clear sight at first and not really grounded in any real sense as a location or a concrete place. The Calypso Island configured in and through Peanuts Taylor's performance is, rather, a space out there to be imagined and enjoyed, or as Mimi Sheller (2003) would say, to be "consumed." Gone are the attempts to incorporate Bahamian markers so prevalent during the 1950s. They are replaced here by a very careful and skillful accommodation to prevailing aesthetics in the North American music industry.

TOURIST HONEYPOT:
BEING A PLACE IN PLAY DURING THE 1960s

It should come as no surprise that the years unfolding between Peanuts's tenure as George Symonette's drummer and his own recording session as a bandleader had

FIGURE 7. Peanuts Taylor (on the congas) performing at the Drumbeat Club with Maureen "Bahama Mama" Duvalier. Photograph courtesy of Da Island Club.

witnessed a great deal of change. Perhaps the most significant development was the rapid growth of the tourist industry between 1959 and 1964. In 1959, some 264,624 visitors disembarked in the Bahamas, and by 1962, tourist arrivals, which had jumped by an average of sixty thousand additional visits per year, stood at 444,870 for the year. By 1964 visits had sharply increased yet again, totaling 605,171. The million-visitor threshold was surpassed in 1968. The political arena was also in flux, as this was the moment when the Bahamas lobbied for and won internal self-rule (1964). With the bourgeoning civil rights movement in the United States as a backdrop, the push toward majority rule was also in full swing, and it was won when the Bay Street Boys (of the United Bahamian Party) were eventually voted out in favor of the predominantly Afro-Bahamian Progressive Liberal Party in 1967.[22]

Accompanying this dramatic increase in tourism was the rapid development of local infrastructure to accommodate the volume of visitors. And starting in earnest around 1963, this growth was no longer confined to New Providence, for Grand Bahama was rapidly becoming another major "place to play" in the Bahamas. The

groundwork for the emergence of Grand Bahama as the other pole of the Bahamian center (until the early 1960s, the center was simply Nassau) was laid in 1955,
when Wallace Groves, a Virginian financier, motivated for and saw the Hawksbill
Creek Agreement signed into law. Angela Cleare describes this agreement, which is
a great example of the increasing role played by foreign capital investment in the
process of "building" the Bahamas, as follows: "In this original agreement, Government conveyed 50,000 acres of land, with an option for an additional 50,000 acres,
to the Port Authority, and promised freedom from customs duty, excise, export and
stamp taxed for 99 years. The Agreement further guaranteed exemption from real
property and personal taxes for 30 years (later extended to 2015). The developers
agreed to create a deep water harbour and to convert the scrubland into a lucra-
tive industrial area, encouraging industries" (Cleare 2007, 119).

The harbor was completed in 1960, and shortly thereafter Freeport became a
bustling center of activity. By the end of 1961, there were already 305 hotel rooms
on Grand Bahama, and as Freeport developed (and more concessions were offered
to investors), hotels were built at a staggeringly rapid pace—397 rooms in 1962; 536
rooms and a new commercial airport by 1963. In 1964 there were 1,444 rooms,
thanks in part to the completion of the Lucayan Beach Hotel; and 1965, which saw
the Holiday Inn and King's Inn open, raised the count to 2,180 rooms (Cleare
2007, 570). This growth was matched by the rapid development of Paradise Island,
including more hotel rooms, nightclubs, restaurants like the Café Martinique,
and golf courses (all connected via bridge to New Providence in 1966), the continuing expansion of the Cable Beach area on West Bay Street, and the beginnings
of tourist presence in what were then still called the Out Islands (especially in
Eleuthera, Bimini, Harbour Island, and Abaco).

Another shift in the tourism sector was accomplished in 1964, and against
great resistance by large sections of the population, when two large casinos
opened on Grand Bahama (the Monte Carlo and El Casino). By 1967, the Paradise
Island Casino opened as well. While casinos had been part of the exclusive private clubs in the Bahamas since the 1920s, no licenses had ever been granted to
facilities catering to the general tourist population. Craton and Saunders characterize this conflict as follows:

> There had been two limited exceptions to the rule against casinos, granted through
> "exemption certificates" to small private clubs in Nassau and on Cat Cay. The au-
> thor of the exemption idea was none other than Stafford Sands as a young lawyer in
> 1939. On April 1, 1963, however, it was announced that the Executive Council had
> granted an exemption certificate to a company called Bahamas Amusements to
> operate an unlimited number of casinos in the Freeport-Lucaya area for a ten-year
> period. Despite the furor raised by this grant, ardent campaigning by the Bahamas
> Christian Council, and, it seems, the personal opposition of Premier Symonette, Sir
> Stafford Sands . . . managed to negotiate a similar exemption certificate on behalf of

the American-owned Paradise Island Enterprises early in 1966. (Craton and Saunders 1998, 343)

The casinos were indeed controversial, and in addition to creating a major
source of social concern within the Bahamas, they presented an attractive reason
for tourists to stay on resort grounds. The impact was not immediate nor was it
isolated, but the effects of this new entertainment draw contributed to an increasingly competitive atmosphere within which the nightclubs began to lose ground,
and this was especially the case for the Over-the-Hill clubs.[23] The cumulative effect of legalized gaming, the development of Freeport, new tourism infrastructure, and the like was that, beginning in the late 1950s, hotels and new clubs on
Bay Street were aggressively pursuing the best local musicians, giving them high
salaries in order to perform at their establishments. Ronnie Armbrister recalls:

> The hotels would open up nightclubs, and their nightclubs would [stay] open later
> than usual . . . and what really changed things a lot was when Paradise Island came
> on-stream [mid-1960s], and they opened a venue whereby they started hiring a lot
> of the groups who were performing at the Over-the-Hill clubs. And they were able
> to pay more monies than the locals who owned these clubs. And also, too, at one
> point I believe that, and this is my observation, I believe that the hoteliers saw
> whereby they were losing a lot of money to Over-the-Hill clubs, so they wanted to
> keep their guests in and make that money. This is my observation, and they would
> hire the bands for lots more money. (Ronnie Armbrister, interview with the au-
> thor, June 8, 2006)

And thanks to the Hawkscreek Bill of 1955, by the early 1960s the action was
also shifting in dramatic fashion to Grand Bahama, where tourism was busily
"building" the resort town of Freeport. As such, Freeport drew a great number of
artists and bands that would otherwise have had occasion to play in Nassau to its
own new nightclubs. A scene that had been localized and relatively contained
throughout the first decade of the tourism surge was growing in ways that forced
musicians and entertainers to make choices about the venues they performed in,
and these developments had devastating effects on the Over-the-Hill clubs—effects
that were just beginning to come to public light right around the time Peanuts Taylor released his recording of "Calypso Island" in 1964. As many as one-third of the
Over-the-Hill clubs closed their doors during the mid-1960s, partially because local musicians were taking advantage of increasing access to higher-paying gigs on
Bay Street, Paradise Island, the Cable Beach strip, and Freeport, and partially because so many good venues for entertainment were now directly competing with
the, by comparison at least, relatively out-of-the-way Over-the-Hill clubs.[24]

One of the bright exceptions to this trend, however, was the Cat and Fiddle
Club. Freddie Munnings Sr. saw this club to its greatest heights during this period. He had added a smaller, indoor room known as the Ghana Room in 1957,

and major international stars continued to move through the venue in the early and mid-1960s. That the Cat and Fiddle was the largest and most renowned of the Over-the-Hill clubs certainly helped to prolong its life vis-à-vis other venues. Ronald Simms remembers it as a major institution in the musical life of the Bahamas:

> At fourteen [in 1968], I joined the last Cat and Fiddle orchestra. [Freddie Munnings] took me under his wing, . . . so I got stuck on the Cat and Fiddle. I practically lived in the Cat and Fiddle. I came from school in the afternoon; before going home I went straight to the Cat and Fiddle. And so I was exposed to all these artists, all these performers, and all these opportunities that presented themselves. Because the Cat and Fiddle was really a school, a breeding ground, and a training ground for musicians dancers and anyone in the performing arts at that time. (Ronald Simms, interview with the author, August 8, 2007)

It would, nevertheless, eventually become impossible to keep even this last vestige of the Over-the-Hill scene profitable, and in the early 1970s, it too closed its doors for the last time.

As the Over-the-Hill scene began to suffer and eventually fail, artists found themselves performing mostly for audiences composed almost entirely of tourists. They were also performing for audiences no longer infatuated with calypso. That trend had passed by the early 1960s, and musicians were searching for a new register within which to locate their sound. The centrifugal exploration was, in this case, not matched by a centripetal grounding like the one that had resulted in the goombay aesthetic, and musicians' repertories began to reflect this new development. Charles Carter has observed: "By the late 1960s many Bahamian entertainers were really just cover artists" (Charles Carter, interview with the author, November 30, 2005).[25]

Taken at face value, Carter's comment could seem pejorative, but I'd like to suggest otherwise. The motivation to explore a different aesthetic and a larger proportion of covers in live shows was not derived from an irresistible drive to transform local bands into lounge acts. There were other issues at stake, not least of which was the political climate within which artists were again negotiating the poetics of representation. The Bahamas were at that moment poised on the verge of majority rule (1967), and independence shortly thereafter (1973), and, as such, deeply invested in a renewed consideration of what face the Bahamas should present to the international community.

Conditioned throughout the colonial encounter to devalue local aesthetic and cultural currents, Bahamians were unsure of how to approach this question. For example, Tinkle Hanna, a leading musician active during the 1970s (in the band Sweet Exorcist), recalls that "many Bahamians became reticent to express aspects of their own culture and heritage in the period from the 1940s through independence" (Tinkle Hanna, interview with the author, December 11, 1997). That

Peanuts Taylor dropped the goombay drum in favor of congas is only one small example of this prevailing trend.[26] According to Tinkle, the real issue was respectability: many felt that their own culture didn't offer the means by which they could become thoroughly modern world citizens in their own right. Radio, television, sound recordings, magazines, and tourists provided ample opportunities for Bahamians to look elsewhere for identity, and it is in this atmosphere of ambivalence toward Bahamian cultural productions that musicians adopted a deliberately transnational aesthetic as opposed to a goombay aesthetic. Not dissimilar in motivation to the calculated, panregional, and obliquely Bahamian goombay aesthetic, then, this new approach privileged the close (and ever-closer) relationship of Bahamians to the United States, further aligning the Bahamas' political and artistic futures with its large neighbor to the north. This tendency was also evident in the growing number of newly composed songs that drew on funk, soul, and Motown for inspiration instead of Bahamian themes and musical ideas.

As I see it, this musical shift was a function of Nassau and Freeport as itineraries just as much as the goombay aesthetic was, though it generated quite different sonic consequences. To illustrate how this transnational aesthetic—signaled in Peanuts Taylor's version of "Calypso Island"—sounded toward the middle and end of the 1960s, and to provide a contrast with the earlier goombay aesthetic, I turn now to a brief analysis of two songs—both covers—recorded by Carl Brice and Richie Delamore.

Excursus V: Broadway, Bossa, and the Bahamas

Recorded by Carl Brice in 1966, "Hello Dolly" is the signature tune from the Broadway show of the same name, first produced in 1964. The arrangement, for flügelhorn, tenor sax, piano, upright bass, drum kit, and congas, was charted by Guillo Carias, the Dominican jazz pianist, and includes solos for both horns. The bass plays a straightforward walking line, and the drummer plays a standard swing feel on the ride cymbal. Carl Brice, for his part, croons his way through the lyrics with distinctly North American inflections and pronunciation. This is a performance that illustrates the degree to which Bahamian artists were in tune with entertainment news and the *Billboard* charts. *Hello Dolly* opened to rave reviews, and when the song itself was recorded by Louis Armstrong in 1964, it gained such popularity that it momentarily dislodged the Beatles from the top of the charts in May of that year. Carl Brice's album, moreover, offers a relatively broad sampling of musical styles. Of the eleven tracks, seven are covers of show tunes or jazz standards, including "Misty" and a version of Tom Jobim's "The Girl from Ipanema." The remaining four tracks are jazz-inflected calypsos, including the ubiquitous "Yellow Bird," as well as the famous "Mary Ann."[27]

Broadway, bebop, and bossa thus dominated Carl Brice's repertory, though he certainly incorporated local and regional songs into his performances as well.

The place of locally driven musical style was, thus, being (re)adjusted in favor of other musical ideas—in favor of an explicitly transnational aesthetic. As I will illustrate at greater length in chapter 5, this trend would accelerate into the late 1960s and early 1970s. For the moment, I turn to a second example of the growing transnational aesthetic that took shape in the 1960s.

Recorded in 1968 at the Junkanoo Club in Freeport, Richie Delamore's album, *Free Again,* features only one "calypso" tune among twelve tracks—"Angelina." The remaining eleven tracks are drawn from the *Billboard* charts and include a version of Tom Jobim's "How Insensitive." The overall shape of the album and the performance of "How Insensitive" combine to offer another illustration of the new direction that Bahamian artists were exploring in the late 1960s. Arranged for a very small ensemble including only electric guitar, piano, electric bass, and drums, the song unfolds in a manner that most audiences would have understood as bossa nova in 1968. Rim shots predominate on the drum kit, the chord changes from the Jobim original are adapted without significant changes, and with the exception of a jazz-inflected guitar solo, the instrumentalists offer a solid but understated foundation for Richie Delamore's vocals to shine. This song is, in short, a vehicle to showcase Delamore's vocal talents—a means to illustrate his cosmopolitan position vis-à-vis the tourists he entertained. There is little in the recording, or in the album for that matter, to tie Delamore to the Bahamas in terms of sound, and this is the major difference between the transnational aesthetic and the goombay aesthetic I traced earlier.[28]

These albums and the performances I briefly introduced here suggest that a shift had occurred in the Bahamas, a shift that engendered new priorities and newly emerging dilemmas for musicians. During the 1950s, the decade when the Bahamas became a "place to play," artists were packaging the Bahamas for sale in a way that Carl Brice and Richie Delamore (among many others) did not feel compelled to pursue by the mid-1960s. Tourism had become firmly ensconced within the Bahamas by the mid-1960s, and musicians and nightclub entertainers began to shift their attention to keeping the Bahamas "in play," as it were. This task had different priorities—it required less centripetal grounding. As the calypso craze died down and other forms of popular music not nearly as compatible with Bahamian social dance musics and their associated rhythms came to dominate the airwaves, musicians had to choose among options that were not easily mapped onto Bahamian aesthetics. The cosmopolitan nature of the nightclub, moreover, necessitated a cutting-edge repertory, and nothing illustrates this better than the track list from Richie Delamore's album—a track list including a majority of songs published or recorded within one or two years of his own album's release.[29] Both "Hello Dolly" and "How Insensitive," then, highlight the seam along which Bahamian musical traditions were being silenced in favor of selecting songs that projected a transnational aesthetic.

This is not to say that everyone agreed on how to negotiate this shift. Indeed, organized dissenting voices accompanied it. In fact, a formal roundtable discussion addressing these questions, titled "Bahamian Music—What It Was—What It Is Now—Where It Is Headed," involving Charles Carter (radio personality), Bert Cambridge (veteran band leader), Count Bernadino (performer), and Sonny Johnson (performer), was organized during the first week of August 1967. Serious concerns were raised about the apparent turn away from centripetal sources of musical inspiration. The following excerpts were included in an editorial printed in the *Nassau Guardian* on August 5: "Most . . . believe that our proximity to the United States and the influx of Americans is responsible for the de-generation and stagnation of anything Bahamian and also the lack of nationalistic pride. . . . In the words of Count Bernadino, the Bahamians should use this American influenced music discretely because so much of it is transitory. 'Calypso will go on and on,' he said. 'Hully gully, rock-n-roll come and go. What we should try and do is to continue to build music and arts that is entirely Bahamian in style and quality'" (Thompson 1967a, 3).

This sentiment has been a consistent rallying cry from the late 1960s to the present, whether in service of explicitly nationalist or cultural and artistic goals. The prevailing trend toward the transnational aesthetic nevertheless continued to gain momentum, and by the time independence was achieved in 1973, the goombay years were relegated to nostalgic memory and a few isolated performers like Count Bernadino, who attempted to retain the goombay aesthetic in the face of these changes.

"BAY STREET ROAD MARCH":
PLAYING TRADITION, SOUNDING PLAY

The shifts in musicians' poetics of representation undoubtedly moved gradually from a goombay aesthetic to an increasingly transnational one. That said, however, it is useful to offer a few counterexamples and caveats in order to offer a more nuanced picture of the scene. First, although the goombay aesthetic generally tended to exclude instruments from and direct references to rake-n-scrape and Junkanoo music, there were plenty of occasions when such artistic choices were deemed useful and were in fact embraced. This was often the case during the floor shows, when small Junkanoo ensembles would festively rush through the crowd. This was, of course, a much less problematic showcase of "native" traditions, given that the Junkanoo ensembles were made up of both dancers and musicians— Junkanooers were, in effect, a self-contained show—meaning that the house band or orchestra did not need to participate musically in the actual performance.

More interesting are the moments when bands or musicians decided to reach centripetally into traditions like Junkanoo and (less frequently) rake-n-scrape and use them in their own performances in explicit ways.[30] Against the backdrop created by the careful references made within the goombay aesthetic to rake-n-scrape and Junkanoo—references that obscured and occluded from clear view these sources of inspiration—and the deliberately transnational emphasis prized in the late 1960s, those moments when explicit references are made to these musical practices stand out in sharp relief. And those moments were numerous enough that several recordings truly foregrounding both Junkanoo and rake-n-scrape were released during the 1950s and early 1960s. I offer this final set of analyses in order to illustrate the kinds of choices that some artists made in representing themselves and their musical ideas in deliberately transparent ways to their audiences.

Excursus VI: "Junkanoo," John Chipman (1961)

I begin by turning to another recording from *Bahamas Treasure Chest,* the album that has provided part of the frame for this chapter. This track, "Junkanoo," was performed by John "Chippie" Chipman and his Junkanoo Champions.[31] The overall structure of the song is A-B-A. The A section's melody and lyrics are drawn from a traditional Junkanoo tune called "Mama Bake the Johnny Cake," and the accompaniment includes a piano playing the chord changes along with the Junkanoo percussion section of drums, cowbells, and whistles (see Example 12). The B section is an extended Junkanoo "rush" performed only with the percussion section, and this works back into a reprise of the A section. "Mama Bake the Johnny Cake" bears many of the hallmarks of the social dance tunes I discuss in chapter 2: it consists of two eight-measure sections (A-B structure) in 2/4 meter, and each of these sections is built from two identical four-measure phrases; it has only a very short text, which is repeated as needed; the end of each phrase (i.e., every fourth measure) culminates on the *and* of the second beat, emphasizing the characteristic rake-n-scrape rhythm illustrated in chapter 2.

The instrumental backdrop to the melody, however, is based on Junkanoo rhythms. The extended "rush," which lasts the better part of four minutes (3:51), is notable for the fact that the bellers (who also play the whistles) do not remain in place during this section of the performance. Instead, they move about the sound stage against a stable background of drums and, in so doing, give the impression of an actual "rush." They move from left to right and closer and farther from the microphones while the drummers remain stationary and steady in terms of volume level. Part of the appeal of including this recording on the album, no doubt, relates to the memories of Junkanoo and floor show routines that the sounds would engender. It is also, however, an effective illustration of the dynamic power of Junkanoo—a subject that I address in greater detail in chapter 4.

Unlike many of the goombay songs of the 1950s and early 1960s, John Chipman's recording does not attempt to meet tourist expectations. This is a recording that showcases the Bahamas, representing in a very direct way the performing

EXAMPLE 12. "Mama Bake the Johnny Cake" (traditional melody).

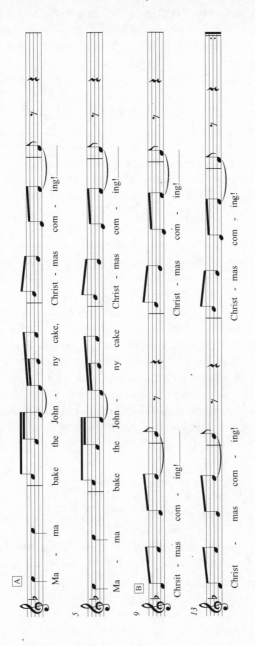

traditions that dominate the Christmas season within Bahamian neighborhoods and households. This is especially the case because the bellers move back and forth between two very distinct rhythmic cells. Indeed, they were distinct enough to have specific names (see Example 13). The first of these is called the Over-the-Hill beat, and the second is simply called the "scrape." Both are distinct from the well-known kalik rhythm (see Example 11). John Chipman's recording also points to a dynamic that needs to be emphasized, namely, that the floor shows did not consist only of limbo and fire dancing, but also included Junkanoos that showcased their "pasting" (costume arts) skills as well as their musical heritage and the basic character of the festival itself. As such, the floor shows were an interesting combination of elements, some of which resonated more deeply with Bahamian audiences than others did, and some of which gave deeper glimpses into local life and musical traditions. Whether or not tourists were able to distinguish between these various registers of the poetics of representation during floor shows remains an open question, for all of these activities were "sold" as Bahamian and "authentic."

Another recording that presents the Bahamas in a particularly direct way is included on an earlier album by Freddie Munnings Sr. Released in 1956, this album, called *Goombay Rhythms* (Bahamian Rhythms, B. Rh. 17), includes two tracks that feature Junkanoo percussion sections (performed by a group called the Jolly Junkanoo Jivers) and for which the lyrics concern themselves with the festival itself—"Bay Street Road March" and "Junkanoo." I explore only the former song here, though both could serve to illustrate this point. Unlike John Chipman's recording, which features the Junkanoo players for most of the performance, Freddie Munnings's effort blends the Junkanoo elements into an arrangement for his orchestra. As such, the cowbells, lead drums, and whistles provide the percussive backdrop for a song that includes horns, piano, guitar, and bass. His lyrics, moreover, narrate the competitive nature of Junkanoo as well as Freddie's own absence from home and happy return.

> This Bay Street carnival
> Goes both ways on Bay in town.
> We bring the place like a battle zone,
> Everyday there's war with bottle and stone.
>
> Beware, Abaco, beware, Bay Street coming down.
> Beware Abaco, beware, Bay Street coming down.
>
> Making fight for forty years,
> My bread is buttered with mayonnaise.
> Let them play the hooligan,
> Freddie is happy in his hometown.
> I was not at home to see,
> But I got the news playing Mayaguana.

EXAMPLE 13. "Over-the-Hill" and "scrape" bell rhythms in "Junkanoo."

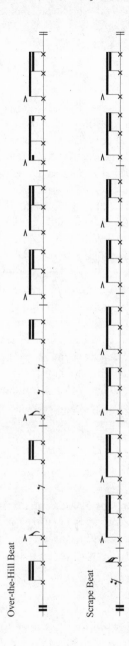

> Beware, Abaco, beware, Bay Street coming down.
> Beware, Abaco, beware, Bay Street coming down.
>
> Yes, man, the Junkanoo fo' day.
> Every New Years' morning, man.
> Before the sun comes up it's the dance of the unknown,
> The dance of the Junkanoo.

The lyrics, combined with the steady kalik of the cowbells and the rhythms played on the lead drums, afford a glimpse into local understandings of the festival, local neighborhood politics, and Freddie's own investment in Junkanoo. This song was not particularly well suited to (targeted for) the tourist market—the lyrics would undoubtedly have been too localized to mean a great deal to the average tourist. It would, more often than not, have served primarily as a vehicle for recalling memories of the Junkanoo floor shows. But for Bahamians, these lyrics would have offered a great deal with which to identify. By way of illustration, the refrain "Beware Abaco" warns the wealthy Bay Street merchants, many of whom were white Abaconians, that the Over-the-Hill Junkanoos were going to take over Bay Street (at least during Boxing Day and New Year's Day). "We're bringing this place like a battle zone" and "everyday there's war with bottle and stone," moreover, acknowledge and revel in the neighborhood clashes between groups that so characterized Junkanoo season during the middle of the twentieth century (more on this in chapter 4).[32]

As such, this song's lyrics are centrally concerned with local knowledge and with Bahamian experience. The arrangement (which, incidentally, makes very sparse use of the horn line) provides a big band vehicle for bringing these lyrics to a wider audience, but it is embedded within a Junkanoo framework. By adopting this strategy, Freddie Munnings created in "Bay Street Road March" the earliest commercial recording for the tourist market of Junkanoo instruments featured as integral elements of a performance. These two examples represent exceptions to the approach that tended to define the goombay aesthetic, and they certainly stand out in sharp contrast to the transnational aesthetic toward which artists began to direct their efforts in the mid-1960s. And yet they also illustrate the constant negotiations between centripetal and centrifugal sources of inspiration that musicians confronted in the course of creating their sound—negotiations that were bound up in local identities as much as in cosmopolitan realities and inextricable from center/periphery dynamics, both at home and vis-à-vis the region.

I conclude these reflections on the poetics of representation during the goombay years by returning to one of the central theoretical models used by Mimi Sheller and John Urry in thinking about tourism in the Caribbean—the idea that places are made into "places to play" and are, as such, also "places in play" (Sheller and

Urry 2004). Their concern for the extent to which these places to play are fluid and constantly moving is crucial to my own understanding of the goombay years. Throughout this chapter, I have argued that the 1950s and 1960s saw the Bahamas become a place to play (with a great deal of assistance from Bahamian musicians) and that during the mid- to late 1960s the emphasis changed from creating a place to play to maintaining the Bahamas' standing as a "place in play." In so doing, I have traced a shift in the poetics of representation—from a goombay aesthetic toward a transnational aesthetic—a shift that I have tied in part to the changing priorities of musicians who were acutely aware of their "place" in Bahamian life.

I have also interrogated the centripetal and centrifugal flows of music and people within the context of the nightclubs, suggesting that the goombay aesthetic drew at least a portion of its inspiration from a centripetal evaluation of Bahamian musical life and combined this with a centrifugal, regional exploration of musical possibilities in the process of developing the goombay sound. The 1960s, however, saw a gradual move away from this centripetal impetus and witnessed an accompanying shift in the focal point of musicians' centrifugal explorations, a shift that found musicians increasingly drawing on North American models for their musical sound. But the formation of these approaches to representation occurred in and through a dialogue with fellow Bahamians and by virtue of the power-laden interactions they experienced with tourists. As Philip Crang has pointed out: "Tourism workers [in this case, musicians] have to inhabit visual practices that are power-laden, in terms of class relations, histories of ethnic power, and sexuality. But . . . they are not just passive recipients of tourist gazes. They actively respond to them. They may hide from them (finding or constructing places shielded from the gazes); they may masquerade within them (using gazes to facilitate the development of one or more personae); and they may pose through them (using the gaze to send a message)" (Crang 1997, 151).

And in the case of musicians, sight was coupled with sound. What, however, did it mean to be heard? What sounds were tourists in a position to hear? To explore this idea, I turn to a theoretical model suggested by Mimi Sheller. Her premise is that tourism (and the consumption of bodies, sounds, foods, and landscapes that accompanies this leisure activity) works in large part through a network of mobilities and immobilities: "Most analysts now recognize the ways in which mobility is embedded in systematically asymmetrical power relations involving a politics of lived forms of mobility and immobility in which these two terms are always already implicated in each other. . . . Rather than a celebration of the postmodern 'nomad,' then, theorists of mobility are asking who or what is able to travel a supposedly 'borderless world,' and who or what is kept in place. . . . The mobilities of consumption are not only material, but also cultural and discursive" (Sheller 2003, 29, 24).

Sheller's idea puts a finger squarely on the aesthetic dilemma faced by Bahamian musicians in the 1950s. To provide sounds that would be "heard," as it were, musicians like George Symonette, Blind Blake, and Eloise Lewis needed to work within the expectations of a pan-Caribbean regional sound that arrived with the tourists. Their sound was, within this reading of the exchange, fixed and immobilized for consumption. But this did not mean that Bahamian musicians were without options in negotiating their place within this dynamic. As I see it, musicians' centripetal exploration of Bahamian sounds and their frequent opportunities for performance in front of Bahamian audiences as well as for tourists, combined to afford these artists a means of absorbing and then refiguring that externally·driven immobility (which, ironically, needed to be imported from Trinidadian, Cuban, and Jamaican models). In so doing, these musicians developed a sophisticated approach to sound, simultaneously offering tourists what they expected to hear and representing a particular place—the Bahamas, that is—for those who would know how to "hear" beyond the sounds of that fixed, generic "Calypso Island."

As Bahamian dependence on tourism increased, the demand for a pan-Caribbean sound was fading (in large part because of the end of the Calypso craze in the United States) and a concomitant increase in the perceived mobility of sound developed. By the mid-1960s, moreover, the Over-the-Hill scene was dying. One of the consequences of this collapse was that musicians were playing fewer shows for fellow Bahamians and spending a greater portion of their creative energies in dialogue with tourists. The gradual move toward transnational styles can be understood as a function of both the willingness of tourists to "hear" a wider range of sounds but also musicians' reaction against the exoticizing constraints that their colleagues in the 1950s had labored to negotiate. Put otherwise, musicians explored cosmopolitan connections in ways that foregrounded their standing as artists, thereby implicitly rejecting their previous immobilization as musicians who inhabited "Calypso Island."[33]

In light of these shifts in economic and political contexts, and taking into account the shifting mobilities and immobilities engendered in the process, I suggest that the "Calypso Island" used as a frame throughout this chapter is much less generically pan-Caribbean than it may seem. It is less ethereal than it is made to sound, for it exists in and is a product of the very process of negotiating the centripetal and centrifugal flows necessitated in an environment where self and other are multiply present and where identity is doubly dependent on both for its shape. As such, the location of "Calypso Island" is subject to shifts and drifts—to migrations, even—and may in fact never be in one place for long. But in the process of participating in the negotiation of new realities, that "Calypso Island" continues to offer insights into new encounters and new itineraries in a place that is often thought of as Nassau (or Freeport) but reveals itself to be so much more than that in the end.

4

"Gone ta Bay"

Institutionalizing Junkanoo,
Festivalizing the Nation

I am a Junkanoo.
—LYNDON PINDLING, *NASSAU GUARDIAN*, SEPTEMBER 1, 2000

I'm on Bay Street with a camera in one hand, a video camera in the other, trying not to get in the way of anyone from Government High School's Junkanoo group as they rush around me. It's about 10:00 PM on December 16, 2004, and the occasion is the annual Junior Junkanoo competition. I'm rushing with the group because Yonell Justilien, one of the main organizers of the group, invited me to join them this evening. I visited the gymnasium over at Government High School just a few days ago, and at that time the lead pieces were not anywhere near finished. The theme of tonight's Junkanoo is centered around dinosaurs, and every conceivable variation of land and air dinosaur was spread around that gym, most at one stage or another of being assembled, pasted, and painted—in fact, only a few looked like they were even close to complete. I remember wondering how these students would be able to find the time to complete their preparations for tonight's event, but by some miracle of the Junkanoo season, they began to marshal at the site of the old straw market a few hours ago with all the loose ends tied up and ready to go.[1] The grade school groups head down Bay Street first, and the secondary schools like Government High bring up the rear.

Some members of the group, mostly instrumentalists and choreographed dancers, are wearing an elaborate headdress and have pasted ordinary clothing to match their headdress. Others, called "toters," are carrying the larger lead pieces, which they climb into (or under) and then hoist onto their shoulders, often having only an eye slit or two to see out of. The heaviest pieces actually require alternate toters, because no single Junkanoo can bear the load through the entire evening's proceedings. Costumes of various smaller sizes are made for frame dancers and

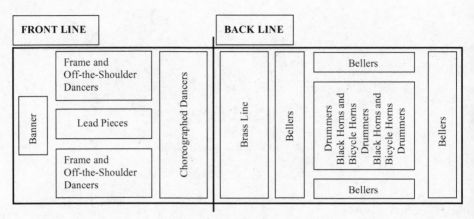

FIGURE 8. Typical Junkanoo group formation. Adapted from Nash-Ferguson 2000, 62.

off-the-shoulder dancers, each of which benefits from a great deal more mobility (and less weight) than do the toters.

The group, with dancers and lead pieces in the front line, rushes down Bay Street behind the group banner. The dancers, incidentally, include both free dancers, who tend to dance alone and play to the crowd watching along Bay Street (frame dancers and off-the-shoulder dancers are part of this group), and choreographed dancers, who organize themselves into dance troupes of various sizes and perform set rehearsed routines as they rush down the road behind the lead and free dancers. They are dancing to the music provided by the back line, and the back line is structured so that trombones, trumpets, and sousaphones are first, followed by a solid block of bellers (cowbells and whistles). Bellers provide the glue for the back line by forming the outside ranks of the back line, much like a frame, so that they extend their ranks down each side and bring up the rear of the back line. The drummers and horn blowers (black [fog] horns and bicycle horns) take up positions in the center of the back line (see Figure 8).

This arrangement is acoustically motivated in that it helps keep the melody instruments roughly in the middle of the group, thereby at least mitigating to some degree the effects of phasing that, if left unchecked, could easily destroy the timing of a large group. And although there are about 150 participants in Government High's Junkanoo group, making phasing a possible issue, the real reason for setting up the order in this way has to do with preparing the "junior" Junkanoos for participation in the largest of the adult Junkanoo groups—groups that regularly bring well over five hundred people to Bay Street. Many Government High Junkanoos are already members of adult groups like the Valley Boys, the Saxon Superstars, One Family, and Roots, but this is their moment to represent their school, and they are leaving it all out on Bay Street tonight.[2]

As we rush down Bay Street, I work my way to the front of the group and stand off to the side, watching as they rush past me in what feels like slow motion. The basic step used in Junkanoo is a double stomp on the right foot (on beats one and two of each measure [2/4 meter]), followed by a weight shift to the left foot, which repeats the double stomp (without missing a beat), but only about four inches farther down the road from where the right foot has just been planted. Variations on this theme seem endless, and I'm very interested in them, not least because I'm currently working to learn all I can for my own use as I try to get up to speed as a guest member of the adult Junkanoo group known as Sting.

Sting is not one of the large adult groups. It does not spend vast sums of money on choreographers, lead brass arrangers, and costumes. Its membership spends as much time eating and drinking and socializing as it does rehearsing, and Sting doesn't even pretend to have a back line of instrumentalists. Sting is, in short, a scrap group, a pejorative used to designate groups that exhibit a relatively informal approach to Junkanoo (i.e., they are thrown together). Sting, though, wears that label with pride.

Given that Sting doesn't actually play Junkanoo per se, it has become the group's custom to commission a song from a local popular musician and—in Trinidad Carnival style—to blast the song from a sound system mounted on a float while rushing down Bay Street. This choice makes the group ineligible for many of the awards that Junkanoo groups compete to earn, solidifying its reputation as a scrap group, but Sting is all about having a good time, not about winning prizes—a strategy that even its critics agree conforms well to the spirit of Junkanoo. This year's song, "Civil Servant," recorded by K. B. (Kirkland Bodie), pokes fun at the perceived lack of work ethic among civil servants in the Bahamas. It has already become a radio hit, and people are excited to see Sting rushin' down Bay Street ten short days from now.[3]

Thankfully, Sting still has those ten days to work out the dance steps and routines, and judging by the amazing performance being put on by Government High School's Junkanoos, I am keenly aware that I, at least, will need every second of rehearsal between now and then in order to have a chance at a decent showing on Boxing Day. Junior Junkanoo finishes at about 11:00 PM. After a solid three hours of rushing, Government High School has won first place, and I am tired but highly motivated for tomorrow's rehearsal—more ready than ever.

The preceding description of Junior Junkanoo and Sting captures the place of Junkanoo in the Bahamas. On the one hand, Junkanoo is widely understood as the quintessential marker of national identity. As such, Junior Junkanoo, inaugurated in 1988, represents a concerted effort to extend opportunities to younger participants whenever possible and to foster a love for the art form from an early age. The activity's stated goals are as follows: "(1) To begin to develop in school age children in general and young Bahamians in particular a greater appreciation for

Junkanoo; and (2) to develop in the young populace a higher degree of interest in participation, separate and apart from major adult groups."[4]

On the other hand, however, the presence on Bay Street of scrap groups like Sting clearly illustrates the differing opinions within the Bahamas about what Junkanoo is or should be. Is it a spontaneous neighborhood-driven celebration of social bonds or an institutionalized, highly competitive, economically driven event? It will become clear in the pages that follow that the answer lies somewhere between these two extremes—and yet, these extremes are, nevertheless, both performed on Bay Street. Perhaps in part because of these very different approaches to and understandings of Junkanoo's place within the Bahamas, the discourse surrounding the festival is often highly charged, a fact that a few hours of listening to the popular weekly radio show *Junkanoo Talks!* will amply reinforce.[5] Junior Junkanoo and scrap groups like Sting thus point to the pedagogical and institutional margins of the festival as it is currently marketed and enjoyed (i.e., as a primarily adult and highly competitive activity) and simultaneously highlight the disagreements over the contemporary shape and practice of Junkanoo.

In chapters 2 and 3 I traced the long history of rake-n-scrape and explored how the rhythms of what was once the primary accompaniment to social dance music were absorbed into the music of Bahamian nightclubs during the 1950s and '60s. Along the way I mentioned the presence of Junkanoo in the nightclubs, especially as part of the nightly floor shows, and analyzed two recordings that made very explicit use of Junkanoo instruments and rhythms (John Chipman's "Junkanoo" and Freddie Munnings's "Bay Street Road March"). And yet I have not, to this point, interrogated the festival itself, nor have I offered a sense of how Junkanoo—which has a history equally as long in the Bahamas as does rake-n-scrape—figures into the musical life of the archipelago.

To that end, this chapter explores festival Junkanoo and places the practice within a larger regional context, thereby providing a working framework for thinking about the extent to which popular musicians turned to festival Junkanoo for inspiration in the years following independence—the subject of inquiry in chapter 5. Accordingly, this chapter is organized into two sections: I begin with an interrogation of nineteenth- and early twentieth-century practices and then turn to an exploration of the gradual and inexorable institutionalization of the festival and the implications of this process for Junkanoo itself.

"RUSHING THROUGH THE CROWD": ROOTS, ROUTES, AND CREOLIZATION

The antecedents and models that Junkanoo was first built on and from which it has developed remain difficult to ascertain with any degree of certainty. That Junkanoo is a thoroughly creolized art form drawing on both African and European sources for its contemporary shape, moreover, increases the complexities attendant to tracing the roots of the festival, leaving more questions than answers. This set of challenges, however, has attracted the interest of a fair number of scholars, making Junkanoo the most researched art form and musical practice in the Bahamas. It is, as such, fruitful to place into dialogue the several theories that have been put forward to explain the etymology of the term itself, the masking practices associated with the festival, and the possible roots of the practice in the New World.

I do so by cycling through three frames for thinking about the history of Junkanoo: (1) roots; (2) routes; and (3) creolization. By viewing the long history of Junkanoo through these interlocking and overlapping frames, I thread questions regarding its sacred roots and seemingly secular contemporary expression, its African antecedents and divergent New World routes, and the processes of exchange between African and European models that have contributed to its varied expression in the region into a close reading of Junkanoo's place (and places) in the Bahamas.

Roots: Sacred Antecedents, Cultural Memory, and the Soul

Whether the tattered rags of slaves, the sponge costumes of grandparents, or the magnificent crepe paper and cardboard structures of today, Junkanoo remains the same: a place to keep our souls, secluded in the intricate steps of the dance, concealed amidst the pounding of our drums, buried deep in the words of our songs.
—ARLENE NASH-FERGUSON, *I COME TO GET ME*, 16

These words, penned by Arlene Nash-Ferguson, are fairly typical of attempts by Bahamians to express in prose the powerful place of Junkanoo in their own lives and within the nation itself. Words searching for ways of describing the ineffable dimensions of the festival and its great value for Bahamian identity are very common and often draw on spiritual metaphors. In this case, Junkanoo becomes a container for the Bahamian "soul," a soul that is carefully guarded (treasured), that is, secluded, concealed, and buried in the dance, drums, and songs of the festival. Another such attempt at describing Junkanoo was made some years earlier by the poet, writer, and musician Pat Rahming. He makes the following claim: "The experience of Junkanoo is not one that can be easily filed into spectator-performer categories. The performers are not minstrels and acrobats providing entertainment for an audience. They are participants in a therapeutic ritual with important personal and natural implications. The fact that the cultural memory is so vague that the 'original' basis for the ritual is foggy is no reason to disrespect the yearnings expressed. In other words, at least for the time being there is still validity in the spiritual 'roots' aspect of the festival/ritual" (Rahming 1992, 32).

Powerful concepts like ritual, spiritual roots, and cultural memory help Rahming make his point about the depth of experience that Junkanoo engenders. And yet the general perception among Bahamians about Junkanoo is that it has no spiritual meaning at all, that it is, in fact, a purely secular activity. E. Clement Bethel (1991), the foremost Bahamian scholar of Junkanoo, goes so far as to flatly deny the possibility that the festival draws on sacred roots. And this argument is extended beyond communal religious traditions to exclude even the individual use of powers (magic or witchcraft).

"Just as there is no evidence to support the religious argument, so too is there no historical indication that John Canoe [an early form of the word *Junkanoo*] was ever associated with witchcraft. Indeed, all the evidence points to the contrary. Those practices which gave the slaves power over their enemies were jealously guarded; those which supported the Europeans' idea of Africans as happy childlike creatures—with a love of singing and dancing, storytelling and drama—were paraded before the planters. Were John Canoe descended from religion or magic, it would have been held in secret" (Bethel 1991, 13).

Bethel's concern over secrecy, however, is not entirely convincing in light of more recent research that seems to suggest that the practice of masking often served to allow religious meaning and ritual to hide in plain sight, as it were (Bilby 2005a; Bilby 2010; Austin-Broos 1997; Aching 2002). I will return to this idea later. Ken Bilby, who has researched in comparative fashion the various instantiations of Junkanoo found throughout the region, concludes that the claim for secularity is not unique to the Bahamas:

> In my very first interview with a Jamaican Jankunu practitioner, in 1974, when I gingerly raised the question of a possible spiritual dimension to his tradition, I was told flatly, "No man! . . . Jankunu is only a pleasure." Three decades later, when I began comparative fieldwork on Jankunu in various other parts of the Caribbean, I heard many similar statements. A respected cultural authority in the Bahamas, who had himself experienced a local version of the Jankunu masquerade every Christmas season while growing up in a small village on Cat Island, told me that "Jankanu was totally separate from religion" and insisted that there was "not a scintilla of spirituality in it." Some weeks later, in Belize, a Garifuna cultural activist and museum director used the term "secular" to describe to me the local version of Jankunu practiced by his own people. Such characterizations remain the norm almost everywhere that variants of the tradition continue to be found (in Jamaica, the Bahamas, and along the Atlantic coast of Central America)." (Bilby 2010)

In spite of the widespread claims that Junkanoo deals only in pleasure and civic enjoyment, it is neither uncommon to find Junkanoo groups incorporating Christian themes in their performances, nor rare to hear spirituals or hymns as part of the musical accompaniment to the parade. Christianity has, it would seem, found a surface space within Bahamian Junkanoo, albeit a space generally understood as wedded directly to a given group's theme for the season (functional) and not as a sacred heritage embedded within the practice (integral).[6]

As I see it, the preceding pages sketch a fascinating nexus of both authorized and devalued discourses that are put in play (or downplayed) in the process of making a case for the importance of Junkanoo in the Bahamas. The authorized discourse connects Junkanoo to African and European musical models, but concomitantly "silences" the possibility that it springs also from deeply sacred roots (Trouillot 1995). Christianity, as an inheritance endowed not by Africa per se, but by the colonizer, is also implicitly authorized. And yet an excess emerges in and through the lived experience of Junkanoo—an excess that can only be described through recourse to sacred metaphors or in terms suggesting its ineffable qualities. In the pages that follow, I take this excess as a starting point for deploying a critique of Junkanoo's authorizing discourses and suggest that the sacred roots of Junkanoo serve as a threatening reminder of the Bahamas' journey through colonialist rule to nationhood. Indeed, I argue that Christianity serves as a "mask" in its own right, a mask that serves to deauthorize African spirituality and does so as the positively charged pole of a binary opposition that always already configures African spirituality as its negative Other. Before further pursuing this idea, however, it is necessary to trace some of the general characteristics of Junkanoo in the New World—some of the routes it has taken—and to offer a context for thinking about the rapid development of the festival in the middle years of the twentieth century.

Routes: Early Accounts, Early Silences

Junkanoo is tightly plaited into the Bahamian psyche, yet seldom do we dwell on its roots, that have been within us since we first became aware of ourselves. But when we do take the time to gather around the rocking chair on the porch in the cool stillness of the evening, our grandparents tell the stories that their parents told to them, of John Canoe. On a lilting voice that is rich with age, we are borne back through the years to understand the drum that beats always within us: the drum that is the spirit of our ancestors, the spirit which survived pain, separation and suffering, on its way to the triumph of today. Their voices call out to us across the centuries. We listen, fascinated to take this voyage into the past, proud that we are part of such a rich heritage.

—ARLENE NASH-FERGUSON, *I COME TO GET ME,* 3

The earliest references to Junkanoo come not from the Bahamas but from Jamaica, where elite observers like Sir Hans Sloane (1707) and Edward Long (1774) attempted to describe the scenes playing out before them, capturing the communal aspects of the festival but failing to register the spiritual dimensions embedded in these festivities.[7] In the process, these early observers also managed to weave their colonial biases into the descriptions they penned, drawing on a vocabulary of revulsion and, in their evaluation of the practice, tending to narrate their unease—either by embedding into their description notions of the aggressive or menacing behavior of the Junkanoos or by offering illustrations of what they considered morally questionable behavior. By way of example, I offer the following passage from Long's *History of Jamaica:* "In the towns during Christmas holidays, they have several tall robust fellows dressed up in grotesque habits, and a pair of ox-horns on their head sprouting from the top of a horrid sort of visor or mask, about which the mouth is rendered very terrific with large boar tusks. The masquerader, carrying a wooden sword in his hand, is followed by a numerous crowd of drunken women, who dance at every door, bellowing out 'John Connu!' with great vehemence" (Long 1774, 424–25).

Indeed, references to "grotesque" dancing and costumes, "terrifying" masks, intemperate behavior, and the like were very common in early descriptions of the festival. The following account comes from the North Carolinian doctor Edward Warren, who witnessed the festivities in Edenton, North Carolina, in 1885:

> The leading character is the "ragman," whose "get-up" consists in a costume of rags, so arranged that one end of each hangs loose and dangles; two great ox horns attached to the skin of a raccoon, which is drawn over the head and face, leaving apertures only for the eyes and mouth; sandals of the skin of some wild "varmint"; several cow or sheep bells or strings of dried goats' horns hanging about his shoulders, and so arranged as to jingle at every movement; and a short stick of seasoned wood carried in his hands. . . . The second part is taken by the best looking darkey of the place, who wears no disguise, but is simply arrayed in what they call his "Sunday-go-to-meeting suit," and carries in his hand a small bowl or tin cup, while the other parts are arrayed fantastically in ribbons, rags, and feathers, and bearing between them several so-called musical instruments or "gumba boxes," which consist of wooden frames covered over with tanned sheep-skins. . . . Coming up to the front door of the "great house," the musicians commenced to beat their gumba-boxes violently, while characters No. 1 and No. 2 entered upon a dance of the most extraordinary character—a combination of bodily contortions, flings, kicks, gyrations and antics of every imaginable description, seemingly acting as partners, and yet each trying to excel the other in the variety and grotesqueness of his movements. (Warren 1885, 53)

The "grotesque" makes another appearance here, as does another feature of Junkanoo that seems to be relatively ubiquitous to the festival—the use of animal imagery and masquerade. This predilection within Junkanoo masquerading is also present in Long's account of Jamaican festivities a century earlier. I offer yet another example of this approach to describing Junkanoo dancing, in this case written by Thomas Young in 1842 and recounting the celebrations in Belize: "Soon after the music strikes up, a dancer appears, who after throwing his body into all conceivable postures, now jumping up and down grotesquely, then advancing and retreating affectedly, then after bending himself on one side so as nearly to fall down, he kicks about with great energy, till at length he gives a whirl, a bow, and retires, another taking his place until they are all exhausted. . . . At Christmas . . . they particularly rejoice; dancing, drumming, and singing, admirably in their way" (Thomas Young 1842, 135).

Young's account traces along the virtuosic characteristics of Junkanoo dancing, embedding it within a "grotesque" context, but also illustrating the exhibitionary qualities prized in the solo dancing (free dancing) associated with Junkanoo.[8] And this aspect of the dance continued to be highly valued well into the twentieth century. In fact, Sweet Richard, the famous Bahamian entertainer of the 1950s and early 1960s, was renowned as a Junkanoo dancer in part because of the flash, virtuosity, and charisma that he brought to the activity. An earlier account, published in 1801 as part of Bryan Edwards's three-volume history of the British West Indies, but written by William Young, who witnessed the festivities in St. Lucia during the winter of 1791–92, opens a window onto another pervasive practice that defined the festival throughout the eighteenth and nineteenth centuries:

> Returning to the villa, we were greeted by a party which frightened the boys. It was the *Moco Jumbo* and his suite. The *Jumbo* was on stilts, with a head, mounted on the actor's head, which was concealed: the music was from two baskets, like strawberry baskets, with little bells within, shook in time. The swordsman danced with an air of menace, the musician was comical, and Jumbo assumed the "antic terrible," and was very active on his stilts. . . . In England, no idea of "jolly Christmas" can be imagined, in comparison with the three days of Christmas in St. Vincent's. (William Young 1801, 258–59)

The "frightening" party, the "menacing" air of the swordsman, the "comical" musician, and the "antic terrible" of the Moco Jumbo all fit into the pejorative colonialist approach to describing a festival for which no ready European analogue existed. But Young's account offers two interesting contributions to a working understanding of Junkanoo in the New World during the nineteenth century. First, he affords a glimpse into the importance of stilt dancers to the festival during the eighteenth and nineteenth centuries. There is, in fact, evidence of the presence of stilts in virtually every local instantiation of Junkanoo in the West Indies (see Bettelheim 1979 and Bethel 1991). Written accounts indicate the appearance of stilt dancers during the eighteenth and nineteenth centuries in Belize, the Bahamas, Haiti (which influenced the shape of Junkanoo in the southern Bahamian Family Island of Inagua—more on this later), Jamaica, St. Vincent, and Bermuda. Though the practice seems to have gradually passed out of practice during the early twentieth century in most of these places, stilt walkers remained central to the Bermudian festival well into the middle years of that century (see De Jon 1956).

Second, Young's account illustrates the terminological slippage that accompanied Junkanoo in its New World settings. The St. Vincentian celebration he witnessed was not called Junkanoo, but rather the Christmas gambols. John Canoe was here replaced by the figure of the Moco Jumbo. In Bermuda, the Christmas gambols became the gombeys. In North Carolina, the festival was variously called John Kuner, John Canoe, or Who's-Who, whereas the Jamaican, Belizean, and Bahamian versions were identified by some version of Jankunu or Junkanoo.

A final example of these early accounts of Junkanoo is drawn from the Bahamas themselves and from an account of the Christmas holiday printed in the *Nassau Guardian* in 1886:

> People were in the streets all night. At midnight brass bands were heard in several directions, while concertinas, banjos, drums, whistles and human voices heralded in the "joyful morn." There were less noisy crackers than usual, while it seemed to us that more blue lights, rockets and other fireworks took their place. At 3 A.M. the Market was "all alive oh!" while at six it was difficult to get along Bay Street in front of the Market in comfort. All Nassau seemed to have turned out! Morris-dancers or some cousins of theirs held revel for an hour or two and then got either too tired with their carnival or too full of spirits from the "vasty deep" or elsewhere, to prosecute their gyrations. One grotesque figure took a snooze in a doorway for a time and then went at it again like a teetotum. The majority of these dancers are graceful in their movements and picturesque in their dress, but others are vulgar and dirty. A shower of rain about nine o'clock sent the revelers and more sober people to their houses where we hope they had a good Christmas breakfast. (*Nassau Guardian*, December 29, 1886)

In addition to contributing yet another illustration of tropes casting revelers as "grotesque," "vulgar," and "dirty," this account is interesting because it opens a window onto Bahamian Junkanoo almost two hundred years after the first accounts of Junkanoo in the New World (1707, Jamaica). It also illustrates the shape of the festival some seventy-five years after the first description of Afro-Bahamian yuletide celebrations was committed to paper in 1811. That initial account was, not coincidentally, penned by a missionary—a Reverend Dowson—who wasted no time introducing into the Bahamian narrative a strong thread of religiously motivated disapprobation of Afro-Bahamian festivities. In this, the very first account of Bahamian Christmastime (though not yet Junkanoo) practices, then, the celebrations of Afro-Bahamians are subject to a negative reading that foreshadows the later, protracted struggle over the value of Junkanoo in and for Bahamian society—a struggle fought on the ground of morality and Christianity. Dowson describes the festivities: "Landed on the largest of the Turks Islands [part of the Bahamas until 1848], by the Spaniards called *Las Amanas,* who probably derived the name from the natives. In the French charts they are called *Les Isles Turques*. . . . I never before witnessed such a Christmas Day; the negroes have been beating their tambourines and dancing the whole day and now between eight and nine o'clock they are pursuing their sport as hotly as ever. How my heart was pained to see the Redeemer's birthday so commemorated" (Dowson 1960, entry for December 25, 1811).

Taken as a whole, these accounts, scattered across two centuries (1774, 1791 [1807], 1811, 1847, 1885, and 1886), and witnessed in five places (Jamaica, St. Vincent, Belize, North Carolina, and the Bahamas) foreground several of the characteristics shared by all of these local traditions: masking of the face (hence the Bahamian nickname for Junkanoo, the "dance of the unknown"); animal or zoological masquerading (including animal hides and horns); drumming and dancing (using a variety of instruments); and the celebrations occurring around the Christmas holiday. This last characteristic is more significant than it may at first appear, for in contrast to the pre-Lenten carnival celebrations that sprang up in colonies where Catholicism was the preeminent religious context (such as New Orleans, Cuba, Haiti, and Trinidad)—Carnival celebrations for which there were already clear European antecedents and active local traditions—Junkanoo festivals in the New World retain their very similar characteristics in the absence of such a European model.[9]

This state of affairs suggests the strong likelihood that a combination of themes or models deriving from African traditions served as the principal sources of inspiration for Junkanoo, providing the underlying coherence embedded within these various local practices and leading E. Clement Bethel to assert: "The Bahamian Junkanoo festival is related to the John Canoe revels held elsewhere in the New World" (Bethel 1991, 10). Just how it is related, however, remains a difficult question to answer, in spite of scholars' examination of the African practices that may have contributed to the creation of Junkanoo.

I outline several of these ideas in the pages that follow, thereby illustrating the complexities involved in tracing these routes with any degree of certainty and also opening the question of the festival's sacred roots to a fresh interrogation. One approach has been to work toward tracing the etymology of the term *Junkanoo* itself, a strategy that is bound up in tying the New World practice to a historical figure by the name of John Konny. Kwame Daaku describes this person as follows:

A contemporary of John Kabes who was economically, socially, and politically as powerful was John Konny (Counie, Kony) of Pokoso, Ahanta. A man of strong personality and character, he ignored Dutch threats, openly defied them, and successfully pitted his power against an Anglo-Dutch alliance in 1711. For almost fifteen years he baffled the calculations of the Dutch and thwarted their designs. John Konny was a ruler with connections reaching as far inland as Asante. . . . His stout defense of the former Brandenburg possessions resulted in their headquarters at

Pokoso being for long known as "Connie's Castle," even after he had been driven away by the Dutch. (Daaku 1970, 127–28)

There is some evidence to suggest that slaves settled in the British West Indies would have had reason to know of John Konny, largely because, as E. Clement Bethel has pointed out, "it is generally accepted, thanks to records of the slave traffic between West Africa and the New World Territories, that the planters in the British colonies, particularly, Jamaica, preferred slaves from the Ashanti-Fanti peoples of the Gold Coast. . . . If the name *John Canoe* is indeed derived from the caboceer. . . . John Conny of the Gold Coast, this would explain why the term is only found among former British possessions" (Bethel 1991, 11). And yet, whether or not this historical figure forms part of the root of the New World name for Junkanoo, this line of thought does nothing to help explain the shape of the festival in its various New World settings.[10] To address that set of concerns, it is necessary to turn to scholars interested in West African agricultural rituals and sacred traditions.

Orlando Patterson has suggested that there are three likely antecedents that may have contributed to New World instantiations of Junkanoo: "the yam festival activities of the *Mno* secret society of the *Ibo* peoples; the recreational activities of the *Egungun* secret society of the *Yoruba*; and the *Homowo* harvest festival of the *Ga* peoples" (Patterson 1969, 245). Each of these possible antecedents involves masked dancing and is closely tied to ancestral rites. They share a great deal with each other, not in the specifics of the festivals themselves per se, but rather through their cosmology and intergenerational and sacred meanings. As such, cross-recognition and mutual adaptation to or adoption of aspects relating to these festivals in the New World context of slavery seems not only possible but plausible.[11] This is the argument that Sterling Stuckey, discussing John Kunering in North Carolina, explores in the following passage: "Africans were so given to secret societies, and their purposes and characteristics were generally so similar, that a great many ceremonies across Central and West Africa involving the use of masks and costumes—signs that ancestral figures are being represented—might resemble and be related to John Kunering, and might have enabled Africans from various parts of Africa to identify with and join in Kunering in North Carolina, since masks are used universally to represent ancestral figures" (Stuckey 1987, 68).

The principle Stuckey is driving toward here can be applied to any of the other instantiations of Junkanoo in the New World in equal measure. And yet the necessarily speculative nature of these musings makes it impossible to construct any definitive statements about these processes. Another possible antecedent is put forward by Robert Dirks and Virginia Kerns, who suggest the following:

We find it irresistible to speculate on some resemblances between John Canoe and a dance performed by the Bambara people of West Africa. The Bambara's tribal domain extends into the Ivory Coast region, an area that was heavily slaved by the European powers. Today, the Bambara still conduct traditional agricultural rites in which the premier dance is the *kono*. . . . Aside from the linguistic similarities, there are two reasons to suspect that the Bambara's *kono* may have served as the model for Jamaica's *Canoe*. In the first place, as an agricultural rite, *kono* shares an affinity with John Canoe, which clearly bore the stamp of a first-fruits ceremony in the early days. Moreover, the *kono,* like the early versions of John Canoe, is performed in animal masquerades. (Dirks and Kerns 1975, 3–4)

This is a particularly attractive suggestion in part because it brings an analysis of both etymological and functional aspects of Bambara ritual to bear on the New World forms of Junkanoo. And yet there is no direct evidence of this connection either, leaving the contemporary shape of Junkanoo, to a significant extent, separated from a grounding narrative. This is, however, merely one more example of the central dilemma of New World societies in general—a dilemma that Stuart Hall characterizes as a "loss of history" (Stuart Hall 2001). E. Clement Bethel takes this collection of ideas regarding Junkanoo's antecedents and, mirroring Mintz and Price (1992), concludes: "It is clear, therefore, that John Canoe cannot be viewed as a single African phenomenon, transported intact to the New World. It is, rather, an intimate mixture of different West African elements, which, having undergone what the Barbadian George Lamming terms a 'sea change,' emerged as a medium of creative expression for the New World African. Whatever its origin, though, one thing is sure about John Canoe: it was this fusion of disparate elements which led all black people, wherever the festival was practiced, to accept it as their own" (Bethel 1991, 14–15).

I will return to this statement later, expanding it toward an exploration of the creolization of Junkanoo in the Bahamian context. Before doing so, however, it is important to consider the overwhelming preponderance of sacred themes and ancestral rites marshaled in these attempts to think about Junkanoo in the New World. Far from being only—or even primarily—a "medium of creative expression," Junkanoo seems likely to have held deep spiritual meanings for its participants.

Recent research on Junkanoo by Ken Bilby suggests that these sacred roots still play a constitutive role in Jamaican contexts. Bilby, researching Junkanoo in rural St. Elizabeth parish in Jamaica, has noted that the celebrations there are still quite heavily invested with religious meaning and ritual power. These celebrations serve as a "year-end component of a larger community religion that is practiced year-round. Throughout the year, as the need arises, local ancestors are called by the gumbay drum and the old *myal* (spirit) songs to come and help the living tackle the problems of daily life. At Christmastime, the focus shifts from healing to feasting, celebration, and Jonkonnu dancing, and the ancestors are very much a part of these holiday observances as well" (Bilby 2005a: 4). The ritual power of Junkanoo, then, is centered primarily on healing from spiritual ailments and on the celebration of such healing. This is in direct contrast to the predominantly "secular" shape that Junkanoo has taken in Jamaican and Bahamian national spaces during the twentieth century. According to Bilby, this state of affairs offers strong evidence for reconsidering the undercurrents of sacred sound and meaning that have been silenced in the modern variants of the practice throughout the region. It also resonates with the claims of earlier researchers on Junkanoo, such as Ira De A. Reid, who, citing fieldwork in North Carolina, Jamaica, and the Bahamas, postulated (as did Orlando Patterson) that the spiritual inspiration for Junkanoo likely derived from a range of West African religious practices (Reid 1942). In this connection, and speaking of both Junkanoo and Buru festivities in Jamaica, Bilby suggests: "These last holdouts in the present are uniquely positioned to help us understand what complex Afro-creole performances such as Jonkonnu and Buru really were—which is to say, what they meant—to those who practiced and cherished them in earlier times. And they offer resounding confirmation of what many in Jamaica and the wider Caribbean have intuitively grasped: both Jonkonnu and Buru, despite their 'secular' appearance in the present, spring from deep spiritual roots" (Bilby 2005a, 5, 9).

Early on, then, Junkanoo provided a context within which community could be reconstituted and fostered and healing could take place—a context that provided a means of rethinking African cosmology, reworking it to suit the current situation. That situation, which I will turn to later, has always included the overarching paradigm of Christianity, and I suggest that the remaining traces of African spirituality are firmly rooted in and routed through the ineffable experiences of the putatively "secular" Junkanoo—a secular festival that Bahamians attempt to describe with recourse to spiritual metaphors. Take the following example from Pat Rahming, who in this passage questions the necessity (and even the validity) of judging Junkanoo:

> Successful junkanoo evokes strong emotional response, which cannot be replaced by intellectual rationale, even concerning so-called "artistic excellence." The judgment of strong emotional response is not easy. . . . If the commitment to judgment is made, then a concurrent commitment must be made to find a way to judge emotional response. "It scared the hell out of me" is a more successful response than "It was nice" or "I'm so excited I can't breathe" is a higher score than "The costumes were very well done." I query the need to judge in the first place. (Imagine determining the best church service every Sunday, and awarding prizes for "having the spirit.") (Rahming 1992, 32)

The imagery used here, it is worth pointing out, traces along some of the same territory as did early accounts of Junkanoo. The unease—even the fear—that observers expressed in describing the "menacing" dancers, who were misread as merely aggressive, resulted in large part from the colonialist frame within which these visitors were operating. Rahming (1992), on the other hand, frames the unease, the "strong emotional response" engendered by Junkanoo, in terms that can be understood as deriving from the deeply spiritual content of the practice. His thought experiment regarding the legitimacy of even attempting to judge the Junkanoo parades—whereby he creates an equivalency between the ineffable effect of Junkanoo and the phenomenon of "having the spirit" in church (at the very least, he conflates the two)—moreover, constitutes a particularly interesting acknowledgment of the uniquely Bahamian context he is describing and the ineffable spiritual content that continues to inhabit Junkanoo.

Creolization: Experiencing Junkanoo in the Bahamas, 1811–1919

I turn now to a specific exploration of the Bahamian version of Junkanoo in the nineteenth and early twentieth centuries. As I have already illustrated, it took a bit longer for accounts of Bahamian Junkanoo to appear in written documents, the first of these appearing almost a century and a half after the initial descriptions of the festival in Jamaica. Several earlier descriptions of yuletide festivities, however, offer glimpses of the disapprobation with which commentators greeted even the celebrations that existed prior to the emergence of Junkanoo (Dowson [1811] 1960; Townsend [1823] 1968, chap. 1). It is significant, moreover, that the very first account of these yuletide celebrations—witnessed on Grand Turk—was penned by a missionary who quickly expressed his displeasure regarding the practice. One of the difficulties in analyzing the shape of Bahamian Junkanoo during the early nineteenth century emerges in direct relationship to the geography of the archipelago. Statements made about Junkanoo in one location—say, Nassau—do not necessarily hold true for Junkanoo as practiced in other places around the Bahamas. The descriptions themselves, moreover, do not describe unequivocally Junkanoo-specific revelry. It is thus possible that Junkanoo was already emerging in the early decades of the nineteenth century, but contemporary written accounts do nothing to shed light on the matter.

Take, for example, the following passage from the plantation owner Charles Farquharson's diary of 1832, which offers a rare glimpse at the social dimensions of slave life in the Bahamas: "Wed. 26. Some of our people gon abroad to see some of their friends and some at home amusing themselves in their own way threw the day, but all of them at home in the evening and had a grand dance and keep it up until near daylight" (Farquharson [1832] 1957). The passage opens a window onto the very particular situation on San Salvador, where Farquharson lived and made his entry, but beyond the fact that it was customary throughout the archipelago to observe a holiday around Christmas, it is unclear how much this entry can be said to reflect practice in communities living on the other Family Islands or in Nassau. It is, furthermore, impossible to ascertain the degree to which these celebrations were tied to Junkanoo proper, if at all. E. Clement Bethel elaborates:

> Unlike their counterparts in the rest of the West Indies, the Bahamian slaves did not even have the fortune of mingling with one another; for the whole of the Bahamian population was scattered among some nine or more islands, each of them isolated from the other and from the capital. As a result, no practice recorded in any single part of the archipelago can be presumed common to the whole colony. The "grand dance" noted by Farquharson in San Salvador was the way Christmas was celebrated on that island. . . . It was observed rather differently in the capital, and each of the other islands, no doubt, had a tradition of its own. Two conclusions, however, may be drawn about the Bahamian Christmas festivities before Emancipation. One is that such activities did exist, and that they involved the slaves. The other is that, wherever these activities were found, they seemed to bear resemblance to the John Canoe celebrations held elsewhere in the Americas. (Bethel 1991, 26)

Although the first of the conclusions drawn by Bethel is fairly straightforward, it is impossible to verify his second conclusion beyond making the heavily qualified (and essentially meaningless) assertion that the celebrations described occurred during the night and on the occasion of the Christmas holiday, thus marking them as occurring in the same seasonal and temporal space within which the Junkanoo festival would emerge in the second half of the nineteenth century.

Less than two decades after Farquharson's diary entry, however, written accounts do begin to bear out hallmarks of Junkanoo. Take, for example, the account of Christmas festivities printed by the *Nassau Guardian* in 1849, which traces a more elaborate celebration—a very different way of celebrating that illustrates several of the central markers of Junkanoo as practiced throughout the region.

> Another Christmas Day has passed, and the festivities of old have commenced "right merrily." The Yule Log and Wassail Cup of our fatherland are not seen here—but these are not the only signs of Christmas. We have in this distant isle other, and as cheering, reminiscences of the period, and, although no carol is sung, the morn is ushered in with music. The Militia Band and the fifes and drums of the Regiment break on the slumberer's ear, and answer for the "Waites"; and the sound of footsteps are the dawn of the day, added to the din of voices and the noise of "crackers," give intimation of the joyous season. The markets were open yesterday until 9 a.m. They were unusually thronged, and the show of meat and vegetables was extremely good. Several prize oxen, decked out in ribbons, were led over the town, previous to falling a sacrifice, and "John Canoe" came forth on stilts in style, much to the gratification of his numerous train of followers. Christmas has commenced well, and we trust that it will end so. We wish our friends and patrons the usual compliments of the season. (*Nassau Guardian*, December 26, 1849, p. 2)

This description of Junkanoo, significant because it offers several insights into the shape of Junkanoo in Nassau's mid-nineteenth-century celebrations, represents several firsts: the first time the term *John Canoe* appears in print in the Bahamas; the first time John Canoe's presence on Bay Street (at the market) is documented in print; and the first postemancipation account of Junkanoo. Two other points are worth mentioning here: some of the music for the occasion is provided by the militia and regiment bands (though it is unclear to what musical accompaniment John Canoe danced around the market); and several oxen are processed as part of the ritual "previous to falling a sacrifice." These insights into the festivities of 1849 provide a context in which to think about the presence of free Africans, the process of creolization, the effects of emancipation on the festival, and the intraregional movement of people and practices during the early to mid-nineteenth century.

That Junkanoo was above all a celebration by and for slaves in the New World is an important dynamic to bear in mind, not least because Junkanoo began a slow and all but inexorable decline throughout the region after emancipation. Unlike Carnival traditions that thrived in part because of the power struggle between former slaves and their former masters, Bahamian elites had no similar vested interest in controlling Junkanoo. As such, Junkanoo stood (mostly) outside of the social, cultural, and political struggles attendant to the development of the "carnival complex" in the New World (Burton 1997). But in part because of the lack of direct engagement with practices brought to the region by European elites, Junkanoo celebrations were not vehicles for resistance or opposition in the same way or to the degree that Carnival celebrations were elsewhere. Consider again the diary entry by Farquharson, which illustrates the extent to which the "grand dance" held on that occasion was separate from white Christmas festivities. E. Clement Bethel notes: "The Bahamian festival of the early nineteenth century was never the elaborate show that John Canoe was in Jamaica; it was a festival celebrated almost exclusively by the slaves. This meant, ironically, that the Bahamian John Canoe (or Junkanoo), never dependent upon the whites for survival, was not affected economically by Emancipation; the festival was still the property of the blacks, and consequently continued to be held long years after that date" (Bethel 1991, 33).

This passage brings into focus another important preemancipation dynamic attendant to Bahamian Junkanoo. The New World context for Junkanoo celebrations was, with the exception of the Bahamas, embedded within the frame of the plantation economy, which was much more developed in places like Jamaica and North Carolina than it ever was in the Bahamas. Bethel (1991), along with Keith Wisdom (1985), points to this lack of effective plantation hierarchies as one of the major reasons for Junkanoo's ultimate survival in the postemancipation era, not least because the preemancipation expression of the festival was "never dependent upon the whites for survival" (Bethel 1991, 33) in the same way that it was in plantation contexts.

One of the paradoxes that this "ownership" engendered in postemancipation Junkanoo is addressed by Bethel: "Ironically, too, the African nature of the festival also worked against it. For the slaves, John Canoe had provided proof that they had identities, despite their condition, and this affirmation of their heritage was a welcome one. As freemen, however, adrift in an alien and often hostile culture, that African identity was more of a liability than a help" (Bethel 1991, 16). And while it is debatable just how adrift or alien they felt themselves to be within the Bahamian cultural milieu, it is nevertheless clear that the regionwide decline in the popularity of Junkanoo after emancipation visited itself on the Bahamas as well, evidence of which comes in the form of two accounts published in the *Nassau Guardian* in 1853 and 1857. The first of these finds John Canoe overshadowed by Neptune and Amphitrite, newcomers to the festivities since 1849 and almost certainly joining the Bay Street crowd from their original home in Inagua, a further confirmation of the idiosyncratic local shapes that Junkanoo took throughout the archipelago.[12]

> Christmas with its customary festivities has been passed by all classes of the inhabitants of our little isle amidst much mirth and gladness. Christmas Day was ushered in by the sound of music from the Militia Band, and closed by the burning of an effigy of the *soi-disant* "Peripatetic," which last contributed not a little towards the amusement of those who live in the Eastern district, where it was burnt. Various grotesque figures intended to represent Neptune, Amphitrite, and others, preceded by fife and tambourines have on the succeeding days exhibited themselves in the usually quiet streets, exciting the greatest merriment among the lower orders. (*Nassau Guardian,* December 30, 1853)

This relatively lively range of activities can fruitfully be juxtaposed with the following account, published only four years later: "If we except the noise made by Chinese Crackers and other fireworks, the festivities of Christmas have passed off quietly enough in our little isle. The representatives of the illustrious 'Johnny Canoe' of former days, have dwindled down to two or three, and as for 'Neptune and Amphitrite,' they have not left their watery domains at all this season. The 'Waits' went their rounds, as usual, and the African 'tom-tom' has done its duty at the Barracks" (*Nassau Guardian,* December 30, 1857).

The rapid decline in participation on Bay Street in evidence here is certainly remarkable, but the apparent lack of enthusiasm was not solely related to uncertainty among ex-slaves and free Africans over what identities could advantageously be mobilized in the postemancipation context. This was, after all, also a moment of unease on the part of the white ruling class, and Junkanoo, while not subject to the same dynamics as Carnival elsewhere in the region, was nevertheless viewed with suspicion and even concern by elite Bahamians. The *Bahama Herald,* for instance, voiced this concern in 1854: "We cannot look with any degree of approbation upon such silly affairs as 'John Canoes' &c. Such harlequinade cannot fail to attract crowds of the idle and profligate, and disorder, vice, and intemperance inevitably follow.... Money acquired by these means is sure to be spent in intemperate pleasures and low debauchery" (*Bahama Herald,* December 30, 1854).

The middle of the nineteenth century, then, saw several delimiting factors, both centripetal and centrifugal, including questions regarding self-representation and concomitant elite disapproval, all of which combined to exert significant pressure on the festival. Unlike many of its namesakes throughout the region, and in spite of the number of "Johnny Canoe" participants dwindling "down to two or three," however, Junkanoo continued to be performed and managed to maintain its presence on Bay Street. Keith Wisdom has suggested that one reason for the festival's postemancipation survival in the Bahamas may be bound up in the celebration of Guy Fawkes Day (November 5), a celebration that offered an analogue sanctioned by patriotism:

> This custom, patriotic in the extreme, was transported by the English to their colonies, where it was adopted whole-heartedly.... On [that] day an effigy was burned and uncostumed Junkanoo bands paraded and danced to the beat of Junkanoo music.... Strange as it may at first seem, Guy Fawkes' Night shared several elements with mid-nineteenth-century Junkanoo. Both fireworks and the burning of effigies have been mentioned as part of the nineteenth-century Christmas festivities in Nassau. This fact, coupled with the proximity of Guy Fawkes' Day to Christmas [November 5], leads almost naturally to an association of the two dates. Guy Fawkes' Day, for the true Junkanoo enthusiast, was as good a time as any to begin earnest rehearsal for the Christmas parade. (Wisdom 1985, 31–32)

By linking the musical content and parading of Junkanoos (uncostumed though they were) to the celebration of Guy Fawkes Day, revelers claimed for Junkanoo a measure of legitimacy that could not otherwise have accrued to the practice.

And while Guy Fawkes Day was undoubtedly celebrated on Bay Street in postemancipation Nassau, several other contributing factors played a role in ensuring Junkanoo's survival into the twentieth century. "The spatial separation of commercial, bourgeois, white elite, and brown middle class downtown Nassau (where Junkanoo was performed) from the predominantly poor and black Over the Hill suburbs (where Junkanoo was prepared and rehearsed)" was one such factor (Craton and Saunders 1998, 488). Though I have thus far juxtaposed Junkanoo with Carnival traditions, pointing to disjunctures rather than similarities, the appeal of taking over the main business thoroughfare—invading and occupying, even if only for a few hours, the spaces ordinarily reserved for the middle and upper classes—was a powerful draw for Junkanoos in the Bahamas just as it was for Carnival revelers in Trinidad (Aching 2002). The attachment to rushing

on Bay Street, in fact, remains so strong in the minds of Junkanoos that a proposed move from Bay Street to the Queen Elizabeth Sports Centre, announced in
1989 (and intended to create more space for the increasingly large groups) was met
with outrage, protests, and the threat of boycotts. The proposal was ultimately
withdrawn. Bay Street, then, became the main space in which to celebrate Junkanoo, was imagined as the symbolic home of the festival by the mid-nineteenth
century, and has been guarded as such ever since.

Another contributing factor was the arrival of liberated Africans who were
brought to the Bahamas and settled outside of Nassau (and eventually in the
Over-the-Hill part of town) between 1811 and 1860. All told some sixty-five hundred Africans were freed—many from Spanish and French slaving ships—during
this half century, adding an intermittent stream of African language, custom,
and ritual to the social fabric of the Afro-Bahamian community.[13] The "revivify-
ing influence" of this African influx is likely also responsible in part for Junkanoo's continuation during the middle of the nineteenth century, not least because liberated Africans themselves served as reminders of African cultural
vitality and value in a colonial context within which European art forms and
cultural practices formed the hegemonic authorizing narrative. Liberated Africans were, for instance, the motivating and organizing force behind founding the
first legally sanctioned and incorporated Friendly Society in New Providence—
the Grant's Town Friendly Society—in 1835. This achievement was followed by
the inauguration of many others in the ensuing years, including the Yoruba and
Egbar societies of Bain Town, and the two Congo societies of Fox Hill and
Grant's Town. (Craton and Saunders 1998, 11). These Friendly Societies provided
for collective action, social and political protest, and community pride. The brass
bands that the societies maintained, moreover, offered another layer of music
and dance to the yearly calendar of festivities. And, very importantly, all of this
activity accompanied both the move from pre- to postemancipation society and
the development of the Over-the-Hill section of town.[14] E. Clement Bethel re-
counts the influence of liberated Africans:

> In 1800, a substantial number of the Bahamian blacks, slave and free, had been
> born in the Americas. As a result, their African heritage was fragmented at best—
> hence the very European air of certain Christmas celebrations, such as the music
> played by the Royal Militia Band. The Liberated Africans, on the other hand, never
> slaves, and forced to settle in communities apart from those already in existence,
> were far more able to preserve that heritage. As well as the appearance of John
> Canoe on Christmas Day, 1849, there was a sacrifice of oxen—evidence of the new
> African presence in the community. (Bethel 1991, 34)

Liberated Africans, then, likely played an important role in the survival of
Junkanoo as a living practice during the middle decades of the nineteenth cen-

tury. And if the sacrifice of Christmas oxen is taken at face value as an indication of religious ritual among Afro-Bahamians, then it is also likely that liberated Africans were in part responsible for keeping open a door to the sacred roots of Junkanoo in those decades.[15] There is little written about Junkanoo in the 1860s and '70s, but the festival could not have passed out of practice during this time if for no other reason than that its reappearance in written accounts during the 1880s indicates that it had grown larger and more organized in the intervening years. According to L. D. Powles, Junkanoo had even garnered some participation by the younger members of the white elite, a seemingly short-lived practice in the preindependence history of the festival, but one that may also have contributed to its staying power during the mid-nineteenth century. "About Christmas time they seem to march about day and night, with lanterns and bands of music, and they fire off crackers everywhere. This is a terrible nuisance, but the custom has the sanction of antiquity, though no doubt it would have been put down long ago if the white young gentlemen had not exhibited a taste for the same amusement" (Powles 1888, 147–48).

In 1886, the *Nassau Guardian* described a festival during which "people were in the streets all night. At midnight brass bands were heard in several directions, while concertinas, banjos, drums, whistles and human voices heralded in the 'joyful morn'" (*Nassau Guardian*, December 29, 1886), But this increase in participation and in the visibility of Junkanoo was accompanied by some serious concerns over hooliganism, violence, and general unrest. According to Michael Craton and Gail Saunders, "The development of Junkanoo toward the end of the nineteenth century pointed up the great social, economic, and political divide between Bay Street and Over the Hill—a division made all the more glaring by the continuing poverty and growing political awareness of the black, the natural healing of the rift between 'old' Bahamian blacks and those who came as liberated Africans, and the almost paranoid fears among the whites stemming from their general ignorance of what life was really like on the other side of Nassau's ridge" (Craton and Saunders 1998, 129).

There was, accordingly, increasing pressure to regulate the festival in some way, and after some years of pressing for legislation (largely by church groups and commercial interests), the Street Nuisances Prohibition Act of 1899 was effected. E. Clement Bethel explains the impact of this piece of legislation:

> As the colony approached the turn of the century the Government became alarmed at the indiscriminate marching about "day and night" at Christmas time. In 1899, a new Act, the Street Nuisances Prohibition Act, came into effect. As its name implies, its purpose was to banish "nuisances" from the streets for most of the year. In order to allow time for legitimate parades, however, the rules of the Act were waived four times a year: from six to ten p.m. on December 24th and 31st, and from four to nine on Christmas and New Year's mornings. The Government was formalizing a

tradition which had until then been simply customary—the practice of holding Junkanoo parades in the early morning. Of the two periods, the participants in the parade quickly demonstrated their preference for the morning times. According to some of the older Nassauvians interviewed in 1977, only semi-costumed stragglers who wished to "let off steam" bothered to come out in the evenings. The "real" Junkanoo parades—complete with costumes and music—took place on Bay Street just before dawn. (Bethel 1991, 37)

And though the law did negatively circumscribe and delimit the celebration of Junkanoo, it managed to hem it in strategically, as it were, successfully locking the festival into a very specific set of hours during the calendar year, times that were, as Bethel points out, sanctioned by tradition. The Street Nuisances Prohibition Act of 1899 is, as such, the first in a long line of strategies whereby Junkanoo came to be institutionalized, regulated, and controlled. Interestingly, though the Street Nuisances Prohibition Act did significantly limit public celebrations, this legislation did nothing to militate against participation in Junkanoo per se, leaving missionaries, priests, and pastors to lament the continued presence of the festival during the Christmas feast. The following complaint is typical of the disapprobation that continued to define discourse about Junkanoo in Christian circles: "The coloured people have their own ways of holiday-making which certainly do not conduce to the religious observance of the festival. On Christmas Eve and throughout the succeeding night, there is an incessant letting off of crackers, beating of drums and blowing of penny whistles and trumpets, crowds are parading the streets, and many wearing masks and dressing themselves up in fantastic costumes" (*Nassau Quarterly Mission Papers* 4 [1890], 245). As the nineteenth century gave way to the twentieth, then, Junkanoo had managed to weather the uncertainty and challenges attendant to the decades following emancipation, becoming popular (and threatening) enough to incur legislative intervention and becoming a fixture of the Christmas season. In short, it had become a tradition that had acquired, as L. D. Powles puts it, "the sanction of antiquity" (Powles 1888, 147–48).

A final point requires mention before I turn to the gradual institutionalization of Junkanoo in the twentieth century—namely, that Junkanoo was primarily (though not exclusively) innovated, performed, and developed in Nassau as opposed to the Family Islands. In contrast to the social dance music that forms the subject of chapter 2, the goombay music that was associated with the Family Islands, Junkanoo is understood as rooted in New Providence. Christmas celebrations throughout the Bahamas took different shapes throughout the pre- and postemancipation years, but Junkanoo increasingly developed into a festival deeply rooted in Nassau, though it was practiced elsewhere as well. Gail Saunders notes:

Out Island communities had special celebrations on Emancipation Day and Christmas Day, but not on the same scale as in Nassau. In black and bi-racial settlements, celebrations bore similarities to the John Canoe parade in Nassau. There was usually dancing, some form of "rushing" to music using drums. In addition to the John Canoe parade, in Eleuthera, entertainment was given by the different lodges on Christmas Eve. In 1897, the Gregory Town lodge, the Grand United Order of Odd Fellows, gave a programme including "dialogues, recitations, addresses, songs, and instrumental music before a large and attentive audience." [*Nassau Guardian*, January 1, 1897] (Saunders 2003a, 68–69)

The flow of Junkanoo from center to periphery, counterbalanced by the movements of goombay music (or rake-n-scrape), flowing in the opposite direction, is one of the factors that continues to play out in places like Cat Island, where it became necessary to import Junkanoo from Nassau in the 1980s because it had passed out of active practice (Bilby 2010) and where rake-n-scrape annually gathers and then releases centrifugal force at the Cat Island Rake-n-Scrape Festival. I will return to this dynamic in chapter 5.

"BACK ON DA SIDE":
SITES, SIGHTS, AND SOUNDS OF JUNKANOO

In the following pages I explore the continued embedding of Junkanoo within Bahamian social life and its increasing institutionalization, as well as the shifts in musical performance and instrumentation that have accompanied these processes. If the nineteenth century can be seen as a test of Junkanoo's social viability in the postemancipation Bahamas, then the twentieth century might be characterized as a test of the festival's ability to serve as a symbol for—an icon of—the nation. That Junkanoo is today the quintessential symbol of Bahamian national culture, however, belies the fraught trajectory that the festival often traveled, especially in the first half of the twentieth century. It also tends to obscure the highly politicized position of Junkanoo, a position into which the festival was increasingly fitted during the second half of the twentieth century.

Junkanoo Sites

The Junkanoo at the beginning of the [twentieth] century consisted of a number of groups or "gangs" from various sections of New Providence. Each gang had a leader who was identified by his solo dance-like performance at the front of the group. The gangs would move down Bay Street "rushing" past each other in opposite directions. This would sometimes result in collisions, some of which were not accidental, between groups.

—KEITH GORDON WISDOM, "BAHAMIAN JUNKANOO," 35

The collisions between participants that Wisdom mentions here were, in fact, often premeditated, intended among other things to settle injuries to pride or person suffered during the year (or, for that matter, during the last Junkanoo parade). But the very tight quarters within which these Junkanoos were "rush-ing" made such nonaccidental incidents—and even unintended interferences—almost inevitable. Until 1973, when the route was changed to a one-way track down Bay Street and back along Shirley Street, Junkanoo groups paraded both ways on Bay Street, passing each other along the way (Wood 1995; Saunders 2003a). One of the goals of a successful "rush" was to disrupt the rhythm and dancing of the other groups, and this could happen in purely musical terms—that is, by playing so loud that the other group lost track of its own pulse—or by adding an elbow or two at an appropriate moment for good measure. And as costumes and groups grew in size and numbers, the width of Bay Street was no longer sufficient to accommodate the revelers.

Not surprisingly, these incidents were part of the reason for elite concern over Junkanoo even in the late nineteenth century, and they undoubtedly contributed to the enactment of the Street Nuisances Act of 1899. As the twentieth century moved into its second and third decades, Junkanoo came under ever-ever greater scrutiny, both from concerned local elites and from academics and visitors, who witnessed and reported on the festival. In addition, the responsibility for manag-ing Junkanoo and developing it on Bay Street was passed through a series of in-creasingly government-driven institutions during the twentieth century. The pa-rade route is one of the aspects of Junkanoo that has been progressively brought under such institutional control, and it is therefore helpful to briefly outline the major shifts in the route during the twentieth century. I then turn to an explora-tion of the legislative interventions and the institutional homes of Junkanoo in order to provide an overview of the sites in which Junkanoo has come to be dis-ciplined and performed.[16]

An account of the festival in the *Nassau Guardian* in 1948 mentions that the Junkanoos paraded Bay Street between Parliament Street and Frederick Street—a two-block stretch in the heart of Bay Street's commercial district (*Nassau Guard-ian,* January 2, 1948, 1). This was likely the basic route for the parade during the late nineteenth century as well. By 1950, the parade route was expanded to run between East Street and George Street in order to accommodate the growing number of participants (see Figure 9) (*Nassau Guardian,* December 27, 1950, 2).

In response to the increasing popularity of Junkanoo in the 1960s, the parade route was extended yet again in 1971, this time extending from Victoria Avenue (just east of Elizabeth Avenue) to George Street. And yet, in spite of the addi-tional linear space, these adjustments did nothing to ease the lateral overcrowd-ing that occurred when groups passed each other on Bay Street (Wood 1995). Liz Nathaniels recounted: "There might be a few moments when no group passes by at all, and then suddenly two groups appear from two different directions and feelings run high—because there is not enough room on narrow Bay Street to allow the two to parade in full strength past each other" (Nathaniels 1971).

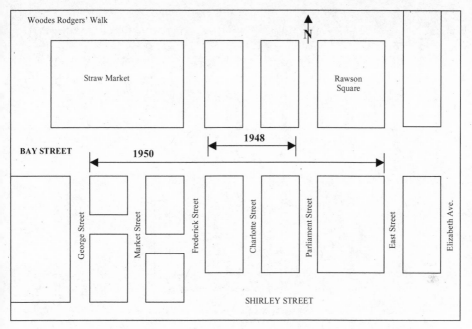

FIGURE 9. Bay Street parade routes, 1948 and 1950. Adapted from Wood 1995.

The continued overcrowding led to the most significant accommodation yet, enacted in 1973 on the occasion of the Independence Day Junkanoo Parade. That year, Bay Street became only one leg (albeit the most important leg) of a one-way circular parade route. This route saw Junkanoo groups rush down Bay Street from Parliament Street to Frederick Street and from there south to Shirley Street. They then rushed down Shirley Street back to Parliament Street and completed the loop back up to Bay Street. The parade route was to stay essentially the same for almost two decades, but by the late 1980s it had again become too constricted. Consequently, a proposal was made to move the festival to the Queen Elizabeth Sports Centre (now called the Thomas A. Robinson Stadium). The outrage and demonstrations that this proposal engendered caused officials to abandon that plan in the end. According to Vivian Nina Michelle Wood, "Group members saw Bay Street as the only possible venue, since it continued to represent a power reversal (White merchants versus the Black masses), and indeed the atmosphere on Bay Street with its closely set buildings which provide excellent acoustics, the Christmas lights that add a sense of mystery to the setting, and the jostling of spectators, are essential to having a true Junkanoo experience" (Wood 1995, 68).[17]

In light of the clear preference of Junkanoos for Bay Street, the circular route was expanded, creating the current route, which was introduced in 1990. This

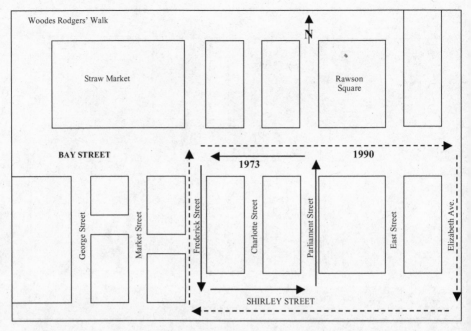

FIGURE 10. Bay Street parade routes, 1973 and 1990. Adapted from Wood 1995.

route changed the direction of the parade so that groups rushed from west to east down Bay Street—or from the straw market past Rawson Square—and increased the length of the route to accommodate the ever-larger groups coming to Bay Street for Junkanoo (see Figure 10).

These changes to the Junkanoo route illustrate the dramatic growth of the festival's popularity, especially during the years that majority rule and independence became realities for the Bahamas. But the early growth, illustrated in the 1950 shift, was realized in the wake of serious legislative injunctions, after periods when the festival was banned outright, and at the expense of submitting Junkanoo to regulatory control in the form of committees and oversight. Next I explore how Junkanoo was strategically situated within the Bahamas and interrogate the extent to which these legal and institutional sites resulted in the formation and consolidation of a national symbol in the second half of the twentieth century.

Although L. D. Powles (1888) mentioned the participation of young white men in the Junkanoo parades, this broad participation in the festival seems to have dwindled during the last decade of the nineteenth century. Consequently, Junkanoo again became, as it had been before and just after emancipation, a festival primarily for and by Afro-Bahamians, and, as such, it was subject to increased scrutiny by middle- and upper-class Bahamians. Newspaper articles printed during the first two decades of the twentieth century illustrate the prevailing attitude toward Junkanoo among those who tended not to participate. The following account comes from the *Nassau Tribune* in 1911: "The New Year holiday was heralded on Monday morning by the customary noise of horns, bells and drums and the grotesque masqueraders disported themselves along Bay Street with an energy and vigour which if put into their pursuit of their avocations during the year will be to some purpose" (*Nassau Tribune*, January 3, 1911). But more than serving as an example of a mere waste of productive energies, Junkanoo also continued to be a nuisance (in spite of the Street Nuisances Act of 1899). Consider this report from the *Nassau Tribune:*

> Yes! In the old days slumbers were undisturbed in the early hours of Christmas morning. . . . When we woke up in the old days it was to hear the melody of the militia band, serenading their officers and local officials, or the less pretentious fiddle and tambourine orchestra serenading their patrons or the revelers enjoying in their own way the pleasing assurance that "Christmas comes but once a year." Things have changed and we are forced to admit not for the better. The dawn of the great festival is now ushered in by a senseless din of discordant horns and bells by no means silver-toned, and the beating of anything that can make noise. A horrible incongruous celebration of the Nativity of "The Prince of Peace." (*Nassau Tribune*, December 24, 1913)

Of interest here is the degree to which the instrumentation recounted reflects the contemporary shape of Junkanoo music. But it is also important to note the continued rhetoric of disapprobation on religious grounds. The "old days," incidentally, could not have been that good, because, as illustrated previously, accounts of nineteenth-century Junkanoo are equally negative and because restrictive legislation was passed in 1899 precisely because it was viewed as a "horrible incongruous celebration."

Though Junkanoo continued to find expression on Bay Street, it was severely circumscribed by the poverty that had set in during the late 1860s and which continued to grip the Bahamas until the Prohibition era poured fresh money, jobs, and infrastructure—all secured by rumrunning—into the Bahamas. Junkanoo, too, was reinvigorated by this sea change, and the 1920s saw rapid development and increased regulation of the festival. According to E. Clement Bethel, this was the first time "Junkanoo drew spectators to Bay Street. . . . The parades took on the air of public performances; costumes and instruments grew in sophistication; and Junkanoo became more orderly, more spectacular" (Bethel 1991, 49).

Not surprisingly, Junkanoo was subject to increasing politicization during these years, an example of which is related to the construction of the Colonial Hotel. Over half of the labor force on that construction project had been brought in from Cuba, causing tension and real grievances on the part of Bahamian workers,

who were not being compensated fairly or offered the better-paying positions secured by the Cuban workers. A near riot in December 1922 erupted over these serious inequities and ultimately saw Bahamian workers placated, but the concern
regarding civil unrest spilled over to Junkanoo. And so the *Nassau Guardian*
printed an announcement just days before Christmas: "We are informed that it
has been decided by the Governor in Council not to suspend this year the Street
Nuisance Rules as is customary during certain hours of the Christmas season.
This decision will, we are sure, meet with the approval of the community and will
be welcomed by those who have long wished for the abolition of this extraordinary manner of celebrating Christmas" (*Nassau Guardian,* December 21, 1922).

Junkanoo, as such, was rapidly becoming not merely a symbol of Afro-
Bahamian custom but a site around which local politics, social policy, and power
were negotiated. And Junkanoo was indeed a power-laden site—a fact recognized and acted upon by the Junkanoos of the day. The ban of the 1922 Christmas
Junkanoo resulted in a strategic retaliation on the part of Junkanoos, who, remembering the injustice throughout the year, chose to celebrate Junkanoo "over
the hill" in 1923 in spite of the ban having been lifted. The *Nassau Tribune* reported this as follows:

> Xmas passed very quietly. The masqueraders . . . behaved themselves very well. . . .
> Although the government permitted them to come "to the market" the men re-
> mained "Over the hill" for the reason that the government refused to allow them
> in the city last year. . . . The stores in the city did practically no business. The stores
> in Grants Town reaped a golden harvest. Many of the shopkeepers in the city, when
> they learnt of the intention of the "boys" to remain in Grant [*sic*] Town offered the
> leaders money to change their plan but they . . . refused the bribe. The "boys" say
> they intend to develop their own district. (*Nassau Tribune,* December 26, 1923)

As economic prospects tied to Junkanoo proved increasingly good (and were
demonstrated as such by the boycott of 1923), so too did official opinion of the
festival improve. As early as 1925, the Development Board began deliberately situating Junkanoo as a tourist attraction, leading to the announcement of a prize
award: "With the object of popularizing the quaint custom of masquerading on
New Year's morning the Development Board has decided to give £25 in prizes for
competitors judged to be wearing the best costume" (*Nassau Guardian,* December 10, 1925). That the Development Board did not recognize the musical aspects
of the festival as worthy of prize money is significant and I will return to this in
the pages that follow. E. Clement Bethel notes: "By 1928, Junkanoo was being
hailed as a native Bahamian custom, a fine example of primitive African ritual,
and an asset to the tourist trade" (Bethel 1991, 54). In that same year, the Development Board attempted to draw some connections to the pre-Lenten Carnival
celebrations throughout the New World, organizing what it called a Mi Careme

Carnival on March 23, an event for which it drafted regulations for participation and again offered prize money (*Nassau Guardian,* March 24, 1928). The following descriptive and analytical account was penned by Robert Curry, who in the late 1920s conducted fieldwork for a monograph on folklore in the Bahamas (first published in 1928 for the American Folklore Society):

> Bay Street has a carnival aspect on two occasions. From midnight to sunrise of Christmas and New Year Mornings the thoroughfare is crowded densely with colored folk wearing the most peculiar costumes. They are taking part in a ritual, the origins of which are not clear. Some suppose it to have a Spanish connotation, but more likely it is a survival of an African practice, which has no meaning today. During the war it was frowned upon by white inhabitants of Nassau as unsuitable celebration in such a crisis; but it has been revived, although not to the extent known before the war. Those taking part in the ceremonies are known correctly as Johnny Canoes and colloquially as Junkanoos. For weeks beforehand their costumes are being prepared. Some are exceedingly clever, being made of colored papers cut into shreds, so that there is a swishing sound as the men walk. With such costumes the headgear is a structure, often the shape of a ship, and covered also with these shredded papers. Other costumes might represent animals, in which cases horns would often project from the covering for the heads. Everyone is masked. All carry horns and many cowbells. Firecrackers are exploded as long as they last. The mob is orderly on the whole, and there are relatively few instances of drunkenness. As in some of the dances of the colored Bahamians and in some of their superstitions and pagan worships—which in solitary cases persist—so in this thoughtless jostling and hurling up and down Bay Street, back and forth, are vestiges of African rituals. So close to the United States, it must seem strange to visitors to find such carnival. Seen in torchlight or in the first streaks of sunrise, the weaving and gesticulating mass presents a curious spectacle. The noise rises to a din as the main body comes opposite you. Only the approach of the day drives them home. Of all the strange experiences of Bay Street, this is the most picturesque. (Curry [1928] 1930, 60–61)

Curry's account illustrates all of the themes thus far explored in this chapter, including the paternalistic and generally negative impression of the costumes and dancing, the masking traditions suggesting African sacred roots, elite disapprobation of the festival (there being "only relatively few instances of drunkenness"), and the increasingly crowded site of Bay Street itself. Far from "thoughtless," the Junkanoos hurling themselves "up and down Bay Street" were at that moment keenly aware of the economic power that Junkanoo represented, and so too were the merchants and officials who increasingly worked to regulate the festival. Curry's account, however, describes Junkanoo just before it began another decline, this one two decades long and fraught with violence, official bans, its use as protest, and general hostility toward the festival.

The end of Prohibition and the worldwide Depression that descended in the 1930s served to reinforce the negative aspects of the celebration in the minds of officials and elites. The Development Board dutifully continued to attempt to keep Junkanoo active enough to support tourism, and so too did a new committee, founded in 1933 and called the Junkanoo Committee. Both organizations worked to promote cash prizes for Junkanoo, but without the success experienced in the 1920s. Without the prospect of profiting from Junkanoo, it seems, the local elite was less willing to grant this "nuisance" much of a place on Bay Street. Church organizations capitalized on this low ebb in enthusiasm and stepped up their opposition to Junkanoo in general and to the Christmas Junkanoo parade in particular. Black Bahamians, for their part, expressed their dissatisfaction with their economic and social standing in and through Junkanoo, adding fuel to the fire even before the 1930s and increasingly thereafter. Predictably, the Christmas Day parade was again banned in 1929 (Bethel 1991), and in 1935, the Christmas parade was permanently banned. Craton and Saunders describe this period as follows:

> In 1932 and 1933 the authorities were concerned about the number of paraders who neglected to wear costumes and were clearly drunk, and after 1934 the Boxing Day Junkanoo was banned because of the disruption it caused both on Christmas Day and the following working day. The New Year's morning Junkanoo continued, the focus of police attention as well as popular participation but also attracting increased commercial support. By 1938, when Boxing Day became an official holiday and the Boxing Day Junkanoo was allowed to revive, both parades were much better sponsored and controlled, setting the pattern for the modern extravaganza: a magnet for tourists yet at the same time regarded as the most important of all manifestations of traditional Bahamian culture. (Craton and Saunders 1998, 266)

It is interesting to note the twin forces at play during the 1930s, when anti-Junkanoo sentiment was high and prohibitions were in force, but also when the Development Board and the Junkanoo Committee nevertheless attempted to reshape the festival as a site around which tourism could be fostered. The reinstatement of the Christmas Junkanoo parade on Boxing Day (December 26) starting in 1938 was, in any case, not to last beyond 1942.[18] This was the year of the Burma Road Riots, which, not unlike the Colonial Hotel incident in 1922, erupted over unfair labor practices. In this case, Bahamian laborers were engaged to help build two air force bases for the United States. One construction project extended the existing Oakes Field; the other site, called Satellite Field, was located at the western end of the island, and Burma Road connected the two. The inequities were staggering: white American workers were brought in and paid at the rate they would have received in the United States; Bahamians, however, were paid at the local rate to perform the same tasks as the Americans—a rate that was further depressed by the serious recession being experienced at the time. The grievance was repeatedly aired, but it became clear that neither local government officials nor the American-based contractors would act on the workers' behalf. This realization led to violent rioting and looting over a two-day period—both on Bay Street and in the Over-the-Hill neighborhoods—and although the workers were appeased with a small raise, the riot shook Bahamian elites to the core (Craton 1986; Saunders 2003a). All public gatherings were banned beginning in 1942. As if for good measure, Junkanoo was made specifically illegal by a special provision in 1944. The total prohibition of Junkanoo was to remain in effect until 1947, and yet newspaper reports from this period make clear that Junkanoo continued to be celebrated in various Over-the-Hill locations, in spite of the threat of arrest.[19]

In 1947, in part because of the efforts of the Junkanoo Committee (now called the Masquerade Committee), the parade was reinstated, beginning with the 1948 New Year's Day parade. The *Nassau Guardian* published a skeptical opinion in advance of the parade:

> A Committee, recently formed [renamed], has raised by public subscription money enough to provide valuable cash prizes for the best costumes, and this incentive will no doubt provoke competitive efforts to restore some of the glories of carnival times of former years. But this in itself is not enough. It will be remembered that it was the gradual degeneration of our annual John Canoe Parade into a mere pretext for hooliganism that eventually led to their disappearance. It is by their conduct—perhaps more than by their costumes—that the public will judge the masqueraders this New Year. . . . The John Canoes are being weighed in the balance; and it rests entirely with them not to be found wanting. The police will be expected to exercise great vigilance. (*Nassau Guardian,* December 29, 1947)

Skepticism aside, the parade was a great success, and Junkanoo entered the second half of the twentieth century with a burst of creative energy. The 1950s witnessed Junkanoo being progressively transformed and institutionalized, not least because of the increasing regulation and greater involvement of the Masquerade Committee, but also because the festival was now understood as a broadly Bahamian activity.[20] The 1950s also witnessed the progressive reshaping of Junkanoo as an art form. As E. Clement Bethel notes, Junkanoo was changing "from a festival in which all were free to take part into a folklore show put on by performers for an audience" (Bethel 1991, 80). This progressive institutionalization was driven as much by the new Junkanoo group leaders as it was by the Masquerade Committee. The prize money created incentive that outweighed whatever regulations accompanied the rewards.

In 1964, when internal self-government was achieved, the Development Board was converted into the Ministry of Tourism (via the Promotion of Tourism Act of 1963), and the Masquerade Committee came under its purview. Upon the achievement of independence, Junkanoo was granted the status of a "national artistic treasure," thereby situating it at the very heart of the Bahamian national project, a site that it had by that time, in any case, already come to occupy for most Bahamians. As if to reinforce this idea, Lynden O. Pindling, the nation's first prime minister, chose to rush with the crowd at the Independence Day Junkanoo Parade, situating himself and the government he represented on Bay Street and symbolically aligning himself through Junkanoo with the nation.

In 1983, the Masquerade Committee was renamed the National Junkanoo Committee and was transferred from the Ministry of Tourism to the Ministry of Youth, Sports, and Community Affairs. One of the principal aims of this shift was to ensure that Junkanoo was fostered as national culture, and Junkanoo has been imported to or reinvigorated on every major Family Island since that time. This export of Junkanoo to the periphery is most interesting in light of the centripetal path taken by rake-n-scrape during the middle of the twentieth century. (I will return to this discussion in chapter 6.) The successful institutionalization of Junkanoo, then, effectively begun in the 1950s and brought to completion by 1973, situated the festival so thoroughly in Bahamian life that it could eventually (by 1983) be moved into this more fitting institutional home, and from this new base in community affairs, the center completed the nationalizing trajectory by fertilizing the periphery, or at least attempting to do so (see Bilby 2010).

Moreover, since the 1950s this nationalizing trajectory has been extending itself well beyond the borders of the Bahamas, for just as the Trinidad Carnival has become a fixture in cities across the world, so too has Junkanoo increasingly become a powerful symbol of Bahamian identity abroad. Miami, for example, has played host to a formal Junkanoo group since 1957, when the Sunshine Junkanoo Band was formed in Overton. Since that time, other groups have formed, including the Bahamas Junkanoo Revue, which came into being in 1993. There is a great deal of back-and-forth travel between the Junkanoos in these groups and the members of Nassauvian groups, leading to an interesting exchange that finds Miami-based groups attending Boxing Day and New Year's Day parades in Nassau and a reciprocal gesture by Nassauvian bands, who attend the annual Goombay Festival in Coconut Grove and the Martin Luther King Jr. birthday celebration in West Perrine, as well as the Rose Bowl parade (Wood 2007). It remains to be seen whether the Miami-based groups will influence Junkanoos in Nassau. What is traceable, however, is an effort on the part of the Miami-based groups to stay abreast of changes in costume design and performance aesthetics in Nassau, which they then incorporate into their own performances (Wood 2007).

Key West, historically linked by migratory patterns to Nassau, has also fostered a Junkanoo tradition that in the middle of the twentieth century was active enough to attract both the interest and resources of Folkways Records (Folkways

FL 4492).[21] Cities such as New Orleans and Toronto also regularly include Junkanoo rushes in their festival programs, and although the international profile of Junkanoo is relatively small in comparison to Carnival, it is interesting to note that Junkanoo is finding its way into the cities where Bahamians are now living abroad, even if it takes the form of scrap groups participating in festivals that are not primarily about Junkanoo.[22] Discussing the growth of what he calls "overseas Caribbean carnivals," Keith Nurse has noted: "Like its parent, the overseas carnival is hybrid in form and influence. The Jonkonnu masks of Jamaica and the Bahamas, not reflected in the Trinidad carnival, are clearly evident in many of these carnivals, thereby making them pan-Caribbean in scope" (Nurse 1999, 674). That said, on those occasions when Junkanoo does take center stage in a festival, the event is scheduled during the late spring and summer, thereby avoiding any potential conflict with preparation for the main event, which remains located on Bay Street in Nassau. In this respect, the Junkanoo festival in Miami reflects the same reasoning that governs the scheduling of other carnivals outside of the Caribbean. At the end of the day, however, it is still Nassau that drives the direction of Junkanoo, and it is still to Nassau that Junkanoos living in diaspora wish to return for Boxing Day and New Year's Day.

Interestingly, however, in spite of the successful linking of the festival with Bahamian national identity achieved during the second half of the twentieth century, the dream of seeing Junkanoo draw huge numbers of tourists has never quite been realized to the degree that the original architects of the strategy had hoped. Ian Strachan reflects:

> Since the 1930s the Bahamian government has had a hand in the coordination of the annual Junkanoo parades in the hope that the parades would be come a tourist attraction. Junkanoo, the Bahamas' Christmastime carnival has remained a staple of postcards and posters: instant "exoticism." The Masquerade Committee, created by the Bahamas Development Board (and now called the Junkanoo Committee), introduced prize money to the folk event and consistently attempts to impose greater "order" and "organization" to an activity that existed for centuries as a resistant cultural form. The majority of Junkanoo performers and spectators continue to resist the appropriation of the parade by the state and the forces of tourism. Today the parade remains an event principally for Bahamians and few tourists frequent it. This fact gives weight to the conclusion that the majority of tourists are more willing to sample local culture in its stereotyped form in the hotel or the lounge rather than in local communities. (Strachan 2002, 129)

This may be another reason why in 1983 the festival's administration was placed under the purview of the Ministry of Youth, Sports, and Community Affairs. Whether or not the majority of Bahamians "continue to resist the appropriation of the parade by the state and the forces of tourism" remains a question that is, I suggest, open to debate, as is Strachan's claim that "few tourists frequent" the festival. The debate over appropriation by the state and the forces of tourism is perhaps best illustrated in the role that scrap groups have historically played in Junkanoo, and it is to this topic that I now turn.

Junkanoo Sights

This section considers the costumes as well as the different kinds of groups (organized and scrap) that have appeared in and peopled Junkanoo during the twentieth century and up to the present, and I begin by returning to the 1930s. During the 1930s in particular, newspaper accounts consistently bemoaned the fact that Junkanoos arrived on Bay Street without the many elaborate costumes that once characterized the festival. The *Nassau Tribune,* for example, lamented: "Masquerading is dying by degrees. This Christmas not one costume with any point to it was to be seen 'in the market.' It is a great pity that this celebration cannot be restored to its former colourful brilliance.... Ten years ago in Nassau masquerading was a distinct art. Today it lacks both point and colour and has nothing to justify its existence" (*Nassau Tribune,* December 27, 1930). It is instructive to consider accounts of Junkanoo costumes in the early twentieth century in order to understand the loss being expressed in the 1930s. In 1916, for instance, Amelia Defries witnessed the Christmas masquerade and described it as follows:

> The general impression I got as daylight broke was a mass of people who had been looting one of the Natural History Museums in New York and had then gone crazy! The masks were cheap and machine made and were in imitation of white people. When dawn broke . . . the Commandant appeared, immaculate in white, and he seemed oblivious to the fact that in the dancing throng there were more than one parody of his uniform! There was even a "kiltie," and there was a parody of a British M.A. The latter never danced at all, but walked sedately, carrying a book and umbrella—always alone. Quite a number—even of the dancers—were alone and I did not once see a male and female dance, as we do, in couples. Some of the dresses would not have disgraced a masked ball; the shapes of the hats worn were very interesting and the effect of them was fine. A few of the tallest hats were surmounted by little Union Jacks. Many of the dresses were variations on Pantaloon, and not the least remarkable thing about them being the choice of colors displayed. The combinations were not only striking and original but often quite beautiful as well. (Defries 1917)

But even though these costumes were, by comparison to the 1930s, elaborate, the masqueraders tended to cobble them together from materials that were inexpensive or readily available. E. Clement Bethel explains: "Newspaper, sponge, banana leaves, tissue paper or 'crocus sack'—the coarse brown sacking in which imported foods were contained—all played their part. The body was always completely covered, the face disguised, and a fantastic hat was worn on the head.... Hats were usually conical with broad brims, like those of picture-book witches, or they took the shape of large wasps' nests; and faces were blackened with charcoal, whitened with flour, or else concealed behind a mask" (Bethel 1991, 42). Parody; whitening or masking the face; tall, conical, wide-brimmed hats; and colorful dresses and costumes were the order of the day in Junkanoo during the early twentieth century. Another description, this one from 1924, further illustrates these trends:

> Christmas Day, 1924. Sleep was obviously impossible to-night during this island festival.... The orgies lasted till eight-thirty, at which hour all the participants melted into thin air in the most orderly manner. The process was the same—just marching up and down with the tom-toms, but some of the costumes were most imaginative. They all had white masks or had whitened their faces. One was dressed like the Englishman in the Boutique, another had on a Shakespearean costume of red velvet with a trench hat; there were three Highlanders, and a quantity decked out as women in the latest Paris fashions. One man especially pleased me: his face was grotesquely whitened, on his head was a little clown's cap, for the rest he was dressed entirely in flour bags. Over his shoulder he carried a vast bundle of sugar-cane, and his middle was wreathed round with twenty or thirty green bananas. On the end of a knotted string he led a whippet. (Parsons 1926, 102)

All of the elements described by Amelia Defries almost a decade earlier remain in place here. But by the 1930s, the situation had changed. The Depression hit the majority of Bahamians very hard, but as Bethel observes, the costumes themselves did not tend to be expensive per se. The waning enthusiasm for and participation in Junkanoo cannot, then, be explained only in economic terms. Some Bahamians attempted to find other reasons for the decline in Junkanoo, and the following paternalistic editorial printed in the *Nassau Tribune* offers one rationale: "The falling off in John Canoeing represents a change in outlook by the bulk of the population, indicating that ... the people are developing a greater sense of pride and self-respect. They very properly feel that they should not make a poppy-show of themselves for the entertainment of the public" (*Tribune*, December 26, 1934). The view expressed by the *Tribune* suggests that grassroots Bahamians were in the process of outgrowing their former pastime. The colonialist value judgments expressed here are typical of middle- and upper-class attitudes toward the festival—tolerance of the "nuisance" when it made them money and complaints about it when no profit was likely—and they illustrate the continued struggle, even in the mid-1930s, attendant to transforming Junkanoo into a national symbol. But this paternalist approach to Junkanoo—expressed so baldly in the *Tribune* editorial—may have caused Bahamian elites to misapprehend the underlying reasons for the decline in Junkanoo. E. Clement Bethel usefully explores this possibility:

> It is possible that when the masqueraders appeared without costumes something more than their poverty was being expressed. Perhaps the labourers, fully aware of

the ruling classes' interest in Junkanoo purely as a tourist spectacle, had decided, consciously or not, to deny them that spectacle. The idea is not so terribly far-fetched when we remember the masqueraders' decision in 1923 not to give the Bay Street merchants their business on Christmas morning; black Bahamians were fully aware of the power of Junkanoo. It is possible, therefore, to read in the rough-ness of the parades the labourers' protest against their conditions—in the only way legally available to them. (Bethel 1991, 71)

Bethel is articulating a dynamic that has been called "social poetics" else-where (Herzfeld 1997). I will return to this idea later, but it is worth noting here that the decision of Junkanoos to appear on Bay Street without elaborate cos-tumes during the 1930s, just like their decision to boycott Bay Street the year after the government banned the Christmas Junkanoo in 1922, is an instance that clearly illustrates a keen understanding of the power that Junkanoo holds. These instances can also be read as the precursors to the appearance of scrap groups on Bay Street in the years after 1948. The scrap groups stand in stark contrast to the increasingly organized Junkanoo groups that began to dominate the festival in the 1950s. It is to an exploration of these Junkanoo sights that I now turn.

In the wake of Junkanoo's reinstatement on New Year's Day 1948, Junkanoo was rapidly pushed in new directions. Many of the shifts in Junkanoo occurred because of the increasing regulation and competition that was imposed on the festival by the Masquerade Committee.[23] The prestige of winning the prizes of-fered by the Masquerade Committee, now including prizes for the best costume and for the best group, became a major organizing principle, and by the mid-1950s, the effects of this competitive draw were being realized in the innovations of Junkanoo groups. Junkanoo was gradually moving away from neighborhood groups of more-or-less loosely organized friends and relatives and toward uni-form groups with themes and coordination of music and costume. The first ex-ample of this, not coincidentally, was to come from several of the nightclub en-tertainers active at that time—including David Kemp, Maureen Duvalier, and Bruce Beneby—who organized a group with matching costumes in 1954 and called themselves the Mexicans.

In 1958, Maureen Duvalier pioneered in another arena. She had already par-ticipated in Junkanoo as an individual performer as early as 1951, breaking the norms of Bahamian society in the process, but it was in 1958 that she became the first woman to organize and then bring a group of women Junkanoos to Bay Street—a group of twenty-five, dressed in costumes of red and black. "I was the first woman. . . . There was no other; I don't mind who comes behind and say they are the queen of Junkanoo. I am the first female to take women to Bay Street" (*Nassau Guardian Lifestyle,* January 12, 2004). Her status as a nightclub entertainer undoubtedly softened the disapprobation of Bahamians, but her ef-forts remain a signal moment in the history of Junkanoo.

By the mid-1950s, groups were beginning to arrange for sponsorships through local businesses, and Junkanoo groups would in turn carry those names to the festival. This practice—not unlike corporate sponsorship of steelband groups in Trinidad (see Stuempfle 1996)—led to Junkanoo winners with names like Fine's Department Store, the East Bay Service Center, and Charley's Men's Shop during the 1950s and '60s. But even these more organized groups were still relatively relaxed compared to the highly disciplined groups that would begin appearing on Bay Street during the late 1960s and '70s. The increasing visibility of Junkanoo as a legitimate (and legitimized) activity, combined with the increasingly complex costumes and "pasting" techniques (using glue to decorate items of clothing with papier-mâché, beads, feathers, etc.), resulted in a gradual shift in public opinion regarding the festival's place in Bahamian life. This is especially evident in the steady growth of interest in Junkanoo among members of the middle class. Keith Wisdom observes: "It was during the 1950s that Junkanoo began to gain acceptance and respectability, via the art of costume design, with middle class Blacks who not only began to participate in 'over the hill' organized Junkanoo groups, but also learned and developed the crafts of Junkanoo and began to organize their own neighborhood groups" (Wisdom 1985, 49).

For instance, one of the most influential and groundbreaking of all Junkanoo groups, the Valley Boys, was formed in 1958 by a group of middle-class high school students led by Winston "Gus" Cooper.[24] The group went on to win first place in the 1960 Boxing Day Parade, entering the parade with an overall theme called "Scottish Highlanders," marching as a coordinated unit with leaders in front and straight lines behind, and generally revolutionizing Junkanoo just as the Mexicans had in 1954.[25] Other organized groups followed suit, and the Valley Boys soon found themselves in stiff competition with the Vikings and the Saxons.

Organized Junkanoo was promoted by the Development Board and legitimized by the Masquerade Committee, and its participants were rewarded with prizes, but the increasing organization and thematic coordination within Junkanoo also served to highlight the reluctance of some Junkanoos to be constrained by an assigned role within an organized group. These dissident Junkanoos, generally derided as scrappers, or "scrap," continued to appear on Bay Street, in spite of the rules and regulations denying them a chance to win any prizes. Vivian Nina Michelle Wood describes scrap groups as follows: "The term 'scrap' is value-laden. It stems from practices in the 1950s when some groups would participate in the parades without costumes, or with costumes that they had hurriedly created. The term also implies that these groups are inferior to the organized groups. Throughout the decades, the scrap groups have developed a reputation for being disruptive because members often drift from group to group during the parade, and aesthetically displeasing because of their hurriedly made, simple costumes" (Wood 1995, 90).

Wood goes on to claim that there is a distinct connection between scrap groups and the "attitudes and philosophies of Junkanooers who rushed as a form of protest, cleansing or celebration, prior to the formal organization of Junkanoo" (Wood 1995, 91). And it is this aesthetic and philosophical linkage between the boycott of the 1923 Christmas Junkanoo, the poor or nonexistent costuming exhibited on Bay Street during the 1930s, and the scrappers that have peopled modern Junkanoo since 1948 that suggests scrap groups as a fruitful site for exploring social poetics in the Bahamas.

The possibility of thinking about scrap groups through the lens of social poetics becomes yet more intriguing when considering Junkanoo sights of the late 1960s and '70s. Among those sights were politicians like Lynden O. Pindling, rushing after majority rule was achieved and again in the Independence Day celebrations. In an interview with Rosita Sands, Maureen Duvalier and Ronald Simms remember the impact of this sighting as nothing short of a paradigm shift for Bahamians:

> Particularly now with the increased sense of awareness—like Maureen mentioned the Prime Minister: he turned the thing around. When he started "rushing" back in 1968 or 1970, when he became Prime Minister, people realized—hey, that's the Prime Minister rushin'. Well if he could do it, God knows who might. And then the other politicians started to get involved. And so there it was that this status kind of a separation thing that we had had, became eliminated. The Prime Minister was out there rushin', to your doctor was out there rushin', your lawyer was out there rushin,' and all these high-falooting people became involved. And so the barriers started to crumble, and the stigma started to disintegrate. (Rosita Sands 1989, 100)

But sighted also, starting in 1966, were metal barricades that barred access to the parade route to all except fully costumed participants, a development that made it more difficult for scrap groups to enter Bay Street during the festival and a rule change that constrained them to adopt at least a minimal level of costuming (*Nassau Guardian,* December 28, 1966, p. 7). The arrival of barricades also had the effect of fixing spectators in their roles, making it impossible for them to spontaneously join groups on Bay Street—a practice that had been a customary part of Junkanoo. Politicians, then, were flowing out into the Junkanoo parades while the festival itself was becoming ever more regulated and more heavily policed. Symbolic unity was being paralleled by a concomitant denial of free access, an issue that scrap groups continued to address. Wood observes: "The attitude of scrap groups is one of nonchalance and rebellion. While they must abide by the rules that the National Junkanoo Committee has established, they flout authority at every given turn. Furthermore, scrap groups embody the desire on the part of some Bahamians to reclaim Junkanoo from the highly competitive, carnival-like event that it has become" (Wood 1995, 92).

The involvement of the state in promoting a sense of shared space and community—a union between state and nation—is indicative of cultural intimacy. Michael Herzfeld suggests that cultural intimacy can be developed through sources of national embarrassment: "National embarrassment can become the ironic basis of intimacy and affection, a fellowship of the flawed, within the private spaces of the national culture" (Herzfeld 1997, 28). The history of Junkanoo is clearly marked with less-than-desirable episodes of social and racial stigma. The deliberate involvement of the state in the festival and the subsequent broadening of social involvement in it, then, both seem to point to a process through which the majority government and the newly independent state shaped and continued to fashion cultural intimacy. Craton and Saunders agree: "The most important change in Bahamian Junkanoo after the mid-century, however, was its adoption by the government once majority rule was achieved and acceptance by the people as the quintessential expression of the new nationalistic ethos. Though transcending mere party politics, it was an occasion when political leaders, following the example of the PLP's [Progressive Liberal Party's] helmsman, Lynden Pindling, made a point of 'rushing' with the people whenever this was permitted" (Craton and Saunders 1998, 489).

But making Junkanoo the "quintessential expression of the new nationalistic ethos" required a particular kind of narrative and a controlled one at that. The particular remapping of history that has allowed Junkanoo to serve as an essentialized representative of Bahamian culture, when peeled back just a fraction, reveals the very real social fissures over which the nationalist narrative has been laminated. Two examples will illustrate this point for the moment. First, the present rhetoric hailing Junkanoo as the great equalizer of all Bahamians is belied by several obvious social distinctions in the practice. Vivian Nina Michelle Wood observes: "Women perform in a capacity that is totally different from that of the men; the middle class dominates the front line [dancers], while the back line [music] remains the domain of the grass-roots; and whites are more likely to be involved in the costume arts than in music" (Wood 1995, 500). The deliberate rhetoric touting unity—a strategy drawing on what Homi Bhabha calls the "double-time" of the nation, and by which leaders assert an as yet unrealized vision of the nation in order to create it (Bhabha 1990)—when articulated in conjunction with the selected forgetting of various all-too-real themes within the history of Junkanoo in the Bahamas, seems to confirm Jonathan Boyarin's conclusion: "What we are faced with—what we are living—is the constitution of both group 'membership' and individual 'identity' out of a dynamically chosen selection of memories, and the constant reshaping, reinvention, and reinforcement of those memories as members contest and create the boundaries and links among themselves" (Boyarin 1994, 26).

And second, this contested ground is exemplified by the spontaneous participation of scrap groups in each Junkanoo festival. These scrap groups (like Sting) do not compete in the festivities, nor do they prepare for the event with the goal of winning. Rather, they deliberately ignore the organized aspects of Junkanoo, participating for the sole purpose of enjoying the spirit of the event. These performers are, in effect, calling attention to the way Junkanoo was celebrated less than sixty years ago (before its institutionalization). They are reminding Bahamians of the "double-time" in which Junkanoo has been implicated. This activity is an example of social poetics in the Bahamas, in that the tension between official and lived understandings of Junkanoo is acted out on a national stage. Herzfeld argues that "it is the specific task of social poetics to reinsert analysis into lived historical experience and thereby to restore knowledge of the social, cultural, and political grounding—the cultural intimacy—of even the most formal power and the most abstract knowledge" (Herzfeld 1997, 26). And scrap groups, by their very visibility—their sightedness—call attention to the disjunctures between the "double-time" of the national narrative and the lived experience of Bahamian Junkanoos.

Junkanoo Sounds

The instruments and music played during Junkanoo have moved through a series of shifts that reflect not only the gradual creolization of Junkanoo, but also the impetus toward organization and competition that has characterized the festival since the middle of the twentieth century. One of the defining features of Junkanoo during the mid- to late nineteenth century was the presence of the militia band, a quintessentially European and colonial sound that was part of, if not necessarily central to, the experience of the festival. Fifes and tambourines are also mentioned in early accounts of Junkanoo celebrations, but the basic instruments that came to be understood as embodying the core of the Junkanoo sound were the drums, bells, whistles, and horns (bugles, foghorns, and bicycle horns). In fact, these instruments became synonymous with the festival, and the practice of opening Christmas with the militia band and parading with fifes and tambourines faded as the drums, bells, whistles, and horns moved to the center of the Junkanoo sound in the early twentieth century (see the previously quoted lament from the *Nassau Tribune,* December 24, 1913).

By the end of the nineteenth century, the drums and whistles were already part of the festival's sound (see, for instance, the previously quoted account in the *Nassau Guardian,* December 29, 1886). By the early twentieth century, cowbells and horns (bugles or foghorns) were also being included in the instrumental line-up of Junkanoo (see, for example, the previously quoted *Nassau Tribune* article from December 24, 1913). These instruments laid a foundation of sound over which it was common to sing and chant songs, songs which could range from well-known tunes to spontaneously composed numbers offering commentary on or criticism of a given person, policy, or event.[26] In this sense, Junkanoo made social commentary possible and, importantly, anonymous. Keith Wisdom describes Junkanoo in the early decades of the twentieth century:

> Characteristic also of Junkanoo during this period was the improvised singing of songs which provided a social commentary on the year's events and the people who were responsible for them. Some of the Junkanoo songs from this period are "Mama, Bake the Johnny Cake" (sung at Christmas Junkanoo), "Spare Me Another Year O Lord" (sung at New Year's Junkanoo), "A-Rushin' Through De Crowd" (sung on both occasions). . . . Pranks and tricks were also part of the Junkanoo at this time. Throughout the city of Nassau, gates, fences, carts, and bridges covering drains would be removed, and some streets would be obstructed. These pranks, as well as being fun, suggest a quality of protest. (Wisdom 1985, 36)

That singing was even possible is indicative of the much smaller groups that were prone to rush on Bay Street before the 1950s. While the groups of the 1990s and later have regularly brought five hundred or more Junkanoos to Bay Street (and have sometimes amassed as many as a thousand people for the parade), the early twentieth-century parades were conducted on a more modest scale. As Wood notes, "In the first half of this [twentieth] century, a total of less than one hundred Junkanooers participated in any given parade. . . . In 1950 the number of Junkanoo participants increased and many people formed small groups with which they rushed" (Wood 1995, 63). By this time, singing had largely disappeared. Junkanoo in the 1950s and '60s, then, was dominated by the rhythms of the drums, cowbells, whistles, and the sounds of the assorted horns that added pitched percussive accents to the proceedings.

In the 1970s, melodies returned to Junkanoo, but not carried on voices. In 1976 a new organized group rushed out onto Bay Street on Boxing Day and won the parade (the group also won the Boxing Day parades in 1977 and 1978). The group featured "not only a fresh approach to costume-making and theme, but also a brass section among its musicians, which played traditional Junkanoo tunes as the band 'rushed.' The 'Music Makers,' as the group was called . . . provided the impetus for a new leg of development in Junkanoo" (Bethel 1991, 86). The use of brass instruments was quickly assimilated by the other organized groups, and in the mid-1980s, when the sousaphone was added to the brass section (by the Valley Boys), groups were able to rush with trumpets, trombones, and sousaphones.

During the 1970s, the tunes played by the brass instruments tended to be traditional Junkanoo songs like "Mama Bake the Johnny Cake" and "A-rushin through the Crowd," a tune particularly suited to the limitations of the bugles of days past—which could play only the notes contained in their key's harmonic series—and songs that connected the singing of the early twentieth century to these new melody instruments, tethering memory to new practice (see Example 14).

EXAMPLE 14. "A-rushin' through the Crowd" (traditional melody).

By the 1980s, however, regional and North American songs became a regular feature of the Junkanoo parades, and tunes were chosen to coincide with or add weight to a given group's organizing theme. Soca tunes, show tunes, songs from movie soundtracks, spirituals, and hymns all found their way into the parade during the 1980s and '90s. The 1980s also witnessed the pioneers of brass section playing, like Christian Justilien (of the group Roots), begin to arrange charts for the brass instruments—a musical choice that created yet more organization and a significant move away from the informal "playing by ear" initially used by the Melody Makers and others. These innovations allowed for much more sophisticated segues between songs, greater cohesiveness within the groups, and a more professional presentation of a given group's brass section.

In 1982, faced with the much more musically active character that the brass sections of Junkanoo groups were adding to the sound of the parade, the National Junkanoo Committee instituted an additional prize for "Best Music." Yonell Justilien recalls: "This new trend to organize brass section playing faced great resistance at first but has gained popularity through the years. By the mid 1980s [1982], the category of 'best music' that was added to the Junkanoo competition was greatly influenced by the presence of the brass section" (Yonell Justilien 2004, 27). One of the hallmarks of Junkanoo parades during the 1990s and early in the first decade of the twenty-first century has been the increasingly rapid tempo maintained on Bay Street. In contrast to the slower tempos of the 1950s and '60s, which generally worked out to a moderate march tempo of approximately 110 to 120 beats per minute, the parade has witnessed a shift in performance aesthetics that prizes a much faster tempo unfolding at a furious 160 beats per minute or so.

One of the consequences of this shift has been a gradual change in the foundational bass drum rhythm, caused not necessarily by a shift in approach but because of the physical strain that the rapid pace places on the drummers' technique. The bellers are also playing much more rapidly, creating more tension in their performance and reducing—over the course of a given night's parade—their accuracy and stamina. Yonell Justilien observes: "Some Junkanoo groups are now solving this timing problem by slowing down their tempos while others still think it is more impressive to keep the tempo at a fast pace" (Yonell Justilien 2004, 30). Before illustrating these changes, however, I turn to a brief exploration of several core rhythms that have defined Junkanoo at different junctures throughout the twentieth century and into the beginning of the twenty-first century.[27]

Junkanoo rhythms can be separated into slow and fast beat configurations, by which Bahamians refer to the relative note density in the rhythmic patterns and not to the tempos per se. The slow beat rhythms that were used in Junkanoo during the early twentieth century are no longer used in the parades. One slow beat in particular, however, maintains a link to memories of earlier Junkanoos, in spite of it rarely being heard anymore. It is kept alive in the Bahamian imagination more through nostalgia than sound.[28] It is called the Over-the-Hill beat, and it unfolds in the moderate march tempo of the midcentury Junkanoo parades (see Example 15).

This beat, incidentally, provides the foundation for John Chipman's 1961 recording of "Junkanoo," discussed in chapter 3. I should clarify at the outset that this schematic representation of the Over-the-Hill beat does not account for each of the lines being played by multiple musicians who are all feeling their way through the performance in an atmosphere in which improvisation is an essential component of the musical experience. As such, the whistles, lead drummers, and bellers deviate from the rhythms transcribed here in order to pursue spontaneous musical ideas, but do so while maintaining an overarching sense of the basic feel of the beat. Wood notes that during Junkanoo parades, "back line musicians communicate through gestures and facial expressions, and tune in to each other by listening to the rhythms of the various instruments and fitting their own patterns into the overall scheme" (Wood 1995, 356). Individual musicians' attention to their fellow performers, then, ensures that the feel is maintained within this flexible, improvisatory framework.

Slow beats like the Over-the-Hill beat have been replaced by fast beats, of which there is a wide range in use today. One beat, however, is particularly prevalent among Junkanoo groups, and I transcribe it in Example 16.

Although tempo is a crucial component to the fast beat, and in spite of the dramatic increase in tempos since the 1970s, the real difference between slow and fast beats has to do with the density of notes played or struck in the basic rhythmic cell. As such, fast beats involve more active playing per two-measure cell than do the older slow beats. This has led to much less space for improvisation within the texture of fast beats, and some Junkanoo purists bemoan the loss of that freedom within Junkanoo music. Tinkle Hanna recalls this transition: "In the old days there was a lot of room to move in and out of the rhythms. If you were a beller, you could add extra notes in between the beat of the drummers. These days, the bellers and lead drummers are playing every note they can already, and there is no room to add that spice. That's why I think of the old, slower tempos as sweeter than what is being played today" (Tinkle Hanna, interview with the author, June 25, 2007).

By filling in every subdivision to the sixteenth-note value with constant playing by the bellers and lead drummers, contemporary Junkanoo groups are sacrificing the "sweetness" that Tinkle refers to in favor of the intensity that the back line generates through the fast beat. And yet, since the late 1990s and early in the twenty-first century, an interesting shift has been increasingly audible in Junk-

EXAMPLE 15. The Over-the-Hill beat (Yonell Justilien 2004).

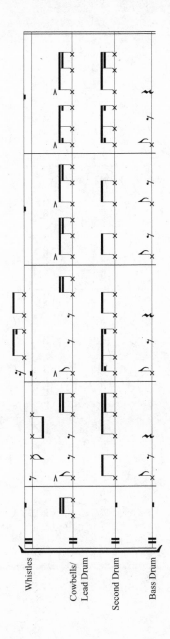

EXAMPLE 16. Contemporary fast beat (Yonell Justilien 2004).

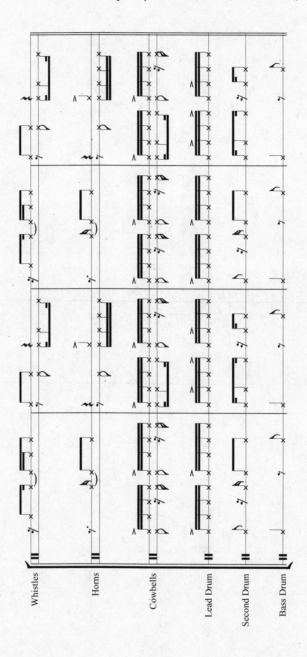

anoo performances. Because of the increasingly rapid tempos, the bass drummers in most groups are being forced to play more rapidly than they can effectively play while maintaining the volume level necessary for the group's cohesiveness. They are asked to play as loudly as before, but the time frame within which they are raising and lowering their arms has become increasingly compressed, making it difficult to sustain the rhythm over long periods of time. As a result, the very even eighth-note rhythm played across each bar line is being strained and stretched to the point that it is no longer possible to hear it as an eighth-note pattern. Some have described this phenomenon as "dragging" the beat (Yonell Justilien 2004; Christian Justilien 2003), but the need for slightly more time between strokes has also tended to manifest itself as an anticipatory syncopation, a choice which allows the performers to continue heavily accenting the downbeat of each measure (see Example 17).

Neither of these results is desirable, because they disrupt the established rhythmic relationships between the bass drum part and the rest of the back line instruments.[29] Junkanoo purists, including Fred Ferguson, moreover, argue that the anticipated syncopation heard in some of today's Junkanoo groups moves the entire performance beyond the space of Junkanoo rhythms. Simply put, "That's not Junkanoo anymore!" (Fred Ferguson, interview with the author, June 5, 2006). The aesthetic shifts that have witnessed faster tempi, a move toward more rhythmic density in the individual instrumental parts, and a concomitant closing up of the rhythmic space traditionally available to musicians in slow-beat Junkanoo have, I suggest, reached a limit test, one that is determined primarily by the physical demands that these shifts have placed on the bass drummers. It remains to be seen whether the foundational bass drum rhythm will shift in order to accommodate these aesthetic ideas or whether the rhythm itself will retain its place at the heart of what Bahamians like Fred Ferguson consider fast-beat Junkanoo.

The contemporary dilemma has not, however, dimmed the desire among popular musicians to imaginatively incorporate the rhythms and sonic markers of Junkanoo into their recordings and performances. Since the middle of the twentieth century, and with greater frequency after independence, the rhythms briefly traced in this section, whether slow beat or fast, and the particular instruments involved, have served as tools through which popular musicians have narrated their place within the nation, offered contributions to the nation-building project, and critiqued the order of things, and it is to an exploration of these musicians and their contributions that I turn in chapter 5. Before doing so, however, and in concluding this chapter, I return to several of the themes raised thus far, including the sacred roots of Junkanoo, the role of Christianity in masking those roots as secular, and the place of Junkanoo since the late 1960s as the quintessential expression of the nation.

EXAMPLE 17. Contemporary challenges experienced by bass drummers.

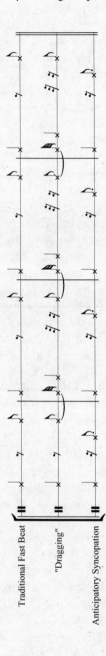

"RUNNIN' HOT":
JUNKANOO AND THE SOUL OF THE NATION

Like all such syncretic phenomena, the Bahamian Junkanoo owes its survival and vitality to its popular relevance, a combination of authentic roots and dynamic adaptability. That it became and remains the essential expression of Bahamian identity owes as much to its shaping in Bahamian social history—from slavery and its aftermath of poverty, race, and class distinctions, to great if uneven prosperity, majority rule, political independence, and national integration—as to its deep roots in Africa and Europe alike and its irresistibly somatic music of goombay drums, conch shell, cowbell, whistle, and bugle.

—MICHAEL CRATON AND GAIL SAUNDERS, *ISLANDERS IN THE STREAM,*
VOL. 2, 487–88

Thus far this examination has lent a great deal of corroborative evidence to the claim for Junkanoo's secular place within the Bahamas. In the decades since independence was won, Junkanoo has become the most institutionalized, marketed, and visible symbol of the Bahamas, lending its name, vibrant colors, sounds, and atmosphere to everything from restaurants (Café Johnny Canoe) to summer festivals (Junkanoo in June) and advertising campaigns (Coral Wave Cable).[30] Indeed, the following passage by Ken Bilby describes quite accurately the contemporary shape of the parade:

Of all the present-day outposts of Jankunu, the Bahamas is surely the society where the tradition (officially spelled "Junkanoo") is most visible, most vigorous, and most ubiquitous; in short, this is where, in some respects, the tradition seems most *alive*. At the same time, it is here that the tradition appears to have strayed farthest from its historical roots, departing in startling ways from older forms while developing rapidly in new directions. In the Bahamas today, Junkanoo is an enormous national festival rivaling in energy and scale the famous pre-Lenten carnival of Trinidad and the numerous Eastern Caribbean festivals patterned after it, as well as a primary symbol of Bahamian identity. Associated with a complex structure of official and commercial patronage, codified and governed by a strict set of regulations, featuring ever more elaborate costumes and thematic displays designed and constructed by competing Junkanoo bands with hundreds of members, this Bahamian festival mobilizes thousands of people and receives a great deal of media coverage. It has also become one of the main tourist attractions of the Bahamas, and is by far the most commercialized of the surviving variants of Jankunu. (Bilby 2010)

It is not difficult to agree with Bilby that the contemporary shape of Junkanoo no longer explicitly foregrounds the sacred roots that so clearly contributed to its early practice in the New World. And yet the rhetoric used to describe the experience of

Junkanoo remains tied in quite significant ways to the sacred or, at the very least, to the discourse of spirituality. So, for instance, Arlene Nash-Ferguson asks: "So what is this strange thing that we call Junkanoo? Why, year after year, do we Bahamians engage in this ritual about which most of the world knows nothing? To Bahamians, it is a most natural part of life, as vital, energizing, and soul quenching as water. Even most of us 'junkanoos' find it hard to explain. It is a door that swings open to that secret place deep within Bahamians, where we keep the real 'us'" (Nash-Ferguson 2000, 2). And Vivian Nina Michelle Wood describes the trance-like state that Junkanoos attain during this "soul quenching ritual" at length in her dissertation—a state that is called "runnin' hot" by performers:

> When the Junkanooer runs hot she/he enters a very brief, trance-like state in which she/he experiences a feeling of ecstasy and intensity . . . the Junkanooer's performance is heightened and becomes more intense, and the Junkanooer has a sense of being outside the realm of the event. . . . During performance the musician is aware of the spectators, the other musicians, and the photographers. However, as the musician gets more and more into the groove this awareness diminishes. The musician knows that there are others around her/him but they become marginal to the musician's experience. When the musician runs hot, she/he drifts out of awareness. Once the run-hot stage has passed, the musician once again becomes aware of the others. (Wood 1995, 410–12)

Keith Wisdom—who calls this experience the ecstatic moment—notes that Junkanoos' "ecstatic moments seem very much like the experience that a number of anthropologists, for example Victor Turner and Jonathan Hill, characterize as 'flow.' Flow in this sense involves 'pleasure' in subordination to ritual forms, a spontaneous and individual joy in expressing oneself through a loss of self in disciplined actions" (Wisdom 2004, 79).

While I am not convinced that runnin' hot—induced as it is through musical performance—constitutes contemporary evidence of a deep spiritual undercurrent in Junkanoo in and of itself, the possibility for sacred meaning suggested within the spaces pried open during these "ecstatic moments" merits a thorough exploration. It is worth considering, for instance, the extent to which these ecstatic moments could be linked to New World religious practices such as Santería and vodou.[31] Two issues immediately militate against any direct correspondences. First, Santería and vodou are explicitly religious contexts within which music is performed for expressly ritual purposes intended to facilitate healing and spiritual insight through possession. Junkanoo is clearly not performed with the same purposes in mind. Second, the musicians in Santería and vodou ceremonies do not, as a general rule, enter trance states during these rituals, rather providing a framework in which others are able to do so. In the case of Junkanoo, however, it is the musicians themselves who enter what Wood and Wisdom describe as trancelike or ecstatic states.

And yet these clear differences should not discourage further exploration, for the Rara bands that take to the streets, crossroads, and cemeteries of Haiti during Lent offer an intriguing combination of spiritual work and carnivalesque play that may offer an analogue (albeit a much more explicitly sacred one) to the current shape of Junkanoo. Elizabeth McAlister observes:

> Rara festivals are Creole performances par excellence, imbued with historical memories so terrible and profound that they are transmitted not in everyday speech, but through the dancing body and in the cryptic texts of songs and rituals. Yet Rara is not only about historical memory. More immediate is what Rara has to say about the present realities of Haiti's disenfranchised poor majority. . . . Rara is about play, religion, and politics and also about remembering a bloody history and persevering in its face. But at its most bare philosophical level, Rara is a ritual enactment of life itself and an affirmation of life's difficulties. (McAlister 2002, 4, 23)

Each year Rara bands engage in a six-week-long process of work masked as play, and while Junkanoo does not participate explicitly in the kind of sacred work associated with Rara bands, it is worth considering the possibility of a sacred core within Junkanoo. Unlike E. Clement Bethel, who chose to deny sacred roots in the case of Junkanoo and did so on the grounds that slaves' religious practices were conducted in secret, I suggest that Rara offers an intriguing example of a practice that combines overt, public, and secular performance with a covert, private, and sacred core and parades it through the streets. Junkanoo in the nineteenth and early twentieth centuries could well have exhibited these same general patterns (albeit within a context dominated by Protestant belief structures). I am thinking here of the clear understanding on the part of white observers in 1849 that oxen were going to be "falling a sacrifice" after the morning's festivities, a knowledge matched by complete silence as to what that might entail and, more importantly, what that sacrifice might mean for the Over-the-Hill community. It seems plausible to suggest, then, that Junkanoo may have provided for sacred registers of meaning among participants throughout its history in the Bahamas— provided for sacred meanings that were hiding in plain sight, as it were. And given the recent research of Ken Bilby (2010) illustrating the extent to which Jamaican practices are concerned with sacred work, I am increasingly convinced that Junkanoo continues to preserve a sacred dimension at its core.

Two other reasons for making this claim suggest themselves. First, the Bahamian practice of obeah, long associated in the Bahamas with individual use of powers and sorcery, but better understood as a communal way of accessing healing (Bilby 2008) continues to serve as a living link to African religious heritage. It is, in other words, the religious practice that has remained active in the face of disapproval by Protestant churches and in spite of the negative appraisal of the practice by most Bahamians. Today it is primarily associated with Cat Island, though it was very prominently a part of the Over-the-Hill communities during the late nineteenth and early twentieth centuries.

Significantly, obeah has come to be used by popular musicians as a means of critiquing the nation. For instance, Exuma (Tony McKay) used obeah in constructing his public personae and referenced it frequently in his lyrics. I will explore the appropriation of obeah into popular music in greater detail in chapter 5, but here I suggest that obeah, which operates as a counternarrative of spirituality within the explicitly Protestant Bahamian context, has historically offered a means of linking power, politics, and play together. Whether or not Junkanoo became a musical site for this type of linkage is unclear, however, largely because the rhetoric surrounding the festival remains so staunchly secular. This rhetoric of secularity is, I suggest, directly related to the masking effect of Christianity with respect to African religious heritage the Bahamas.

And this brings me to the second reason for considering the possibility of a sacred core that continues to survive, for the excesses that take hold in performance (runnin' hot) and flow out in rhetoric (invocations of the metaphysical and sacred tropes and metaphors) are too bound up in the ineffable and in the numinous—too connected to African understandings of spirituality—to be merely coincidental or purely utilitarian. Whether or not Junkanoos consider their performances to be imbued with sacred content or spiritual undercurrents is less interesting than the presence of these excesses in their acts of performance and in their efforts to describe the experience of Junkanoo. I am not concerned, then, with pointing out clear examples of sacred practice in contemporary Junkanoo, but rather with illustrating the continued presence of a phenomenological layer that defies description without recourse to the sacred.

I submit, therefore, that the roots of Junkanoo—almost certainly bound up in sacred practices—have been silenced in direct relationship to the dominant authorizing discourse of spirituality, in direct relationship to Christianity, that is. The collection of papers titled *Junkanoo and Religion: Christianity and Cultural Identity in the Bahamas* (Junkanoo Symposium 2003) offers an excellent example of the discursive spaces within which these roots have systematically been muted. While many of the contributors acknowledge that slave spirituality incorporated African cosmologies and religious practices, none explore the extent to which these roots may continue to exist in an uneasy relationship to Christian belief and practice. Junkanoo is, rather, seen as a social practice that needs to be further incorporated into Christian worship and liturgy. And yet in the foreword to the volume Gail Saunders remarks: "The spirit of Junkanoo is truly the soul of the Bahamian people" (Saunders 2003b, 4). She thus offers at the very outset of that collection an excellent instance of precisely the kind of excess I am attempting to trace here.

In the final analysis, it is necessary to leave these questions concerning the place of the sacred within the contemporary expression of Junkanoo unanswered, but I do suggest that the excesses I have pointed to both in its performance and in the discourse surrounding it have not been overlooked by those charged with nurturing the Bahamian state. Quite to the contrary, I maintain that the conflation of national politics with Junkanoo, effected in the late 1960s and increasingly perfected after independence, is calculated to take advantage of precisely these excesses—excesses which politicians know are rooted in deeply held understandings of self and intimately connected to identity (and this, I argue, is due to their sacred roots).

Since the 1960s, then, Junkanoo has increasingly provided a site wherein both government and people interact with and restructure the face of the nation. It is embodied and located in a specific place. In addition, myths surrounding the origins of Junkanoo lend the event and its roots (sacred or otherwise) a certain timelessness, which is reinforced by the actual performances. As groups rush down Bay Street, the music of one group blends into the music of the next, fashioning the performance and, by extension, Bahamian history, as a long and seamless event; the people, and by extension the nation, as a large but unified family. Thus, Junkanoo offers a very specific image of the nation, one that is timeless and mythical, spatially bounded, and embodied in community performance—secular, that is, and nationalistic. This historicized approach to the nation is counteracted by the commentary on history and the nation introduced by the performances of the scrap groups and, as I illustrate in the following chapter, by popular Junkanoo as well. It is also counteracted by the excesses I have traced here, for though they have provided a vehicle for solidifying Junkanoo as the quintessential expression of Bahamianness, they also trace along the very tensions in Bahamian life that threaten to unravel the seamless narrative of nation and kinship adopted since independence. Junkanoo is, as such, a tool—an idea and a practice—that can be used in multiple ways and to varying effects, both by politicians and by grassroots "scrappers," to mythologize the nation or to illustrate, expose, and amplify the fissures in that self-same national myth. Junkanoo, then, has been and remains much more than a symbol of the nation. Perhaps Gail Saunders has it just right—perhaps "the spirit of Junkanoo is truly the soul of the Bahamian people" (Saunders 2003b, 4). The musicians I explore in the following two chapters certainly see the potential and power of Junkanoo, and the varied approaches that they have taken to incorporating Junkanoo sounds, but also the "soul of the Bahamian people," into their performances speak to their willingness to direct that powerful collection of sounds and ideas toward making their visions of the nation a reality.

5

"A New Day Dawning"

Cosmopolitanism, Roots, and Identity
in the Postcolony

Lift up your head to the rising sun, Bahamaland!
March on to glory your bright banners waving high;
See how the world marks the manner of your bearing!
Pledge to excel through love and unity
Pressing onward, march together to a common loftier goal,
Steady sunward, tho' the weather hide the wide and treacherous shoal.
Lift up your head to the rising sun, Bahamaland!
'Til the road you've trod lead unto your God,
March on, Bahamaland!

—"MARCH ON, BAHAMALAND," BAHAMIAN NATIONAL ANTHEM,
   TIMOTHY GIBSON, 1973

Actually, once the government changed to a predominantly black
government in '67, that's when really the music died.

—RAY MUNNINGS, INTERVIEW WITH THE AUTHOR, JULY 11, 2009

Forward, upward, onward, together

—BAHAMIAN NATIONAL MOTTO

The postcolony was born on July 10, 1973, and the newly independent Bahamian nation celebrated with Junkanoo, a new national anthem, and monuments to music and culture such as the album *A Nation Is Born: A Musical History of the Bahamas*. Released in 1973, the album's cover depicts the national crest of the Bahamas breaking out of an egg against a white background, stylized sunbeams of gold, aquamarine, and black spreading out toward the edges of the record jacket; spreading the birth announcement along with the national motto—"Forward, upward, onward, together"—to any who would see the light.[1] And yet this album is not a musical history per se. There is no traditional rake-n-scrape here. No sea shanties are included. Not a single anthem is recorded (though a traditional African American spiritual makes the cut).[2] *A Nation Is Born* seems, rather, to go about the business of showcasing the novel, the popular, and things recent, thereby aligning the nation with cosmopolitan spaces and urban places and situating it within an explicitly contemporary milieu.

To be sure, the pioneers of Bahamian music memorialized here, including artists like Alphonso "Blind Blake" Higgs, Eloise Lewis, and Ronnie Butler, offer a nostalgic reflection on mid-twentieth-century musical life in Nassau. And yet their contributions are significantly outweighed by the many younger, more transnationally oriented artists popular in the Bahamas during the early 1970s—such as the Beginning of the End, Biosis Now, the Mighty Makers, Rupert and the Rolling Coins, and Bobby Smith. In short, this album is not a musical history, as such, but instead very much a monument to the present and the future of the Bahamas—it serves as a powerful statement of arrival.

This moment of arrival, though, was manufactured against a cultural, political, and economic background that was ambiguous at best and contradictory at worst. Ambiguous because independence was fought for and won with recourse to a cultural nationalist platform, which had been articulated in direct opposition to the colonial condition.[3] In the wake of independence, the cultural nationalist platform began to reveal the legacy of that colonial past, a legacy manifested in a very real lack of confidence in things Bahamian. What international face should this newly emergent nation place before the world? Put otherwise, the conversation leading up to independence had benefited from a specific interlocutor— a clearly defined antagonist—in opposition to which the cultural nationalist platform could efficiently be articulated. The postcolony, however, faced a conversational vacuum, and the album *A Nation Is Born* is an indication of one of the ways Bahamians responded to that new state of affairs. They responded, that is, by reaching outside the nation for interlocutors, finding in Motown and Soulsville—and, by extension, the civil rights movement and black power—some powerful possibilities for articulating the concerns of the present moment in "Funky Nassau."

Contradictory because, although the Bahamas had enjoyed majority rule since 1967, the hope associated with that development was, at least among musicians, nightclub owners, and taxi drivers, revealed as a chimera by the mid-1970s. This became especially evident in the first years after independence, when, in addition to wrestling with the effects of the economic downturn of the early 1970s, the new government was increasingly pressured by international business conglomerates (such as cruise lines and multinational hotel chains) to continue offering them financial concessions. Ironically, one of the sectors most adversely affected by the continued growth of tourism within the Bahamas was entertainment. The government was making choices that seemed to counter the interests of the many

Bahamians employed in that sector, but with the goal of further solidifying networks within the mass tourism industry.

To make matters worse, the government felt it necessary to strategically distance itself from the very black nationalist rhetoric it had used to great effect during its rise to power. As far as most musicians were concerned, all other issues aside, the minority rule of the Bay Street Boys had been very good for entertainment. And now, when all signs pointed to a new, better day, the opposite trends seemed to be playing themselves out at government house. And this is one of the main reasons why Ronnie Butler's remarks are so vituperative: "My government done fuck me. Print that! The government ain't worth shit since Stafford Sands" (Ronnie Butler, interview with the author, June 27, 2007).

BLACK POWER, BLACK RULE: ("BACK-TO-THE-BUSH") COSMOPOLITANISM?

The remainder of this chapter unfolds as a series of case studies. The first two explore the difficult, even impossible choices that the Bahamian government faced from the moment of majority rule through the mid-1970s. Even as the government's nation-building impulse was inexorably channeled into the narrow terrain of financial and economic policy, the resulting decisions, pragmatic though they were, generated quite seriously negative consequences throughout the Bahamian entertainment sector. The decisions also illustrated that the journey initiated by the majority government, which had been ideologically driven by black nationalist ideas, had become a long march into a nonradical and cosmopolitan future, a vision not shared by the entertainment sector. The remaining three case studies focus on the very different ground on which several musicians between the early 1970s and the 1980s attempted to "build" the Bahamian nation. These musicians, each in his own way, continued to journey to the black nationalist destination originally hailed as the goal of majority rule and independence. This parting of the ways, as it were, found the musicians gravitating toward forms of expression that would enable them to continue articulating a sufficiently radical (read postcolonial) understanding of (Afro)Bahamian identity. To that end, they latched onto obeah, rake-n-scrape, and Junkanoo and coupled these deeply Afro-Bahamian practices with the ideological core of the civil rights movement and black power in the United States.

Excursus I:
Jumbey Village, Goombay Summer, and the Use-Value of Culture

I begin by returning to the creation and eventual razing of Jumbey Village, drawing several themes from this ill-fated cultural village that inform both its place within the national discourse about postcolonial identity and its vulnerability in the face of tourist development projects. Edmund Moxey remembers the story as follows:

> Jumbey Village . . . started as an offspring from the Jumbey Festival. The name Jumbey is symbolic of a Bahamian tree, plant, shrub, that we call the Jumbey tree. The leaves are thick, all right? And the roots, if you cut it down and burn it down, all you need is a good squall of rain and it come back. So it is symbolic of the Bahamian people. I thought that, going for independence at that particular time, it was a symbol of the Bahamian people growing together from strength to strength—root, branches.
>
> We started the festival in 1969, and we held it in the heart of Coconut Grove. And we built indigenous structures and the side . . . so we built all the structures as it relate to what is known today as the Big Yard. And the first year we did it we had to take it down. Second year, in 1970, we had to take it down. Third year, Jumbey Festival coming up, so we said, "It doesn't make sense to build all these structures and have to tear them down. The best thing to do is to look for a permanent place." And that's how we got over to a four-and-a-half-acre [site] which was a dump. And everybody says Moxey is crazy. A dump on a swamp. And what I did, I got together with . . . three ministers of government at that particular time: Carlton Francis, who was wearing two hats because he was . . . minister of education and culture and finance. So I had his ear. The minister of transport, where we got the fill from to fill in the swamp. Dr. Doris Johnson, she was minister of transport, and she had control of thousands and thousands of tons of fill on Arawak Key . . . and she said, "Go ahead." And Winston Coakley, he was minister of works, and he had a D8 tractor [Caterpillar] . . . and that's how we cleared that place down and bring in the fill. . . . [We] put the homestead site up, and in '73, in January of '73, we had a meeting with all the teachers. And at one of those meetings I suggested, I said, you know, "We should do something. Teachers and students should make a gift to the nation." And everybody start, "Yeah, that's a good idea." And then I said, "What I really had in mind," I said, "it would be a good thing if we get a museum and art center." Everybody jump for that. And they agreed right there on the spot that all the teachers in the system would donate a half day's pay and every school would have a function.
>
> And we launched that program and came up with one hundred thousand dollars in the space of three months. Art museum [and] cultural center was built. I went to Carlton Francis and said, "Well, now I have some money." And we did an arts and crafts center plus eight gift shops. The arts and crafts center was a production area, and the gift shops was available for them to sell the wares that they made in arts and crafts. I got some money for them for an auditorium, which we got up and was using. And then in '73 I said to them, I said, "Listen, we got to develop a program in social, cultural, and economic development of the country as a commitment to independence." And everybody—you had them in the palm of your hands. Could do anything with them, and they asked us to set up the program. So we set up the program financing, had all the personnel to operate the program, and

we didn't have to bring in one person from the outside. Everybody was in the system. [We] put up a special cabinet paper, cabinet agreed, and when I pick up the budget [in] December, everything was cut out of the budget. Everything. Nothing! I said, "You all don't need me around. You know, I gone!" That was a little bit too much. Village lingered, lingered, lingered . . . just keep on deteriorating, deteriorating until they came up with this grandiose scheme to put national insurance there. And when they was ready, they blow the whole thing down. (Edmund Moxey, interview with the author, August 11, 2007)

Moxey's vision for a permanent cultural center in the Bahamas grew out of the success of his Jumbey Festivals, which started in 1969 (see chapter 2). The project constituted a truly bold move, because the site where he chose to build the village was located over-the-hill. It was also innovative in concept, for it was designed not only with a view toward generating tourist visits, but rather primarily as a site by and for Bahamians. The project, in short, participated in the continued reclamation of confidence in Afro-Bahamian cultural heritage. This was, it is worth remembering, the time when black power reached its apex throughout the Caribbean, and many Bahamian artists, writers, artisans, and musicians were powerfully drawn to the ideological and sociopolitical direction that black power represented.

Ironically, the majority government (elected in 1967), which had swept to power on a black nationalist platform, found itself busily blunting the more radical voices within its own ranks in an effort to assuage international investors' fears of political instability within the country.[4] These efforts at mellowing the ruling party's discourse constituted a reaction to a real, but certainly not the only (or even the most dire), threat to the political power of the Progressive Liberal Party (PLP), however, for the PLP's rise to power was followed in short order by a worldwide economic slowdown that had significant effects in the Bahamas.[5] For instance, 1970 saw the first drop in tourist arrivals since World War II, a fact that the opposition party quickly seized upon as evidence of the lack of direction and poor governance offered by the PLP. In any case, it was clear that the government and, by extension, the crucially important Ministry of Tourism would need to offer effective solutions in order cope with what was, at best, a serious budget shortfall in the short term and, at worst, a possible long-term structural problem for the industry.

One suggested solution involved hosting a summer festival, called Bahamas Goombay Summer. Initiated in July 1971, the festival was an unqualified success, drawing record numbers of tourists during that summer season. Clement Maynard, the minister of tourism at the time, recalls:

Bahamas Goombay Summer was created as a possible solution to two problems that loomed on the horizon of summer tourist volume—low European fares, and the rash of negative publicity concerning the Caribbean. Under captions such as *The Palm Tree Revolution,* and *Black Power in the Islands,* there were reports of wide political unrest. In the first instance, Bahamas· Goombay summer was an added "product benefit" for the visitor; a built-in value to his holiday. Secondly, it was a means of exposing visitors to Bahamians and Bahamian culture, so that visi-· tors could see for themselves that none of the negatives was true of The Bahamas. Bahamas Goombay Summer was a 13-week festival staged in both Nassau and Freeport. It included such events as closing the main street (downtown) one night a week and converting it to a ̈shopping mall, followed by a Goombay parade with "Jump-in" dancers and goatskin drums. Vendors sold from gaily decorated carts such Bahamian specialties as conch fritters and soursop ice cream. Afterwards, there was dancing in the street for all, to music by popular bands. What in concept had been a planned festival became a carnival because of spontaneous Bahamian involvement. (Maynard 2007, 308–9)

The obvious benefit to the tourist industry, coupled with the ability to defend Bahamian culture, proved important to the festival's survival, and Bahamas Goombay Summer was indeed celebrated annually for some twenty consecutive years thereafter. By the time Moxey's Jumbey Village was ready for government funding in 1973, then, Goombay Summer had already proved itself an effective event for three years. As the majority government wrestled with the nation's budgetary concerns, there were real arguments to be made for directing money to tourism promotion instead of cultural heritage projects. In the final analysis, the government determined that it was more important (and less risky) to incorporate a few well-planned cultural productions into a tourist-centered event than it was to fund, at some financial sacrifice, a truly Bahamian cultural enterprise.

That decision relegated Jumbey Village to slow but inexorable decline, culminating in its destruction by explosives in 1987. The unrealized promise of a place like Jumbey Village, however, continues to generate debate even now, in large part because it encapsulates both the unrealized possibilities envisioned by cultural activists, but also because it serves as a perfect, if discouraging, metaphor for the nation's lack of commitment to its own cultural and creative life. Two recent reflections on the failed project provide a case in point. The first is an editorial by Oswald Brown that appeared in the January 16, 2009, edition of the *Freeport News:*

[Jumbey Village] was a concept that could have had a profound and far-reaching impact on many aspects of Bahamian life and culture if those in the seats of power at the time had the good sense to recognize its full potential. Why this happened is still a mystery, considering that Jumbey Village politically was one of those projects that the Progressive Liberal Party (PLP) government could have benefited from tremendously for many, many years, and quite possibly it could have been enshrined in its legacy as one of the PLP's most important accomplishments. But in the end, the lack of vision and foresight by the principal decision-makers in the party—and quite possibly petty politics—resulted in the demise of Jumbey Village during its infancy.

And the following assessment by Arthur Foulkes appeared in the blog Bahama Pundit a few years earlier:

> Nearly four decades ago Mr. Moxey had the brilliant idea of creating a comprehensive national cultural village Over-the-Hill. It would have been a permanent exhibition of Bahamian culture in all its aspects and a centre for the development of Bahamian arts and crafts. One can only imagine the positive impact Jumbey Village might have had on succeeding generations of Bahamians—and the nation as a whole—in terms of cultural advancement, personal development, national pride and economic opportunities. The project was actually started, but petty politics got in the way and it was aborted. Now, as the Bahamas struggles against a sea of negative cultural influences and so many of our young people are adrift, the deferral of Mr. Moxey's dream is to be especially lamented. It was a colossal mistake. (Arthur Foulkes, *Bahama Pundit* (blog), June 2006, http://bahamapundit.com)

Both of these reflections, framed by the clarity achieved in hindsight, nevertheless highlight the main reason why this failure continues to live on in discussions about Bahamian life. That Jumbey Village was to be a Bahamian enterprise promoting Bahamian creative arts and culture placed it in an entirely different category vis-à-vis any of the events sponsored by the Ministry of Tourism, and it offered tantalizing possibilities for consolidating the nation's arts and culture discourse around an active, lived focal point. The lack of support Moxey's project received from the government, coupled with the failure of any government since that time to pursue similar projects, has installed Jumbey Village at the heart of regional jokes (i.e., "Name the country who blow up the culture!") but has also had the—no doubt unintended—consequence of creating a symbolic and physical monument to the government's low valuation of Bahamian culture. The irony that Jumbey Village was razed to make way for the national insurance building is not lost on many, rather starkly underscoring the economic imperatives that continue to drive government policy.

The late 1960s and early 1970s thus saw a new government, both in its transition to independence and thereafter, struggling to balance the clear need to project the Bahamas as a modern, stable, and nonradical haven for investors and tourists against the equally clear cultural imperatives that were at the time being articulated within a black nationalist and black power paradigm. The horns of this dilemma did not offer much in the way of a middle ground, partially because the government needed to safeguard itself against losses during this period of global economic downturn. Put otherwise, the potential gains associated with supporting Moxey's vision for Jumbey Village were outweighed by the feared losses that could accrue if tourists had less incentive to visit during the summer months. Sponsoring cultural productions, moreover, would cost the government money that would not be recovered in kind, whereas an investment in Goombay Summer would be paid for many times over in tourist dollars.

Excursus II: Cruise Ships, Cruise Shops, and Entertainers

This same pragmatic gain-loss calculus was at the heart of another major policy decision implemented just a little more than a year later, in 1975. The Ministry of Tourism decided to actively support local native shows aboard cruise ships that were docked at Prince George Wharf in Nassau. This decision was particularly controversial, not least because it served as a final blow in a fierce struggle that had occupied musicians, entertainers, and taxi drivers from majority rule to independence. The beginnings of this struggle trace back to 1968, when after months of discussion the government renegotiated its contracts with several cruise ships, curtailing subsidies paid and thereby affording the ships more freedom to operate shops and entertainment on board. The reaction among entertainers was fierce. In fact, even the news that the government was considering this course of action engendered heated public discourse.

In order to contextualize the strong reaction to the government's initial decision and the long struggle it precipitated, it is helpful to bear in mind that it was in the late 1960s that nightclub owners and entertainers in the Bahamas were beginning to feel in earnest the negative effects of the growing tourist market. I asked Ronald Simms to outline the factors that he felt contributed to the rapid decline, from the mid-1960s on, of the nightclub scene in the Bahamas. He enumerated several and included the cruise ship issue:

Once the hotels became year-round operations, the hotels had this need for entertainment. Obviously the only entertainment existing [after the dinner hour] was the entertainment in these Over-the-Hill clubs. The hotels, of course, then offered these guys contracts way beyond what they were getting playing in the local establishments, so all the performers emptied out into the hotels because they now had a steady job. Right? In addition to that, other factors that contributed to the demise of the Over-the-Hill entertainment was [the increase in] alternatives—casinos, movie theaters, television, video machines, all this stuff. People did not have to go out for these entertainments anymore. The Over-the-Hill clubs could not compete with the hotels in terms of dollars paid, in terms of work conditions. So as a musician, if I had the opportunity to work in a hotel six night a week, I'll take it. That's really the nuts and bolts of what happened. The other factor that came into play was, when the industry was very successful, all cruise ships coming into port had to shut down three miles out of port. Totally shut down. Their food-and-beverage operations, whatever activities that existed on the ship had to shut down. That then forced people to go out to eat, to go out to be entertained. I think it was sometime

around 1969 or thereabouts, around the turn of the '70s, when the government allowed the cruise ships to open in port. So you have this mass volume of people now
not filling your establishment because they have alternatives. There's entertainment on the ships, you can eat on the ships, so you don't have to come off the ship
anymore. (Ronald Simms, interview with the author, August 8, 2007)

Compare Ronald's reflections with an editorial printed in the *Nassau Guardian*
in June 1968:

Native night clubs in Nassau are being adversely affected by cruise ship floor shows
and the absorption of their best acts by the big hotels. . . . "Business has been drop-
ping off for some time" said Mr. W. Sweeting, operator of the Big Bamboo on Bay
Street. "I believe this is because the cruise ships are now putting on floor shows
while they are docked here. This means passengers can see the show on the ship for
nothing so they don't come ashore in the evening to visit local shows" he said.

Charles Lehmann of the famous Charley Charleys said . . . "The big hotels are
cutting down the business of the native clubs . . . and so are the cruise ships by putting on shows. Not only are the hotels taking customers away, but they are also
taking the acts away from local clubs." He pointed out that the big hotels were willing to pay more than the smaller clubs, so consequently they got all the best acts.
There was a tendency lately for the top hotels to favour native Bahamian talent and
they were draining the local acts from the clubs. . . . The Blue Note native club on
Wulff Road is to close, it was announced this week, the Playboy Club closed some
time ago and the Lemon Tree, run by Ritchie Delamore, failed to re-open after a
fire on the premises.

Mr. Freddie Munnings, Entertainment Director for the Ministry of Tourism,
told the Guardian-Observer that the native clubs had been suffering for about four
years now. "Naturally the big hotels offer much more money to local acts—so they
get them," he said. ("Talent Drain Hurts Native Night Clubs," *Nassau Guardian*,
June 13, 1968)

This, then, was the backdrop against which entertainers, taxi drivers, and
nightclub owners reacted to the news that their government was considering a
curtailment of the subsidies to cruise ships. When viewed in conjunction with
the pressures brought to bear by hotels and casinos, it is understandable that the
entertainment sector felt as though government was out of step with their needs
and challenges. In fact, the government seemed to be actively exploring a policy
decision that would materially harm the entertainment sector.

The government's decision itself, however, revolved around a strictly monetary
concern, one that was quite clear from a profit-making standpoint. The leadership was attempting to answer the fundamental question of whether it remained
necessary in 1968 to subsidize cruise ship companies in order to bring their passengers to Nassau.[6] In 1964, the year the subsidies were first enacted, the scale of

the tourism industry dictated that the Bahamas incentivize and cultivate as fully as possible all potential revenue streams. That year, a total of 605,171 tourists visited the Bahamas. Of these, 240,560 arrived via ship (Bahamas 1967, 9; Cleare 2007, 574). Fully 40 percent of the potential tourist revenue, then, was tied directly to the cruise ship industry. By 1968, the situation had changed considerably, primarily owing to tourist volume. In this milestone year, for the first time the Bahamas attracted more than 1 million visitors (1,072,213), and of these, 253,219 (less than 25 percent) arrived by sea (Cleare 2007, 224). Taking into account that stopover visitors spend a great deal more than do cruise passengers by virtue of the length of stay, the consensus within the government was that revenue lost by restructuring contracts with a few cruise ships would be more than compensated for in sheer volume.[7]

The subsidies that since 1964 had helped a few cruise companies to defray advertising costs and berthing fees carried the condition that cruise ships benefiting from these incentives not operate any duty-free shops on board in order to encourage their passengers to spend additional money in Nassau. The three principal ships that the government subsidized at the time were not merely symbolic in this regard, for they were responsible for very regular traffic on the Nassau/New York and Nassau/Miami routes. Importantly, however, all cruise ships, subsidized or not, were under obligation to close their shops and entertainment while in port in the Bahamas. And it is with reference to this larger question that the discourse regarding the subsidies played out, for the government was regularly charged with turning a blind eye to the cruise ships operating shops and entertainment in port in violation of their agreements. The truest threat, then—far more threatening to the entertainment sector than the proposed curtailment of subsidies—was the governmental inaction that implicitly encouraged cruise ships to remain open for business while in port. The news that the government was leaning toward removing the subsidies for several ships served as a tangible and strategic lever that entertainers pulled to call attention to their critical situation.

The government's pragmatic position on this issue was thus preemptively subjected to vigorous critique. Nightclub operators, taxi cab drivers, entertainers, and Bay Street business owners viewed the government's potential withdrawal of subsidies as concrete evidence of their leaders' lack of interest in truly fighting for local business and entertainment interests. From the perspective of these constituencies, every tourist and every purchase mattered. The *Nassau Tribune*, for instance, ran a front-page story summarizing the situation:

> Shops aboard cruise ships coming to the Bahamas may soon be in strong competition with Bay Street stores catering to the tourist industry. The rumoured "no holds barred" attitude on the part of liners now subsidized by the Bahamas government is believed due to the possibility that government may decide to lop off

these subsidies when the four-year contracts terminate at the end of this year. . . . If subsidy cuts are made, subsidized ship operators have reportedly threatened to allow duty-free shops aboard to operate on a wide-open basis, with possibly serious repercussions on tourist buying in Nassau. It is understood that the question of subsidies is still under consideration by government, which is not yet prepared to make any statement on the matter. ("'Cruise Ships to Open Shops to Compete with Bay St.' Rumour—Question of Subsidies Will Decide," *Nassau Tribune*, August 31, 1968)

In September, a concerned Chamber of Commerce issued its own formal statement to the press in which the leadership urged the government to continue subsidizing the cruise ships, not least because of the threat that direct competition with the cruise ships would represent to tourism-related businesses.

The Bahamas Chamber of Commerce has expressed its concern at the possibility of Government's discontinuing subsidies granted to cruise ships. A statement issued by chamber president Bryan Moody said that discontinuance of these subsidies could result in the ships not calling here or in curtailing their stop-overs. "With the tourist duty allowance at its present $100 as opposed to $200 in the Virgin Islands, the people most likely to be affected by this would include taxi drivers, straw vendors, night club operators, etc.," said the statement. "Another important factor would be the loss of revenue to the colony." ("Chamber's Plea to Govt.: Don't Cut Cruise Ship Subsidy," *Nassau Tribune*, September 6, 1968)

Nightclub operators joined the discussion as well. Their concerns were set forth in the *Nassau Tribune* as follows:

"A most unfair monopoly exists in New Providence because when we consider the decreasing number of visitors to our night-clubs then we are faced with a dilemma." He [Basil Cooper, secretary of the Nightclub Owners and Operators Association] added that the dilemma was now reaching a crucial stage because many clubs had closed through lack of tourist business. "One of the main distractions as far as night-clubs are concerned is the Paradise Island gambling casino. Most tourists are lured there repeatedly and they seldom hear of Nassau's night life." Another factor was that most major hotels had night-club shows in their lounges and bars. "So naturally, the tourists are enticed to remain at these resorts rather than take night-club tours." . . . Mr. Cooper said that he was also concerned about Miami cruise ships putting on shows and opening their bars while "in port." As a result, most cruise ship passengers never even got in the clubs on Bay Street, he maintained. ("Night Club Men Blame Casino for Trade Drop," *Nassau Tribune*, October 2, 1968)

Over these objections and concerns, the government nevertheless made what appeared to be a solid fiscal decision, if also one detrimental to the entertainment sector, seriously curtailing the subsidies built in to the new contracts.[8]

Prime Minister Lynden O. Pindling yesterday announced a cut-back in subsidies to cruise ships operating between Nassau and the United States and the introduction of a new cruise ship next year. At a brief meeting of yesterday's House of Assembly he told members that a new contract had been signed with the Oceanic reducing the advertising contribution paid by the Bahamas government to that ship from $275,000 a year to $100,000. Mr. Pindling said that according to three contracts entered into by the previous government with the Oceanic, the S.S. Miami and the Bahama Star, the Ministry of Tourism was paying more than half a million dollars a year either as direct subsidies or as contributions to advertising costs incurred by the shipping companies. The S.S. Miami has since been withdrawn by its owners. He said that concern had been expressed that the elimination of subsidies would lead to the cancellation of cruise ship visits and to reduced shopping in the city. "I acknowledge that it may have been necessary five years ago to give incentives in the form of subsidies, but today, it would be difficult to justify that more than half a million dollars should be paid out of the public exchequer mainly to promote shopping in Nassau," he said.

He said the Ministry of Tourism and the Ministry of Finance had carefully considered the "pros and cons" of the situation and had decided that things had changed and it was no longer necessary to offer substantial subsidies to any ship. Noting the increase in tourist figures, he said the Bahamas was likely to receive 1.2 million visitors next year. And "noting that the cruise ships that now run to Nassau without a subsidy do now operate shops on board ship, remembering that more and more tourists are arriving by air, and considering the overall increase in tourist numbers, it is more than likely that the extra numbers will be able to take up any slack in shopping due to onboard purchasing."

He added that "the effect on revenue had been carefully and closely studied and "we are now satisfied that the loss in customs duty would be only a fraction of what is being paid in subsidies." Mr. Pindling was "completely satisfied" that the lack of subsidies was not going to deter the cruise ships from coming to Nassau, and announced that at the beginning of next year there would be four cruise ships from Miami instead of three.... "Finally it should be made clear that, while the ships are in port, they will not be allowed to open or operate their own shops." ("Government to Lower Cruise Ship Subsidies," *Nassau Guardian*, November 28, 1968)

Importantly, the last line of the editorial reveals that the government had become aware of how much attention was being directed at their lack of enforcement while ships were in port. It comes as no surprise that the nightclub owners filed a petition shortly thereafter, protesting their untenable position within the tourism sector.

Nightclub owners in New Providence have drafted a five-point protest "petition" against mounting competition from hotels and cruise ships and will present it to Prime Minister Lynden O. Pindling and his cabinet. The depleted Bahamas Nightclub Owners and Operators Association met Friday to discuss the mounting crisis facing local nightspots—16 of which have closed in the past 18 months because of what they claim to be unfair competition. However, two of the clubs listed—the Conch Shell and the Goombay Club—burned down. They complain that incoming tourists are not given sufficient information about the locally-run nightclubs and are escorted straight to the big hotels. They suggest that cruise directors should re-organise their programmes so that passengers are not all in one place at the same time. They also maintain that: Literature on local nightspots should be made available on cruise ships and in hotels. Hotels should programme their shows so that guests can be allowed out at about 9:45pm. The Paradise Island Casino should be excluded from organized tours. The government should enforce the closing of clubs, theatres and shops aboard cruise ships while in port. The term "over-the-hill" which often discouraged people from travelling away from the city area, should be dropped. One member said that cruise directors and the hotels displayed "wanton disregard" for local businesses by deliberately dissuading tourists to go over the hill. ("Nightclub Owners to File Petition," *Nassau Guardian,* February 24, 1969)

Shortly thereafter, in an obliquely related development that highlights the central issue in this debate, then minister of tourism Authur Foulkes announced a new agreement with the Bahamas Taxi-Cab Union (BTCU) that satisfied, for the time being, the concerns of the nightclub owners. Importantly, one of the assurances offered, though tellingly not included in the formal announcement of the agreement, was that the cruise ships would stop all entertainment while in port.

Over-the-hill nightclubs which have suffered from a trailing tourist appeal because of the major hotels received a shot in the arm from Tourism Minister Arthur Foulkes Wednesday. After successful talks with cruise ship operators and taxi men, Mr. Foulkes pledged in the House of Assembly: "It won't be too long when nightclub space we have over-the-hill will not be enough for the tourists, who will want to go over there." Mr. Foulkes congratulated cab drivers who had agreed to go to the wharfs at the arrival of cruise ships and transport passengers to over-the-hill nightclubs for $2 each including waiting time. Although it was not included in his speech, Mr. Foulkes said after the session that cruise ship operators had agreed to stop all entertainment on board while ships were in port. ("Nightclubs Get Boost from Cab Driver Deal," *Nassau Guardian,* March 20, 1969)

Entertainers soon realized, however, that the imperatives of economics and expediency were overriding factors justifying why the cruise ships should be able to operate shops and entertainment in port in spite of their agreements to the contrary. Cruise ships could, quite simply, make a great deal more money if they offered these services while in port. The government, for its part, recognized that other ports in the region would be happy to accommodate any ships that became displeased with their terms in the Bahamas.[9]

Mutually beneficial expedience on the part of cruise ship companies and the Bahamian government, however, led to a very different economic result among the musicians and entertainers. In fact, one of the most troubling long-term consequences of these shifts in tourist mobility (and spending) on performance venues (and the increasing lack thereof) and new possibilities for individual careers (in the hotels) was that the system of tutelage—the training ground for aspiring musicians—which had been in place since the 1940s, was progressively lost. During the 1950s and early 1960s, for instance, long-standing Over-the-Hill house bands like the Freddie Munnings Orchestra were constantly rejuvenated by the addition of younger players, who in turn benefited from a wide range of musical experiences during their tenure with the group. These experiences were often parlayed into successful careers once musicians left the Munnings Orchestra.[10] The dozens of Over-the-Hill clubs provided the initial venues for first-time band leaders, new ensembles, and aspiring soloists. Once a measure of success had been reached in these clubs, musicians could transfer their skills to the hotels with confidence. To be sure, many bands were able to find success without the help of the Over-the-Hill scene (T-Connections and Beginning of the End, for example), but these ensembles generally reflected only the most talented among a relatively large pool of musicians.

Once the Over-the-Hill clubs began closing in rapid succession, there was little room for the larger number of musicians that the scene had supported in the 1940s and '50s. As career possibilities began to be circumscribed by these practical considerations, the gap between excellent bands and mediocre ensembles grew wider and fewer amateur musicians chose to pursue professional careers in the entertainment industry. By the early 1980s, the Bahamas could still boast many excellent bands, but these bands consisted of personnel from the last generation of trained and highly skilled musicians.[11] The effects of this state of affairs were not felt until the late 1980s, when the working bands of the 1970s were coming to the end of their careers and found that there were no suitable younger professional musicians waiting to take their places. By the 1990s, the idea of the full-time professional musician in the Bahamas had effectively died.[12]

And even as entertainers struggled to come to terms with the new realities, the government introduced what amounted to the final policy blow. In October 1975, the Ministry of Tourism announced that it had begun to actively sponsor local shipboard entertainment.[13] Not only was this a clear acknowledgment that cruise ships were free to open in port at will, but this decision also had the effect of further diminishing the pool of tourists willing to pay for entertainment in Nassau. The musicians and entertainers were distressed by the news. The entire Over-the-Hill scene had been broken by this time, leaving many clubs reduced to mere drinking establishments with radios, and many more closed for good. This latest decision now threatened the few locally owned clubs still surviving on Bay Street (such as the King and Knights Club and the Drumbeat Club), and King Eric Gibson, then president of the Nightclub Owners and Operators Association, responded immediately. In a front-page story in the *Nassau Tribune,* he called for the removal of Clement Maynard, the minister of tourism:

> "It is time they move this damn man," he declared bluntly. "Maynard has insulted the musicians and entertainers time after time and has proved over and over again that he is not thinking Bahamian. He already killed all the clubs over the hill and now he's killing the ones on Bay Street," Mr. Gibson alleged.... Mr. Gibson's outburst has opened the latest round in a long-standing battle between the nightclub owners and the Ministry over what the operators see as unfair competition from the cruise ships moored at Prince George Wharf.... The Ministry has for years rejected Association appeals for Government action to stop entertainment and the sale of alcoholic beverages aboard the liners while they are in Nassau harbour. Now, Mr. Gibson pointed out, the Ministry has gone a step in the opposite direction by sponsoring its own shows aboard the ships, to further discourage passengers from seeing entertainment ashore. (Mike Lothian, *Nassau Tribune,* October 23, 1975)

The following day, King Eric was joined by Duke Hanna and Richard Moss—presidents of the Bahamas Musicians and Entertainers Union (BMEU) and the BTCU, respectively—who also called for Clement Maynard's resignation. Interestingly, Richard Moss made a direct reference to the Jumbey Village controversy in his comments: "We see this whole concept of having native shows on the ships as very detrimental to the taximen's livelihood. If the Tourism Ministry wants cultural exposure for visitors, then they should exercise their influence to fix up Jumbey Village so the taximen, the people in the area, and the country in general can benefit" (Mike Lothian, *Nassau Tribune,* October 24, 1975). Clearly evident in Moss's comments are the early beginnings of Jumbey Village's transformation from a physical place to a symbolic space—a transformation that continued to gain strength during the 1970s and '80s, in large measure because the government continued to show little political interest in supporting the cultural nationalist priorities that had been at the core of Jumbey Village. When these priorities were seemingly neglected in other registers of Bahamian life—such as the controversy over shipboard entertainment—then Jumbey Village could easily be mobilized as an archetype.

Two political cartoons satirizing the government's policy decision reflect the concern among the leadership of the BTCU, the Nightclub Operators Association, and the BMEU over the effects that this agreement would have on their members. Created by Eddie Minnis—himself an artist and musician of national fame with a stake in this policy change—the first cartoon caricatures Minister of Tourism Clement Maynard in a small rowboat, labeled as an "In Port Cruise Ship." Minister Maynard is sporting floor show attire, and dancing while he explains, "I only tryin' ter make der tourist happy!" (see Figure 11. Published in the *Nassau*

FIGURE 11. Eddie Minnis, "I only tryin' ter make
der tourist happy!" Used with permission.

Guardian on October 27, 1975, the cartoon also makes the most of the fact that
the Bahamian single "Funky Nassau" (performed by the Beginning of the End)
was still very popular, invoking the structure of the first verse as the soundtrack
for Maynard's show. The lyrics of the song read, "Nassau's gone funky, Nassau's
got soul."

The second cartoon, published by Minnis the very next day, shows the presidents of the two unions most affected by this policy asking themselves, "What dat
man tryin' ter do ter we?" as they watch Minister Maynard dancing for the tourists who are standing on the deck of a cruise ship. He is singing again, this time
pleading, "If you go please come again" (see Figure 12). Both of these cartoons illustrate with sharp wit the reaction of musicians and entertainers to the government's

FIGURE 12. Eddie Minnis, "What dat man tryin' ter do ter we?"
Used with permission.

decision while simultaneously holding up for ridicule a minister of tourism who, according to the musicians, was literally taking their jobs.

The calls for cultural awareness and cultivation of a national heritage rooted in blackness did not emanate solely from the margins of the sitting government, however, nor did they emerge only in the form of political satire or as calls for economic protectionism by various constituencies. These calls were amplified and elaborated on by a handful of musicians who consistently wrote music that pointed out the need for (and general lack of) national attention to cultural productions and who often did so in direct opposition to the dominant cosmopolitan discourse of modernity favored by most business leaders and politicians. One song in particular, "Back to the Bush," written by Frank Penn, became an anthem of sorts. Recorded in 1978, it directly challenged this dominant discourse and offered a radical black nationalist alternative. The song's lyrics call for a measure of cultural pride among Bahamians: "In this year, before it's too late / We've got to get one thing straight / Take some pride this place we call home / By playing music of our own." The refrain then makes the source of the music explicit by exclaiming, "In the bush, Lord, in the bush / We've got to stay in the bush."

Although Frank Penn, the noted Freeport-based musician and producer, arranged the song for a dance band (bass, guitar, synths, drum kit) and included a steelpan, the underlying rhythm, as expressed in both the bass guitar line and on the hi-hat, is structured around Ronnie Butler's approach to popular rake-n-scrape (see chapter 3).[14] John Boy and the Mustangs, a band based in Freeport, performed "Back to the Bush." Their dance band sound, combined with the Freeport nightclub scene they performed in, however, suggests a somewhat more complex position, a position that might be called back-to-the-bush cosmopolitanism or, following Kwame Appiah (2006, xvii), a partial cosmopolitanism. This back-to-the-bush movement corresponds in many of its aims to the "cosmopolitan nativist" perspective that Tejumola Olaniyan (2001) articulates in exploring Fela Kuti's career. Bahamian musicians who adopted this back-to-the-bush approach to their material were, in many cases, articulating what their government could not—that is, a progressive, ultramodern sound tied in important ways to the long history of the Bahamas and in particular to the Afro-Bahamian dimensions of that historical experience.[15]

This middle ground took shape in a variety of ways during the 1970s and '80s, as the case studies that follow illustrate, for artists pushed at the boundaries of this middle ground in both directions. These efforts were contrary to the trend, begun during the mid-1960s, toward embracing a musically more transnational aesthetic in the nightclubs of Nassau and Freeport at the expense of local musical conventions (see chapter 3). The rather subtle forms of localizing sound prevalent within the goombay aesthetic were, moreover, dramatically extended, such that local sounds, instruments, and rhythms were often explicitly foregrounded. The musical alternatives to this transnational aesthetic and the earlier goombay aesthetic thus relied heavily on the musical streams of both rake-n-scrape and Junkanoo for their articulation and provided a sonic means of exploring the Bahamas simultaneously as "bush" and cosmopolitan milieu.

"GONNA BUILD A NATION": PERFORMING THE POSTCOLONY

Given the political landscape and the choices available to musicians during this seminal period in Bahamian history, it is not surprising that artists had very different ideas of what "building a nation" might sonically entail. The three case studies that follow illustrate this rich context for performing the nation, for they each articulate in sound a cosmopolitan nativist position deeply informed by and in solidarity with the possibilities of the black power movement and politically invested in the role that Afro-Bahamian heritage should play in shaping the newly independent nation. These case studies, moreover, open a window onto the very different spaces that musicians occupied vis-à-vis the nation during the 1970s and early 1980s.

Tony McKay, better known by his sobriquet Exuma, the Obeah Man, and Tyrone Patrick Fitzgerald, whom most people knew simply as Dr. Offfff, both created music heavily marked as Bahamian in both sound and lyrics. But while Exuma lived and performed abroad throughout most of his career, Dr. Offfff remained in the Bahamas for much of his life, and their respective musical horizons are shaped in part by the fact that they inhabited such different spaces. The members of the Beginning of the End, by contrast, approached their craft with a view toward reminding their audiences in rather more subtle ways of their Bahamian roots while offering an ultramodern and contemporary interpretation of funk, soul, and R&B, as well as an affirmation of black power. Like Dr. Offfff, the Beginning of the End worked by and large in the Nassau scene, and the itineraries that these musicians followed—the spaces they occupied during the course of their careers—are significant in that they reinforce the center-periphery model within the nation (i.e., none of these musicians could have made a career on Cat Island or Long Island). Their careers, moreover, clearly link transnational spaces to local ones, both in the performances of the musicians themselves (i.e., their musical itineraries) and through the very audiences that attended their many performances.

Excursus III: Exuma, the Obeah Man

> Don't molest nobody, unless they mess with somebody.
> —TONY MCKAY, "OBEAH, OBEAH"

Tony McKay was born in Tea Bay, Cat Island, on February 18, 1941, and was christened McFarlane Gregory Anthony Mackey. Though he was born on Cat Island, his family moved to Nassau when he was just six weeks old and took up residence on Canaan Lane in the vicinity of Mason's Addition—a historically Afro-Bahamian neighborhood. He recalls those days and the musical atmosphere in that neighborhood:

> "When I was up in Canaan Lane all the people like Ma Gurdy, Tonka, and Nassi [common names for older Afro-Bahamians] used to come up and go up on Black Hill by the factory and build a big fire and have the jump-in dance and the fire dance.... Any old can, any old goatskin drum. Tonka used to play his nose, and

even used to take his nose to weddings. They were exciting days as things were only just beginning in the entertainment field. There were the pace-setters, Freddy Munnings, George Symonette, Blind Blake, Spence—now Spence is one of the greatest guitarists in the world—Sweet Richard, Peaches, my friend Fireball Freddy." (Duggan 1973)

The performances McKay remembered were backed by makeshift rake-n-scrape accompaniment and referenced both African and "Out Island" memories, reminding those present of the legacy to which Afro-Bahamians held claim. These performances were only part of his musical experience in Nassau, however, because McKay happened to grow up during the formative years of the entertainment industry, gaining firsthand exposure to the great performers of the 1940s and '50s. These formative experiences notwithstanding, McKay was not at first interested in pursuing a musical career. In fact, he relocated to New York City to study architecture when he was seventeen, and it was not until he immersed himself in the Greenwich Village scene of the late 1950s and early 1960s that he found himself compelled to create music and art (see Figure 13). McKay recalled: "I found I was more drawn towards music. . . . I had an old beaten guitar that I used to play. It was cold in New York and I got lonely and fantasized a lot. I started writing songs and that eased the loneliness some" (*Nassau Tribune*, December 24, 1982). The social and political power of the scene was as significant as the musical draw, for he came to identify with the civil rights movement and with black power and applied his understanding of these U.S.-based movements to an exploration of Bahamian life.

McKay made his debut in Greenwich Village at the Café Wha? in 1963 amid a whole generation of artists who have since risen to international prominence—Bob Dylan; Joan Baez; Peter, Paul, and Mary; and Richie Havens to name but a few. By this time, he was already well on his way to becoming Exuma, the Obeah Man. Exuma was not merely a stage name—it had deep spiritual significance for McKay, because he was deeply invested in the practice of obeah even before he began performing. His lyrics, art, and approach to creating music all drew on the power of obeah, its subversive place within the Bahamian imagination, and his convictions regarding its relevance as a site of meaningful resistance. Given the place obeah occupies in the Caribbean and Bahamian popular imagination—marked by associations with evil and harm more than with good, with illicit rather than licensed spirituality—Exuma's approach to obeah was doubly powerful, for he mobilized obeah in a postcolonial Christian context and reconfigured it as a force for good.[16] McKay's approach to obeah was captured in an interview he gave in 1973. Ann Duggan of the *Nassau Guardian* asked him this question: "Obeah features very largely in your compositions. Do you have any experience of the workings of Obeah?" Tony answered:

FIGURE 13. Tony McKay, a.k.a. Exuma, the Obeah Man.
Photo by Derek Smith. Used with permission.

Well, I don't like to discuss it in public and all I can tell you is that obeah is the sky, the sea, the spirit what we are drinking now, cerasee [herbal remedy], it is the spirit of past, present, and future. Obeah is God. A lot of people misunderstand it. Moses, for example, was the biggest obeah man ever. . . . Obeah is spiritual, physical, life and death. It can be used for good or evil. I myself never use it for evil. It is being aware of forces around you that are here on earth. We are not the only living organisms in this atmosphere. There is a fifth, sixth, and seventh plane. (Duggan 1973)

Exuma also said that "the Obeah Man knows of all the things that bother people and how to make them feel good. . . . I am an Obeah man of music" (*Nassau Tribune,* December 24, 1982). So he was careful to emphasize the positive power of obeah, but the implicit threat that, if the need arose, obeah could be turned toward malevolent or retributive ends remains part of the context in which Exuma's claim is situated. And it is precisely this threat that forms the basis of the power of his lyric included as the epigraph to this section—"Don't molest nobody, unless they mess with somebody."

In a religious climate in which Christianity explicitly figured in the new nation's constitution, and in a political atmosphere more interested in fostering cosmopolitan connections than supporting Afro-Bahamian cultural reclamation, Exuma's career was particularly salient. It signaled a clear counternarrative of belief and practice that, it is worth remembering, had a long-standing presence in Bahamian life. It also provided a foundation for the project of cultural reclamation that would accompany Exuma throughout his career, in that he was laying claim to practices that could be tied to African cosmology and could therefore be understood as a spiritual antecedent to the Christianization of the Bahamas.

Ken Bilby points out that "because the semantic domain of this term [obeah] almost always overlaps with spiritual concepts that have profound existential significance—and because, in the minds of those who speak it, the term almost invariably remains associated with an ancestral African past—it occupies a particularly prominent and highly-charged place in this zone of cultural contestation" (Bilby 2008, 1). Exuma worked to ensure that his point could not be missed, adopting larger-than-life costumes that included flowing capes, oversized hats with beadwork or feathers, and percussion instruments (rattles and noisemakers) variously attached to his body, all designed to complement his lyrics and his writing. The resonances (real or imaginary) with African musical aesthetics and cosmology were calculated and deliberate: "I fashioned my costumes after those worn by African witch doctors," he said (*Nassau Tribune*, December 24, 1982). His musical style, moreover, was deeply influenced by the rake-n-scrape and Junkanoo he had grown up listening to—a sound that he fitted easily to the folk music scene in 1960s New York City. This approach translated to a productive career in which Exuma developed a powerful lyrical style and an eclectic musical vocabulary, "introducing the Bahamas to the world and reintroducing Bahamians to themselves" (Charles Carter interview with Tony McKay on *Bahamians*, radio program aired February 3, 2001).

Alfred Sears, one of Tony's close friends, reflects on McKay's career:

An aspect of our emerging sense of nationalism was to examine those things about ourselves that connected us to Africa. And as you know our history was one where anything associated with Africa was denigrated. He celebrated the knowledge of medicine and herbs and plants that was passed down from generation to generation for hundreds of years from Africa through the Middle Passage and in the Bahamas. And you know, whenever you visited him at his apartment on Fourteenth Street in Manhattan down at the Village, he always gave you, you know, some cerasee. Especially in the winter, you know, he gave you a bottle of cerasee to take. In other words, it was real; he lived it. And I think that the celebration of our heritage, especially the African aspect of our heritage, was one that helped to affirm us as a people and helped to nourish our evolving sense of nationalism. (Charles Carter interview with Alfred Sears on *Bahamians*, radio program aired February 3, 2001)

Exuma's musical approach was informed, then, by his commitment to alternative readings of Bahamian spirituality, by his clear sense that the African diaspora in general, and Afro-Bahamians in particular, had important stories to tell and a significant heritage to claim, and by his consistent use of Bahamian musical language to frame these aesthetic and sociopolitical concerns. Exuma spent much of his adult life abroad, living in New York, New Orleans, and Miami when he wasn't touring. At the height of his career, he played with artists like Patti La-Belle, Curtis Mayfield, Toots and the Maytals, Steppenwolf, Peter Tosh, the Neville Brothers, Sly and the Family Stone, and the Edwin Hawkins Singers. He played the New Orleans Jazz and Heritage Festival consistently from 1978 to 1991, but his place as a Bahamian musician of international fame was never quite solidified within the Bahamas until after he passed away on January 25, 1997. Alfred Sears remembers this well:

> So as an artist we see this incredible struggle with limited resources to maintain the integrity of his voice. And I think that we as a country, we really need to reflect, because I can say, having represented him during the later part of his life, that it was very difficult for him in the Bahamas. He was not accorded the respect of an artist who had made the contribution that he had made and was still making. He was not accorded the opportunities to maintain a source of earnings, to maintain a dignified existence. And I think that, you know, Bob Marley says, "How long shall they kill our prophets while we stand aside and look?" And I think that it is very interesting that we allow one of our prophets, someone who celebrated us, whose only purpose in life was to really project the Bahamian cultural heritage and folklore, in his own country was not given or allowed to have the kind of dignified existence that he deserved. (Charles Carter interview with Alfred Sears on *Bahamians*, radio program aired February 3, 2001)

Exuma, then, found it easier to live and work abroad than at home. Part of the equivocal reception he experienced in the Bahamas, undoubtedly, stems from the controversial nature of his explicit references to obeah—the uncomfortable claims he made through his music—especially at a time when modernity and cosmopolitanism were the principal mode of authorized expression in Nassau's political and economic discourses. His song "Exuma, the Obeah Man" illustrates his departure from that discursive frame quite well (see Example 18):

> I came down on a lightning bolt,
> Nine months in my mother's belly.
> When I was born, the midwife scream and shout.
> I had fire and brimstone coming out of my mouth.
>
> I'm Exuma, I'm the Obeah Man.
> Exuma was my name when I lived in the stars.
> Exuma was the planet that once lit Mars.

I have the voices of many in my throat.
The teeth of a frog and the tail of a goat.

I'm Exuma, I'm the Obeah Man.

Recorded and released in 1970, "Exuma, the Obeah Man" was McKay's first single, and it incorporates several stylistic markers that would become hallmarks of his style throughout his career. First, the song is designed to work as a voice-and-guitar coffeehouse number—it would work well, that is, even if the accompaniment were reduced to syncopated chordal strumming on the guitar. Second, the performance is driven by its rhythmic possibilities more than by its melodic content—the highly syncopated performance of the lyrics and the percussive shout that characterizes his vocal delivery in the upper register of the melody are more important to the song's musical statement than the actual pentatonically driven melodic content. Third, McKay explores and even exploits the ineffable aspects of obeah through his lyrics. He consistently performs an alternative belief that predates the Christian foundation proclaimed in the Bahamian constitution. Fourth, many ambient noises are incorporated into the song, including, crickets, footsteps, dogs, whistles, and shouts.[17] These sounds are as much a part of the soundscape of Exuma's performances as the instruments and vocals he layers into the mix. The effect of these additional sound sources is to create a deep sound field, one that is "live"—even "lived"—in a way that traditional "studio" recordings rarely project. It also serves to decenter the musical content of the track, forcing on the listener an awareness of other people, sounds, and agendas. And fifth, the rhythmic base of the tune is drawn straight from rake-n-scrape and Junkanoo sensibilities—in this case, the cowbells play a skeletal rake-n-scrape rhythm while simultaneously invoking Junkanoo through sonic association.

These features remained prevalent markers throughout McKay's musical and artistic life. He wrote songs that musically enact séances and graveyard rituals ("Séance in the Sixth Fret" and "Paul Simon Nontooth," respectively), songs that offer strong references to obeah throughout (e.g., "Obeah, Obeah," "Damn Fool," and "Exuma's Reincarnation"), songs that illustrate his commitment to foregrounding Junkanoo and rake-n-scrape (e.g., "Junkanoo," "Cat Island Rake-n-scrape Band," and "Rushing through the Crowd"), and politically powerful songs such as "Pay Me What You Owe Me," a song that speaks out in favor of reparations for slavery.

The themes McKay drew on in his lyrics and the prevalence of Junkanoo and rake-n-scrape in his musical style combined with his magnetic and otherworldly stage presence afforded McKay fame abroad. But these very same characteristics caused his reception in the Bahamas to remain equivocal and somewhat ambiguous. He had his loyal fans, to be sure, but he remained a threatening (or at least a potentially threatening) presence in the newly independent Bahamas. An open

EXAMPLE 18. "Exuma, the Obeah Man."

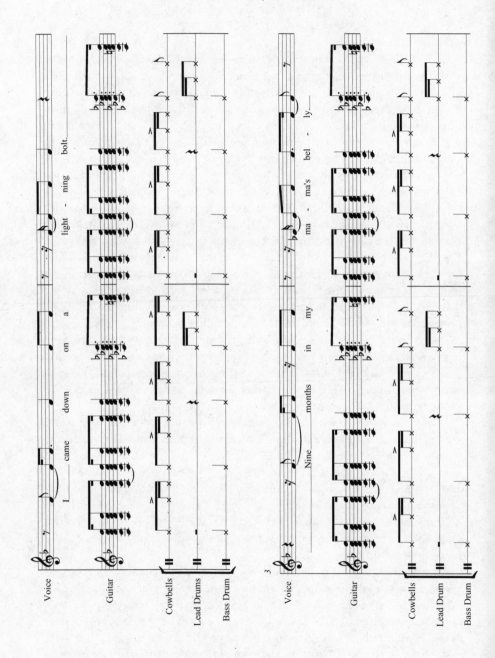

EXAMPLE 18. *continued*

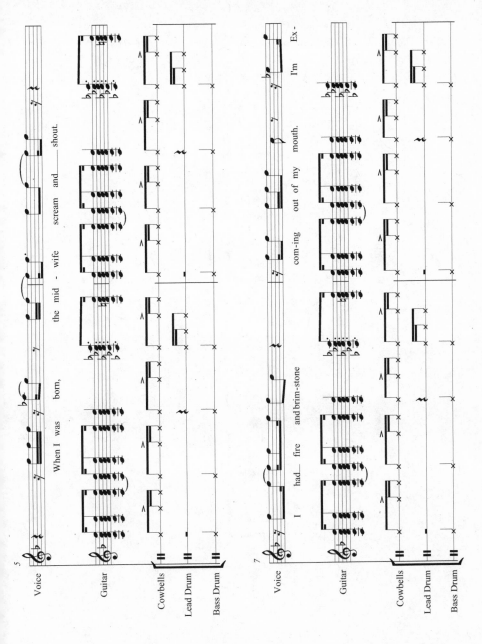

(continued)

EXAMPLE 18. *continued*

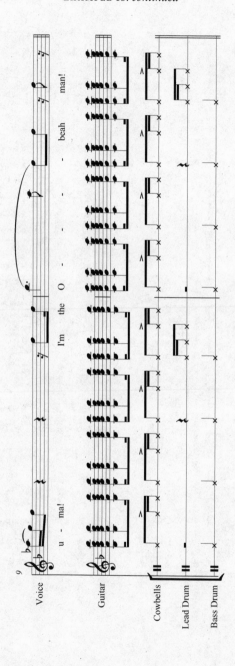

letter, written by Jackson Burnside (renowned architect and close friend of Exuma's) on the occasion of the seven-year anniversary of Exuma's passing, offers an incisive treatment of Bahamians' ambivalent relationship to the musician:

> I started this letter a few days after Tony died, and had to stop because I was too angry. I was angry, not at God's infinite wisdom, but at the flood of recognition that came to this true Bahamian Hero after his death. Many of the tributes were genuine, I am sure. However, it is my opinion that a significant portion of the praise was not only too late but, in Tony's words, not "true-true." I was angry and bitter because, in my opinion, it was precisely a lack of recognition and respect from his own that caused Tony McKay's broken heart. His heart was broken long before he died. His soul cried because, in a world that would have loved "pasteurized" culture, Tony stayed true-true and in his own home town he was denied. . . . I was angry and bitter at what I saw as hypocrisy. We are so quick to deny ourselves. Our "education" has so conditioned us, that we voluntarily reject our own culture. We refuse to recognize our own value when we see it. We seem to insist that we define ourselves by somebody else's definition, to be valid. A wise old Bahamian grandfather used to say "You better see what you lookin at." We looked at "Exuma," but as is typical of the treatment of hometown prophets, we did not see him. . . . How long will it take before we see that the best people to promote our rich legacy to the world are those who thoroughly immerse themselves in our culture and traditions? . . . I was angry and bitter, because the emotions I felt did not allow me to feel love in the face of what I saw as rejection; respect in the face of dishonesty. (Jackson Burnside, "A Tribute to the Obeah Man," *Nassau Guardian,* January 16, 2004)

Tony McKay showed Bahamians a way to be Bahamian after colonialism. He helped to nourish a sense of Bahamian nationalism, as Alfred Sears put it, but his was a "true-true" path that necessarily included obeah, incorporated direct references to African antecedents, ascribed to black power, and drew heavily on traditional Bahamian musical materials. For many Bahamians, this path was tantamount to an antimodern, anticosmopolitan stance, in spite of the PLP having seized power from the United Bahamian Party by setting the Bahamas on this very path. While it is clear that Exuma's career did not hew to the modernist, cosmopolitan (and pragmatic) stance now promulgated by the government, it did offer a compelling, cosmopolitan nativist alternative. The truly subversive nature of his project has yet to be fully explored as an artistic inheritance.

Excursus IV: Dr. Offfff

Tyrone Fitzgerald, or Dr. Offfff, as he came to be known, was born on March 17, 1948, and passed away on November 27, 2002, at the age of fifty-four. His career was rooted in Junkanoo and informed by the formative experiences of "rushin'" in a Junkanoo group. In a reflection on his early musical experiences, Dr. Offfff explained his fascination:

My first contact with Junkanoo began as a child of five, growing up in Centreville in the heart of Nassau, the capital of the Bahamas. I had heard of Junkanoo before but I was frightened because I didn't know what it was. The music sounded fine; it was the people, the way they acted, the way they looked that seemed wrong. Everybody seemed to be happy but in a trance. They wore masks and all kinds of paintings on their faces. Some jumped up and down, some just let out loud screams. All I could do was hold on to my mother's neck and pray because my father, who had brought us to the celebration, had vanished into one of the groups. He had a drum on his shoulder and, as he began to beat, the crowds opened and sucked him in and he was gone. That was 4 a.m. in the morning. I didn't see him anymore until a day later. On that day my mother swore that was her last day at a Junkanoo celebration, because she too was afraid. She had only decided to go to the celebration because I asked her, over and over again. But that was all right by me if she said she wasn't going back, because I had already decided that I wasn't going back no more. And I didn't for three years, but during that time rushed up and down the road with my friends, using a paint kettle for a drum with a piece of plastic pulled around one end and fastened with tube rings cut from the inner tubes of car tires. The cowbells were made from empty tomato paste cans mashed at the open end with small stones placed inside for sound. But it was not until the age of eight that I got my first real contact with Junkanoo. It was during the month of October. My father and his group were practicing for the upcoming Guy Fawkes celebration; it was the day before Halloween. They were practicing in the street next to our house. I was standing on the side watching them. Suddenly my father stopped beating his drum, raised his hand in the air, and the music stopped.

He then turned to one of the other drummers and began shouting at him, asking him if he could not beat any better than that! The drummer muttered a few words back at him, and that's when my father told him, "I bet even my young son there can beat better than that." Then the drummer turned towards me and said, "Who, him?" My father said, "Yeah, him!" The drummer laughed, took off his drum, passed it to me, and said, "Here Boy, go make your pa shame." I didn't know what to do so I hesitated, then my father said "Go on, show him. Beat the drum." I put the drum over my shoulder (it was very heavy), closed my eyes, and began to beat. There was silence, I could only hear the sounds of my drum. "Boom stick boom ka stick-boom stick boom ka stick." And then I heard it: the cowbells started ringing, the whistles started blowing, then the other drums joined in, and immediately I was caught up in the magnificent sound of sounds, the sounds of the Unknown, the sound of Junkanoo.

It was then that I realized what I had witnessed three years before—the trance, the happy faces. Those were the faces and expressions of the feeling of freedom, of inner peace—peace of mind that one feels once they have been caught up in the sounds of Junkanoo. It is a feeling one can't fully explain. Try it!

Since that first contact that October night, the sound has haunted me ever since—like a spirit within me it keeps begging to come out. (Fitzgerald 1981)

This account draws attention to the spiritual depth so consistently attributed to the experience of Junkanoo (see chapter 4). It offers a glimpse into the power of Junkanoo as religious experience. Trance, joy, and inner peace are the product of participation (contact), the result of involvement in the celebration of Junkanoo. Like Exuma, the Obeah Man, Fitzgerald saw the implicit spirituality of musical performance as a form of power. While Exuma chose to explore this power primarily through recourse to obeah, Fitzgerald found himself drawn to Junkanoo as a deeply spiritual practice. The rather less proscribed character of Junkanoo compared to obeah within the Bahamas afforded Fitzgerald less ambiguous and generally more enthusiastic local support than Exuma was granted, but a claim to the power of spirituality as a pre-Christian, Afro-Bahamian heritage was explicitly articulated in both of their careers.

As Tyrone Fitzgerald began to immerse himself in Junkanoo, he gradually became aware of the potential of these rhythms as vehicles for popular music. He continued to perform as a Junkanoo, forming his own supremely successful and famous group, called PIGS (Power, Integrity, Guts, Strength) in the early 1970s. But he also began to write music that incorporated Junkanoo rhythms into a dance band format. His initial explorations in this vein, also during the early 1970s, included cowriting the hit song "Funky Nassau" with Ray Munnings. I will discuss this song later in the context of the Beginning of the End, but it is important to note here that Fitzgerald rapidly gained a reputation as a particularly talented songwriter and performer during the 1970s.

By the early 1980s, Fitzgerald had successfully innovated a sound that combined the power of festival Junkanoo with an electric dance band. Unlike Ronnie Butler, who had deliberately translated the rhythms of rake-n-scrape into a dance band context without recourse to the saw, goat-skinned drum, and accordion, Fitzgerald chose to augment his dance band with a full complement of Junkanoo percussion (a Junkanoo side), thereby making Junkanoo central to the sound and visual character of the group (see Figure 14). Not only were these Junkanoos part of the band, but also the entire aesthetic of the band's performances was driven by the ineffable qualities of festival Junkanoo. Fitzgerald, who by this time was better known as Dr. Offfff, always performed as a Junkanoo (i.e., masked), and the percussionists, who were also masked, were tasked with rushing through the crowd, parading on stage, and in general making the experience as participatory as possible for the audience. When asked by Charles Carter about his practice of masking, Dr. Offfff remembered:

I know that presenting the Junkanoo just like that—everybody wear whatever they wanna wear—it didn't have that right presence, or the presentation wasn't proper enough. So we came up with a costume that we can all dress alike. One of the

FIGURE 14. Tyrone Fitzgerald, a.k.a. Dr. Offfff, at right, at the New Orleans Jazz and Heritage Festival in the 1980s. Photo courtesy of Ronald Simms.

mystiques of Junkanoo is what they call the faceless face. And so the mask[s] preserve that image. And so as a result of that, if you notice that Junkanoo was held first thing in the morning, that's like 4 o'clock in the morning. It's dark. Nobody could hardly see anybody, but at that time they would paint up their face with coally [charcoal] or flour, or something like that, but they always sorta hide their identities. And that's, like I say, I took that as a spinoff to carry straight through. (Charles Carter interview with Tyrone Fitzgerald on *Bahamians*, radio program aired March 21, 1998)

Dr. Offfff, in short, found a way to compress (translate) the vitality of festival Junkanoo into a staged popular music performance. Asked to explain this approach, one of Dr. Offfff's bell players, Patrick Cash, reflected:

"We play a traditional form of Junkanoo music that is very basic; we concentrate on the down beat, in this aspect we are not commercial. We scare the shit out of a lot of people, but then, too, you must remember that Junkanoo is 4 a. m. music, when no one on this planet is sure of what's going on and that's scary, terrifying if you ask me. . . . We try to make/take whatever is happening in Junkanoo and electrify it," maintains Cash. "Our blend of music fits the 'Mythos' of now and goes strictly back into the past—right into the embryo—the bloodstream (and the heart). Every group doesn't have that. We don't like to say pop, we like to say the sound of Junkanoo because anybody can dance to it, or participate. There's a

sound that is familiar to everybody, plus tension—lots of tension." (H.W. Munnings, "Dr. Offfff," *Junkanoo* August/September/October 1981, 15)

This explicit link between Junkanoo and "the past," between Junkanoo and
"the bloodstream" constitutes an unequivocal statement of Afro-Bahamian power
within a cultural nationalist frame—an affirmation of Junkanoo's place within
Bahamian life (in this case both temporal/historical and physical/biological).
And this affirmation, whereby Junkanoo is equated to being Bahamian, also makes
a powerful political claim in that it reinforces the value and importance of Afro-
Bahamian cultural heritage. That said, Dr. Offfff's musical choices were far more
palatable to the government than were Exuma's, in part because the work of sub-
suming Junkanoo within a Christian context had already enjoyed a long history
within Bahamian society. Dr. Offfff's musical and artistic project was, as such,
considerably less threatening to the vision of a modern, cosmopolitan Bahamas
than was Exuma's.

Another factor contributing to Dr. Offfff's less ambiguous reception, however,
is rooted in his very different engagement with black power vis-à-vis Exuma.
While Exuma wrote songs explicitly linking himself to the sharp edge of civil
rights and black power (e.g., "Pay Me What You Owe Me"), Dr. Offfff chose to
draw on the rhetoric of social uplift and national solidarity, further ameliorating
the potentially subversive aspects of his Junkanoo-based performances in the
process. As such, he wrote songs like "Get Involved" and "Let's Do More" instead
of engaging with the more radical themes that animated the discourse of black
power in the late 1970s and early 1980s. "Get Involved" gently exhorts the younger
generations of Bahamians to get socially and politically involved: "Leave all the
people things alone / There are other ways to get involved" and "Don't be no fool,
stay in school / Let your mind become a tool."

"Let's Do More," moreover, overtly serves the interests of the Ministry of Tourism, for it is addressed to Bahamians and encourages them to make a better impression on the tourists that continue to flock to the Bahamas. The chorus intones,
"Let's do more in '84 / let's keep it up, just like before / Let's do more in '84 / and
bring more people to our shores." This song points to the deep sense of national
solidarity that continued to pervade public discourse in the Bahamas even in
1984, eleven years after independence. Dr. Offfff was not the least bit averse to
writing a song reminding his fellow Bahamians that their livelihoods and the nation's future rested on the quality of their relationship to the tourist sector.

It is significant, however, that Dr. Offfff effectively inverts the intended audience of the long-standing genre of tourist-driven songs in the Bahamas. Unlike
songs such as "Island in the Sun" and "Calypso Island," written in the middle of
the twentieth century and directed at tourists themselves, "Let's Do More" is directed at Bahamians. Bahamians are reminded of the great benefits that they

have on offer for the tourists; Bahamians are reminded that they need tourists. Also significant here is the link established between the contemporary moment (of struggle) and the pre-national past (the golden age of tourism of the 1950s and '60s). In 1984, when the song was released, Dr. Offfff pointed his audience to a past when Bahamians knew how to draw tourists to Nassau: "Let's keep it up, *just like before.*" This inversion of audience and the concomitant idealized invocation of the past are themselves signs of significant shifts in the market, which had matured into mass tourism by the 1980s and was experiencing and exhibiting the ambivalence and even the resentment of a postcolonial local service industry.

When he wasn't writing songs in this vein, Dr. Offfff was explicitly promoting the art of Junkanoo by producing songs such as "Junk, Junk, Junkanoo" and the instrumentals "Last Lap" and "Straight Through." The instrumentals are eminently danceable versions of Junkanoo rushes, and the band's sound is driven and anchored by the powerful Junkanoo section. "Junk, Junk, Junkanoo" celebrates dancing to the Junkanoo: "Listen all you people, all around / Listen to the sound we're putting down. / Now that's right girls, you're doing it, get in line / Just move on the side, let the gentleman take his time / and dance the Junkanoo." Dr. Offfff discussed this song in an interview with Charles Carter:

> The first song that we actually recorded was "Junkanoo," which was released as "Junk, Junk, Junkanoo." But "Junkanoo," when we recorded "Junkanoo," we recorded that at Elite Studios. And to be as authentic as possible, we didn't begin to record until four o'clock in the morning. So we camped out in the studio until four o'clock to start to record Junkanoo, so that we could have that actual feeling, you know, that Bay Street, that natural feeling. We went on for about half hour, because you know, when Junkanoo start you can't stop it. Once the rhythm got going and we really got into it like that, and so, as a result of that, we tried to keep as close to the tradition as possible, and we were able to come up with something that everybody, like I say, could identify with because that was sure energy and feeling. (Charles Carter interview with Dr. Offfff on *Bahamians,* radio program aired March 21, 1998)

I now turn briefly to the nature of the sounds that Dr. Offfff was "putting down" in order to illustrate that the sonic and visual dimensions of his performances remained much more open to political and cultural mobilization than did his lyrics. Dr. Offfff's sound consisted primarily of installing the and-ONE and kalik rhythms of Junkanoo as the dominant markers of his arrangements. The drum kit reinforced the kalik of the cowbells on the hi-hat and also assisted the goat-skinned drums in achieving a powerful accent on the downbeat by playing on the ONE while the goat-skinned drummers played and-ONE. This rhythmic idea is at the heart of most of Dr. Offfff's recordings, and it is augmented by the remaining Junkanoo instruments as well as the melodic and harmonic instruments of the electric dance band. Isaiah Taylor, the leader of High Voltage, the band that accompanied Dr. Offfff in concert, explains: "The bass, the goatskin drums, the kick drum supposed to lock with the down at all times—always—'cause you have to think Bay Street. If you're not thinking Bay Street, you not gonna get it right" (Charles Carter interview with Isaiah Taylor on *Bahamians*, radio program aired March 21, 1998). The active role played by the "Junkanoo side" in the band instills some of the same "live" or "lived" quality into Dr. Offfff's recordings that is present in Exuma's recordings. One of the ways that this "liveness" is created in Dr. Offfff's recordings is by creating short breaks during which the Junkanoo side "solos." At the 2'55" mark of "Get Involved," for instance, the entire band drops out and the Junkanoo side "rushes out" for approximately 30 seconds. The Junkanoo side is, in this sense, treated as a whole—as an instrument—within the arrangements.

All of these arranging techniques, however, worked on record only to the extent that people knew what Dr. Offfff was attempting to achieve during live performances. His stage performance relied heavily on the visual artistry of Junkanoo costumes, the conventions of Junkanoo dancing and rushing, the sheer size of his band and the musicians' interactions on stage, and the willingness of his audience to participate in the show as though they were attending Junkanoo on Boxing Day. Dr. Offfff thus mobilized the long history of Junkanoo in order to promote a vision of Bahamian culture that, while drawn from Afro-Bahamian roots, was simultaneously modern and cosmopolitan in presentation—the electric dance band wedded to the Junkanoo mask. Dr. Offfff was, in this sense, the consummate cosmopolitan nativist, and he was not satisfied with the role of pioneer, for he was convinced that his innovations could provide a foundation for contemporary Bahamian popular music and afford Bahamian musicians entry into the international market. In fact, in an editorial published in 1981, he succinctly prefigured the words and approach of Nicolette Bethel (see epigraph to chapter 1): "Dr. Offfff has set out to prove that the Bahamas musical heritage and national beat, Junkanoo, has a place in the world of music. 'We have something nobody else in the world has—the down beat,' Fitzgerald said, 'and the sooner our musicians realize this, the better it will be for them'" (H. W. Munnings, "Dr. Offfff," *Junkanoo* August/September/October 1981, 15–16).

Unlike many of his contemporaries, Dr. Offfff never chose to pursue music as a full-time career, but he nevertheless managed to make a significant impact on how a whole generation of musicians interacted with the rhythms of Junkanoo in their performances and compositions. Musicians did, in fact, begin writing songs in Dr. Offfff's popular Junkanoo idiom, and it should come as no surprise that the Bahamian band that has achieved the most international notoriety since the 1990s—the Baha Men—began its career as the electric dance band backing Dr. Offfff.[18]

Excursus V: The Beginning of the End and "Funky Nassau"

The Beginning of the End was a project deeply rooted in the Munnings family. The band formed in 1969 and included three sons of Freddie Munnings Sr.: Raphael "Ray" Munnings on vocals and organ (see Figure 15); Roy Munnings on guitar; and Frank Munnings on drums. A cousin, Fred Henfield, rounded out the quartet on bass, and the band rehearsed at the Ghana Room (which had been renamed the Lion's Den by Ray Munnings in the late 1960s). The Ghana Room/ Lion's Den, owned by Freddie Munnings Sr. and originally named in honor of Ghanaian independence, was an indoor club that had been added to the Cat and Fiddle complex in 1957. Because of the general decline in nightclub business, the club offered an excellent and relatively uninterrupted rehearsal space for the Beginning of the End, and it was here that they developed their musical approach. All four of the core members were already veterans of several cover bands of the sort discussed in chapter 3, and they were not interested in continuing their careers in this transnational aesthetic.

The band ultimately developed a sound best exemplified by their hit song "Funky Nassau," which was cowritten by Ray Munnings and Tyrone Fitzgerald (Dr. Offfff). In an interview with Charles Carter, Dr. Offfff recalled how the song was composed:

> Myself and Ray, we got together. Ray and those, they were practicing in the Ghana Room. And I would go and attend the practices because I enjoyed their music. They had a rhythm that was truly their own. They weren't copying anybody else per se. They came up with a natural rhythm that they felt for each other. And during one of their sessions practicing, I just sat there, and as I listened, I could hear these words coming out the music they were playing. They weren't playing anything particular. They just, what you would call, jamming. And as a result of that, myself and Ray got together with the words that we had come up with, and we came together and filled the words in with the rhythm that we decided would be the best way to present the song. (Charles Carter interview with Tyrone Fitzgerald on *Bahamians,* radio program aired March 21, 1998)

The Beginning of the End went on to record the song as the B-side of a forty-five in November 1970 (the A-side was "Gee Whiz It's Christmas"). The band had borrowed two thousand dollars from Ray's uncle, Vernal Percival Munnings, which was just enough to cover travel to Florida and studio time at Miami's Criteria Studios and a pressing of five thousand copies. When they returned to Nassau with the forty-five, the A-side received quite a bit of attention from deejays because it was the right season for "Gee Whiz It's Christmas." In fact, the first pressing sold out in a matter of four or five weeks. As Ray Munnings tells it, however, "Funky Nassau" did not generate any airplay in Nassau at first. The story of "Funky Nassau" is itself a story of itineraries and travels (of both sounds and bodies):

FIGURE 15. Ray Munnings. Photo courtesy of Ray Munnings.

We were driving around Nassau listening to WMBM, you know, one of the major black radio stations in Miami, when we heard this deejay, Fred Hanna was his name, play "Funky Nassau" and say right on the air, "You guys better get up here, because you've got a hit on your hands." He had heard the recording at the Elk's Lodge on Seventh Avenue in Miami. You know, he had Bahamian roots and would go there, 'cause lots of Bahamians living in Miami would, you know, visit the lodge there. Anyway, another Bahamian who worked and lived in Miami had traveled to Nassau for the holidays and picked up the forty-five, and he had put it in the juke-box at the Elk's Lodge. So in comes Fred Hanna, and he's like, "How come I'm program director at WMBM and I haven't heard of this?" So he started playing it on the air and asking people to guess who this band was. And of course nobody knew, because nobody ever heard of the Beginning of the End. But people were loving it, and it started to get picked up on other radio stations. So when he said that on the air, and we heard him, we jumped on the next plane to Miami, and the rest, as they say, is history.

We got up there, and that's when we got to know Henry Stone at Alston Records. This was like January or early February 1971, and we signed a distribution deal with Henry Stone. So he said, "Of course you'll need to replace 'Gee Whiz It's Christmas.'" So he had a small studio called Tone Distributors, and we sent back to Nassau for the rest of the band and recorded "Funky Nassau Part 2." We slid the original "Funky Nassau" to the A-side and put Part 2 on the B-side, and that forty-five just took off. In the meantime, we started working on the album, and that was released in August or September 1971. But the problem was that we could have jumped on an east-coast tour in the early summer, but the rest of the band didn't think we were ready and wanted to go back to Nassau to rehearse. You know, "Funky Nassau" peaked in July, and we made the mistake of not touring. So the single went out there and did what it should have done, and we let it pass us by.

A few years later, we tried again with a different record label and released an album called *Superwoman,* and we had two more chances to go on big tours. The first was that we were supposed to open a series of shows for Marvin Gaye in New York, but there was no reciprocal agreement with the Bahamas musicians union, so that deal fell apart. The union in New York just said, "Why should we bring a band in here all the way from the Bahamas when our guys can't go there and play?" And then we were supposed to go out and open for the Babylon by Bus Tour that Marley had planned, but he broke his toe and had to change the plan, and we fell out of that plan in the end. It's like it wasn't meant to be for us, but "Funky Nassau" keeps on going. It just left us behind back then, and we haven't caught up yet. (Raphael Munnings, interview with the author, July 11, 2009)

The single did experience a rapid ascent up the charts. The band, having signed on with Alston Records in January 1971, repackaged "Funky Nassau" as Part 1 and Part 2, and by May the single had made it into the Hot 100 Pop-Single-Chart.[19] "Funky Nassau" quickly climbed the charts in the United States, sailing to number 15 on the *Billboard* Hot 100 Pop-Single-Chart, to number 10 on the Cash Box Top 100 Singles Chart, and to number 7 on the *Billboard* Best Selling Soul Singles Chart, and all signs pointed to a long and productive international career for the band.[20] Unfortunately, a string of bitter disappointments cut short any hope of capitalizing on the band's promising start. After rapidly writing and recording the material included on their debut album in the spring of 1971, the Beginning of the End chose to return to Nassau and rehearse instead of going on an east coast tour that was being organized by Burt Oceans and Henry Stone. The rationale was good, in that band members wanted to be musically as tight as possible before they exposed themselves to new audiences, but the opportunity to tour passed as the success of their single waned. This meant that their LP, released in the summer of 1971, languished without any promotion and did not sell as well as it would have with a concerted marketing and touring schedule. The Beginning of the End thus found itself relegated to playing the club scene in the Bahamas, isolated from the market in which their music was being played and sold. These developments effectively stopped the band's career in its tracks.

Several years later, Ray Munnings attempted to break through once more, this time with a different management group headed by Don Taylor (then Bob Marley's manager). The band recorded and released an album in 1976, called *Superwoman*, but this album did not succeed at the level of "Funky Nassau." Another series of potential concerts in support of the project was planned and subsequently cancelled.[21] These developments left a disappointed Ray Munnings playing around Nassau when he could and eventually turning his attention to a new career as a videographer.

The Beginning of the End's short burst of creative energy, however, made a lasting impression on a whole generation of musicians in the Bahamas. This was due in part to their unapologetic integration of traditional rake-n-scrape rhythms with core Junkanoo rhythms. The "natural rhythm" that Dr. Offfff refers to in his remarks about "Funky Nassau" is perhaps the best illustration of Ed Moxey's contention that "rake 'n scrape is not really rake and scrape, it is really goombay music, an African sound . . . the music for Junkanoo is not 'Junkanoo music' but 'goombay music at the Junkanoo festival.' It's all just a variation of goombay music" (quoted in Lomer 2002, 125–27). The band simultaneously deployed core rhythms from both rake-n-scrape and Junkanoo within the arrangement, thereby creating a sound that was "truly their own."[22]

Though the song is performed in 4/4 meter, each measure develops as two cells of 2/4. Within this structure, the band creates an alternating flow between a relatively static antecedent cell and a heavily marked consequent—heavily marked, that is, by accent patterns particular to rake-n-scrape and Junkanoo. The importance of the *and* of two (or the upbeat) in rake-n-scrape is made explicit through the kick drum's involvement on the *and* of the fourth beat of each measure during the verse (see Example 19, measures 4–8). The dominant role of the downbeat in Junkanoo, often in combination with the upbeat (i.e., ONE or and-ONE), is also present in this performance. The first four measures find the tom and kick drum combining to achieve the and-ONE feel of Junkanoo, and this feel continues into the downbeat of measure 5, when the rake-n-scrape rhythm takes over. The phrase structure after the four-measure introduction develops as follows: 4 + 4; 4 + 2; 4 + 4, 4 + 2. The Junkanoo beat reappears at the beginning of each new phrase group, providing closure to the preceding phrase and opening onto the next group in the process (i.e., on the first beat of measures 13, 19, 27, and 33 [not transcribed]). It is preceded, moreover, by a short fill on toms and snare that

EXAMPLE 19. "Funky Nassau," the Beginning of the End. Cowritten by Tyrone Patrick Fitzgerald and Raphael Munnings. Transcription used with the permission of Raphael (Ray) Munnings.

EXAMPLE 19. *continued*

(continued)

EXAMPLE 19. *continued*

EXAMPLE 19. *continued*

(continued)

EXAMPLE 19. *continued*

EXAMPLE 19. *continued*

builds momentum into the downbeat (see measures 4 and 12). In this sense, the recurring Junkanoo downbeat performs a reinforcing role similar to that of the bar in rake-n-scrape performances, though it occurs on the first beat of the measure here (whereas the bar occurs on TWO in rake-n-scrape contexts). The kick drum, then, performs very distinct Junkanoo and rake-n-scrape rhythms, which are amplified, made explicit, and extended by the corroborating rhythms played on the hi-hat and congas.

The hi-hat of the drum kit is charged with playing a very common rake-n-scrape saw rhythm while the congas perform what amounts to a distillation of standard lead drum rhythms from Junkanoo. It is this backdrop of explicit Bahamian rhythmic markers that the Beginning of the End uses as a foundation for the arrangement. And it is precisely the juxtaposition of these rhythmic markers that the Beginning of the End innovated in "Funky Nassau." The horns, guitar, organ, and bass all operate within a recognizably "funk" vocabulary—that is, they each play short, repeating, predominantly percussive lines within a i—ii⁶—i—v⁷ harmonic progression. The lyrics furthermore invoke the clear connection that the Beginning of the End was making to soul, R&B, and funk.

> Nassau's gone funky, Nassau's gone soul.
> We've got a doggone beat now, we're gonna call our very own.
> Nassau rock and Nassau roll, Nassau's got a whole lot of soul.
> Mini skirts, maxi skirts, and afro-hair do's,
> People doin' their own thing, don't care about me or you.
> Nassau's gone funky, Nassau's got soul now.

The overall effect created by this song, then, is a layered, ultramodern yet thoroughly grounded expression of Bahamian popular music. "Funky Nassau," that is, clearly expresses the strong connection to African American musical life felt throughout the Bahamas during the early 1970s, but simultaneously stakes a claim to the possibilities that exist for Bahamian rhythmic markers and sensibilities. The government, for its part, was pleased to appropriate this song for its own purposes, eventually including it on *A Nation Is Born* for good measure. Because the song could be interpreted as an entirely cosmopolitan engagement with popular music and African American fashion and musical genres, it did not strike the subversive chord explicit in Exuma's project and implicit in Dr. Offfff's. It was a song that by its sound and poetry celebrated the basic tenets that, by independence, had become of paramount concern to the government. "Funky Nassau," then, was mobilized as an example of the future of the Bahamas, of the modernity inherent in Bahamian musical life, and, by extension, of the nonradical and stable character of this new nation-state among nation-states.

Mobilizing the song in this fashion necessitated a "hearing" of "Funky Nassau" that downplays the Bahamian roots of its rhythmic structure while simultaneously highlighting the transnational connections that it invokes along the way (downplaying the centripetal while highlighting the centrifugal). It is interesting to note here that the numerous cover versions of this song that have been released over the years also fail to "hear" the juxtaposition of rake-n-scrape and Junkanoo rhythms as central to the song (though for different reasons). The richly Bahamian rhythmic core of the song is, thus, generally neglected in favor of highlighting the rhythms of the drum break that the Beginning of the End introduces later in the song (following the line "Listen to the drummer, playing his beat" at the one-minute-mark of the recording).[23]

One of the aims of this book is to illustrate the degree to which itineraries of sound affect sound practices themselves. Put otherwise, the process of moving from one place and context to another generates crises of translation that are rarely fully resolved—partial resolutions that initiate not only new uses of and new meanings for sound, but also new sound, as such. So, for instance, the movement of rake-n-scrape from social dance contexts in the Family Islands to nightclubs in Nassau was only a partial translation—no instruments, save the goat-skinned drum survived this itinerary. Similarly, the international itinerary of "Funky Nassau" occasioned a crisis of translation that resulted in its eventual identification with disco and in multiple covers that simply excise the Bahamian rhythmic markers in favor of privileging the break-beat.

The situation is much the same when the itineraries are inverted. Funk, soul, and R&B, as well as calypso, son, and bossa nova, were all translated into the Nassau and Freeport context in bits and pieces as they became useful and "heard." Tourists visiting the Cat and Fiddle Club during the late 1950s were in a position to "hear" only part of what musicians layered into their arrangements, consuming the sounds with reference to their own expectations and prior experiences— "hearing" Bahamian music quite otherwise than did the musicians themselves. As such, sounds are always "heard" against a backdrop of other local sounds, and these local sounds participate in the very process of "hearing." The cover versions of "Funky Nassau" provide a particularly salient example of this creative mishearing. This pattern is intimately linked to centrifugal and centripetal patterns of listening and influence, and I suggest that the ways through which sound is made multivalent across space and within new performance contexts are in fact made possible by the acts of partial translation that occur along these routes—by creative mishearings that enable new aural itineraries.

"SLEEP ON, DREAM ON":
IDENTITY AS MEMORY WORK?

In the foreword to *Independence for the Commonwealth of the Bahamas*, the most pressing argument for independence reads as follows: "Above all, Independence will enable the Bahamian people to find their true identity and to establish that freedom toward which all men aspire and to which all are entitled" (Bahamas Cabinet Office 1972, 7). How Bahamians would find their true identity, however, was a source of great concern. Catherine Hall has pointed out that questions such as "Who are we? Where do we come from? Which 'we' are we talking about when we talk about 'we'? . . . have a new salience in the contemporary moment" (Catherine Hall 1996, 65). And indeed these questions were being answered in very different ways during the 1970s and '80s. The government offered a particular set of answers, predicated on their need to, in Timothy Brennan's formulation, "manage" the newly independent nation-state. "Nation-states are not only, as we customarily hear today, imagined communities: they are also, and no less fundamentally, *manageable* communities. The state as coercive negotiator presides over a community it must, by definition, be capable of managing" (Brennan 2003, 46). The pragmatic choices that dominate the first two case studies detailed in this chapter illustrate this point clearly. Fiscal policy and economic imperatives consistently outweighed the cultural life of the Bahamas, such that musicians and entertainers became convinced that the government was no longer in the business of answering the same set of questions that had accompanied them to majority rule and independence. Put otherwise, the "we" that the government was focused on no longer seemed to include musicians and entertainers—at least not in a way that was recognizable to artists like Ray Munnings and Ronnie Butler.

The last three musical case studies, for their part, illustrate the varying approaches that artists took in attempting to craft their own answers to this set of questions. They also illustrate the spaces they came to occupy within the nation as a result of their artistic and political choices. The more subversive the project was—that of Exuma, for instance—the less likely that the artist was unambiguously welcomed into the political context of postindependence Bahamian life. For instance, it is telling that Exuma, who released "Exuma, the Obeah Man" in 1970, was not included on the LP *A Nation Is Born,* while the Beginning of the End was featured on side A, track 1. The question of what we are talking about when we talk about "we," then, was answered by pointing to the modern, the cosmopolitan, and the (at least nominally) Christian.

Approaches ranging from rather overtly subversive and unapologetic claims to black nationalist and Afro-Bahamian heritage (Exuma) to more subtle yet still transformative explorations of these same themes (Dr. Offfff) were marginalized voices in the dialogue about identity. This marginalization had a great deal to do with both of these artists referencing alternative sources of the sacred in making their claims. Obeah and, to a lesser extent, the spiritual dimensions attendant to Junkanoo were not considered part of the core identity of the Bahamas, and this is best illustrated by Christianity being installed as the national religion within the constitution itself. John Gillis has pointed out that "the core meaning of any individual or group identity, namely, a sense of sameness over time and space, is sustained by remembering; and what is remembered is defined by the assumed identity. . . . We need to be reminded that memories and identities are not fixed things, but representations or constructions of reality, subjective rather than objective phenomena" (Gillis 1994, 3). With this in mind, the easiest project to assimilate into the contemporary political moment was that of the Beginning of the End. Their music was, on the surface, quite cosmopolitan, modern without fail; their lyrics exhibited none of the potentially subversive themes present in Exuma's compositions; their stage attire was as cutting-edge as Dr. Offfff's was "bush"; and there was no appeal to the ineffable in their sound, stage presence, or lyrics. And yet their project was deeply informed by the sense that their sound was Afro-Bahamian at its core. This subtle approach led to widespread acceptance within the Bahamas and almost secured for the band an international career. No one would have mistaken Exuma or Dr. Offfff for mainstream artists, but the Beginning of the End made a play at that label while exploring their musical roots without recourse to the sacred, thereby aligning themselves with the international scene as much as they appealed to the core identity of the Christian, cosmopolitan, and newly independent Bahamas.

As the 1980s wound on, the entertainment sector in the Bahamas continued to grind out the momentum it had established in the previous two decades. By the time the Baha Men signed with Big Beat records and recorded their debut album, *Junkanoo!*, in 1992, the prospect of a viable music scene in the Bahamas was beginning to fade. The album is itself a monument to the past in a way that *A Nation Is Born* is not. It is explicitly about the past and, more importantly, posits the idea that individuals need to reconnect to the past, to the Family Islands, and to past lifeways in order to remember what it is to be Bahamian. It is a project that explicitly explores the future (and futures) of nostalgia (Boym 2002). A mere twenty years after independence, then, the focus of a seminal album is explicitly set in the past, looking archeologically beyond independence to roots while the musical optimism of the future-looking memorial album at independence seems misplaced as a projection—already a failed project. The questions of identity that abounded during the push for and in the wake of independence were clearly not yet answered, and the Baha Men looked backward in order to look forward. It is to this question of "re-membering" the nation, to the itineraries of memory work, that I turn in the final chapter.

6

"Back to the Island"

Travels in Paradox—Creating the Future-Past

*Tourism is a sort of chemotherapy. You have cancer and it's the only pos-
sible cure, but it might kill you before the cancer does.*
—JUAN ANTONIO BLANCO, QUOTED IN JOHANNA MCGEARY AND
CATHY BOOTH, "CUBA ALONE," *TIME* MAGAZINE, DECEMBER 6, 1993

*To unearth the fragments of nostalgia one needs a dual archeology
of memory and of place, and a dual history of illusions and of actual
practices.*
—SVETLANA BOYM, *THE FUTURE OF NOSTALGIA*, XVIII

*If we don't find a way very quickly from our leaders, to decide and say
what Bahamian music is, and believe what it is, promote what it is . . .
without that happening then we are on a spiraling path to hell!*
—FRED FERGUSON, *NASSAU GUARDIAN*, JUNE 16, 2005

It's past midnight on January 10, 2010, and Fred Ferguson and I are sitting in his
home studio. We've spent the best part of the night rummaging through boxes
full of old cassette tapes and listening to several of his old projects with High
Voltage, the band he joined in 1982 and which eventually came to be known as
the Baha Men. Fred hasn't listened to this material in years, and this occasions a
conversation about his early career and his own background as a musician.[1]
Along the way, he tells me a bit about the itineraries that marked his childhood—
itineraries that illustrate the gravitational pull of the national center but which
also confirm for me why Fred is particularly well suited to his current role as
cultural activist within the Bahamas:

> I am grateful I was born in the era I was born in. And I'm also further grateful that
> I was born *where* I was born, which would be in Acklins, 'cause that gave me the
> root, my Baptist roots. We didn't have any instruments, that's the first thing. You

know the church that I grew up in, we had just a pump, one of those organs that you pump the pedals to put the air in the thing, and then there's the thing on your right leg that you open to make the swell a little bit louder. And that was the instrumentation that we had, if we had any, in the church. And then there were some persons who had, someone might have had a guitar or something like that, but all the rhythms were played with sticks on the benches or stuff like that. . . . So my grandparents would have gone to church, and they would sing stuff from the hymn books, and my parents also had that same thing. So I heard that stuff growing up, and so my sense of harmony, even if it's limited to an extent, is rooted on that four part SATB kind of thing. . . . My parents were both teachers, and after moving between Crooked Island and Acklins a few times, because my dad is from Crooked Island and my mother is from Acklins . . . we got transferred to Nassau for a short moment. And then we got transferred to Long Island. . . . When I got to Long Island I would have been in my sixth grade, and then I would have been playing organ in the church . . . then I would have passed my common entrance exam, which moved me to Nassau to high school.

My parents would still have been on the island, but I was living in boarding school. . . . After coming to Nassau for a while and moving to another school with my sister, when she came, then I discovered girls. And then I wasn't doing any work in school, and my father moved me back to Long Island. Now understand that I was playing guitar and stuff while I was still in school here, but my father moved me to Long Island 'cause girls had taken over. Then while in Long Island, they would have rake-n-scrape dances, and they would have a couple of bands that would play around. . . . I was still in the eleventh grade then. My father would take me to play the dances at nights and wait for me to go home afterward, so that kind of like opened my eyes to that kind of playing. . . .

So I was playing with a band there, called Smacky and the Boys, but they also had serious rake-n-scrape dances in the church hall on the weekends and stuff. . . . So I graduated high school in Long Island and then my parents didn't figure that I should come to Nassau on my own, and they got transferred to Eleuthera. So I went to Eleuthera and just did another year in school . . . so I played in quite a few bands. I think we moved to Eleuthera, say, on a Wednesday, and on Friday night someone came and picked me up to play in a band, 'cause they heard from Long Island that I was playing and was coming there. So this guy named Charlie Cooper, he said, "I heard you could play, man. Come play with me." And they drove me like a hundred miles to Waterford from Palmetto Point, and I played my first gig with him. (Fred Ferguson, interview with the author, January 10, 2010)

Fred moved to Nassau for good around 1976, and his early travels clearly orbited around the center in obvious ways. Unlike many families around this time, however, Fred's parents' skills were needed in the Family Islands, and this likely kept his family from simply settling down in Nassau or Freeport. Instead, Fred lived on four Family Islands in the formative years of his life (Acklins Island, Crooked Island, Long Island, and Eleuthera). He participated in Baptist services throughout his youth, learning to sing the hymns, anthems, and rhyming spirituals from his parents and grandparents. He experienced rake-n-scrape music and dancing on Long Island when that tradition had all but fallen out of active practice elsewhere in the Bahamas. But he also experienced dance bands like Smacky and the Boys in Long Island and Charlie Cooper's bands in Eleuthera. Those bands, such as Ophie's roughly contemporaneous band on Cat Island (Eddie and the Educators), offered a poignant counternarrative to the center-dominated notion that the Family Islands were out of step with modernity and peripheral to national culture. Fred was living on Long Island when independence arrived, but he had also experienced life in Nassau during majority rule. By the time he came to Nassau, he was already an accomplished musician, and though it was not immediately obvious to him, he was also already committed to both the roots and routes of Bahamian musical life. His current projects are all informed by these early experiences (I will return to these later), and he has consistently been drawn to work with artists who share his aesthetic and cultural goals—Dr. Offfff, Ronnie Butler, High Voltage, and, for a time, the Baha Men.

I foreground Fred's career here because it represents an excellent case in point for what can be considered the last generation of professional musicians to enliven the nightclubs of the Bahamas. Born on December 15, 1959, Fred is among the youngest of the musicians who finished the run of live music making in Nassau and Freeport during the 1980s. By the 1990s, bands with members around his age (mid-thirties and forties) were the only game in town.[2] Younger musicians were either playing in church or not performing at all.[3] It was during the 1990s, moreover, when musicians like Fred began to realize that the foundation required for live music in the Bahamas—the pedagogical base as well a wide range of venues in which to work—had all but vanished between the late 1970s and the late 1980s.

For musicians of Fred's generation, however, the late 1970s and 1980s had still been fertile ground for training up and working themselves into truly professional outfits. Fred distinctly remembers the first time he heard High Voltage during the late 1970s, not long after he had moved to Nassau:

> By chance, I went into this place called Fore and Aft in the Emerald Beach Hotel. And there was Isaiah, Moe, Pat Keary, Portia Butterfield, Oni Martin on keyboards, Garfield on conga drums, and I learned these names later, but what an experience that was for me. I couldn't believe that live musicians sounded that good. Isaiah used to trip me out as a bass player because he was, you know, short and had energy, plenty energy on stage. And then Pat, they played stuff by Steely Dan, you know. They did "Josie" and "Peg," and then they did all the Bob Marley stuff, which Isaiah sang, and then they were able to do the rake-n-scrape stuff that they did. And I was like, man, band could sound like this? (Fred Ferguson, interview with the author, January 10, 2010)

Fred had arrived in Nassau fresh from playing in bands around Long Island and Eleuthera, and he was both impressed with and inspired by the music of High Voltage. More importantly, he arrived in Nassau at a moment—and at an age (late teens)—that afforded him the chance to sit in with bands, to get studio work from time to time, and in general to integrate into the live music scene in Nassau. During the late 1970s and early 1980s, Fred (though working full-time) dedicated himself to his craft, playing with a gospel group called the Love Singers, filling in with a band led by Frankie Victory called Laser, sitting in from time to time with the VIPs at the Crystal Palace, and joining a band called the Backstabbers and playing with them in the Tradewinds Lounge for a few months. In this fashion, Fred gradually developed a reputation for excellence, and by the early 1980s he had distinguished himself as one of the best guitarists in Nassau. His first real break came in 1982. Fred remembers it as follows:

> I was still working at the bank. Isaiah came to the bank and said, "Uh, I heard you can play, man. You want to join?" 'Cause High Voltage was back now; they had broken up, so [it] was just Isaiah, Moe, and Herschel left. Pat had gone with T-Connections [they were based in Freeport], Portia had gone somewhere else . . . and so I said, "Okay." So on my lunch breaks we'd practice at the union. So four of us in the musicians union. No girls, just four of us, no keyboards, just us, man, and we played, and we played a lot of functions with just only us four, too, in '82. (Fred Ferguson, interview with the author, January 10, 2010)

Fred played with High Voltage throughout the 1980s, eventually quitting his day job and becoming a full-time musician. The band played a series of clubs, backed Dr. Offfff for his occasional concerts, recorded with Eddie Minnis, cycled through several lead singers, and by the early 1990s High Voltage was as popular as a band could get in the Bahamas without expanding into international markets. Throughout this journey, the leadership of the band was unquestionably in Isaiah Taylor's hands, and according to Fred, he had a very specific musical vision for the band—one that aligned High Voltage with some of the aims and ideals of the back-to-the-bush cosmopolitan strategies of Exuma and Dr. Offfff:

> Isaiah was very, I tell you, he was Hitler, man. You know, we never did any dancehall stuff, we never did any rap, so to speak, 'cause Isaiah wasn't into that. He said, "We got to keep it Island, man." Every time we played like maybe three, four American songs, we had to go in the bush. . . . He was very stickler, man, about this bush thing. . . . We always played rake-n-scrape stuff, always, brother. He always say, "Let's go in the bush." When Herschel [the band's other guitarist] and I get away from that, no, we got to go in the bush, man. (Fred Ferguson, interview with the author, January 10, 2010)

It is this emphasis on maintaining a focus on Bahamian musical heritage that determined the shape of the band's debut album, *Junkanoo!* Steve Greenberg from Big Beat Records (a subsidiary of Atlantic Records) visited the Bahamas during High Voltage's peak popularity in 1991 and expressed interest in signing the band. The demos the band recorded at Compass Point Studio were the band's ticket to a record deal and international distribution, but High Voltage became the Baha Men in the process.[4] According to Fred, "Steve Greenberg felt we needed another name, as there were other bands with the name High Voltage out there, and he wanted something more catchy" (Fred Ferguson, personal communication with the author, February 11, 2010). Fred remembers the events just prior to getting signed:

> Waterloo was the turning point for us. And Waterloo is where we got signed. Steve Greenberg came there, and we were smoking, brother. I mean crowds were everywhere. . . . We really rocked that place, and Steve Greenberg from Atlantic records came there one night and heard us and said, "I want to sign you all." So when that happened, you know, we didn't have any material. We just said, "well, we'll borrow some money." And that's what we did. We borrowed some money from I think Moe's father or somebody, and we went into the studio and wrote songs. We got Kendal [Stubbs] 'cause we all knew Kendal. Isaiah had spoken to Kendal. And Kendal came in and we just sat around in a meeting and decided we'll do remakes of old standard songs "Home Sweet Home," "Mama Lay, Lay, Lay," "Land of the Sea and Sun," and we just took the chance, man, went in the studio and just worked those songs. And the stuff was so good it made it into a movie, actually—*My Father the Hero.* (Fred Ferguson, interview with the author, January 10, 2010)

The Baha Men would go on to tour in the United States and Japan and parlayed their international success into a standing gig at the Culture Club in Nassau. When they were in town, the band set up shop at the club, and when they were abroad, touring or recording, they were replaced by an up-and-coming band called Visage. By 1994, they had released their second album, *Kalik*. During the recording sessions for their third album, *Here We Go Again,* the band began to move away from the back-to-the-bush cosmopolitan sound that had defined the first two albums. The band had stopped working with Kendal Stubbs (engineer and producer for the first two albums), and Isaiah Taylor felt that the musical direction suggested by their new producer, John Ryan, was worth exploring on the current project.[5] Fred had, by this time—ironically, thanks in part to his experiences "in the bush" with High Voltage/Baha Men—become committed to producing music clearly marked as Bahamian. This musical and ideological disagreement ultimately led to his departure from the Baha Men in 1996.[6]

Fred has spent the subsequent years pursuing various opportunities to showcase Bahamian music. He has written songs for and produced recordings of a range of artists, including Ronnie Butler, K. B., Sweet Emily, Geno D, and Funky D; he has recorded traditional rake-n-scrape and released it on his own label (Blue Hole Records); he has served as a consultant in the Ministry of Tourism, where he promoted festivals such as Junkanoo in June and the Cat Island Rake-n-Scrape Festival; he produced important concerts such as a reunion show featuring the T-Connection; he has written numerous editorials for local newspapers and given radio interviews encouraging awareness of Bahamian musical and artistic heritage; and most recently, he has joined forces with Ronald Simms, opening a club called Da Tambrin Tree in a bid to revive live music in Nassau. In all of these ventures, Fred has become increasingly discouraged by what he sees as a lack of interest on the part of the government and the national media in encouraging Bahamians to take their musical heritage seriously, a point driven home by his comments to the *Nassau Guardian* quoted in the epigraph to this chapter.

Throughout the remainder of this chapter, I am interested in the degree to which heritage becomes a space and provides a set of itineraries that can in turn be mobilized in order to envision possible futures. The current lack of an active live music scene in Nassau effectively precludes practice-based futures, and this has been the case since at least the 1980s. I will illustrate through a series of case studies that a vision of the future built on successful mobilization of nostalgia has become a dominant means of attempting to reinvigorate the present. In this connection, it is helpful to remember Svetlana Boym's assertion: "Nostalgia is not always about the past; it can be retrospective but also prospective. Fantasies of the past determined by the needs of the present have a direct impact on realities of the future. Consideration of the future makes us take responsibility for our nostalgic tales" (Boym 2002, xvi).

In contrast to the back-to-the-bush cosmopolitan projects discussed in chapter 5, the mobilization of nostalgia during the 1990s and the first decade of the twenty-first century was clearly driven by a need to (re)connect to an elusive core of Bahamian identity that the artists of the 1970s and early 1980s took for granted in the process of connecting, as Bahamians, to other streams of identity (such as the black power movement). Nostalgia thus became useful in direct proportion to the extent that cosmopolitanism eclipsed the back-to-the-bush projects of the 1970s and early 1980s. As nostalgia developed into a useful critique of the nation and of cosmopolitanism, artists turned to space (geography) and time (memory), along with culturalisms (lifeways), in their efforts to articulate "true-true" Bahamian music and identity. Boym is again helpful in summarizing nostalgia's role in shaping this kind of discourse: "Nostalgia tantalizes us with its fundamental ambivalence; it is about the repetition of the unrepeatable, materialization of the immaterial. . . . Nostalgia charts space on time and time on space and hinders the distinction between subject and object; it is Janus-faced, like a double-edged sword. To unearth the fragments of nostalgia one needs a dual archeology of memory and of place, and a dual history of illusions and of actual practices" (Boym 2002, xvii–xviii). To begin exploring these ideas, I turn to a close reading of the Baha Men's debut album, *Junkanoo!*

"HOME SWEET HOME":
IDENTITY AS ARCHAEOLOGY?

The Baha Men produced an album incorporating "remakes of old standard songs," rearranging them and, in the process, infusing them with a rhythmic base drawn from Junkanoo. What emerged was in essence a concept album, and it was the first of its kind in the Bahamas. The songs the band chose to include on the album mapped the history of Bahamian entertainment from the 1940s through the 1980s and did so while clearly articulating a musical model for other entertainers to follow. Predicated as it was on the work of Bahamian legends, the project accomplished an archaeology of sound. This archaeological dimension, moreover, lent the lyrical content of the songs a decidedly anachronistic quality—a quality that provided a foundation upon which to articulate a prospective nostalgia. Taken as a whole, this album can be considered a seminal attempt to design the Bahamian future-past, and the following pages trace some of the interrelated themes that made this musical statement of identity possible.

The first three songs on the album are cover versions of tunes generally acknowledged as classics within the Bahamian music scene: Ronnie Butler's "Crow Calypso" (called "Back to the Island" on this album); Dr. Offfff's "Junk, Junk, Junkanoo" (called " Junk Junkanoo" here); and the Beginning of the End's "Funky Nassau." The Baha Men thus open their debut project by setting up an explicit homage to three of the great entertainers in Bahamian history, gathering musical statements accumulated across three decades into their understanding of the present in the process ("Crow Calypso," 1969; "Funky Nassau," 1971; and "Junk, Junk, Junkanoo," 1981). In appropriating these songs and presenting them as part of their own musical heritage, the Baha Men nevertheless arrange them quite differently than the original recordings, making the most dramatic changes to Ronnie Butler's "Crow Calypso." This song, analyzed in chapter 2, has served as a quintessential model for the popular rake-n-scrape sound, but the Baha Men turn it into a Junkanoo tune instead. The essential changes include incorporating a goat-skinned drum playing a pattern ending on the downbeat instead of the *and* of two (as would have been common in rake-n-scrape), through which the Baha Men shift the rhythmic structure to fit more squarely into a Junkanoo frame; adding cowbells playing the classic kalik rhythm; and arranging the song such that one or the other of these structural rhythms is always present in the mix. The drum kit and the bass guitar are thus free to explore rhythms that complement the Junkanoo feel but that are not necessarily marked as such (see Example 20).

The lyrics of "Crow Calypso" were deliberately nostalgic even when Ronnie sang them in 1969, but by 1992 they were positively anachronistic (see lyrics in chapter 2). Reminiscing about the island to which he intends to return by

EXAMPLE 20. "Back to the Island," transcribed from 2'14" to 2'39." Transcription used with the permission of Isaiah Taylor and the Baha Men.

(continued)

EXAMPLE 20. *continued*

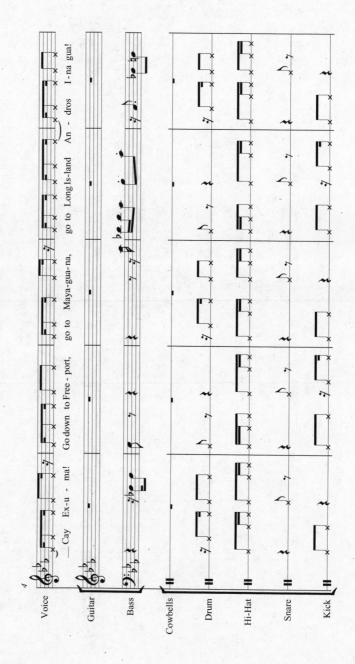

EXAMPLE 20. *continued*

(continued)

EXAMPLE 20. *continued*

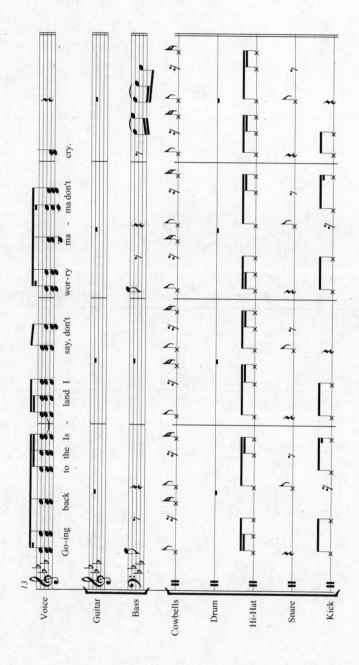

afternoon mail boat, the narrator sings of swimming in blue holes, cooking in iron pots, catching black crabs, growing corn, and attending Saturday night goombay dances. Although some of the images invoked are readily understood as referencing a physical return, the nature of the activities offer insight into the narrator's agenda, for Ronnie's lyrics are at least binary in nature, a fact which the additional decades between his original recording and the Baha Men's revival serve only to further highlight. On the one hand, the lyrics clearly write the narrator's itinerary in terms of physical space. Current home (Nassau) and prior Home (the Family Islands) are thus easily defined in geographic relation to one another, reinforcing the suspension of these spaces within a center/periphery model of the Bahamian nation. On the other hand, the lyrics simultaneously posit the act of return as involving a double movement addressing temporal as well as spatial itineraries. In other words, the lyrics also narrate a return through time to the "true" Island.

Boym's assertion that nostalgia "charts space on time and time on space and hinders the distinction between subject and object" is clearly illustrated here, as are the ambiguities that this type of discourse instantiates. I conceptualize the physical and temporal movements required of the traveler as playing out along parallel trajectories. The physical journey unfolds as a kind of centripetal movement (from away to home), while the temporal itineraries attendant to this prospective nostalgia are, necessarily, also centripetally focused. Importantly, outward motion—the appearance of return—is only useful insofar as it is accompanied by a concomitant inward journey in search of the ever-elusive goal of nostalgia—a stable core, a home. Perhaps the most telling illustration of this dynamic is offered in the chorus of the song, when the narrator, who is already "home" in Nassau, wakes up and announces that he is heading back to the Island—his "Home."

Reinforcing this idea, the Baha Men include a bridge in their version of the song in which they shout out to Ronnie Butler, "Hey Ronnie, how you gonna get there?" Making a guest appearance on the recording, Ronnie calls back, "By mail boat." After repeating this exchange, the Baha Men encourage Ronnie and their listeners to journey to a number of places throughout the Bahamas (see Example 20, measures 1–8). Among the locations mentioned are Nassau, Eleuthera, Cat Island, Rum Cay, Exuma, Freeport, Mayaguana, Long Island, Andros, and Inagua. The reference to a physical return is clear here, but the Baha Men's implication of a temporal dimension is inescapable. As Bahamians, Ronnie and the song's narrator are equally "at home" in the Bahamas no matter on which island they happen to be. The distinction made between the islands thus has more to do with temporal perception, with centripetal trajectories of self. Nassau, the capitol city, is considered to be just that—a city, cosmopolitan, modern, central, and no longer possessed of the core Bahamian identity that appeals to the narrator.[7] The other islands in the narrator's list are perceived very differently: they are understood as hewing more closely to the cultural heritage of the Bahamas. They are selected from among the Family Islands and, as such, are considered "true-true" Bahamian, understood as participating in Bahamian identity as counterexamples of Nassau—as Nassau's antipodes. That is, the Family Islands are "true-true" Bahamian to the extent that they are perceived as rural, insular, antimodern, and peripheral.[8] In order to satisfy the demands of a temporal return, then, Ronnie and the song's narrator need to complete a journey to one of the other islands listed in this text.

It is important to note here the degree to which these perceptions of the Family Islands were themselves already rooted in myth. Since the 1950s the Family Islands had gradually moved into the orbit of the tourism industry. This was a slow process, but by 1992 the Family Islands were generating approximately 20 percent of the total tourist visits to the Bahamas. By 2005, the Family Islands were responsible for roughly 25 percent of tourist visits (see Table 7). The perception that the Family Islands have remained locked in time, untouched by the forces at play within Nassau, and that they thereby offer a safe haven for Bahamian identity, is, then, a strategic inversion of the equally untenable stereotype that Nassauvians fostered during the 1950s and '60s. During the move toward mass-tourism, self-rule, and independence, the Family Islands were viewed through the very same lens—that is, as antimodern, provincial, insular, and rural. The sociopolitical realities of the time, however, tended to code the Family Islands pejoratively. Samuel Charters's recollections of Nassauvian responses to musical practices emanating from the Family Islands—"those boys a little behind"—provide a case in point (Charters 1999, 167). After independence, and in the wake of the back-to-the-bush movement, the Family Islands were at least partially rehabilitated within the Bahamian social imaginary, factoring now as the progenitors of true Bahamian identity. And yet the basis for these perceptions remains rooted in myth and stereotype. The Family Islands, as such, continue to play the role of foil, conforming within the national imaginary to provide the balancing antipode (antidote?) to the itineraries of the center.

This elusive home, then, located in the Family Islands but, more problematically, in a mythologized Family Islands located in a "sometime," nevertheless instantiates precisely the ambiguity that Boym points to when she asserts that nostalgia "hinders the distinction between subject and object." The paradoxical nature of this form of travel can be summed up in the form of a question: is it possible to return when that journey necessitates returning to a "when" instead of a "where"? Because most Nassauvian families or their forebears have at some point during the nineteenth or twentieth century migrated to New Providence from the Family Islands, the narrative of return—through routes that involve time as well as space—to the roots of Bahamian identity finds a receptive audience. The call for return signals the need to generate a poetics of representation

TABLE 7 Tourist visits to the Family Islands, 1970–2005

Year	Family Islands	Bahamas Total	Percent of Total
1970	71,700	1,298,351	5.5
1975	119,010	1,380,860	8.6
1980	273,620	1,904,560	14.4
1985	294,400	2,631,970	11.2
1990	495,069	3,628,519	13.6
1995	566,463	3,239,155	17.5
2000	841,917	4,203,834	20.0
2005	1,156,134	4,779,417	24.2

SOURCE: Condensed from Cleare 2007, 565–66.

that incorporates the past as it looks to the future. But this discourse remains ambivalent as to what could constitute a "true-true" return, what would qualify as a successful mobilization of the past for use in the present, and who could claim to have traveled the appropriate routes to engage with the roots of Bahamian identity. The prospective nostalgia mobilized in "Back to the Island," then, maps the past onto the periphery and prescribes this itinerary as a means for moving the center into the future.

A second trio of songs on the Baha Men's album hearkens back even further into the history of Bahamian entertainment. "Mama Lay, Lay, Lay," "Gin and Coconut Water," and "Home Sweet Home" are traditional songs that have been sung around the Anglophone Caribbean since at least the 1940s, and each of these songs has been recorded by numerous Bahamian musicians throughout the years. By including their own versions of these songs on this album, the Baha Men create a connection to Bahamian legends from the 1940s, '50s, and '60s—artists such as Blind Blake, George Symonette, Charlie Adamson, Tony Seymour Sr., Count Bernadino, and King Eric and His Knights. By instantiating sound connections to these histories within their own album, the Baha Men stake their claim to the "golden years" of entertainment in the Bahamas and ground their own approach in that very heritage. These songs, moreover, afford the band opportunities to reflect on the position of the Bahamas vis-à-vis the United States and its many Caribbean neighbors.

Although the starting point of "Back to the Island" is Nassau itself, "Gin and Coconut Water" along with "Home Sweet Home" trace a geography of the Bahamas from an explicitly transnational perspective. Throughout "Gin and Coconut Water" the journey home is defined in relation to a specific location—the United States—and the lyrics catalog the negative long-term effects of diasporic existence for those who for education or employment have moved abroad. The symptoms of the narrator's malady can be understood as physical manifestations of homesickness—nostalgia.

> Gin and coconut water,
> Gin and coconut water,
> Gin and coconut water,
> Cannot get it in America.
>
> 1. Honey child come go with me,
> back to the West Indies.
> Baby, can't you see,
> I lost my strength and my energy. (What I need is . . .)
>
> 2. I remember when I was young,
> I was healthy and very strong.
> But now I'm feeble and weak,
> My knees keep a-knocking when I walk the street. (What I need is . . .)
>
> 3. Medical center whatcha think?
> Now the doctor say you gotta drink.
> He said, take this advice from me,
> You gotta go back to the coconut tree. (What I need is . . .)
>
> 4. Now mi family was glad to see,
> Me go back to the coconut tree.
> Mi family was glad to see me,
> Climb the tree like an ol' monkee. (What I need is . . .)

The Baha Men's lyrics remain faithful to earlier recordings of this song, made by Blind Blake (1951), George Symonette (1951), and Kasavubu and Lord Cody (1961), with the exception of one key departure. All of the earlier recordings reference the West Indies more often than do the Baha Men. For instance, both Blind Blake and George Symonette use "West Indies" in the last line of verse three, whereas the Baha Men insert "coconut tree." In that same verse, moreover, Blind Blake includes the name "Houdini" in line four, where the Baha Men simply sing "you." This is undoubtedly a reference to the Trinidadian calypsonian Wilmoth Houdini, whose recording of this song in 1945 was the likely model for the Bahamian versions of the 1950s and '60s.[9] In verse four, Blind Blake again references "West Indies" instead of the "coconut tree." George Symonette and Kasavubu, however, both sing about going back to "Trinidad" in verse four, conforming to the lyrics sung by Houdini.

With the exception of verse one, the Baha Men thus choose to focus on the symbolically neutral coconut tree instead of on the much more regionally and politically specific notion of the West Indies or on the Trinidadian model the older Bahamian versions are based on. In the context of the album, this affords the Baha Men the opportunity to tether the song to a Bahamian orbit instead of a regional one. This is accomplished in large part by combining a lack of lyrical specificity with explicit musical markers; the Junkanoo rhythm central to the arrangement, along with the sonically marked cowbells and goat-skinned drum, combine to ground this song squarely in the Bahamas (see Example 21).

The overall effect of this song is similar to the musical representations achieved by the goombay artists during the 1950s—that is, the song is heard as pan-Caribbean, understood as having a history of wide circulation in the region, but possessed of qualities marking it as specifically Bahamian in the face of this regional connection. That said, the Baha Men make the local markers much more explicit in their version than did the artists of the goombay years. The lyrics, meanwhile, offer a further meditation on nostalgia, positing only one cure for homesickness. The itinerary prescribed as a tonic for this ailment involves a return to home and, more specifically, a return to roots.

Another song on the album, "Island Boy," explores the very same condition. Each verse unfolds as a list of the things the narrator misses about Nassau: the foods, sights, smells, and sounds that are at the root of his homesickness. These include things like goombay summer, the sailing boats beneath the bridge (to Paradise Island), the cowbells and drums on New Year's morning, the smell of hibiscus, and the conch and fish at dawning. The lyrics to this song illustrate the sentiment embedded in a popular Bahamian aphorism: "Ya could take da man from out of de island, but ya cannot take de island out of da man" (Minns 1981, 59). Consider, for example, the following refrain:

> Island Boy, you got your mind on your job in New York but your
>   heart's in the Caribbean.
> Island Boy, when you look at the concrete walls can't you hear them say,
> Come Back Home, to the land of the sun and the sand and the
>   palmy beaches.
> Where your heart has always been since the very first day.

Lyrics of this sort in fact mirror a trend found in Bahamian literature of the 1970s and 1980s. Anthony Dahl observes: "We find in the overwhelming presence of themes relating to national culture such as Bahamian customs, foods, institutions, flora, fauna and people, symbols for the Bahamas as a space to belong to and be proud of, a space related to the archetypal motif of the Promised Land" (Dahl 1995, 123). And this motif of a Promised Land ties in well with the production of prospective nostalgia, in that the Promised Land is, in this Bahamian context, at once about roots and about future possibilities. The narrators in "Island Boy" and "Gin and Coconut Water" are engaged in a process of remembering in order to envision possible futures—futures that necessarily involve both recovering the past and returning to the Bahamas.

Voice

Guitar

Bass

Cowbells

Goat-Skinned Drum

Hi-Hat

Snare Drum

Kick Drum

EXAMPLE 21. *continued*

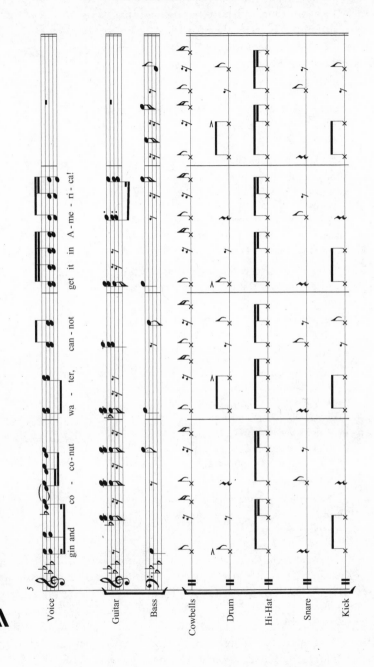

The mention in verse four of "Gin and Coconut Water" of the narrator's family and their joy at his return to the "coconut tree" is significant in this regard, because the multigenerational nature of family life can be helpful in bridging the conceptual distance between geographic and temporal itineraries. The trope of the family is usefully invoked in the song "Home Sweet Home," the lyrics for which follow:

> 1. I have traveled to Germany, enjoyed myself in Atlantic City.
> I've been to all of the great countries, now I'm living like a king
>   down in Bimini.
>
> Just talkin' 'bout, home sweet home.
> Singin' 'bout, home sweet home.
> No matter which part of the world I roam, little Nassau is my
>   happy home.
> Talkin' 'bout, home sweet home.
> I'm singin' 'bout, home sweet home.
> No matter which part of the world I roam, the Bahamas is my happy home.
>
> 2. I love the land, I love the fun, I love the taste of the bitter rum.
> I love the people of this country, but the young girls are more
>   important to me.
>
> 3. Nassau's the home of Junkanoo, Barbados is where the sugar cane grow.
> Jamaica is where the rum come from, but Baha Men are
>   natural-like Bahamians.
>
> [Bridge:] Been around the world, been down the way,
> Been to the big city, been going astray.
> I still remember my grandpapee when he say,
> "Ain't no place like home my boy!"
> Been to China, been to London town,
> Been to Jamaica, oh! been all around.
> I thank me mother for bringing me in this town,
> 'Cause there ain't no place like home my boy!
>
> 4. Three years ago back in Trinidad, oh what a lovely time I had.
> They gave me a name for my Junkanoo, now I'm taking it
>   everywhere I go.

In this song, the narrator reflects on the Bahamas as the Promised Land, comparing it to all of the other places he's been able to visit throughout his life.[10] The physical return inscribed here is readily apparent—the narrator has traveled widely and has finally settled down in Bimini, where he is "living like a king." Particularly interesting in this narrative of return is the role the grandfather fulfills. The grandfather, temporally separated from the narrator by two generations, has (or had) intimate and much longer experience of the Bahamas than the narrator has had. The grandfather stresses that there is "no place like home," and the narrator, who has traveled far and wide, has come to full agreement with his grandfather on this claim, actually restating this sentiment and making it his own in the process of thanking his mother for "bringing him in this town." As such, the narrator reenacts a scenario not unlike that of the biblical prodigal son, first "going astray" and ultimately coming back home, significantly after engaging in an act of memory involving his grandfather's words. Once again, then, nostalgia drives a new future, in this case instantiating an itinerary that involves a reevaluation of the Bahamas as the Promised Land accompanied by a physical return.[11]

The Baha Men, however, do not wholly rely on cover songs or traditional tunes to populate their debut album. They incorporate two original songs, "Mo' Junkanoo" and "Let Your Body Move to the Rhythm," as well. Both of these songs situate the Baha Men as firmly engaged with the live music scene in Nassau's hotel clubs, as illustrated by the lyrics of "Let Your Body Move to the Rhythm":

> Let your body move to the rhythm now.
> Let your body move to the rhythm now.
>
> 1. You say you want this party started, say you want to have some fun.
> You know you don't, don't need a permit, you don't need
>   permission from anyone.
> Just move your body, move your feet. Feel the rhythm feel the beat.
> You wanna party, you wanna dance, so listen up y'all, here's your chance.
>
> 2. Ease your tension, remove your stress. Don't you worry about the rest.
> There's no need to, to hold it back. There is no need for you to be depressed.
> There's a time to party and this is it. Move to the rhythm, then you may quit.
> And when it's over make a call, and tell everyone you had a ball.

The lyrics of this song ground the Baha Men in the live music scene in Nassau, illustrating that the band had risen to popularity by performing a mixture of traditional and dance tunes for audiences predominantly consisting of tourists in the local hotel clubs. The lyrics suggest that dancing to the music provided by the Baha Men is confirmation that you're in the Bahamas and that it must be time to party, to blow off stress, and to enjoy yourself. Significantly, however, the musical register remains firmly rooted in Junkanoo. Although the Baha Men were able to play all of the popular dance tunes on the pop charts, and in spite of the inclusion of these songs in every set they played in Nassau, the band had a clear vision of what it was attempting to accomplish with this album. It was to be a total Junkanoo effort.

To that effect, the arrangement once again deploys a Junkanoo rhythm and the sonic markers that accompany it, such as cowbells and goat-skinned drums. The chorus, transcribed in Example 22, is sixteen measures long and consists of two eight-measure phrases (only the first of which I transcribe completely). The Baha Men build the groove for each eight-measure phrase as follows: the cow-bells play the kalik rhythm twice per measure, while the kick drum hammers out the and-ONE once per measure. Against this, both the hi-hats and the bass guitar play two-measure repeating figures. The keyboard, for it's part, plays two four-measure phrases, the first of which includes two rest measures (measures 3–4). This sets up a percussive and harmonic context in which the lead vocalist utilizes the first two measures and the last two measures of each eight measure phrase to set up the background vocalists, who sing "Let your body move to the rhythm now" from measures three to six, effectively arching across the two four-measure units delineated by the keyboards and supported by the bass and percussion.

The arrangement illustrates a keen sense of how the percussive building blocks of the phrases can be fitted together to generate inexorable forward momentum while simultaneously incorporating syncopated melodic and harmonic material that sutures the two four-measure units into a larger eight-measure arc. "Let Your Body Move to the Rhythm" thus represents both an excellent illustration of the performative context in which the Baha Men were operating throughout the 1980s and early 1990s—the clubs of Nassau, that is—but also an example of the innovative approaches the band was exploring in order to extend the conventions of writing explicitly Junkanoo-driven material.

The Baha Men are not, then, interested in adhering to the customary phrase structure that informs the traditional repertory in the Bahamas. The four-by-four-times-two formula $[(4 + 4) \times 2 = 16]$ that drives so much of the rake-n-scrape and Junkanoo repertory is here modified so that a four-by-four-times-two rhythmic base is combined with a melodic line that cuts across the four-by-four division, thereby making an eight-times-two hearing of the chorus more normative. Driving a chorus with two eight-measure phrases instead of four discreet four-measure phrases that combine to form eight-measure units conforms more closely to the pop aesthetic that animated much of the repertory that the Baha Men performed in the clubs. It provides a means for integrating the Junkanoo rhythm into sets without marking it as folk or traditional by virtue of its phrase structure. While this is a subtle shift, it is indicative of the Baha Men's constant exploration of how to incorporate Junkanoo rhythms into popular dance music.

The song "Mo' Junkanoo," written by Kendal Stubbs, the band's close friend and engineer on the project, takes these explorations a step further. The lyrics revolve around the power of Junkanoo, both as a symbol of national pride and as a vehicle for spirituality, and the Baha Men thereby contribute yet another statement to the ongoing discourse on Junkanoo and its relationship to the ineffable. One of the exclamations that ties the song's rather sparse lyrical content together is the short phrase "spirit of Junkanoo," which is repeated throughout the arrangement. The phrase "gotta feel the rhythm in your soul," which appears toward

EXAMPLE 22. "Let Your Body Move to the Rhythm."
Transcription used with the permission of Isaiah Taylor and the Baha Men.

(continued)

EXAMPLE 22. *continued*

EXAMPLE 22. *continued*

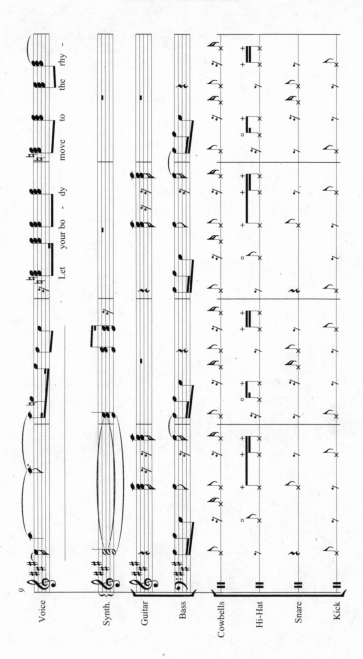

(continued)

EXAMPLE 22. *continued*

the end introduces the excess I highlighted in chapter 4. The message of the song, then, is about the centrality of Junkanoo to Bahamian national identity, but also about the centrality of Junkanoo to Bahamian conceptions of spirituality.

> 1. Over one hundred years, we've had a rhythm pent up in our souls.
> There's a message in this rhythm, and the time has come for it to be told.
> I guess it can be said, we've got a sound that's second to none.
> There is a special reason their rushin' is for fun.
>
> 2. Do you feel it (Junkanoo), like I feel it (Junkanoo).
> Do you want it (Junkanoo), like I want it (Junkanoo).
> Do you need it (Junkanoo), like I need it (Junkanoo).
> Cause I need it (Junkanoo), I got ta have it (Junkanoo).
>
> [Bridge:] This rhythm makes us proud (Junkanoo).
> We love to make it loud (Junkanoo).
> There's a rhythm in our souls (Junkanoo).
> It's gotta be under control (Junkanoo).
>
> (Spirit of Junkanoo)
> (Gotta feel the rhythm in your soul)

And yet the musical context in which these lyrics are delivered is perhaps less precisely Junkanoo than any of the songs on the album. The kick drum plays a very basic pop pattern that actually works against the and-ONE of Junkanoo rhythms. The only musically unambiguous markers of Junkanoo included in the arrangement are the cowbells, which play a very basic reduction of the Over-the-Hill beat throughout the entire track (see Example 23). This, then, is a song that finds the Baha Men exploring the extent to which musical style can be stretched at the boundaries while still retaining a connection to a core set of ideas and conventions. "Mo' Junkanoo" illustrates the fact that the Baha Men were performing in contexts where Junkanoo was generally still coded as "island music" and offers a concrete example of their attempts to bridge that perception in their arrangements.

I turn now to a brief discussion of a final track on the Baha Men's album. This is a cover version of a song made famous by Harry Belafonte's 1961 recording "Land of the Sea and Sun."[12] Written by the Bajan singer/songwriter Irving Burgie, the song narrates a love story begun in the Caribbean and interrupted by the narrator's inability to stay (the reason is never stated). The narrator, who has "memories by the score," resolves to go back and "give her my name" before his "days are done." The song was a commercial success upon its release, and numerous Bahamian artists, including Freddie Munnings Sr., Roy Shurland, and Ronnie Butler, recorded it in the early 1960s. As such, like the other traditional songs included on the Baha Men's album, "Land of the Sea and Sun" was a staple of the live scene in Nassau.

EXAMPLE 23. Drum kit and percussion in "Mo' Junkanoo."

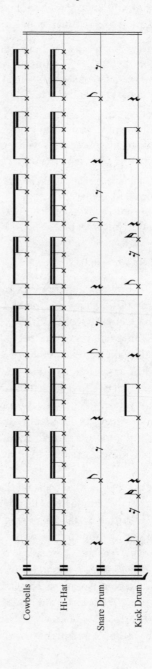

Once again, the Baha Men shift the lyrics just enough to obscure the regional roots of the song, singing of a "Nassau girl" instead of a "Bajan girl." By way of comparison, Roy Shurland sings the original lyrics and Freddy Munnings chooses to sing of a "Bahamian girl."[13] Nostalgia is again the principle driver of the lyrical content, and by incorporating a commercially successful pan-Caribbean song from the 1960s into their album, the Baha Men signal the extent to which the great Bahamian entertainers were connecting with the sounds of other artists around the region, while they fulfilled the expectations tourists brought with them when they swarmed to see their shows. The Baha Men were themselves intimately familiar with the pressures attendant to representing themselves and their musical performances as both sufficiently pan-Caribbean and adequately Bahamian, as both cosmopolitan and native. Though the venues and politics and particularities associated with live performance had shifted dramatically since the "golden years" of Bahamian entertainment, the Baha Men nevertheless still wrestled with the act of representation. By closing their album with a version of "Land of the Sea and Sun," the Baha Men acknowledge this long struggle while simultaneously paying tribute to the many artists who addressed themselves to these issues in the decades before their own careers had even begun. Indeed, the Baha Men close their liner notes as follows: "This album is a tribute to all Bahamian artists who have paved the way" (Baha Men, *Junkanoo!* liner notes).

As the first section of this chapter has amply illustrated, *Junkanoo!* succeeds as a tribute, as a vehicle for prospective nostalgia, and as an advertisement for Bahamian music on the world scene. For my purposes, however, the Baha Men's debut album accomplishes a great deal more as well, because *Junkanoo!* also offers a lens through which to revisit in a single artistic statement the three overarching themes that have informed this book: the physical interposition of the Bahamas between the United States and the rest of the Caribbean; tourism; and the nation's colonial and postcolonial histories.

The album forges an amalgamation of the influences that have crisscrossed the Bahamas since the 1940s (and long before that). It offers anyone interested in these geographies of sound a monument to the varied ways Bahamian artists have responded to these influences, pressures, and challenges. The regional songs, such as "Gin and Coconut Water," "Mama Lay, Lay, Lay," and "Home Sweet Home" all locate the Bahamas firmly within the Caribbean. And yet the band's careful Junkanoo-informed arrangements effectively tether the songs sonically to the Bahamas. "Funky Nassau" and "Junk, Junkanoo," for their part, are covers of songs that in their original contexts illustrated the strong connections that artists like the Beginning of the End and Dr. Offfff had established with African-American musical genres. And yet both the original recordings and the Baha Men's cover versions demonstrate a strong commitment to crafting specifically Bahamian approaches to these transnational sounds.

The Baha Men extend these sonic reflections on the Bahamas' interposition between the United States and the rest of the Caribbean by including songs that specifically concern themselves with diaspora and itineraries of return, and this in particular with reference to the United States ("Gin and Coconut Water" and "Island Boy"). That the Trinidadian Wilmoth Houdini in all likelihood provided the model that jump-started this song's long tenure in the Bahamas and the Baha Men's strategic occlusion of this progenitor in their own performance of the song illustrate the regional particularities that continue to shape the nationalist representations of identity within the Caribbean. That is, common histories and shared aesthetics nevertheless operate within a context of regional competition and neighborhood rivalry. As such, it becomes strategically necessary to highlight the local while homogenizing and departicularizing the regional. Interestingly, this representational strategy seems to have been at least as important (if not more so) in the 1990s as it was in the 1950s, when Blind Blake and George Symonette first recorded the song. Another example of this pattern finds the Baha Men recording a Bahamianized version of an Irving Burgie song, erasing lyrical cues to it's Bajan roots and reframing it as a (pan)Caribbean song.

Tourism's role in the production of Bahamian music is evinced forcefully throughout this album. The Baha Men's two original tracks ("Mo' Junkanoo" and "Let Your Body Move to the Rhythm") offer a glimpse into the poetics of representation driving the Baha Men's arrangements. Both songs clearly explore the musical possibilities of Junkanoo within a popular music frame, while simultaneously articulating both national pride and a clear sense of their primary audience (tourists) in the process. The inclusion of "Land of the Sea and Sun" and "Mama Lay, Lay, Lay," moreover, affords powerful reminders that these negotiations have been a constant companion to performances within the Bahamas. These "Island songs" have formed the backdrop to tourist entertainment throughout the region since at least the 1940s, and this was certainly the case within the Bahamian musical landscape. These musical statements, driven by stereotypes of sun, sea, sand, and romance, encoded with recourse to calypso and goombay and delivered with a smile, have accompanied Bahamian entertainers from Blind Blake to the Baha Men. Perhaps most significantly, the Baha Men make no attempt to engage critically with this repertory, seeing in these songs merely an extension of the heritage they are claiming as contemporary artists. As such, they understand themselves as purveyors of a tourist product, but also as Bahamian artists who are articulating a fundamentally unified approach to musical identity—an approach grounded in Junkanoo.

The album's connection to the colonial and postcolonial history of the Bahamas is driven by nostalgia. The insistence on prospective nostalgia conveys a deep sense that national identity as such is not being adequately articulated. In fact, *Junkanoo!* reflects a sentiment common throughout the Bahamas during the 1990s, which is aptly summarized by Michael Craton and Gail Saunders. In addressing the question of national identity, the authors highlight the extent to which the three themes under discussion here are interdependent, cross-cutting, and, in the final analysis, inseparable:

> As the tumultuous twentieth century draws to its close . . . it is clear that more than a quarter-century of political independence, even a conscious policy of Baha-mianization by the two counterpoised political parties, have not been enough in themselves to provide Bahamians with a coherent sense of national identity. Inter-nal divisions (of color or class or even between the subcultures of different islands) and powerful external influences (of modernization in general and the United States, Britain, and the West Indies in particular) confuse and diffuse. . . . Being a small and young country set between the millstones of dominant North American and Caribbean cultures, the Bahamas is hard put to claim the distinctiveness of its folklore, crafts, and architecture, to preserve its distinctive styles of music and dance, or to develop a national literature. (Craton and Saunders 1998, 435, 476)

This passage reveals much about the pre- and postcolonial life of the Baha-mas, the difficulties attendant to national identity formation and the production of locally distinctive musical performances, and the external forces that continue to participate in shaping the everyday realities of Bahamian life. For Craton and Saunders, the question is one of exploring, as historians, the roots of Bahamian life in order to articulate a basis for national identity. The Baha Men, however, are interested in routes as well as roots, in itineraries as well as practices. They ex-plore these routes and roots throughout *Junkanoo!* by instantiating an insistent exploration of the mythical past, searching for a core Bahamian identity, seem-ingly located in the stereotyped Family Islands, and performing their resistance to an unproblematical cosmopolitan stance. In so doing, the Baha Men seek to build a foundation for envisioning a productive future identity.

The Baha Men saturate their project with allusions to and invocations of many great Bahamian performers, thereby tying their own musical performances to a long history of such musical statements and simultaneously suggesting that the best of Bahamian entertainment lies in the past to be recovered for use in the pres-ent. In multiple ways they explore the preindependence culturalisms of the Bahamas in order to envision a postindependence mode of living. They question the present with recourse to a particular vision of the past, all with the goal of generating a new and ostensibly better vision of the future. The ambiguities in-herent in this exercise, notwithstanding, the Baha Men stood at the threshold of the 1990s and judged that the past held more promise than did the future. The musical bankruptcy of the moment did not touch them—they were signed and at the height of their popularity—but the signs of this bankruptcy were visible to any who were willing to critically examine the entertainment sector. In produc-ing this particular album at this specific moment, the Baha Men proffered both a diagnosis and a prescription for Bahamian entertainment, the inherent ambiguities and paradoxes of which continue to be played out. To illustrate this, I turn now to a brief review of musical life in the Bahamas after 1992.

"BRING BACK DA GOOD OLE DAYS": ARCHAEOLOGY AS IDENTITY?

Recognizing his increasingly deep aesthetic and ideological differences with the rest of the band, Fred Ferguson left the Baha Men in 1996 during the recording sessions for their third studio album, *Here We Go Again*. His subsequent career serves as a particularly good model for framing the kinds of possibilities that have accompanied Bahamian musicians into the twenty-first century. Our conversation on January 10, 2010, eventually arrived at this juncture of his career, and he described the gradual move from producer to cultural activist:

> So I bought my first set of equipment, which would have been like an eight-track recorder, had little sequencer stuff, drum machine, and I started producing, and K.B. would have been the first person. The first song I would have done would have been "Just 'Cause She Fat," which took off, huge. It was a big song for K.B. and gave me a name. After that, I did more K.B.'s, and then K.B. and I coproduced Emily [Sweet Emily] with her first album, and I wrote stuff like "Why You Bodder Me," and K.B. and I did "Send Him Home" and lots of stuff like that.... Then I got Geno D, his first song I did took off also, was called "Da Gal Look Good." I did that. I did Funky D, "Start Me Up," which I cowrote with K.B. I just have a lot of work that I would have done in that period. It was my only income then. I had always thought that I should move on to the next level in the industry. Playing was there always. The next thing is to move to the next level, and production was that. And then, you know, I learned a lot from Kendal [Stubbs], just watching him work, and I'd question him and so forth, watch what he does. And so I never saw myself as an engineer, but I ended up doing all my own stuff, recording it, mixing it. I made quite a bit of mistakes, too....
>
> [During this time] I came back to the roots. You know, I started to get a little historic and understanding. I started to get an urge to understand our own culture. Then I became an activist for it, got myself in lots of problems.... My first main project I did [from a specifically roots-oriented perspective] would have been Ronnie and Emily. It really was an Emily project that she wanted me to do for her. And I wrote the duet, I wrote a number of songs on that album, but I also wrote the duet "Look What Ya Do" that I got her and Ronnie together. So this would have been my connection to Ronnie Butler. And that "Look What Ya Do" turned the whole industry around because that was the song of all songs, man, that played forever. That song did well for me. And with that, that kind of woke me up even more into the rake-n-scrape thing. Even though I was there, that really made me say, you know, this thing could work, man. 'Cause I went to the Dominican Republic and that song was played over there.... And so then, you know, I just like, man, we

need to focus on this thing. I start writing more of the rake-n-scrape; I start fighting for it, you know. I get on the radio stations and talk about it. And yeah, then I started producing lots of people. Ronnie Butler, his album came, and I had "Age Ain't Nothin' but a Number." I had hits coming one right after the other, so I was pretty popular then. (Fred Ferguson, interview with the author, January 10, 2010)

When read against each other, two of the songs Fred mentioned during our conversation illustrate the gradual shift in direction he describes. The first is the song that Fred cowrote with K. B. for Sweet Emily, "Why You Bodder Me," and the second is the duet sung by Ronnie Butler and Sweet Emily, "Look What Ya Do." Released in 1996, "Why You Bodder Me" is a Junkanoo track, written and arranged in the same manner as the Baha Men's work on *Junkanoo!* The song is driven by an and-ONE kick drum, and this rhythm is reinforced by goat-skinned drums and the bass line. The Junkanoo model, promulgated by Dr. Offfff and codified by High Voltage/Baha Men, had become sufficiently established by the mid-1990s that songs in this vein were expected from Bahamian artists.[14] Fred's long experience with this compositional approach thus helped to ensure the success of "Why You Bodder Me." The lyrics consist of Sweet Emily's humorous reflection on her own plus-sized body and sexual energy and her simultaneous derision of any man who would dare attempt to pick her up without fully considering and being ready to respond to the great demands that this would place on him. The celebration of fun in the lyrics and the strong Junkanoo groove made this song a local radio hit, and it was eventually included in the compilation CD *Best of the Best, Volume 1*.[15]

One of the most significant itineraries highlighted by this song is bound up in the fact that it managed to find its way onto local radio and into compilation CDs, but not, like the Baha Men's work, into international distribution. This is representative of one of the main post–Baha Men difficulties faced by Bahamian musicians. The Baha Men were not, as it turns out, the first of many artists to break out of the Bahamian scene and onto the transnational circuit, as might have been expected—they were instead the only band to do so in any sustained way in the 1990s and the first few years of the twenty-first century.[16] The doors to international distribution were open in the early 1990s, but only the Baha Men were prepared to cross that threshold. Compare this lack of a broad base of success within the Bahamas to the international growth of soca in the 1990s, with artists such as David Rudder, Atlantic, Super Blue, Xtatik, and Machel Montano taking advantage of the transnational possibilities open to soca and successfully creating a base that younger artists like Destra, Bunji Garlin, Shurwayne Winchester, Kevin Lyttle, and others were subsequently able to build on. The growth of dancehall traces along a similar, if even more successful trajectory, finding artists such as Gregory Isaacs, Buju Banton, and Shabba Ranks, along with many other artists, making significant strides in the international scene during the early 1990s, thereby paving the way for Beenie Man, Elephant Man, Capelton, Lady Saw, Sean Paul, and a host of other artists.

This comparison to regional neighbors like Trinidad and Jamaica is not entirely fair, however, because the case of the Bahamas is complicated by the loss of the live scene's younger base during the late 1980s. Indeed, because there were only one or two veteran bands capable of breaking into the international scene, and because no younger artists were actively training to follow their lead, success could not follow in the same way it did for Trinidadian and Jamaican artists, who had the benefit of being able to draw on a much more vibrant and eager core of younger musicians just waiting for their opportunity.[17] The itinerary of "Why You Bodder Me" thus highlights this narrowing of horizons for Bahamian musicians.

The relatively few Bahamian artists who have attempted to pursue a career in music since the early 1990s are, by and large, singers like Sweet Emily, who rely on songwriters for material and on backing bands for their live shows (of which there are few). Bands as such have virtually disappeared, with the exception of the four or five outfits I've mentioned previously—Tingum Dem, Visage, Spank Band, Baha Men, and the Falcons.[18] The songwriters, for their part, consist of a very small number of individuals—Fred Ferguson, K.B., Ira Storr, and Eddie Minnis are the most active—and these writers have, more often than not, settled into composing songs in formats they know will generate airplay. The result is an industry environment in which singers are recording material that is lyrically novel but sonically very similar to the last batch of singles.

Unfortunately, this rather strategic approach to composing new material, which has generally discouraged songwriters from embracing innovation and experimentation, has dovetailed with an increasing dearth of performance opportunities, consequently forcing new releases to be consumed within an increasingly local market. That is, a single is no longer released as a sonic incentive to go see a given artist live at weekly shows, because the live scene is no longer active in this fashion. Rather, the single has become a platform from which—if the song does well enough—a singer might be able to secure an invitation to perform at a festival or in a one-off concert. Though tourists can still buy CDs at the airport and in hotel shops and Bay Street's bookstores, the point of releasing a single has shifted away from competing for the best gigs, enticing huge crowds to your venue, and making sales at shows, to securing a tenuous local popularity through exposure to predominantly local listeners. The Baha Men constitute the exception that proves the rule in this context, but the extent to which the local music industry has narrowed its scope and target audience since the 1980s is nevertheless quite remarkable.

Another conceptual shift made explicit in "Why You Bodder Me" concerns the emphasis on prospective nostalgia, which was so fundamentally expressed throughout the Baha Men's debut album and then was gradually abandoned in favor of more immediate concerns during the mid-1990s. This trend was, I should point out, if not initiated, then certainly sanctioned by the Baha Men themselves when they released their sophomore album of 1994—an album brimming with Junkanoo grooves but no longer mobilizing nostalgia as explicitly as had their debut album. Bahamian artists soon followed suit, layering topical and humorous lyrics over their Junkanoo grooves, and Fred and K. B.'s song for Sweet Emily fits well within this lyrical paradigm. The new thematic material for Junkanoo songs also gravitated toward the experience of Junkanoo itself.

The Baha Men, for instance, included "Dance to the Junkanoo" on their sophomore effort. In this song, they remind their audience what should happen when experiencing the sounds of Junkanoo:

> Listen everybody, let me tell you something. It's time to change
>   the way you move.
> You don't have to worry, or even say you're sorry, when you hear
>   the Junkanoo.
> If you feel a rhythm, or a new sensation, makes you wanna get up and dance.
> Shake your body like you're crazy, jump around and carry on like you're mad.
> Dance (to the Junkanoo), shake (to the Junkanoo),
> Jump (to the Junkanoo), wine (to the Junkanoo).
> Move (to the Junkanoo), groove (to the Junkanoo),
> Twist (to the Junkanoo) on time (to the Junkanoo).
> Dance (to the Junkanoo), shake (to the Junkanoo),
> Jump (to the Junkanoo), and wine (to the Junkanoo).
> Everybody join the party, this [is] what Junkanoo's about. (Big Beat 92394–2)

The lyrics explicitly narrate the experience of hearing Junkanoo, reminding would-be dancers that this is what it should feel like to be overcome by Junkanoo. This is clearly a song about being "in the moment" as opposed to reconfiguring the relationship between the future and the past. The same can be said for Visage's "Das Junkanoo!" released in 1996. Consider these lyrics: "And the drums start to play, and the cowbells ring, oh Lord, that's the sweetest feeling. / If you're losing control, 'cause the rhythm's in your soul—Das Junkanoo!" (Stars SCD-1290). The sonic markers of Junkanoo are thus easily paired with direct lyrics related to embodied experiences of the festival, each reinforcing the other in the process. It is worth pointing out here that the underlying excesses tied to the ineffable that I explore in chapter 4 continue to surface in the lyrics of current Junkanoo songs.

In addition to such pointed references, artists began to incorporate more oblique connections to festival Junkanoo, which necessitated at least some local knowledge of the event. As Junkanoo groups rush down Bay Street during the competition, for example, they often engage the crowd in short call-and-response chants that identify the group while drawing spectators (especially their supporters) into an active, participatory role in the parade. The Roots Junkanoo group chants "Roots! There it is!" while the Valley Boys call out "Who are we? The Valley!" Vivian Nina Michelle Wood notes that this type of chant is repeated "until the crowd has reached a frenzy, thus heightening the excitement of the parade" (Wood 1995, 354). Drawing on this practice, the band the Falcons has adopted the Valley Boys' chant, incorporating it into a song called "Go Down to Raysha": "Who are we? The Falcons!" (Stars SCD-1290). Topical/humorous songs and reflections on Junkanoo itself, then, became the general themes for Junkanoo songs during the second half of the 1990s, marking a clear shift away from deploying prospective nostalgia.

The second song Fred mentioned in our conversation charts the beginning of a dramatic shift toward popular rake-n-scrape that can be traced to "Look What Ya Do," released in 1998. Fred wrote and arranged this song, and it serves as a particularly excellent example of the popular rake-n-scrape feel pioneered by Ronnie Butler in the late 1960s. Although the sounds of popular rake-n-scrape were never out of earshot in the Bahamas, partly because Ronnie Butler had inspired other artists to experiment with this sound and had himself continued to perform, the late 1980s and early 1990s belonged to Junkanoo in that the most creative work focused on how to incorporate Junkanoo into dance band formats.[19] To be sure, artists like Eddie Minnis, Ira Storr, Geno D, and Funky D were all producing rake-n-scrape songs during the mid-1990s, but it was "Look What Ya Do" that proved a breakthrough hit. This song, as Fred recalls, "turned the whole industry around" by paving the way for a resurgence of popular rake-n-scrape among songwriters.

One measure by which a resurgence of this sort can be gauged is the proportion of rake-n-scrape songs included in the annual *Best of the Best* compilations. Volume 1, released in 1999, included nine Junkanoo tracks and two rake-n-scrape songs; only two years later, volume 3, released in 2001, featured only four tracks that were driven by Junkanoo rhythms, while fully seven were rake-n-scrape songs. By 2006, when volume 6 was released, the collection included one Junkanoo song and fourteen rake-n-scrape tracks. It is no coincidence that the beginnings of this significant shift away from Junkanoo and toward rake-n-scrape can be traced to Fred Ferguson's release of Sweet Emily's "Look What Ya Do."

Firmly grounded in Ronnie Butler's approach to popular rake-n-scrape, "Look What Ya Do" deploys a two-AND rhythmic structure articulated by the bass and kick drums. This foundation is reinforced by the yuk (performed by the rhythm guitar) and the characteristic saw pattern (performed on the hi-hat in this recording) (see Example 24). This approach quickly became a template that many songwriters used successfully, and by 2006 the popular rake-n-scrape sound dominated the (still limited) windows devoted to local music on the airwaves as well as the major compilation CDs devoted to Bahamian artists.[20]

The shift away from Junkanoo, however, represents more than a musical or stylistic choice. It is perhaps more usefully characterized as a change in emphasis

EXAMPLE 24. "Look What Ya Do." Transcription used with the permission of Isaiah Taylor and the Baha Men.

(continued)

EXAMPLE 24. *continued*

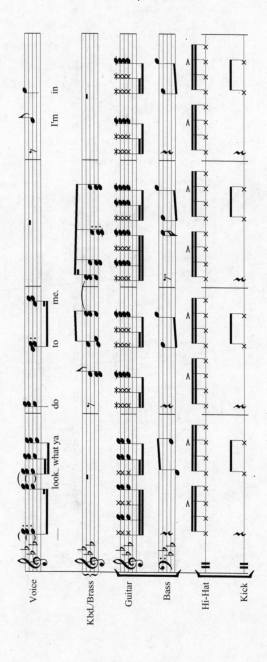

EXAMPLE 24. *continued*

(continued)

EXAMPLE 24. *continued*

on the part of musicians. During the early 1990s, the question of national identity was heavily invested in exploring the roots of Bahamian culture—in performing identity as archaeology. Conversely, by the late 1990s it was more common to perform archaeology as identity. The nuances involved here play out as follows. In the course of their debut recording, the Baha Men were explicitly concerned with performing the act of archaeology itself as a means of generating identity. As I illustrated earlier, however, the ambiguities instantiated in the process of "doing archaeology" reflected back onto identity with open questions, which made it difficult to articulate in any uncomplicated manner answers that could combine to consolidate an adequate expression of Bahamian identity.

And yet, as "Why You Bodder Me" highlights, it is clear that popular Junkanoo itself was stabilized in the process of the Baha Men's efforts and that it was gradually inserted into the very fabric of Bahamian musical life. Although by the middle of the 1990s popular Junkanoo came to be considered a quintessentially Bahamian musical model, it continues to be associated most closely with Nassau and with the center, and not, as it were, with the periphery. As such, popular Junkanoo performances that rely only on the musical heritage claimed in and through the sonic markers of Junkanoo struggle to address the larger questions of identity that the Baha Men explored in and through their lyrics.

This is not, in and of itself, an issue that would have rendered Junkanoo less popular among artists, but it does emerge as a subtle difference in emphasis and function in comparison with popular rake-n-scrape, because rake-n-scrape remained identified with the Family Islands throughout the twentieth century and into the twenty-first. Ironically, the call for a return to roots, issued so compellingly by the Baha Men on *Junkanoo!* is actually somewhat less ambiguously accomplished using the vehicle of rake-n-scrape over Junkanoo. With this in mind, once artists became comfortable working in a genre that was openly (if stereotypically) acknowledged as "roots," questions of identity were further stabilized. In this musical context, archaeology (rake-n-scrape) effectively stands in for questions of identity, allowing anyone performing in that style to claim an unambiguous relationship to Bahamian heritage. Place is mapped onto time through sound. Lyrics of nostalgic character are no longer necessary to prompt this cartographic accomplishment. Rake-n-scrape itself is always already marked as nostalgic, as timeless, and as premodern. To be sure, questions of identity remain open here, as they did in the Baha Men's debut album. But the subtle difference concerns the degree to which sound maps onto the national imaginary. Put otherwise, the "good ole days" are sonically more thoroughly enacted through the performance of rake-n-scrape than they are through Junkanoo.

It was at this moment, moreover, that the saw itself began to find its way back into the musical textures of popular rake-n-scrape. This prompted a general exploration of the musical possibilities opened up by adding the accordion and goat-skinned drum back into the popular rake-n-scrape ensemble, and a deeply roots-oriented sound developed side by side with the more dance-band driven arrangements. Ancient Man, Elon Moxey, the Lassido Boys, and the Brilanders, among others, are all considered exponents of this style, and one of the significant aspects of roots-oriented rake-n-scrape is the extent to which its itineraries of sound crisscross the Bahamas throughout the twentieth century and into the twenty-first. Goombay would not have been possible as such without the influences drawn from traditional rake-n-scrape. Popular rake-n-scrape would have been unthinkable without the demands of the nightclub scene and the experiences of the goombay years. And the roots-oriented rake-n-scrape sound takes this dance band sound and combines it with traditional rake-n-scrape instrumentation, producing a particularly salient example of the center-periphery dynamics at play within the Bahamas. It is also, I suggest, a poignant example of the degree to which the musical landscapes of the Bahamas have been shaped by itineraries of both centripetal and centrifugal trajectories.

It should not come as a surprise, however, that this shift toward popular and roots-oriented rake-n-scrape did not translate into more performance venues, additional sales, or multiplying transnational opportunities for Bahamian artists. Instead, the industry found three or four producers doing the majority of the writing, a small group of singers ready to record that material, and radio stations that (with the notable exception of Island FM) continued to prefer spinning hip-hop and dancehall to rake-n-scrape. And it was in this environment that Fred began to advocate more actively for increased government and local support for the arts. In 2003, he was hired as an entertainment consultant at the Ministry of Tourism, and he was heavily involved in suggesting musical possibilities for the tourism calendar during the four years he served in that capacity. He recalls that his responsibilities at the ministry compelled him to form his current band:

> While in Ministry of Tourism, one of my goals was to lift the level of entertainment. I was the entertainment consultant, and I said, you know, one way I could do that is to put a band together to show the persons what I'm talking about. And this happened around the thirtieth anniversary, so this would be 2003, the thirtieth anniversary of independence. So I put this band together to back all these artists. So here I am—this was the show that we put together. I got Ronald [Simms] to work with me; I just had to put this whole production. I brought home T-Connection for one of their first reunions, brought home Baha Men—they performed also. We had three stages set up, and we had this thing televised live. It was a production, brother—it rained and nobody moved—it was like a massive production. So we pulled that off, and so Tingum Dem [the band] was born there. (Fred Ferguson, interview with the author, January 10, 2010)

Tingum Dem thus became a vehicle for promoting Fred's vision of Bahamian music, which was ultimately bound up in finding ways to foreground both Junkanoo and rake-n-scrape in every possible venue. Fred articulated this vision in radio interviews, at board meetings, in newspapers, and in his concerts and festival performances. But Fred's sense of urgency was not felt by many of his contemporaries. As a result, the discourse about Bahamian musical life came to take on polarized extremes. A few examples should suffice to illustrate this point.

Obie Pindling, the leader of Visage, has consistently approached Bahamian music from a very different perspective. For him, the fact that the membership of his band is Bahamian is sufficient, regardless of the musical genres that they play. In fact, Visage is known regionally as a soca band that also happens to play Junkanoo, and the band has attempted to develop a hybrid of sorts that they call soca-noo. When asked by the *Nassau Guardian's Weekender* magazine about his goals as leader of Visage, Obie offered the following response:

> Our goal is to make Bahamian music as recognizable and as internationally (starting with our region) accepted as music from Trinidad, Barbados, Antigua and Jamaica and our regional neighbours. The Bahamas is not known in our region as a music-making or producing country.... Our goal is to put The Bahamas on the map regionally and to open the door for all our fellow Bahamian brothers and sisters and to break down the barriers so that they too can get their music played and eventually sold in the region and in Caribbean music stores around the world. We want to get our foot in the door and once Visage becomes a household name, then we can drop the Junkanoo sound on them in full force so that everyone everywhere will know that we as a musical nation ... yeah, we reach!! And what will the sound be when the barriers come crashing down? "BRIGGA DUM BRAM!" (Michelle Wells, "Face to Face with Visage," *Nassau Guardian Weekender*, July 30, 2004, p. 1)

It is clear that Obie finds it useful to present audiences with sounds that they will enjoy and to make a name for his band in this fashion before presenting the full force of the Junkanoo sound. This approach has not yet paid off in the way that Obie envisioned back in 2004, and the band has actually moved away from their earlier emphasis on soca in order to more explicitly explore Bahamian arrangements in recent years. And yet the idea that artists need to explore beyond Bahamian genres and aesthetics in order to reach beyond a local market is clearly shared by others within the community, including Devlynn Stubbs, better known as Jah Doctrine, who is currently making a name for himself as a dancehall artist. He has consistently and explicitly chosen to reference his Bahamian roots, but to place these lyrical ideas into a musical context heavily indebted to dancehall.[21] Chris Justilien, a lecturer at the College of the Bahamas and one of the best brass players in the Bahamas has maintained a significant presence on the scene for several decades. He agrees with Obie and Jah Doctrine. In an interview with the *Nassau Guardian*, he offered his assessment of the Bahamian music industry:

Chris Justilien, local music composer and a music Lecturer at the College of The Bahamas, said that he feels that there must be an international dimension to "our music," if we are to achieve global success. "When a young person is exposed to the different styles of the Bahamian music, they can say I like rap music. How can I do rap and put rake'n scrape and reggae in there? And as a result, they come out with a new Bahamian sound." Mr Justilien said that before we can add different dimensions to our music culture, we must first understand what our heritage is all about. "If a young person is then exposed to the different styles of Bahamian music, he or she can then find a way to combine portions of rap music or reggae to it," he said. Mixing international and Bahamian music would produce a fresh new sound, he suggested. "As a people, we are already borrowing influences from all around the world. It's just a matter of how we interpret those sounds [with respect] to our culture." Justilien added that this is something that has been done many times in the past among Bahamian artists. "When I listen to Blind Blake, I hear blues, I hear the influence of the big band era. In George Symonette's music, he is playing jazz, but we don't usually notice and hear those things," he said. (Viraj Perpall, "Our Music Needs a Wider Audience," *Nassau Guardian*, March 15, 2006)

Although Fred Ferguson does not see Chris's comments as antithetical to or incompatible with his own stance (or his own career), he worries that Chris's remark regarding the need for younger artists to know the heritage of Bahamian music—the point he finds most significant and needful—gets lost in translation more often than not. And while Fred understands what Obie is saying when he maintains that Junkanoo comes later, he is concerned that the "later" may never come. The open question, and the issue which polarizes this discourse, revolves around what is necessary in pursuing Bahamian music in the present. Both the popular Junkanoo codified by the Baha Men and the popular rake-n-scrape that has regained the stage in recent years operate, to one degree or another, on the basis of nostalgia. While the explicit prospective nostalgia embedded within the Baha Men's debut album has been muted somewhat since the mid-1990s, both popular Junkanoo and popular rake-n-scrape continue to derive their symbolic power from the links they create with the past. Sonic enactments of place, they map onto the space-time of the Bahamian postcolony in ways that afford a relatively stable vehicle for the production of national identity. In the process, these sonic markers of heritage reify the past in a manner that creates certain challenges, for they point a way toward a future, but can also circumscribe current possibilities. Creating the future-past, it would seem, threatens to obscure the present. Nowhere is this more obvious than in some artists' attempts to create music other than Junkanoo or rake-n-scrape. Artists such as Obie, Jah Doctrine, and Chris subscribe to a present open to the future, but not circumscribed by the past. Theirs is decidedly not a nostalgic approach to identity, but rather a radically presentist one. Fred understands this but worries about moving into a future that no longer references or even remembers the past, heritage, and roots that this approach seeks to (re)present.

The open question that continues to drive this polarizing discourse revolves around the proper place of nostalgia and the past in addressing current needs, for any answer here is transferred through the present onto the conditions of possibility for envisioning productive futures. It is this question to which a nuanced and middle-way answer is required (in spite of the ease with which the opposing positions can be debated) and that continues to follow Bahamian musicians into the second decade of the twenty-first century. It is this question that sits uneasily at the heart of the current musical life of the Bahamas and which, as Fred, Obie, Jah Doctrine, and Chris have all suggested, requires a musical answer. But there is another, larger debate within which this open question must be situated—a debate surrounding the way forward for cultural development in the Bahamas in general. The final section of this chapter, then, explores the debate regarding what forms cultural development and (national) identity might take in the Bahamas as the nation moves toward its fortieth year of independence.

WHAT HAPPENS IF YOU SURVIVE?

This book has thus far traced the musical itineraries of rake-n-scrape and Junkanoo and explored them with respect to geographic, economic, and political frames. I have illustrated that both rake-n-scrape and Junkanoo have repeatedly been mobilized and deployed in the process of representing the Bahamas both to Bahamians themselves and to tourists. I have also demonstrated the ways these musical trajectories have informed identity and the national imaginary in the process. Risking, for a moment, an overly reductionist summary, the 1950s and '60s found Bahamian musicians deploying rake-n-scrape (and in some cases Junkanoo) within the Nassau scene and crafting a subtle poetics of representation that I call the goombay aesthetic. But the 1960s also found many artists taking a deliberately transnational approach to their craft, representing themselves as quintessentially cosmopolitan while simultaneously downplaying specifically Bahamian sounds. During the 1970s and '80s, artists were again engaged in attempts to represent the Bahamas, this time focusing on a cosmopolitan nativism which, I suggest, sought a middle ground between the two approaches prevalent during the previous decades.

By the 1990s, the conditions of possibility for live music had changed considerably, and the Baha Men posited yet another style of representation, this one grounded in Junkanoo but lyrically indebted to prospective nostalgia—essentially a cosmopolitan nativist approach onto which a powerful emphasis on nostalgia was grafted. This approach effectively codified Junkanoo as a viable popular music, but it also marked the first time that the goal of representation was addressed by rethinking the past in such a sustained fashion, both lyrically and musically (identity as archeology). By the turn of the twenty-first century, popular Junkanoo had been, if not supplanted, then certainly outstripped by the resurgence of popular and roots-oriented rake-n-scrape, both of which constitute a reevaluation of the Family Islands as important and useful sites of heritage—a reevaluation made explicit in and through the performance of heritage (archaeology as identity). Both Junkanoo and rake-n-scrape performances, nevertheless, turn to nostalgia to ask (subtly different) questions about the present and future, even as the nostalgia driving their explorations hinders "the distinction between subject and object" (identity as archaeology? archaeology as identity?).

In the process of outlining these itineraries, this book has traced a parallel and quite insistent trajectory of decline in the Bahamian live music scene. To suggest that the scene is currently in dire straights would be to merely state the obvious and perhaps even to understate the situation. And yet, as I have illustrated, there is little agreement regarding a way forward for Bahamian music. This disagreement, moreover, is part of a larger debate within the Bahamas concerning cultural development in general. It is to this larger debate that I now turn.

In October 2004, Vincent Vanderpool-Wallace, then the director-general of tourism for the Bahamas, made a presentation to the Cultural Commission, inaugurated by Prime Minister Perry Christie in 2002, in which he asserted that the central dilemma facing the government remains the same as it was in the early days of tourism under Sir Stafford Sands. That is, tourism sells experiences, and while it recognizes the importance of cultural development, it is not equipped to handle culture except as a commodity. Tourism will attempt to package culture in order to sell it, but the process of supporting, defending, and promoting the cultural life of the Bahamas (upon which tourism depends for its commodities) must be fostered elsewhere. The urgent question remains the same as in previous decades. Where should this cultural work take place? Vanderpool-Wallace's comments, summarized well in an editorial for the *Nassau Guardian,* are worth quoting at length here:

> How can The Bahamas market a tourism product to its visitors that will be etched in their minds and guarantee their return? Vincent Vanderpool-Wallace, Director-General of Tourism, declared to the Cultural Commission that this goal can be achieved through the development of cultural tourism. Mr Vanderpool-Wallace passionately presented the case for the development of the valuable resource of culture as a saleable asset on Wednesday afternoon at Royal Victoria Gardens. . . . Mr Vanderpool-Wallace said exposing visitors to Bahamian culture and making broadly available "parts of the culture that resonate with the visitor" will bind tourists to this destination, making them more than just visitors who only "skim" the sun, sand, and sea "surface." He said, "The value of the culture is to identify elements of it that people seem to like and make it available far more broadly. Then one would suddenly discover that we have a true person for life."

Mr Vanderpool-Wallace stated that tourism ascertains what the customer wants and sells it at a price that he is willing to pay, while cultural development has to do with "finding out what our people want, and celebrating it." . . . Bemoaning the fact that technological developments, such as satellite radios and triple digit cable channel options, have led to the deluge of foreign cultures onto Bahamian society, in may ways displacing its own culture, Mr. Vanderpool-Wallace cited the need for a sole ministry dedicated to Culture. He stated, "Why don't we have a Ministry of Culture that does nothing but maintain a focus on this thing that is so important to all of us?" "Unless we do that, we are going to find ourselves fighting a tidal wave that we can't possibly survive," he said. (Thea Rutherford, "Bringing Culture to the Tourism Market," *Nassau Guardian*, October 14, 2004, p. 1)

So a prominent member of the tourism industry makes it clear that the Ministry of Tourism is the wrong venue for accomplishing the kind of cultural work that individuals like Fred Ferguson are calling for. The Ministry of Tourism is willing to attempt to package and sell culture as long as it can return a profit, and in this sense, Vanderpool-Wallace is arguing for an investment in culture as difference, for the continued exploration (exploitation) of successful ventures such as Goombay Summer and, more recently, Junkanoo in June. Arjun Appadurai insightfully characterizes the agenda that fuels such cultural tourism: "Culturalism . . . is the conscious mobilization of cultural differences in the service of a larger national or transnational politics. It is frequently associated with extraterritorial histories and memories . . . and almost always with struggles for stronger recognition from existing nation-states or from various transnational bodies" (Appadurai 1996, 15). In the case of the Ministry of Tourism, culturalisms serve to generate tourists "for life" by particularizing and differentiating the Bahamian experience from competing destinations.

And yet this type of investment does not, by Vanderpool-Wallace's own admission, constitute cultural development. For that type of cultural work, Bahamians should, according to him, demand an effective and focused Ministry of Culture. Nicolette Bethel, for one, has given up on that prospect. She served as cultural affairs director in the Ministry of Culture from 2003 until 2008, when she resigned her position. In a productive exchange on the prominent blog *Bahamian Pundit*, Nicolette states her case bluntly: "For a generation and a half—the entire time since Independence—our national policies have been shaped by a group of men and a handful of women whose actions and behaviour cumulatively suggest that they would rather erase Bahamian culture than invest in it. Our cultural industries are in effective decline" (quoted in Larry Smith, "Culture Wars in the Bahamas," *Bahama Pundit* (blog), April 22, 2009, http://www.bahamapundit.com/). And according to Larry Smith, this claim can be quantified in that the operating budget for the Ministry of Culture is largely given over to infrastructural and prize-related expenses in support of the annual Junkanoo season. In other words, the Ministry of Culture is charged with cultural development and simultaneously underfunded to such a degree that it cannot adequately fulfill its mandate.[22]

In January 2009, Nicolette Bethel's frustration led her to call for a Day of Absence. Inspired by Douglas Turner Ward's 1965 play of the same name, this day was intended to illustrate just how integral the arts are to Bahamian society. Not surprisingly, this idea generated both support and criticism, though even the criticism was concerned with highlighting the underlying issues in a more productive fashion, and not with discouraging the attempt to draw attention to the state of things. Larry Smith, a frequent blogger on *Bahama Pundit* and a weekly contributor to the *Nassau Tribune,* was generally supportive of the call for such a day, writing himself of the plight of artists in the Bahamas and the generally sparse funding for and institutionalized spaces available to support their creative efforts.[23] Ward Minnis, son of artist and musician Eddie Minnis and an artist in his own right, however, suggested a different way of conceptualizing the work that such a day might accomplish:

> To ask what the Bahamas would be like without *Bahamian* artists is like asking what 100 Jamz would sound like without *Bahamian* music. Artists in the Bahamas have not only had days of absence but have had years, and even decades, of absence. We do not need any more absence. . . . I will say it plainly: it is necessary for Bahamian artists to come out and do something on the Day of Absence because if they stayed home one day, or even a whole week, no one would notice. The metaphor of absence is in error. . . . Ironically, everything I have read about the Day of Absence points at the concept of presence. It is the presence of the arts community that is sorely lacking in the Bahamas. The wider society needs to be reminded that we do exist. We need to put our distinctive stamp on Bahamian living and let our voices be heard. We need to stop waiting for government, to stop pointing fingers at everything "out there" and realize that the greatest hollow is actually in our own back yard. We need to be here—really here. Or, to paraphrase the words of Helen Klonaris, the new day will be born only when we come out of absence. (Larry Smith, "An Abridged Critique of Nicolette Bethel's 2005 Day of Absence," *Bahamian Pundit* [blog], January 1, 2010)

This powerful reframing of the very point of the Day of Absence revolves around the metaphor of presence, but it also obscures the frustrating institutional and governmental itineraries that have driven Nicolette to resign her position and have pushed Fred to pronounce the Bahamas well on their way down a "spiraling path to cultural hell." Minnis's prescription for a Day of Presence in which Bahamian artists need to collectively "be here—really here" articulates a sit-in as opposed to a walk-out mentality, but it misses the appeal of a walk-out for those artists who have "sat in" for as long as Nicolette and Fred have. In any case, the sobering realities of the cultural landscape in the Bahamas suggest that a collaborative answer to this question—one articulated by artists, cultural activists, and government officials alike—is necessary if a productive future is to be imagined in the present. And this is, ironically, as important for artists and ordinary Bahamians as it is for the Ministry of Tourism.

And this brings me to a final reflection on how the metaphors of absence and presence can productively be placed into dialogue with the idea of nostalgia. The Baha Men's experiment with prospective nostalgia produced an album that prescribed a particular relationship to the past in which archaeology becomes the means through which identity can be crafted for use in the future, but one that at least potentially "hollows" the present by privileging the past. In this sense, one of the consequences of prospective nostalgia is the potential to absent oneself from the present, to stop "being here," where "here" refers to a time as much as, if not more than, a place. The ambiguities inherent in the process of producing identity through recourse to prospective nostalgia stem, then, as much from the difficulties related to ascertaining who can claim "true-true" readings of the past and, for that matter, who can claim to adequately apply them in the current moment, as they do from the here/not here slippage that these itineraries can create. In other words, if the present has reached the point of requiring rescue from the past, how is it possible fully to inhabit the present? The call to "Bring Back da Good Ole Days" summarizes well the double bind of prospective nostalgia. The time traveler still occupies the present but runs the risk of not being fully "present." And yet the absence that this call signals is one of deep significance, for it illustrates an antipathy with the present that, if not addressed in productive fashion, results in events like Nicolette's "Day of Absence."

The resurgence of rake-n-scrape was driven by a commitment to performing heritage as a template for identity (archaeology as identity), by which I mean that the very performance of rake-n-scrape (regardless of lyrics) qualified as participating in the project that the Baha Men had set out to complete. As such, rake-n-scrape performances rely far less on prospective nostalgia, thereby also running less risk of "hollowing" the present. And yet the production of heritage as a template instead of as an active engagement with the past potentially creates an absence in the realm of creative vision, in that the parameters of performance have become increasingly fixed. The risk in this case is an (unintended) absence potentially affecting visions of the future. It revolves around whether rake-n-scrape artists will actively engage in envisioning possible futures while churning out music dictated by a relatively fixed template rooted in heritage.

Musical approaches bound up in mobilizing nostalgia to one degree or another thus risk, on the one hand, not fully engaging with or being present in the contemporary moment (that is, not being able to deploy a critical and productive intervention in the present)—Junkanoo!—or, on the other hand, not being able to adequately generate the creative vision necessary to engage with and project presence into future possibilities—rake-n-scrape. The musical approaches concerned with current trends, such as those promulgated by Visage in the early years of the twenty-first century and Jah Doctrine more recently, by contrast, are particularly adept at projecting presence and are in a strong position to articulate new visions regarding the future of Bahamian music. The potential absence here, then, is concerned with the past. In reacting against the circumscribed approach to identity proffered by approaches that mobilize nostalgia (i.e., Bahamians play Junkanoo and rake-n-scrape), they run the risk of silencing history, of muting the past, and of disconnecting their practice from narratives of cultural identity and heritage (assuming, that is, that they would be interested in remaining connected to these narratives in the first place).

Each of these approaches brings powerful representational tools to bear on Bahamian music, and all constitute valuable contributions to the scene. And yet all of the artists involved find themselves in a political and economic situation the realities and frustrations of which prompted the "Day of Absence." As part of a broad-based vision for cultural development, each of these approaches could add unique perspective and depth to the arts, but that vision has not emerged as a policy priority in the itineraries traced throughout this book. As a result, these creative projects stand on their own, present, to be sure, but not visible or audible enough to constitute a vital "presence." I should be clear that this book is in no way intent on providing a way forward for cultural development in the Bahamas. It is, if anything, an account of the deep roots, the multiple routes, and the creative approaches to representation that have defined Bahamian musical life since the 1950s.

And yet, in the process of exploring the centripetal and centrifugal patterns of musical production and consumption that have accompanied the Bahamas from Crown Colony to nationhood, it has also become clear that the musical life of the Bahamas, as it currently stands, finds itself in a considerable crisis. Changes in the way tourists travel (all-inclusive resorts, cruises, etc.), continued lack of political will to invest in the arts, and the near total disappearance of truly skilled musicians have all contributed to this state of affairs. It remains to be seen whether a productive vision of the future can be articulated and then enacted or whether the scene will continue to dissolve into a few isolated home studios producing a trickle of singles for use on local radio and performance at a handful of concerts a year. I end where this chapter began, agreeing with Juan Antonio Blanco that, with respect to musical life, at the very least, "Tourism is a sort of chemotherapy. You have cancer and it's the only possible cure, but it might kill you before the cancer does" (McGeary and Booth 1993). The question is, what happens if you survive?

Epilogue

It's about 7 PM on July 10, 2009. I've just walked into Da Tambrin Tree Club in the Summer Winds Plaza off Harrold Road. It's a nice space, complete with a restaurant and bar, an outside patio, a dance floor, and a raised stage for bands. I order some grouper fingers and fries, along with a Kalik, and settle down at the bar to talk with Fred Ferguson and Ronald Simms, the proprietors of the club. On the way over here, I noticed that the club is a bit out of the way, especially if you count Nassau's Bay Street shopping district as central to New Providence. It's not downtown at all. In fact, it's located strategically between the Cable Beach Strip and downtown, but on an east-west artery that remains over the hill (i.e., south of Bay Street). The logo for the club depicts a tamarind tree, a tree particularly well known for its wide canopy and deep roots and associated in local lore with providing soothing shade for storytelling sessions and general relaxation. It is, as such, a deliberately nostalgic and distinctively Bahamian symbol to mobilize for the purposes of generating solidarity and a shared sense of history.

The club opened in August 2008 and serves as a great place to grab a drink with friends and, most nights, to dance to deejay sets or sing karaoke. But on Friday and Saturday nights, the club plays host to a live band called Tingum Dem. This is one of only two clubs in Nassau to feature live music outside of the hotels and resorts (the other is the Backyard Club, owned and operated by Ira Storr and featuring the Spank Band). Fred and Ronald have chosen to market the live music to a demographic they calculate will become loyal customers—the forty- and fifty-something crowd. These two generations of Bahamians would have been clubbing during the last two decades of active musical life in Nassau, would remember what it's like to dance to live music, and would—both Fred and

Ronald hope—have the resources to support this kind of nightlife. To that end, the repertory is decidedly old school, featuring a heavy dose of local and international hits from the 1970s and '80s.

Fred grabs a stool next to me, Ronald leans against the bar facing us, and they begin talking about the struggles of keeping the club open, the difficulties they face in generating a consistently strong base of support from locals, and the obstacles to getting tourists, especially those staying in all-inclusive resorts, to venture out to the club. Their vision is to develop this club on the model so successfully deployed by Freddie Munnings Sr. during the late 1950s and '60s, when his Cat and Fiddle Club was the jewel of the local entertainment industry. This model provided experiences for both local and tourist audiences, including live music, special programs and concerts, and floor shows that showcased so-called native traditions (like limbo and fire dancing). Fred and Ronald are hoping to establish Da Tambrin Tree as a truly local venue that can offer a range of experiences to its patrons.

The floor shows Fred and Ronald envision are intended primarily for tourists. As Ronald tells it, they are proposing to the Ministry of Tourism, along with the cruise ship companies and the taxi companies, a floor show they call "From Then 'Til Now." It is intended as a review of Bahamian entertainment from the 1950s to the present and will also feature a "driving tour" of the island. The idea is to get passengers on the cruise ships to buy tickets in advance, meet them at the dock in taxis equipped with good public address systems, and then bus them to Da Tambrin Tree, regaling them with sights and sounds of the Bahamas en route. Once in Da Tambrin Tree, Tingum Dem will cycle through a series of hits from each decade starting with the 1950s. This soundtrack will be accompanied by choreographed dancing in different styles (based on the decade being reviewed), interspersed with a few looks back at fire dancing and limbo, and all managed by two masters of ceremony.

Fred and Ronald are hoping that the club can host a number of these tours during the week, a venture that would more than cover their overhead costs and allow them to focus on developing their local clientele. They are also hoping that the show will grow so that they can afford to offer more live music at the club. I'm listening with interest, not least because Fred sent me the script for the show a few weeks back and I've been wondering about how the logistics would work and how the show fits into the other offerings at the club. Fred and Ronald are clearly excited about the possibilities that could grow out of the show, and more urgently, they are counting on it to materialize as a revenue stream to alleviate their tenuous financial situation. Almost a year into this venture, they are, by their own accounts, just barely hanging on, and neither of them sees any way that their cash flow situation can improve without the influx of tourist dollars.

I returned to Da Tambrin Tree in January 2010 and the negotiations with government, cruise ships companies, and taxi outfits were still ongoing. The latest issue was that the cruise ships wanted a different venue entirely, owing to concerns over insurance and liability issues. Bottom line: the venue had to be closer to the ships so the taxi ride could be eliminated. Fred and Ronald screened for me the demonstration video they had shot of the show and remained optimistic as they discussed progress with me, but both of them indicated that they couldn't wait much longer for this to happen without being forced to close the club. Eighteen months into their joint venture, they were at the brink of gaining some success or conceding failure.

As it turns out, the government came through with an ideal space in the spring of 2010. The space is in the (unused) Junkanoo Museum in Festival Place, which is right on the docks and therefore central to all of the cruise-tourist foot traffic. The Ministry of Tourism even agreed to allocate money to renovate the space and provide the necessary furnishings, lighting, and sound system to make this show at home in that space. As I write these words, all of these commitments are still in their early stages, however, and it would not surprise me in the least to see the preparations falter. That said, the prospect of being able to put on several shows a week, and perhaps even multiple shows per day, has encouraged Fred and Ronald to continue pushing through with their idea. The bittersweet reality they now face, however, is that they were forced to close Da Tambrin Tree. They simply could not keep up with the overhead and are now looking for a less expensive venue in which to reopen the club in the future. Their dream of creating a space in which both tourists and local clientele could encounter each other and share musical experiences has, for the moment at least, been put on hold, but the revenue stream they consider crucial to making that dream a reality seems tantalizingly close at hand.

I relate this story here because it highlights many of the struggles explored throughout this book. Da Tambrin Tree, by its very existence, fought against the prevailing economic pressures militating against operating a locally owned club. It resisted the notion that live music is a thing of the past in Bahamian clubs. Da Tambrin Tree proved—again—that it has become exceedingly difficult to attract tourists to local venues, and it also illustrated that there is only a moderate amount of support for clubs among local audiences. Like so many clubs that came before it, moreover, Da Tambrin Tree closed.

"From Then 'Til Now," for its part, is a project predicated on a nostalgic approach to representation similar to that in evidence on the Baha Men's album *Junkanoo!* Unlike that project, however, Fred and Ronald's show is focused squarely on the story of the center itself instead of on the periphery. It mobilizes the past in the present, envisioning a future when these memories could again be lived experiences—the Bahamas, imagined once again as a "tourist honeypot." That it is marketing this prospective nostalgia to tourists and selling the idea of bringing back "da good ole days" to cruise passengers hearkens back to the self-exoticizing floor shows put on at local nightclubs in earlier decades and also draws a direct connection between local solvency and the excesses of tourist itineraries. Fred and Ronald both recognize that tourist "buy-in" has historically been crucial to the live scene in the Bahamas and "From Then 'Til Now" is an attempt to restore at least some of those connections and to explore anew the encounters they would enable.

Both Da Tambrin Tree and the show that Fred and Ronald have designed offer poignant examples of the continued struggles facing those who wish to promote live music, local entertainment, and a sense of "presence" for Bahamian arts in general. They also engage with the many itineraries related to roots, routes, and representation that have animated the pages of this book. As such, they provide a fitting and open-ended reminder that the questions raised here remain open and contested and that Bahamian musicians continue to turn their creative vision toward accumulating possible (and necessarily partial) answers to those questions.

NOTES

PREFACE

1. Further illustrating the trends affecting locally owned and operated nightclubs in Nassau, Da Island Club closed in the summer of 2008 because the Nassau Beach Hotel was being renovated. No space will be available for this nightclub when the hotel reopens.

2. See, for example, Inderia Saunders's front-page editorial "'The Reef' Officially Opens," *Nassau Guardian*, December 20, 2007.

1. NASSAU'S GONE FUNKY

1. Anthony Dahl is, of course, not alone in his assessment. Questions of colonialism and the postcolony have shaped works as diverse as Jamaica Kincaid's novel about Antigua, *A Small Place* (2000); Jocelyne Guilbault's ethnographic study of music and cultural politics in Trinidad, *Governing Sound* (2007); and Deborah Thomas's anthropological reflection on race in Jamaica, *Modern Blackness* (2004), to offer only three important explorations of these ideas.

2. *The Real Bahamas in Music and Song* is the title of a recording originally released in 1966 by Elektra and recently rereleased by Nonesuch Records in its Explorer series (2003: CD 79725). It contains a selection of folk music performed by various artists and participates in the same logic that drives cultural nationalist ideas about Bahamianness, featuring musical traditions that, by 1965, when the recordings were made, had already become largely folklorized for lack of active and widespread performance. This musical monument to folklore was then titled *The Real Bahamas*, thereby suggesting that the real or essential culture of the Bahamas remains located in the past.

3. This peripheral status, incidentally, holds for the academic community as well. Very little work has been published on the Bahamas relative to other locations around the region, and that is especially the case in musical scholarship.

4. The material presented in this section has benefited tremendously from the careful and thorough historical research compiled by Michael Craton and Gail Saunders in their two-volume *Islanders in the Stream: A History of the Bahamian People*. Michael Craton's earlier work, *A History of the Bahamas*, has also proved indispensable. Their work stands as the best overarching account of the social and political history of the Bahamas to date.

5. The economic ventures that have historically sustained the Bahamas, for instance, can themselves be read as trafficking at the interstices and seams of established markets. These ventures have taken myriad forms, including the siphoning off of excesses (wrecking, privateering, piracy) and practices that offered for sale goods and services that were in some way regulated elsewhere (blockade running, rumrunning). Even tourism can be read in this light, capitalizing as it does on other kinds of surpluses, in this case vacation time and excess income.

6. For more detailed information about the Eleutheran Adventurers, including William Sayle, their leader, see Henry C. Wilkinson, *The Adventurers of Bermuda* (New York: Oxford University Press, 1958), and John Bregenzer, *Tryin' to Make It: Adapting to the Bahamas* (Washington, DC: University Press of America, 1982). The adventurers' articles of incorporation are reprinted in Robert Curry, *Bahamian Lore* (Paris: Private printing, 1930), 115–22.

7. See John Oldmixon's account in *The History of the Isle of Providence* (Nassau: Providence Press, 1949), which is excerpted from *The British Empire in America*, 2 vols. (London: Brotherton and Clarke, 1741), and John Graves, *A Memorial or Short Account of the Bahama Islands* (London, 1708), for more details concerning the relationship between governors and population in the Bahamas during the late seventeenth century.

8. A vast amount of material (much of it mythologizing or sensational) has been generated regarding piracy in the Caribbean. See the following sources—only a few of the important contributions to that literature—for detailed accounts of this period in Bahamian (and Caribbean) social and economic history: Charles Johnson [Daniel Defoe], *A General History of the Pyrates* (London, 1724; reprint, Nabu Press, 2010); Marcus Rediker, *Between the Devil and the Deep Blue Sea: Merchant Seamen, Pirates, and the Anti-American Maritime World, 1700–1750* (Cambridge: Cambridge University Press, 1987); Peter Galvin, *Patterns of Pillage: A Geography of Caribbean-Based Piracy in Spanish America, 1536–1718* (New York: Peter Lang, 1999); Kris Lane, *Pillaging the Empire: Piracy in the Americas, 1500–1750* (New York: M. E. Sharpe, 1998); and C. R. Pennell's edited collection, *Bandits at Sea: A Pirates Reader* (New York: New York University Press, 2001).

9. According to Cluster and Hernández (2006), "In 1762 it [Havana] was significantly larger than Philadelphia and about three times the size of New York" (2006, 22).

10. The Bahamas were briefly occupied by the American Navy in 1776 and then captured by the Spanish in 1782, only to be liberated from that indignity by American loyalist Andrew Deveraux in 1783. From that point on, the Bahamas remained under British rule until its independence in 1973.

11. Although this influx of people significantly altered the demographics of the Bahamas, they represent only a very small fraction of the some hundred thousand refugees who sought new homes in Nova Scotia, Canada, and the West Indies in the wake of the Revolutionary War. For more detailed information on the loyalists, see Wallace Brown, *The Good Americans: The Loyalists in the American Revolution* (New York: Morrow, 1969); Gail Saunders, *Bahamian Loyalists and Their Slaves* (London: Macmillan Caribbean, 1983); and Michael J. Prokopow, *"To the Torrid Zones": The Fortunes and Misfortunes of American Loyalists in the Anglo-Caribbean Basin, 1774–1801* (PhD diss., Harvard University, 1996).

12. Samuel A. Floyd Jr. has discussed the importance of the ring shout within African American music in several of his publications. The influx of such a large number of slaves and free blacks from the new United States into the Bahamas makes the ring shout and ring dances in general of signal importance to the musical life of the Bahamas. See Floyd, *The Power of Black Music: Interpreting Its History from Africa to the United States* (New York: Oxford University Press, 1996), for a detailed discussion of this practice.

13. See Bridget Brereton, *A History of Modern Trinidad, 1783–1962* (New York: Heinemann, 1982), for a detailed discussion of this period in Trinidad.

14. For detailed accounts of the abolitionist movement and its impact on the West Indies, see Christopher Brown, *Moral Capital: The Foundations of British Abolitionism* (Chapel Hill: University of North Carolina Press, 2006), and David Davis, *Inhuman Bondage: The Rise and Fall of Slavery in the New World* (New York: Oxford University Press, 2006). For specific information relating to the Bahamas, see Whittington Johnson, *Race Relations in the Bahamas, 1784–1834* (Fayetteville: University of Arkansas Press, 2000), and Howard Johnson, *The Bahamas from Slavery to Servitude, 1783–1933* (Gainesville: University Press of Florida, 1996).

15. An account of these festivities was also included in Charles Farquharson's journal of 1831–32. Farquharson was a planter living in San Salvador, and the entry for Wednesday, December 26, 1832, reads as follows: "Some of our people gon [*sic*] abroad to see some of their friends and some at home amusing themselves in their own way threw the day, but all of them home in the evening and had a grand dance and keep it up until near daylight" (Farquharson 1957, 82–84).

16. In a truck system, employees are often paid with commodities in advance, thereby initiating a cycle of debt from which they cannot extricate themselves. Once indebted to the company, they are paid in credits that must be spent at a company store where goods are expensive and of poor quality.

17. The practice of maintaining mutual aid and burial societies was, of course, a longstanding tradition among Afro-Bahamians dating from well before emancipation.

18. The Bahamas' historical reliance upon events in North America for its own economic health is one of the principal means through which the Bahamas has come to occupy a place "apart" from the rest of the West Indies and the Caribbean more generally. The Revolutionary War, the Civil War, and Prohibition each provided opportunities for economic growth that found the Bahamas looking north instead of to the British Empire for direction.

19. A grim account of the vicious cycle endured by the spongers was offered by L. D. Powles in 1888: "He applies to the owner of a craft engaged in the sponge or turtle fisheries, generally the two combined, to go on a fishing voyage. He is not to be paid wages, but to receive a share of the profits of the take. . . . At once comes into play the infernal machine, which grinds him down and keeps him a slave for years and years. . . . His employer invariably keeps, or is in private partnership with someone who keeps, a store, which exists principally for the purpose of robbing the employé. . . . As soon as a man engages he has to sign seaman's articles, which render him liable to be sent on board his vessel at any time by order of a magistrate. He is then invited, practically forced, to take an advance upon his anticipated share of profits. . . . Preliminaries settled, the fisherman starts on his sponging or turtle voyage, and remains away from six to twelve weeks, when he returns with his cargo of sponges. These he cannot by law take anywhere except to Nassau, where they have to be sold in the Sponge Exchange by a system of tender. The seller is a Nassau merchant, the buyer—usually the agent of a New York firm—is also a Nassau merchant; and that the two agree together and arrange a bogus sale, by means of which they rob the unhappy fisherman, I am convinced. The sale over, the amount realized is declared, and owner and fisherman proceed to share. The fisherman is already liable to the owner for his original advance, and his share of the expense of provisioning the vessel. Nine times out of ten the former makes out that there has been a loss and the fisherman is in debt to him, or, at any rate, that there is nothing to divide. The latter has then no recourse but to sign articles for a fresh voyage, in return for which the merchant advances him the wherewithal to keep body and soul together . . . the relations of master and slave are established!" (Powles 1996 [1888], 85–89).

20. Craton and Saunders point out that the Out Islands remained "fixed in the age of sail well into the twentieth century. This difference intensified the traditional division to the point that Nassau, 'a sleepy Rip van Winkle sort of place' to outside visitors, appeared a virtual dynamo compared with Out Island settlements sunk in a timeless torpor" (1998, 74).

21. The Royal Victoria Hotel was a major step forward from what had, until that time, been a rather informal lodging situation based on private residences. Advertisements placed in the Nassau Guardian offer some sense of this early scene. On November 29, 1844, for instance, Nathaniel French placed this advertisement for his Victoria House on West Hill Street: "Where Gentlemen and Ladies can be accommodated with Board and Lodging by the day, week or month. This house is located on one of the pleasantest and most healthy situations of the town, and its accommodations are adapted as well for families or for single persons." The lodging house eventually came to be called French's Hotel.

22. A systematic rebuttal of Froude's book, titled Froudacity: West Indian Fables, was published by the Trinidadian John Jacob Thomas in 1889.

23. Peter Henry Bruce describes the Bahamas as follows: "The Bahama Islands enjoy the most serene and the most temperate air in all America, the heat of the sun being greatly allayed by refreshing breezes from the east; and the earth and air are cooled by constant dews which fall in the night. They are free from the sultry heat and little affected by frost, snow, hail, or the northwest winds, which prove so fatal both to men and plants in our other colonies. It is therefore no wonder the sick and afflicted inhabitants of those climates fly hither for relief, being sure to find a cure here" (Bruce [1782] 1949, 44).

24. The following passage betrays Ives's paternalistic and romanticized view of Bahamian life: "Nobody appears to be at work. In sunshine or shadow, having nothing and wanting nothing, taking no thought for tomorrow, they live on like the birds from day to day, not needing to take lessons of the ant nor of any other of the world's greedy and grasping toilers. All are merry, lighthearted, and joyous; nobody frets or scolds; not a child cries; and the dogs, crouching beside their indolent masters, are literally too lazy to bark. All the thieving is of the petty kind—it would be too much like work to plan and execute robbery on a large scale—and what is the use of committing burglaries and grand larcenies when a little sugar-cane or a handful of fruit fills to overflowing the measure of their wants! There are no trades-unions, no commercial revulsions, and no strikes for higher wages. No heads ache from the pressing weight of the crowns they wear, and no brains give out in the ceaseless and crazy struggles for wealth and power. Voluptuous idleness is the happy offspring of these charming isles of the sea, where frosts are unknown, and health and happiness float on each passing wave of the soft, perfumed air" (Ives 1880, 55–56).

25. The four hundred rooms of the luxurious Hotel Colonial, however, never lived up to their builder's dream of hosting waves of tourists. The building burned down on March 31, 1922, just before the real era of tourism began in the Bahamas. It was rebuilt as the New Colonial in 1923 under American ownership.

26. "For some days after we first arrived at the Royal Victoria, young Africa gave frequent vocal entertainments in the court of the hotel. The voices of some were soft and musical, and they sang the religious songs which they had learned in 'the shouting meetings,' with perfect abandon. . . . The songs sung on these occasions probably have never been printed or reduced to writing. Having taken some of them down, we subjoin them for the benefit of those of our readers who may have a curiosity to know something in regard to their character, although the words alone give only a faint representation of their merits when wedded by these uncultured people to music, and sung with a fervid enthusiasm, born of a native love of melody and of genuine devotional feelings" (Ives 1880, 73–74).

27. These figures are derived from the census taken on April 14, 1901. Of the 57,735 Bahamians accounted for in the census, roughly 22 percent (12,534) lived on New Providence. The remainder of the population was dispersed throughout the Out Island settlements (Craton and Saunders 1998, 176).

28. These first flights by Pan American World Airways were made with seaplanes (Sikorsky-38s), and they landed and tied up right in Nassau Harbor. The first flight arrived on January 2, 1929 (Cleare 2007, 73–74). According to Stafford Sands, "Nassau became the second overseas city to be served by scheduled commercial service (Havana was first a few months earlier)" (Sands 1960: 180).

29. The Over-the-Hill clubs were locally owned clubs located in the Afro-Bahamian neighborhoods of Nassau. These clubs catered to clientele that included both Afro-Bahamians and tourists, making them important social crossing places within the Bahamas.

30. The Cambridge Orchestra, the first professional Bahamian orchestra, was founded in 1923 by Bert Cambridge (piano). This seven-piece orchestra included Harold Curry (violin), John Coakley (saxophone), Oliver Mason (trumpet), Mannaseh Strachan (bass),

Arthur Pinder (trombone), and Harold Deveaux (drums), and the ensemble was instrumental in fighting for local performers' rights to play at the hotels along Bay Street. Maxwell Thompson also played sax and clarinet with the Cambridge Orchestra. The Chocolate Dandies, active during the 1930s, served as a training ground for two musicians who would go on to become fixtures on the Bahamian entertainment scene—George Symonette and the bandleader and trumpeter Lou Adams Sr.

31. This pattern of migration from the periphery to the center had begun in earnest during the Prohibition era (i.e., in the 1920s), but was to accelerate during the ensuing decades, creating significant challenges for communities living in places like Cat Island, Eleuthera, and Long Island.

32. Unfortunately, there is no way to verify Moxey's account, because ZNS-1 did not archive its materials, habitually reusing tape (recording over existing programs) and failing to store those master tapes that did survive in appropriate fashion. As a result, no tapes of this landmark radio program have survived into the present.

33. See Michael Eldridge, "There Goes the Transnational Neighborhood: Calypso Buys a Bungalow," *Callaloo* 25/2 (2002): 620–38, and Ray Funk and Donald Hill, "Will Calypso Doom Rock 'n' Roll: The U.S. Calypso Craze of 1957," in *Trinidad Carnival,* ed. Garth Green and Philip Scher (Bloomington: Indiana University Press, 2007), for more detailed information about the calypso craze and its impact on popular music in the United States during the 1950s.

34. Among the various cultural reasons for relegating the goat-skinned drum to traditional and exoticized spaces within the nightclub scene in Nassau was the very practical fact that the head of the drum needed to be "fired" every forty-five minutes or so in order to maintain the appropriate amount of tension. This meant that the drummers either took the time between sets to place their drum close to a fire or, later, placed a Sterno lamp inside the drum. This later practice was, of course, a fire hazard. Another practical reason for choosing conga drums over the goat-skinned drum is that congas are easily mounted on stands, making it much more practicable for the drummer to stand and interact with other performers and audience members during the performance.

35. For a detailed account of Trinidadian Carnival, see John Cowley, *Carnival, Canboulay, and Calypso: Traditions in the Making* (New York: Cambridge University Press, 1999). For overarching explorations of Carnival in the Caribbean, see Gerard Aching, *Masking and Power: Carnival and Popular Culture in the Caribbean* (Minneapolis: University of Minnesota Press, 2002), and Richard Burton, *Afro-Creole: Power, Opposition, and Play in the Caribbean* (Ithaca, NY: Cornell University Press, 1997).

36. The Street Nuisance Act of 1899 was particularly restrictive of Junkanoo celebrations because it proscribed musical and social activities during nighttime hours. Although a waiver was built in to the law which legalized Junkanoo celebrations, it restricted the event to the hours between 4AM and 9AM on December 26 and January 1, thereby shortening it considerably. This legislation remained in effect until 1954, when the ban was lifted with a view toward promoting more tourist involvement in the celebration.

37. Many thanks to Ken Bilby, whose research on Junkanoo confirms that Cat Island Junkanoo had to be imported from Nassau toward the end of the twentieth century for lack of local Junkanoos (personal communication, 2007).

2. "MUDDY DA WATER"

1. Take for instance the following passage published by the Society for the Propagation of the Gospel in 1901: "The greater number of the islands are peopled entirely by negroes, who, 'though nominally Christian, are to a great extent practically heathen.' . . . Even with all their love of witchcraft, their riotous wakes and dances, and other enormities, the blacks are still a delightful people, whom to teach and train is as happy an employment as Missionaries could desire." Relatively clear from this short excerpt are the blatantly paternalist attitude toward Bahamians and the general attitude taken by nineteenth-century missionaries toward practices that fall into the category of social dancing (Pascoe 1901, 226–27a).

2. Pindling's remarks, delivered at the National Conference on Independence, April 12, 1972, and Moxey's efforts at recovering cultural markers for use in the present can fruitfully be compared to the strategic hybridities envisioned in Trinidad and Jamaica a decade earlier, as Eric Williams and Norman Manley worked to unite their respective populations around images of "Mother Trinidad" and mottos such as "Out of Many One People." Shalini Puri, *The Caribbean Postcolonial: Social Equality, Post-nationalism, and Cultural Hybridity* (New York: Palgrave Macmillan, 2004), explores these ideas in particularly productive ways.

3. This lack of documentation has a long history in the Bahamas. L. D. Powles, resident in the Bahamas during 1886–87, wrote in his memoirs: "The people of New Providence have been at so little trouble to preserve any records of their history that in this [history of Fort Charlotte], as well as other matters, it is difficult to arrive at the truth" (Powles 1996 [1888], 193).

4. This was a repeating pattern throughout the region. For a particularly rich and useful study of these practices and processes and additional case studies along these lines, see Rebecca Miller, *Carriacou String Band Serenade: Performing Identity in the Eastern Caribbean* (Middletown, CT.: Wesleyan University Press, 2007).

5. That the accordion would gradually assume a central place in rake-n-scrape ensembles beginning in the late nineteenth century is consistent with the rapid opening of markets for accordions throughout the world at this very moment. For a detailed history of the globalization of accordions, see Christoph Wagner,ed., *Das Akkordeon oder die Erfindung der populären Music* (New York: Schott, 2001).

6. See, for example, the *Caribbean Voyage* series of recordings released by Rounder, throughout which Lomax recorded both African-derived and European-influenced musical styles and made a point of exploring the interconnections between them.

7. Many thanks to Ken Bilby, who shared with me some of his unpublished field notes by virtue of which I have been able to corroborate my own research and gain some valuable insights into the idiosyncratic nature of quadrille performance in the archipelago.

8. It is interesting to remember that goombay was the name used to discuss the entire spectrum of traditional music in the Bahamas before 1968, when Charles Carter coined the term *rake-n-scrape*. The entertainers working in the nightclubs were, thus, appropriating a name that carried a great deal of local meaning and translating it into popular use, strategically marking their product as specifically Bahamian, though none of them

wished to actually incorporate the sounds or instruments associated with goombay into their sets.

9. According to Basil Hedrick and Jeanette Stephens, "The word 'goombay,' as it is broadly used today [1976], appears to have come into being in the 1950s, when Bahamian musicians (such as Edward 'Apple' Elliott, George Symonette, 'Blind' Blake Higgs, and Berkeley 'Peanuts' Taylor) decided to coin a name for the music indigenous and exclusive to the Bahamas. They appear to have used the word 'goombay' since it was the already existing local term for a drum" (Hedrick and Stephens 1976, 45).

10. Ronnie named this song "Crow Calypso" because it borrows its melody from an earlier goombay song of the same name.

11. This song was written for Ronnie by singer/songwriter Alia Coley and as such illustrates the kinds of lyrical themes that local artists associate with Ronnie's career.

12. A great wealth of scholarship has been devoted to exploring the folklore of the Bahamas. For some representative examples, see Daniel Crowley, *I Could Talk Old-Story Good: Creativity in Bahamian Folklore* (Berkeley and Los Angeles: University of California Press, 1966); Basil Hedrick and Cezarija Abartis Letson, *Once Was a Time, a Wery Good Time: An Inquiry into the Folklore of the Bahamas* (Greeley: University of Northern Colorado, Museum of Anthropology, 1975); Elsie Clews Parsons, *Folk-Tales of Andros Island, Bahamas* (New York: American Folk-lore Society, 1918); and Charles Edwards, *Bahama Songs and Stories: Memoirs of the American Folklore Society III* (New York: Houghton, Mifflin and Co., 1895).

13. Ronnie Butler was, in fact, articulating in song a sentiment that would become ever more prevalent as the Bahamas moved toward national independence. The back-to-the-bush movement of the late 1970s, for example, was built on the same ideology.

3. "CALYPSO ISLAND"

1. Paradise Beach is located on Paradise Island, which is located just off New Providence and connected to Nassau by bridge (since 1966). But Paradise Island was originally known by the much less inviting name of Hog Island. In 1959 Huntington Hartford purchased it from Axel Wenner-Gren and changed its name to the much more appealing Paradise Island. Since that time, the island has been heavily developed. Today, Paradise Island is home to the sprawling Atlantis Resort, which is the largest nongovernment employer in the Bahamas. The history of Paradise Island illustrates the degree to which the best land and best beaches have been controlled by foreign investors. For a more detailed exploration of this particular case, see Paul Albury, *The Paradise Island Story* (London: Macmillan Caribbean, 1984).

2. The liner notes, as such, attempt to incorporate senses other than sight—more than the tourist's gaze, that is—into the range of possibilities for Bahamian tourist experiences. Though the eye has, for a variety of reasons, remained one of the most powerful ways of engaging with questions of power and inequality in colonial and postcolonial encounters, Tim Edensor has recently attempted to take seriously the entire range of sensory experiences that together make up tourist encounters. His approach, to which I will return later, is helpful in carving out space for sound in the analysis of tourist experience.

For details of his argument, see Edensor, "Sensing Tourist Spaces," in *Travels in Paradox: Remapping Tourism,* ed. Claudio Minca and Tim Oakes, 23–45 (New York: Rowman & Littlefield, 2006).

3. This is Manning's way of rethinking the actual impact of the "demonstration effect" that tourism is often accused of generating among local populations. For a discussion of the demonstration effect, see Polly Patullo, *Last Resorts: The Cost of Tourism in the Caribbean,* 2nd ed. (New York: Monthly Review Press, 2005).

4. The songs included on *Bahamas Treasure Chest* include "Calypso Medley," Roy Shurland; "Conch Ain't Got No Bone," Eric Gibson; "The Crow," Peanuts Taylor; "Goombay," Richie Delamore; "Calypso Island," Eric Gibson; "Bahama Lullaby," Roy Shurland; "The Wreck of the John B. Sail," Roy Shurland; "The Limbo," Richie Delamore; "Gin and Coconut Oil," Kasavubu; "Little Nassau-Bahama Mama Medley," Eric Gibson; "Bellamina," Roy Shurland; and "Junkanoo," John Chipman.

5. Alice Simms wrote a number of calypsos, including "Calypso Island," "Stranded," "Coconut Fall on De Head," "Like Ma-ad," "Lizzie Carry Basket on Head," "Island Woman," "Liza, Open Up De Door," "Coconut Water, Rum, and Gin," "All Suit No Man," and "De Eye to Big for De Belly."

6. By the mid-1960s, the Bahamas Ministry of Tourism would make these associations a great deal more explicit than did the lyrics of "Calypso Island." I offer as an example one print advertisement from 1967. The advertisement consists of a photograph and a caption with a bit of narrative printed below. The photograph is of a (Caucasian) woman clothed in a sundress, lying half on her side and half on her back, propped up on her elbows. She is lying in about a foot of ocean water, and the water extends to the horizon behind her and to the edge of the frame on the sides. The caption reads "Let's assume I'm an Island." The narrative text reads: "I've got a casino that looks like the Taj Mahal. Golf courses men adore. And if skin diving's your pleasure, I've got that, too. The best in the world. I'm Grand Bahama Island. Just 2½ hours from Times Square and that's what I call conveniently located." Other variations on this theme include several women arranged in roughly the shape of the Bahamian archipelago and labeled with names of the various islands (i.e., New Providence, Cat Island, Bimini, Eleuthera, etc.). This unabashed marketing of sex is already present in the lyrics of "Calypso Island" and has continued to define the advertising campaigns of the Bahamas since that time. "Are You Big Enough for the Bahamas?" and "It's Better in the Bahamas!" are only two examples of this trend.

7. The Development Board was inaugurated in 1914 but had not yet moved the Bahamas aggressively toward making tourism a viable sector of the economy. That said, the board had secured contracts with steamship companies, facilitated hotel encouragement acts, and made available favorable terms for investments.

8. Stafford Sands points out: "The last of Nassau's "Flagler-Florida Boom Era" hotels—The Fort Montagu Beach (now The Montagu Beach)—was erected in 1926. More than a quarter of a century was to pass before another major hotel would be built in Nassau" (Sands 1960, 179–80). However, significant improvements in airport facilities were achieved during the 1940s.

9. In terms of print advertising, the Bahamas material was regularly featured in major magazines and newspapers during the 1950s, "including *Business Week, Esquire,*

Cosmopolitan, Times, Mademoiselle, Harper's Bazaar, Ladies Home Journal, House Beautiful, and fishing magazines" (Cleare 2007, 128). Sales offices were initially opened in Miami, New York, Chicago, Dallas, Toronto, and Los Angeles (Sands 1960, 188). The public relations aspect of the strategy included the deliberate creation of special events that could be advertised as such. The Out Island Regatta (later renamed the Family Island Regatta), various fishing tournaments, and Speed Week (a racing event), were all designed to entice off-season visitors to the Bahamas.

10. It would take another decade before foreign capital investors and the leverage they held in negotiations owing to the Bahamian economy's deep dependence on tourism began to temper the optimism of the 1950s in earnest.

11. Eloise Lewis's familiarity with bolero should not come as a great surprise. The success of Cuban bolero-son groups like the famous Trio Matamoros, for example, was widespread, and their music was popular throughout the Caribbean. For discussions of the influence of Cuban ensembles during this time, see Deborah Pacini Hernandez, *Bachata: A Social History of Dominican Popular Music* (Philadelphia: Temple University Press, 1995), and Gage Averill, *A Day for the Hunter, a Day for the Prey: Popular Music and Power in Haiti* (Chicago: University of Chicago Press, 1997).

12. George's arrangement also makes use of a long-short-short pattern in the bass, but it is performed at a much faster tempo and, as such, does not invoke the bolero in the way that Eloise's arrangement does.

13. For some excellent reflections on this moment in calypso's heyday within the realm of popular music, see Michael Eldridge, "There Goes the Transnational Neighborhood: Calypso Buys a Bungalow," *Callaloo* 25/2 (2002): 620–38, and Ray Funk and Donald Hill, "Will Calypso Doom Rock 'n' Roll? The U.S. Calypso Craze of 1957," in *Trinidad Carnival: The Cultural Politics of a Transnational Festival,* ed. Garth Green and Philip Scher (Philadelphia: Temple University Press, 2007).

14. See chapter 1, note 30, for more information regarding the Cambridge Orchestra. The Chocolate Dandies were notable in part because both George Symonette and Lou Adams emerged from that orchestra and became leading figures in the musical life of the Bahamas. The Lou Adams Orchestra, for its part, initially included Adams himself (trumpet), Bruce Coakley and Eric Cash (saxophones), Morris Harvey (piano), Fred Henfield (bass), and Leonard Perpall (drums). Another ensemble that proved to be an important training ground for many of the horn players who performed in Bahamian nightclubs during the 1950s and '60s is the Royal Bahamas Police Force Band.

15. Racial discrimination was to continue throughout the 1950s, necessitating hotels for colored guests—including the guest house attached to the Chez Paul Meeres, the Rhinehart Hotel, the Alpha Hotel, and Weary Willies, among others. The year 1956 proved an important turning point in the fight for social justice in the Bahamas, as the question of discrimination in businesses and hotels was openly debated in the House of Assembly. The debate led to a gradual shift toward equal access during the late 1950s and early 1960s.

16. Munnings's orchestra was a major training ground for young Bahamian musicians, and many foreign musicians (notably Jamaican guitarist Ernest Ranglin, who played with the orchestra during the mid-1950s) spent time in the ensemble as well. Just

before he left the Zanzibar, the orchestra included Munnings himself on clarinet; Eric Russell, alto sax; Blanche Horton-Stuart, violin; George Wright, trumpet; Walter Neville, trumpet; Anthony Woodside, trumpet; Leonard Johnson, drums; Simon Rolle, bass; and John Clarke, piano.

17. Freddie Munnings enrolled in the popular music program of the New England Conservatory. He studied there for a semester (September 1954 to January 1955), taking voice lessons, arranging, piano lessons, and solfège.

18. *Troubadour* is also used to designate singer-songwriters in Haiti. Gage Averill describes them as singer-composers, called *twoubadou-s,* who often play with a guitar and sing "Haitian *mereng* in pan-Latin style, sometimes backed up by a small string-based trio or quartet. . . . Troubadours are expected to communicate truthfully and with irony, humor, and a lot of strategic ambivalence and wordplay" (Averill 1997, 15).

19. By contrast, one of the principal dehumanizing aspects of the panopticon was that the prisoner was made acutely aware of uninterrupted, unremitting surveillance. The prisoner came to understand that no action, however small, would go unnoticed. The desired psychological effect of this type of surveillance was that it would lead in due time—in theory, at least—to compliance even without surveillance.

20. As it turned out, Freddie Munnings eventually invited Ronald to play in the last incarnation of the Cat and Fiddle Band when Ronald was fourteen.

21. The monthly arrivals figures for the 1950s indicate that year-round tourism stabilized around 1957, when each month of the year saw more than ten thousand visitors (194,618 total for the year). By comparison, 1954 saw six such months (109,605 total); 1955 generated seven such months (132,434 total); and 1956 raised this number to ten (155,003 total) (Cleare 2007, 557).

22. The Progressive Liberal Party, formed in 1953, gained popular support in the late 1950s. The push for majority rule, however, was a long-fought process. As early as 1958, one of the major figures in the party, Milo Butler, taking advantage of the economic and political unrest generated in the wake of that year's general strike, called on Bahamians to look closely at their representatives (who were mostly white and wealthy). He publicly agitated for majority rule, encouraging Bahamians to "get rid of white man rule in this country" (Craton and Saunders 1998, 311). It would take almost a decade to realize this goal. The central dilemma was that people were being asked to vote for real representation in government at a time when tourism was expanding at record-breaking rates, for though these changes served to exacerbate the economic inequalities within the country, they simultaneously made a change of government seem extraordinarily risky.

23. Angela Cleare illustrates the extent of the anticasino lobby: "To reduce the negative influences on the local community, Bahamian citizens and residents have always been barred from gambling in any of the casinos and initially Bahamians were not allowed to take employment in the gaming industry" (Cleare 2007, 158).

24. The following is a list, by no means exhaustive, of the nightclubs operating in the hotels of Nassau and the Family Islands during the 1950s and 1960s. The list is excerpted from the document "How to Correct at Least 90% of the Problems That We Are Now Experiencing in the Business of Music in the Bahamas Today," compiled by Ronald Simms, Freddie Munnings Jr., and Cedric Munnings in the 1990s. These three entertainers

created a company called Premier Entertainment Promotions in the 1990s in order to lobby the Bahamian government to provide more support for local musicians. In the document they divide the clubs into two categories: those located in the hotels of Nassau and the Family Islands and those located outside of hotels in Nassau and the Family Islands. Clubs in hotels, Nassau and the Family Islands included the Back Room, Out Island Bar, Silk Cotton Tree, Buccaneer Lounge, Coyaba Room, Pastiche, Harbour Club, Rat Trap, Cinnamons, Sugar Mill Pub, Mystique, Sultan's Tent, Trade Winds, Palm Pavilion, Pilot House, Pino's, and The Crow's Nest. Clubs outside of hotels, Nassau and the Family Islands included Backside, Piece & Plenty (Exuma), Glass Bucket, Club Yama-Bahama, Purple Mae, Sandpiper, Joker's Wild, Pink Pussycat, Bayside, Dirty Dicks, Junkanoo, Adastra Gardens, Banana Boat, Drum Beat, Zanzibar, the Native Club, Yellow Bird, Vicky's, Sugar Hill, Fox Hill Jungle Club, African Clubs, Silver Slipper, Oasis, King and Knights, Clipper Lounge, Johnson's, Miller's, Pieces of Eight, Blue Marlin, Chicharney, Tide Out, Rumours, the Junkanoo Lounge (Freeport), Island House, Charlie Charlie's, Big Bamboo, Bar Mar, Black Beard, Cat and Fiddle, Lemon Tree, Conch Shell, Hutch, Bird Land, Central Highway, Lovers Holiday, Moon Glow, Golden Isles, Playboy, Flying Dutchman, Tropicana, Sin, Blue Note, Club 36, Shoal, Family Island, the Palace, Ronnie's Rebel Room, Sloppy Joe, Buena Vista, Waterloo, Poinciana, Roselawn, and the Calypso Club

25. Charles Carter is referring here to Richie Delamore, Pat Rolle, and Carl Brice, among others.

26. Goombay drums needed to be "fired" every forty-five minutes or so and were therefore a nuisance in floor shows. This was especially the case in productions that were intended to keep everyone hopping for hours at a stretch. Peanuts Taylor tells of a time in the early 1950s when he was performing in Los Angeles, and the fire he had built to heat his drum caused a serious disturbance. He credits his move to the conga drums (in part at least) to this early experience (Peanuts Taylor, *Bahamians* [radio program], May 3, 2003).

27. The tracks on *This Is Carl Brice* (Tropical Recording Co., 3218, 1966) include "Back to Back," "Birth of the Blues," "Girl from Ipanema," "Hello Dolly," "Island In the Sun," "Mary Ann," "Misty," "My Funny Valentine," "Old Black Magic," "When I Fall in Love," and "Yellow Bird."

28. The tracks on Richie Delamore's *Free Again* (Carib LP-2035, 1968) include "Always Something There to Remind Me," "Angelina," "Free Again," "Goin' Out of My Head," "Honey," "How Insensitive," "Look of Love," "Love Is Blue," "MacArthur Park," "My Cup Runneth Over," "What the World Needs Now," and "Windy."

29. A few examples of this move to record recent hits include: "Always Something There to Remind Me" (recorded by Dionne Warwick in 1967), "Honey" (recorded by Bobby Goldsboro, 1968), "How Insensitive," "Look of Love" (recorded by Dusty Springfield for the *Casino Royale* soundtrack, 1967), "Love Is Blue" (performed as the Luxembourgish entrant in the 1967 Euro Vision song contest), "MacArthur Park" (recorded by Richard Harris, 1968), and "Windy" (recorded by the Association, 1967).

30. Junkanoo instruments were far more likely to find their way into recordings and floor shows than were the saw and accordion of traditional rake-n-scrape ensembles. I discuss musicians' reticence to use rural and peripheral sounds and instruments in nightclub performance in chapter 2. That said, one quasi exception to this prevailing

trend is the "Calypso Medley" performed by Roy Shurland and the Big Bamboo Orchestra and included on *Bahamas Treasure Chest*. In this performance, the standard rake-n-scrape saw rhythm is scraped out on a wooden scraper (instead of maracas), and the characteristic accents are vigorously emphasized. Though not played on a saw, that rhythmic cell thoroughly dominates the percussive backdrop to the medley and is one of the more unambiguous and explicit references to rake-n-scrape practice recorded during the goombay years.

31. John Chipman was one of the premier Bahamian drummers and dancers during this period, and he continues, incidentally, to welcome tourists to the Bahamas, performing at the Prince George Wharf as cruise passengers arrive.

32. With the increasing institutionalization of Junkanoo during the middle decades of the twentieth century, the competitive clashes were virtually eliminated from the festival.

33. Interestingly, no sustained attempt was made to incorporate Jamaican musical style into the sonic palette of Bahamian nightclubs. The sounds of ska and, later, reggae were envied by Bahamians (and the rest of the region), who saw the international success of these genres as a great achievement. In the 1970s and 1980s, Bahamian musicians attempted to achieve a parallel success with Junkanoo-based popular music. I address this effort in greater detail in chapter 5, but suffice it to say here that I know of only one recording by a Bahamian of ska—Smokey 007, backed by the Treasure Isle All Stars, recorded a seven-inch of "Jambalaya"/"Laura" on Dutchess Records (Tel. 25629) in the mid-1960s.

4. "GONE TA BAY"

1. The design, pasting, and painting of set pieces for Junkanoo happens in what are called shacks. Each group has its own shack (Government High School happened to use their gym), and each group somehow manages, in the days just before Junkanoo, to turn what looks (and must feel) like an insurmountable mountain of work into magnificent finished pieces in time (usually just barely in time) to hit Bay Street.

2. Junkanoo groups engender a great deal of pride in their membership and among their fans, so much so Yonnell had to institute a rule stipulating that no Government High Junkanoos are allowed to come to Junior Junkanoo wearing any paraphernalia relating to their adult group affiliations. In other words, the only group they are representing tonight is Government High.

3. "Civil Servant," cowritten by K. B. and Samuel Heastie, went on to win the People's Choice category during the tenth annual Cacique Awards in 2005.

4. Goals posted to the cultural affairs section of http://www.bahamas.gov.bs (as of June 26, 2008).

5. *Junkanoo Talks!* is broadcast every Saturday morning at 11:00 AM on ZNS 1540 AM.

6. Attempts to interrogate the extent to which Junkanoo can be understood from (and as growing out of) a Christian perspective have been increasingly pursued by church groups and academics alike within the Bahamas, so much so, in fact, that a symposium called "Junkanoo and Religion: Christianity and Cultural Identity in the Bahamas" was convened in March 2002.

7. This section is indebted to the excellent research of E. Clement Bethel (1991) and Judith Bettelheim (1979; 1988). Their research was groundbreaking in that it identified and collected many of the sources that subsequent scholars of Junkanoo have relied on.

8. Another interesting aspect of Young's description concerns the degree to which this account seems to parallel descriptions of Bahamian ring dances like the jumping dance.

9. It is important to keep in mind, however, that the earliest accounts of yuletide celebrations in the Bahamas do not offer accounts of Junkanoo per se. Rather, they describe celebrations that were antecedent to but not generative of the later emergence of Junkanoo in the 1840s.

10. For a more detailed exploration of the etymology of *Junkanoo,* see Michael Craton, "Decoding Pitchy-Patchy: The Roots, Branches, and Essence of Junkanoo," *Slavery and Abolition* 16/1 (1995): 14–44.

11. This idea regarding cross-recognition and mutual adaptation motivated Sidney Mintz and Richard Price's groundbreaking attempt to explore the complexities attendant to New World cultural formations. See Mintz and Price, *The Birth of African-American Culture: An Anthropological Perspective* (Boston: Beacon Press, 1992 [1976]).

12. The appearance of Neptune and Amphitrite as characters in the Christmas Junkanoo was rather short-lived in Nassau, roughly spanning the 1850s (first reported in the *Nassau Guardian* in 1854). The practice most likely came to the streets of Nassau by way of the southern island of Inagua, where the community had a great deal of trade contact with Haiti. In fact, wealthy Inaguans would often travel to Port-au-Prince instead of Nassau for their shopping and trade. E. Clement Bethel suggests that the vodou festival of *Agwé* may have provided inspiration for incorporating these characters of the sea. Neptune and Amphitrite continued to appear in Inagua's Junkanoo celebrations for many more years (Bethel 1991, 30–31).

13. Liberated Africans were considered quite troublesome before emancipation. To mitigate their influence on the rest of the population, they were settled in an area about seven miles southwest of Nassau proper in 1825. That settlement was initially called Headquarters and later renamed Carmichael. Adelaide and Gambier, located even farther from Nassau, were founded to ease overcrowding in the 1830s. Closer to town, in the Over-the-Hill section of Nassau, Grant's Town was also eventually heavily settled by liberated Africans, as were Bain Town and Fox Hill. Fox Hill, for instance, contained three loosely bounded sections, or towns, called Congo, Nango, and Joshua Town, each settled by liberated Africans. Concerns over adding too many liberated Africans to the population of New Providence found approximately half of the sixty-five hundred settled in various Out Islands (Craton and Saunders 1998, 3–9, 103).

14. See Gail Saunders's account of the growth of Over-the-Hill communities in *Bahamian Society after Emancipation,* 2nd edition (Princeton, NJ: Marcus Wiener, 2003).

15. Though not directly related to Junkanoo, it is nevertheless significant that until the 1950s, Grant's Town, Fox Hill, and Bain Town were renowned for their obeah experts. Though not sanctioned by the Christian context in which they practiced their craft, the communities they lived in were very aware of obeah and it was part of their collective experience.

16. The excellent dissertations of Vivian Nina Michelle Wood (1995) and Keith Gordon Wisdom (1985), along with E. Clement Bethel's book on Junkanoo (1991), are good sources for the history of Junkanoo in the Bahamas. The following sections have benefited immeasurably from those earlier efforts.

17. Junkanoo group leaders, interestingly, were more open to moving the parade to the sports center because the diminutive physical dimensions of Bay Street restricted the extent to which they could innovate in the areas of costume design and group size (Wood 1995).

18. But it is important to recognize that Boxing Day was officially made a holiday in 1938, allowing Junkanoo to be moved out of the Christmas Day slot it had previously occupied, thereby offering some concession to those opposed to Junkanoo on religious grounds.

19. In fact, the *Nassau Guardian* published reports of illicit Junkanoo parades in 1942, 1943, and 1944. The account from 1944 also featured news of arrests: "During New Year's Eve and New Year's morning the Police were obliged to disperse several crowds of men who were parading through some streets ringing cowbells and making other noises. Several men were arrested and convicted in the Magistrate's Court this morning on charges of disturbing the peace" (*Nassau Guardian*, January 3, 1944).

20. The parallels here to Carnival and calypso in Trinidad during the same decade are striking (Cowley 1999; Dudley 2007; and Stuempfle 1996). It was during the 1950s that steel pan gained social legitimacy in Trinidad and calypso tents were slowly being reconsidered in positive terms. It was also when Junkanoo was reconfigured as a national symbol and a legitimate activity in its own right.

21. The resulting album, *Junkanoo Band–Key West,* recorded by Marshall W. Stearns in 1964, is still available through Smithsonian Folkways at http://www.folkways.si.edu/albumdetails.aspx?itemid=897.

22. Scrap refers to groups that participate in Junkanoo without paying too much attention to their overall theme, their costuming, or their music. In other words, it is about the experience of "rushin'" in Junkanoo itself that motivates scrap bands, as opposed to the desire for national recognition within the framework of the institutionalized Junkanoo competition.

23. For a detailed interrogation of the rules and regulations, the categories for judging, and the competition more generally, see Vivian Nina Michelle Wood, "Rushin' Hard and Runnin' Hot: Experiencing the Music of the Junkanoo Parade in Nassau, Bahamas" (Indiana University, 1995). Arlene Nash-Ferguson also offers a glimpse into these aspects of Junkanoo in *I Come to Get Me: An Inside Look at the Junkanoo Festival* (Nassau: Doongalik Studios, 2000).

24. It is interesting to note that during their first two years on Bay Street, the Valley Boys paraded behind the banners of their sponsors—Model Bakery (1958) and City Lumber Yard (1959) (Wood 1995, 88).

25. For an excellent review of the winners and participants in Junkanoo since 1948, see Anthony B. Carroll's two-volume *History of Junkanoo* (Bloomington, IN: AuthorHouse, 2007)

26. The social commentary made possible through Junkanoo is not dissimilar in scope and effect from the musical invectives offered by Trinidadian calypsonians and

carnival groups during the same decades. For discussions of these themes in Trinidadian calypso, see Donald Hill, *Calypso Calaloo: Early Carnival Music in Trinidad* (Gainesville: University of Florida Press, 1993); Hollis Liverpool, *Rituals of Power and Rebellion: The Carnival Tradition in Trinidad and Tobago, 1763–1962* (Chicago: Research Associates School Times, 2001); and John Cowley, *Carnival, Canboulay, and Calypso: Traditions in the Making* (New York: Cambridge University Press, 1996).

27. This section adapts and synthesizes some of the materials assembled by Vivian Nina Michelle Wood (1995) and Yonell Justilien (2004).

28. That said, however, the Over-the-Hill beat (sometimes just called the hill beat) tends to be played during the Labor Day Celebrations in June (Wood 1995).

29. To be clear, my transcription of the dragging beat is not intended to communicate that the bass drummers are always exactly one thirty-second note late, but rather to illustrate the slightly delayed arrival of their downbeat drum stroke.

30. The Café Johnny Canoe incorporates a small group of Junkanoos into its dinner-hour entertainment. These performers "rush" through the restaurant, playing Junkanoo for the guests. Junkanoo in June is a large cultural festival designed to introduce tourists to the arts, crafts, food, and music of the Bahamas. It is held at the Fish Fry on Arawak Cay.

31. For detailed studies of Santeria and vodou, see Margarite Fernandez Olmos and Lizabeth Paravisini-Gerbert, eds., *Sacred Possessions: Voodoo, Obeah, Santería, and the Caribbean* (New Brunswick, NJ: Rutgers University Press, 1997); David Brown, *Santería Enthroned: Art, Ritual, and Innovation in an Afro-Cuban Religion* (Chicago: University of Chicago Press, 2003); Katherine Hagedorn, *Divine Utterances: The Performance of Afro-Cuban Santería* (Washington, DC: Smithsonian Institute Press, 2001); Elizabeth McAlister, *Rara! Vodou, Power, and Performance in Haiti and Its Diaspora* (Berkeley and Los Angeles: University of California Press, 2002); Claudine Michel and Patrick Bellegarde-Smith, eds., *Invisible Powers: Vodou in Haitian Life and Culture* (New York: Palgrave Macmillan, 2006).

5. "A NEW DAY DAWNING"

1. Black, aquamarine, and gold are the colors of the national flag of the Bahamas.

2. The songs presented on *A Nation Is Born* include "Oh Freedom" (spiritual); "I'm a Better Woman Than You" (calypso); "Upward, Onward, Forward, Together" (popular rake-n-scrape); "The Mail" (popular rake-n-scrape); "Run, Come See" (goombay); "Exodus" (R&B); "Rushing through the Crowd" (popular Junkanoo); "Funky Nassau" (funk); "Independent Bahamas" (funk); "A New Day Dawning" (soul/R&B); "Pumpkin, Bananas, Peas, Corn" (goombay); "March On, Bahamaland" (national anthem).

3. In fact, between 1967 and 1973, Lynden Pindling, the leader of the Progressive Liberal Party, was deliberately styled as the Bahamian Moses, leading the people out of Egypt (colonialism).

4. Some of the more radical voices formed the Vanguard Party of the Bahamas in 1972. See John T. McCarthy, "The Influences of the Black Panther Party (USA) on the Vanguard Party of the Bahamas, 1972–1987," in *Liberation, Imagination, and the Black Panther Party: A New Look at the Panthers and Their Legacy*, ed. Kathleen Cleaver and George Jatsiaficas, 156–63 (New York: Routledge, 2001).

5. See Craton 2002 and Craton and Saunders 1998 for more detailed discussions of the economic factors facing the Bahamas in the early 1970s.

6. Sir Stafford Sands, the former minister of tourism, had entered into such contracts with three ships in 1964. The contracts were due to expire in 1969, and the Pindling-led government felt the expenditure hard to justify going forward.

7. In 1968, for instance, stopover visitors spent $168,726,000 compared to the $11,668,000 spent by cruise visitors (Cleare 2007, 225)

8. As logical as this decision appeared at the time, this calculus proved, in the long term, to be based on the flawed premise that arrivals by air would continue to outpace arrivals by sea. In fact, the decision was reached at the very height of the imbalance between air and sea arrivals, when three out of every four tourist arrivals were by air. Throughout the 1970s, the balance shifted so that approximately two out of every three arrivals were by air. By the early 1980s, arrivals by sea began to outpace those by air. Today, the ratio is inverted, with approximately two out of every three arrivals coming by sea. In order to give a rough sense of how radically different the expenditures of stopover (mostly by air) compared to cruise arrivals are, I offer the statistics on these categories from 2004: Cruise visitors: 3,360,012; cruise expenditure: $185,817,482. Stopover visitors: 1,561,312; stopover expenditure: $1,693,486,565 (Cleare 2007, 373). This translates to an average expenditure of fifty-five dollars for cruise visitors and $1,085 for stopover visitors. The difference is staggering. The government's decision was based, in part at least, on the continued dominance of stopover arrivals. The consequences of this trend for the entertainment sector cannot be overstated.

9. See Polly Patulli, *Last Resorts: The Cost of Tourism in the Caribbean,* 2nd edition (New York: Monthly Review Press, 2005), for a more detailed discussion of the cruise ship industry and its economic and ecological effects on the region.

10. Ronald Simms's career with the Soulful Groovers, a band he formed subsequent to his stint with the Munnings Orchestra, is just one example among many.

11. These included the T-Connections, Frank Penn, the Beginning of the End, Tony McKay, Dr. Offfff, the Soulful Groovers, the Mighty Makers, Willpower, Average Age, and High Voltage.

12. By the mid-1990s, only four viable bands remained active—the Baha Men, Visage, the Spank Band, and the Falcons. Of these, only the Baha Men played at a level of proficiency comparable to the bands of the 1970s.

13. The first of these acts secured by the Ministry of Tourism was the dance and Junkanoo troupe led by John Chipman.

14. Including a decidedly nonlocal instrument may seem incongruous in a song that encourages confidence in things Bahamian, but the steelpan had achieved a measure of local acceptance from the 1950s on and several local performers were associated with the instrument (including Count Bernadino). The Afro-Creole roots of the instrument, moreover, afford a measure of solidarity—a solidarity that is not out of step with Frank Penn's suggestion that Bahamians should stay in the bush.

15. This back-to-the-bush cosmopolitanism, it should be noted, was not unique to the Bahamas. In fact, the Caribbean was home to multiple experiments along these lines during the late 1970s and 1980s. Take, for example, the song "Milk and Honey," recorded in

1977 by the Dominican cadencelypso band, the Midnight Groovers. This song posits the same nostalgic view of local traditions as do the songs by Ronnie Butler and Frank Penn: "Bring back the milk and honey . . . cane juice and bush medicine, vanilla and cassava . . . we've got to remember the good old days." Similar patterns can be traced a bit later (during the late 1980s) in Haiti as well, where the recordings of *mizik rasin* bands like Boukan Ginen and Boukman Eksperyans were motivated, in part at least, by concerns for cultural reclamation.

16. For a more detailed discussion of this negative appraisal of Obeah within the Caribbean, see Jerome Handler and Ken Bilby, "On the Early Use and Origin of the Term Obeah in Barbados and the Anglophone Caribbean," *Slavery and Abolition* 22 (2001): 87–100; and Jerome Handler and Ken Bilby, "Obeah: Healing and Protection in West Indian Slave Life," *Journal of Caribbean History* 38 (2004): 153–83.

17. Exuma even incorporates a bit of throat singing into this track.

18. The band that backed Dr. Offfff in concert and in the studio during the 1980s was called High Voltage. It changed its name to the Baha Men in 1991.

19. Alston Records was a subsidiary of Atlantic Records and was distributed by Atco Records, based in New York City.

20. This was a relatively healthy trip up the Hot 100 Chart. "Funky Nassau" stayed on the charts for fourteen weeks, debuting at number 94 the week of May 8, 1971, and steadily climbing to no. 15 by the week of May 17. The single's fifteen-week Cash Box run was similar. It debuted at number 97 the week of May 1, 1971, peaked at number 10 the week of July 24, and ended its run at number 38 the week of August 7. Thereafter it fell off the charts rather quickly, hanging on through the week of August 7, when it placed at number 34. "Funky Nassau" peaked at number 7 on the Best Selling Soul Singles Chart on May 29, 1971, and managed an eleven-week run on that chart. In addition, a six-week UK Chart run began some years later, when "Funky Nassau" debuted at number 47 the week of February 23, 1974, and rising to number 31 the week of March 16. It finished at number 50 the week of March 30.

21. The basic issue surrounding the chance to open for Marvin Gaye revolved around the lack of a reciprocal agreement between the United States and the Bahamas with regard to entertainment. The concert organizers thus felt it more appropriate to hire musicians from within the United States to perform with Marvin Gaye. An agreement of the sort that would have made it feasible for the Beginning of the End to play New York that year wasn't put in place until 1977.

22. This strategy was not completely unique within Bahamian musical life, as evidenced by the combination kalik and saw rhythms in George Symonette's version of "Calypso Island" (see chapter 3). It is nevertheless a bold and thoroughgoing example of the rhythmic possibilities available to musicians willing to combine rake-n-scrape and Junkanoo, and one that, in contrast to Symonette's composition, highlights rather than obscures the sources of these rhythmic markers.

23. A notable exception to this general trend was the version of this song included on the Baha Men's debut album, *Junkanoo*, which does feature the simultaneous performance of Junkanoo and rake-n-scrape rhythms throughout the arrangement.

6. "BACK TO THE ISLAND"

1. Fred's studio is currently an entirely digital affair. It has been so long since he has needed to play a cassette tape that he doesn't even have a tape deck in his rack. In order to listen to these tapes, we had to haul an old boom box out of the closet and connect from the headphone output into his mixing board.

2. A notable exception to this trend is the singer/songwriter Kirkland Bodie (K. B.). Born in the early 1970s, he played for several years with a the Freeport-based Ego Tripp band during the 1980s. He has written and produced several albums showcasing younger artists in the company of more established musicians—albums with names like *Best of the Best, Island Jams,* and *Island Classics.* The songs on these compilation albums, however, predominantly feature vocalists who have recorded over K. B.'s tracks. When K. B. himself performs, he does not bring his own band, but rather supplies the house band for the given festival or show with a set list that they then rehearse prior to the show. The number of house bands upon which any such festival or concert can draw is, today, limited to three or perhaps four groups; Tingum Dem, Visage, the Spank Band, and the Falcons. Moreover, the core musicians in all but Visage, are Fred's age.

3. In a twist of irony, it has been the churches of the Bahamas that have benefited most from the decline in the entertainment sector. These days, when Fred needs a new bass player or drummer for a project, he often has to pry them out of a church gig, because these remain the most consistent jobs available to musicians.

4. Compass Point was built by Chris Blackwell of Island Records and became a major studio destination in the Caribbean during the 1980s and early 1990s. An excellent retrospective, "Funky Nassau: The Compass Point Story, 1980–86" was released in 2008 by Strut Records (Strut-033CD). Compass Point has since been superseded by less cost-prohibitive digital studios.

5. *Here We Go Again* was released in Japan under the Toy's Factory label (TFCK-87702) in 1996.

6. Perhaps illustrating that both Isaiah and Fred had good points in their disagreement, in 2001 the Baha Men broke into the United States market with a cover of an Anslem Douglas soca tune called "Who Let the Dogs Out?" The song soared onto the *Billboard* charts and became one of the most successful sports anthems of the year, heard in virtually every stadium in the country. Isaiah's decision to experiment with other sounds paid off, but at the cost of recording a cover of a soca tune, a cost that Fred believes was too high.

7. This represents a significant reevaluation of the merits of cosmopolitanism within the Bahamian national imaginary. During the push toward independence and in the decade after achieving that goal, the Bahamas was actively engaged in presenting itself in precisely these terms. During the late 1970s and into the 1980s, however, artists like Dr. Offffff, Exuma, and Frank Penn questioned this approach to national identity, and the Baha Men clearly continue to question it in their debut album.

8. As I illustrated in chapters 2 and 3, the mythology of the Family Islands as locked in time and antimodern has been flawed from the start. And yet the stereotype persists, in large part simply because the Family Islands are not Nassau.

9. Wilmoth Houdini's recording was released as a 78 by Decca (23543) in 1945.

10. The theme of the Promised Land, incidentally, maps well onto the theorization of narrative utopias that occupies Phillip E. Wegner in *Imaginary Communities: Utopia, the Nation, and the Spatial Histories of Modernity* (Berkeley and Los Angeles: University of California Press, 2002).

11. Phillip Wegner, writing about utopian fiction, makes a similar point: "The narrative utopia is a specific kind of representational act, and also a particular way of conceptualizing the world . . . [that] occupies a middle ground between the phenomenological concreteness of the literary aesthetic and the abstract systematicity of the theoretical, working instead to develop . . . a figuration of a space whose lived experience and theoretical perception only later become possible." (Wegner 2002, xviii).

12. The song was included on Harry Belafonte's album *Jump Up Calypso* (RCA LSP-2388) in 1961.

13. In a humorous twist, Ronnie Butler sings of having a notion about this "pagan girl."

14. Sweet Emily's album *Sweet Emily* was released on Stars (CD Star 8100) in 1996. The Baha Men had released their second album, *Kalik,* in 1994, and this album included a number of Junkanoo songs, though it was not a concept album in the same way that *Junkanoo!* was. In 1995, Ira Storr, one of the major singer/songwriters in the Bahamas, released his first solo album, *Island Life* (IS Records CD 6350), which included several Junkanoo tracks as well as some rake-n-scrape-driven songs. His 1996 follow-up album, *Bread and Butter* (Stars Records CD 6300), incorporated even more arrangements drawing on Junkanoo and rake-n-scrape models.

15. *Best of the Best, Volume 1.* Stars (SCD-1290), 1999.

16. Visage's song "I Still Need a Man" was licensed for inclusion on VP Records' *Soca Gold 2003* (VP1690). The band has also played at the Miami Carnival and the Trinidad Carnival.

17. It is also important to remember that Trinidadian and Jamaican expatriates far outnumber Bahamian expatriates, whether in New York, Toronto, or London. As a result, the market for transnational expansion exists for Trinidadian and Jamaican artists in a way not even possible within Bahamian diasporal networks.

18. There are, of course, also a handful of groups that have played together for some time, including the Brilanders, Da Energizers, and the Lassido Boys, but these are, by and large, not professional bands by comparison to, say, Visage or the Falcons.

19. To conceptualize this, consider Ronnie Butler's innovations in the late 1960s as a step toward codifying a popular rake-n-scrape sound. The work of Dr. Offfff, High Voltage, and the Baha Men during the 1980s and early 1990s are the corollary of Ronnie's work, this time focused on Junkanoo.

20. For programming schedules and live streams of broadcasts of Island FM 102.9, see http//www.islandfmonline.com. For ZNS broadcasting schedules and live streams, see http://www.znsbahamas.com.

21. Jah Doctine's MySpace page (http://www.myspace.com/jahdoctrine) includes several videos and downloads that are worth exploring to get a sense of what is going on at the margins of the already marginal musical scene in the Bahamas.

22. "Currently, our Ministry of Tourism spends most of its $91 million budget over-seas. The Ministry of Culture has a $2 million allocation—less than Bahamas Informa-tion Services—and most of that goes to fund the annual Junkanoo parades. The remain-der is used to finance festivals throughout The Bahamas, maintain a "national theatre," and run the National Arts Festival" (Larry Smith, "Culture Wars in the Bahamas," *Ba-hama Pundit* (blog), April 22, 2009, http://www.bahamapundit.com/).

23. Smith wrote two responses, the first of which was published on April 22, 2009 and can be accessed at http://www.bahamapundit.com/2009/04/culture-wars-in-the-baha mas.html. The second response, "More Culture Wars in the Bahamas," was posted on April 29, 2009, and can be accessed at http://www.bahamapundit.com/2009/04/more -culture-wars-in-the-bahamas.html. This second response provides an overview of the funding and granting agencies as well as the established venues such as museums and galleries that form the support network for artists in the Bahamas. It is a bleak list, offer-ing very little support for musicians in particular.

Abrahams, Roger D. 1972. "Christmas and Carnival on Saint Vincent." *Western Folklore* 31/4: 275–89.

———. 2002. Liner notes to *Nevis and St. Kitts: Tea Meetings, Christmas Sports, and The Moonlight Night.* The Alan Lomax Collection: Caribbean Voyage. Cambridge, MA: Rounder Records (Rounder 82161–1731–2).

Accaria-Zavala, Diane, and Rodolfo Popelnik, eds. 2004. *Prospero's Isles: The Presence of the Caribbean in the American Imaginary.* London: Macmillan Caribbean.

Aching, Gerard. 2002. *Masking and Power: Carnival and Popular Culture in the Caribbean.* Minneapolis: University of Minnesota Press.

Adderley, Rosanne Marion. 2006. *"New Negroes From Africa": Slave Trade Abolition and Free African Settlement in the Nineteenth-Century Caribbean.* Bloomington: Indiana University Press.

Albury, Paul. 1984. *The Paradise Island Story.* London: Macmillan Caribbean.

Alexander, M. Jacqui, and Chandra T. Mohanty, eds. 1997. *Feminist Genealogies, Colonial Legacies, Democratic Futures.* New York: Routledge.

Alexander, Robert. J. 2004. *A History of Organized Labor in the English-Speaking West Indies.* Westport, CT: Praeger.

Allahar, Anton L., ed. 2005. *Ethnicity, Class, and Nationalism: Caribbean and Extra-Caribbean Dimensions.* New York: Lexington Books.

Andrews, George Reid. 2004. *Afro-Latin America, 1800–2000.* New York: Oxford University Press.

Appadurai, Arjun. 1996. *Modernity at Large: Cultural Dimensions of Globalization.* Minneapolis: University of Minnesota Press.

Appiah, Kwame Anthony. 2006. *Cosmopolitanism: Ethics in a World of Strangers.* New York: W. W. Norton.

Archibugi, Daniele, ed. 2003. *Debating Cosmopolitics*. New York. Verso.

Armbrister, Ronnie. 2006. Interview with the author, June 8.

Austin-Broos, Diane. 1997. *Jamaica Genesis: Religion and the Politics of Moral Orders*. Chicago: University of Chicago Press.

Averill, Gage. 1997. *A Day for the Hunter, a Day for the Prey*. Chicago: University of Chicago Press.

Bahamas. 1952. *Bahamas: Report for the Years 1950 and 1951*. London: Her Majesty's Stationary Office.

Bahamas. 1959. *Bahamas: Report for the Years 1956 and 1957*. London: Her Majesty's Stationary Office.

Bahamas. 1961. *Bahamas: Report for the Years 1958 and 1959*. London: Her Majesty's Stationary Office.

Bahamas. 1963. *Bahamas: Report for the Years 1960 and 1961*. London: Her Majesty's Stationary Office.

Bahamas. 1965. *Bahamas: Report for the Years 1962 and 1963*. London: Her Majesty's Stationary Office.

Bahamas. 1967. *Bahama Islands: Report for the Years 1964 and 1965*. London: Her Majesty's Stationary Office.

Bahamas Cabinet Office. 1968. *Bahamas: Report for the Years 1966 and 1967*. Nassau, Bahamas: Government Information Services.

Bahamas Cabinet Office. 1972. *Independence for the Commonwealth of the Bahamas: Presented to the Parliament by the Prime Minister, 18th October 1972*. Nassau, Bahamas: Cabinet Office.

Bahamian Anthology: College of the Bahamas. 1983. London: Macmillan Education.

Banfield, Stephen. 2007. "Anglophone Musical Culture in Jamaica." In *Art and Emancipation in Jamaica*. Edited by Tim Barringer, Gillian Forrester, and Barbaro Martinez Ruiz. New Haven, CT: Yale Center for British Art and Yale University Press.

Barry, Tom, Beth Wood, and Deb Preusch, eds. 1984. *The Other side of Paradise: Foreign Control in the Caribbean*. New York: Grove Press.

Baver, Sherrie, and Barbara Deutsch Lynch, eds. 2006. *Beyond Sun and Sand: Caribbean Environmentalisms*. New Brunswick, NJ: Rutgers University Press.

Baxter, Ivy. 1970. *The Arts of an Island: The Development of the Culture and of the Folk and Creative Arts in Jamaica, 1492–1962*. Metuchen, NJ: Scarecrow Press.

Beckwith, Martha. 1969 [1929]. *Black Roadways: A Study of Jamaican Folk Life*. New York: Negro Universities Press.

Bell, Hesketh J. 1893. *Obeah, Witchcraft, in the West Indies*. London: Sampson, Low, Marsten.

Benítez-Rojo, Antonio. 1996. *The Repeating Island: The Caribbean and the Postmodern Perspective*. Translated by James E. Maraniss. Durham, NC: Duke University Press.

Bethel, Clement E. 1978. "Music in the Bahamas: Its Roots, Development, and Personality." M.A. thesis, University of California, Los Angeles.

———. 1983. "From Quadrilles to Junkanoo: Bahamian Music," 81–95. In *Bahamas Handbook and Businessman's Annual*. Nassau, Bahamas: Dupuch.

———. 1991. *Junkanoo: Festival of the Bahamas*. Edited and expanded by Nicolette Bethel. London: MacMillan Caribbean.

Bethel, Nicolette. 2004. "On Cultural Production." *Nassau Guardian*, May 20, p. A7.

Bettelheim, Judith. 1979. "The Afro-Jamaican Jonkonnu festival: Playing the Forces and Operating the Cloth." PhD diss., Yale University.

———. 1988. "Jonkonnu and Other Christmas Masquerades," 39–83. In *Caribbean Festival Arts*. Edited by John W. Nunley and Judith Bettelheim. Seattle: University of Washington Press.

Bhabha, Homi, ed. 1990. *Nation and Narration*. New York: Routledge.

Bilby, Kenneth. 1985a. "Caribbean Crucible." In *Repercussions: A Celebration of African American Music*. Edited by Geoffrey Haydon and Dennis Marks. London: Century Publishing.

———. 1985b. "The Caribbean as a Musical Region." In *Caribbean Contours*. Edited by Sidney Mintz and Sally Price. Baltimore and London: Johns Hopkins University Press.

———. 1999. "Gumbay, Myal, and the Great House: New Evidence on the Religious Background of Jonkonnu in Jamaica." *ACIJ Research Review* 4: 47–70.

———. 2005a. "Christmas with the Ancestors: Jonkonnu and Related Festivities in Jamaica." *Cariso!* Newsletter of the Alton Augustus Adams Music Research Institute (winter), 1–5, 9.

———. 2005b. *True-Born Maroons*. Gainesville: University Press of Florida.

———. 2007. "More Than Met the Eye: African Jamaican Festivities in the Time of Belisario." In *Art and Emancipation in Jamaica*. Edited by Tim Barringer, Gillian Forrester, and Barbaro Martinez Ruiz. New Haven, CT: Yale Center for British Art and Yale University Press.

———. 2008. "An (Un)Natural Mystic in the Air: Images of Obeah in Caribbean Song." Paper presented at the conference *Obeah and Other Powers: The Politics of Caribbean Religion and Healing*, Newcastle University, Newcastle, UK, July.

———. 2010. "Surviving Secularization: Masking the Spirit in the Jankunu (John Canoe) Festivals of the Caribbean and the Southern United States." *New West Indian Guide* 84, nos. 3–4: 179–223.

Bilby, Kenneth, and Daniel Neely. 2009. "The English-Speaking Caribbean: Re-Embodying the Colonial Ballroom," 231–70. In *Creolizing Contradance in the Caribbean*. Edited by Peter Manuel. Philadelphia: Temple University Press.

Block, Alan A. 1998. *Masters of Paradise: Organized Crime and the Internal Revenue Service in the Bahamas*. New Brunswick, NJ: Transaction Publishers.

Boswell, Thomas, and Anderson Chibwa. 1981. *Internal Migration in the Commonwealth of the Bahamas, 1960–1970*. Nassau, Bahamas: Clyde-Berren Associates.

Boyarin, Jonathan. 1994. "Space, Time, and Politics of Memory," 1–27. In *Remapping Memory: The Politics of TimeSpace*. Edited by Jonathan Boyarin. Minneapolis: University of Minnesota Press.

Boym, Svetlana. 2002. *The Future of Nostalgia*. New York: Basic Books.

Bregenzer, John. 1982. *Tryin' to Make It: Adapting to the Bahamas*. Washington, DC: University Press of America.

Brennan, Timothy. 2003. "Cosmopolitanism and Internationalism," 40–50. In *Debating Cosmopolitics*. Edited by Daniele Archibugi. New York: Verso.

Brereton, Bridget. 1982. *A History of Modern Trinidad, 1783–1962*. New York: Heinemann.

Brown, Christopher. 2006. *Moral Capital: The Foundations of British Abolitionism.* Chapel Hill: University of North Carolina Press.

Brown, David. 2003. *Santería Enthroned: Art, Ritual, and Innovation in an Afro-Cuban Religion.* Chicago: University of Chicago Press.

Brown, Wallace. 1969. *The Good Americans: The Loyalists in the American Revolution.* New York: Morrow.

Browning, Barbara. 1998. *Infectious Rhythm: Metaphors of Contagion and the Spread of African Culture.* New York: Routledge.

Bruce, Peter Henry. [1782] 1949. *Bahamian Interlude: Being an Account of Life at Nassau in the Bahama Islands in the 18th Century, Reprinted from the "Memoirs of Peter Henry Bruce, Esq."* With an Introduction by Richard Kent. London: John Culmer.

Bruner, Edward M. 2005. *Culture on Tour: Ethnographies of Travel.* Chicago: University of Chicago Press.

Burnside, Jackson. 2004. "A Tribute to the Obeah Man." *Nassau Guardian,* Social and Community News Section, January 16, p. 1.

Burton, Richard. 1997. *Afro-Creole: Power, Opposition, and Play in the Caribbean.* Ithaca, NY: Cornell University Press.

Butler, Judith, and Gayatri Chakravorty Spivak. 2007. *Who Sings the Nation-State?* New York: Seagull.

Carpentier, Alejo. 2001. *Music in Cuba.* Edited and with an introduction by Timothy Brennan, and translated by Alan West-Durán. Minneapolis: University of Minnesota Press.

Chakrabarty, Dipesh. 2000. *Provincializing Europe: Postcolonial Thought and Historical Difference.* Princeton, NJ: Princeton University Press.

Chamberlain, Mary, ed. 1998. *Caribbean Migration: Globalized Identities.* New York: Routledge.

Charters, Samuel. 1999. *The Day Is So Long and the Wages So Small: Music on a Summer Island.* New York: Marion Boyars.

Chasteen, John Charles. 2004. *National Rhythms, African Roots: The Deep History of Latin American Popular Dance.* Albuquerque: University of New Mexico Press.

Cheah, Pheng, and Bruce Robbins, eds. 1998. *Cosmopolitics: Thinking and Feeling Beyond the Nation.* Minneapolis: University of Minnesota Press.

Clark, Maribeth. 1995. "The Contredanse: That Musical Plague," 61–70. In *Border Crossings: Dance and Boundaries in Society, Politics, Gender, Education, and Technology* (proceedings of the Society of Dance History Scholars)

———. 2002. "The Quadrille as Embodied Musical Experience in 19th Century Paris." *Journal of Musicology* 19/3: 503–26.

Clarke, E. A. 1927. "The John Canoe Festival in Jamaica." *Folklore* 38: 72–75.

Cleare, Angela B. 2007. *History of Tourism in the Bahamas: A Global Perspective.* Self-published at www2.Xlibris.com.

Clifford, James. 1997. *Routes: Travel and Translation in the Late Twentieth Century.* Cambridge, MA: Harvard University Press.

Cluster, Dick, and Rafaél Hernández. 2006. *The History of Havana.* New York: Palgrave.

Conniff, Michael L., and Thomas J. Davis. 1994. *Africa in the Americas: A History of the Black Diaspora.* Buffalo: Caldwell, NJ.: Blackburn Press.

Conzemius, Eduard. 1928. "Ethnographical Notes on the Black Carib (Garif)." *American Anthropologist* New Series 30/2: 183–205.

Corona, Ignacio, and Alejandro Madrid, eds. 2008. *Postnational Musical Identities: Cultural Production, Distribution, and Consumption in a Globalized Scenario.* New York: Lexington Books.

Cowley, John. 1999. *Carnival, Canboulay, and Calypso: Traditions in the Making.* New York: Cambridge University Press.

Crang, Philip. 1997. "Performing the Tourist Product," 137–54. In *Touring Cultures: Transformations of Travel and Theory.* Edited by Chris Rojek and John Urry. New York: Routledge.

Craton, Michael. 1986. *A History of the Bahamas.* 3rd edition. Waterloo, Ontario: San Salvador Press.

———. 1995. "Decoding Pitchy-Patchy: The Roots, Branches and Essence of Junkanoo." *Slavery and Abolition* 16/1: 14–44.

———. 2002. *Pindling: The Life and Times of the First Prime Minister of the Bahamas.* London: Macmillan Caribbean.

———. 2007. *A–Z of Bahamas Heritage.* Oxford: Macmillan Caribbean.

Craton, Michael, and Gail Saunders. 1992. *Islanders in the Stream: A History of the Bahamian People.* Volume 1, *From Aboriginal Times to the End of Slavery.* Athens: University of Georgia Press.

———. 1998. *Islanders in the Stream: A History of the Bahamian People.* Volume 2, *From the Ending of Slavery to the Twenty-first Century.* Athens: University of Georgia Press.

Crouch, David, Rhona Jackson, and Felix Thompson, eds. 2005. *The Media and the Tourist Imagination: Converging Cultures.* New York: Routledge.

Crowley, Daniel, J. 1966. *I Could Talk Old-Story Good: Creativity in Bahamian Folklore.* Berkeley and Los Angeles: University of California Press.

Curry, Robert A. [1928] 1930. *Bahamian Lore.* 2nd edition. Paris: Private printing.

Curtin, Philip. 1969. *The Atlantic Slave Trade: A Census.* Madison: University of Wisconsin Press.

Cyrille, Dominique. 2002. "Popular Music and Martinican-Creole Identity." *Black Music Research Journal* 22/1: 65–83.

———. 2004. "Dance Competition, Tradition, and Change in the Commonwealth of Dominica." *Cariso!* (Newsletter of the Alton Augustus Adams Music Research Institute) Spring: 8–12.

Daaku, Kwame. 1970. *Trade and Politics on the Gold Coast, 1600–1720: A Study of the African Reaction to European Trade.* New York: Oxford.

Dahl, Anthony. 1995. *Literature of the Bahamas, 1724–1992: The March Towards National Independence.* Lanham, MD: University Press of America.

[Dallas, Robert Charles]. 1790. *A Short Journey in the West Indies, in which are interspersed, Curious Anecdotes and Characters.* 2 volumes. London: J. Murray, Fleet Street, and J. Forbes, Covent Garden.

Daniel, Yvonne. 2006. "Come with Me and Let's Talk about Caribbean Quadrilles." *Cariso!* (Newsletter of the Alton Augustus Adams Music Research Institute) 6: 6–12.

Davis, David. 2006. *Inhuman Bondage: The Rise and Fall of Slavery in the New World.* New York: Oxford University Press.

Defries, Amelia. 1917. *In a Forgotten Colony: Life Among the Negroes.* Nassau, Bahamas: Guardian.

DeGarmo, William B. 1870. *The Prompter: Containing Full Descriptions Of All The Quadrilles, Figures Of The German Cotillon, Etc.* New York: Raymond and Caulon.

De Jon, Lythe Orme. 1956. "The Gombeys of Bermuda." *Dance Magazine* 30/5.

de Jong, Nanette. 2003. "An Anatomy of Creolization: Curaçao and the Antillean Waltz." *Latin American Music Review* 24/2: 233–51.

Dirks, Robert, and Virginia Kerns. 1975. "John Canoe." *National Studies* 3/6: 1–15.

Dobbin, Jay D. 1986. *The Jombee Dance of Montserrat.* Columbus: Ohio State University Press.

Dowson, W. [1811] 1960. *A Mission to the West India Islands: Dowson's Journal for 1810–1817.* Nassau, Bahamas: Deans Peggs Research Fund.

Dudley, Shannon. 2007. *Music from Behind the Bridge: Steelband Aesthetics and Politics in Trinidad and Tobago.* New York: Oxford University Press.

Duggan, Ann. 1973. "McKay Show Bursts on Audience with Rage of a Tropical Storm." *Nassau Guardian,* August 10, p. 6.

Edwards, Andrew. 2006. "Bahamian Identity Crisis, Part 1." *Nassau Guardian Weekender,* May 19, p. 10.

Edwards, Bryan. 1801. *A History, Social and Commercial, of the British Colonies in the West Indies.* 3rd edition. 3 volumes. London: John Stockdale.

Edwards, Charles L. [1895] 1942. *Bahama Songs and Stories.* Vol. 3 of *Memoirs of the American Folklore Society.* New York: Houghton, Mifflin and Co. Reprint, New York: G. E. Steckert. Reprint, New York: G. E. Steckert.

Eldridge, Michael. 2002. "There Goes the Transnational Neighborhood: Calypso Buys a Bungalow." *Callaloo* 25/2: 620–638.

Eneas, Franklin ("Count Bernadino"). 2007. Interview with the author, August 9.

Epstein, Dena. 1973. "African Music in British and French America." *Musical Quarterly* 59/1: 61–91.

Farquharson, Charles. [1832] 1957. *A Relic of Slavery: Farquharson's Journal for 1831–32.* Nassau, Bahamas: Deans Peggs Research Fund.

Fiehrer, Thomas. 1991. "From Quadrille to Stomp: The Creole Origins of Jazz." *Popular Music* 10/1: 21–38.

Fitzgerald, Tyrone. 1981. "First Lap." *Junkanoo* August/September/October: 17.

Floyd, Samuel A., Jr. 1996. *The Power of Black Music: Interpreting Its History from Africa to the United States.* New York: Oxford University Press.

———. 1999. "Black Music in the Circum-Caribbean." *American Music* 17/1: 1–38.

Forbes, Monique. 2004. "Junkanoo Queen." *Nassau Guardian,* January 12, p. 1.

Funk, Ray, and Donald Hill. 2007. "Will Calypso Doom Rock 'n' Roll? The U.S. Calypso Craze of 1957," 178–97. In *Trinidad Carnival: The Cultural Politics of a Transnational Festival.* Edited by Garth Green and Philip Scher. Bloomington: Indiana University Press.

Galvin, Peter. 1999. *Patterns of Pillage: A Geography of Caribbean-Based Piracy in Spanish America, 1536–1718.* New York: Peter Lang.

Gibson, Chris, and John Connell, eds. 2005. *Music and Tourism: On the Road Again*. Buffalo, NY: Channel View.

Gillis, John R. 1994. *Commemorations: The Politics of National Identity*. Princeton, NJ: Princeton University Press.

Giordano, Ralph G. 2007. *Social Dancing in America: A History and Reference*. Volume 1, *Fair Terpsichore to the Ghost Dance, 1607–1900*. Westport, CT: Greenwood Press.

Glinton-Meicholas, Patricia. 1993. *An Evening in Guanahani: A Treasure of Folktales from the Bahamas*. Nassau, Bahamas: Guanima Press.

Gmelch, George. 2003. *Behind the Smile: The Working Lives of Caribbean Tourism*. Bloomington: Indiana University Press.

Gomez, Michael A. 2005. *Reversing Sail: A History of the African Diaspora*. New York: Cambridge University Press.

Graves, John. 1708. *A Memorial or Short Account of the Bahama Islands: of their situation, product, conveniency of trading with the Spaniards . . . deliver'd to the lords proprietors of the said islands and the honourable Commissioners of Her Majesty's Customs by John Graves, collector of Her Majesty's customs in those islands, and now humbly presented to both houses of Parliament*. London: Colonial Administration.

Green, Garth L., and Philip W. Scher. 2007. *Trinidad Carnival: The Cultural Politics of a Transnational Festival*. Bloomington: Indiana University Press.

Greene, Oliver. 2007. *Play, Jankunú Play: The Garifuna Wanaragua Ritual of Belize* (Film/DVD). Watertown, MA: Documentary Educational Resources.

Guilbault, Jocelyne. 1985. "A St. Lucian Kwadril Evening." *Latin American Music Review* 6/1: 31–57.

———. 1993. "Musical Traditions of St. Lucia, West Indies." Liner notes for *Musical Traditions of St. Lucia, West Indies*. Smithsonian/Folkways (SF 40416).

———. 2007. *Governing Sound: The Cultural Politics of Trinidad's Carnival Musics*. Chicago: University of Chicago Press.

Hagedorn, Katherine. 2001. *Divine Utterances: The Performance of Afro-Cuban Santería*. Washington, DC: Smithsonian Institution Press.

Hall, Catherine. 1996. "Histories, Empires, and the Post-Colonial Moment," 65–77. In *The Post-Colonial Question: Common Skies, Divided Horizons*. Edited by Iain Chambers and Lidia Curti. New York: Routledge.

Hall, Gwendolyn Midlo. 2005. *Slavery and African Ethnicities in the Americas: Restoring the Links*. Chapel Hill: University of North Carolina Press.

Hall, Stuart. 2001. *New Caribbean Thought: A Reader*. Kingston: University of the West Indies Press.

Handler, Jerome, and Ken Bilby. 2001. "On the Early Use and Origin of the Term "Obeah" in Barbados and the Anglophone Caribbean." *Slavery and Abolition* 22: 87–100.

———. 2004. "Obeah: Healing and Protection in West Indian Slave Life." *Journal of Caribbean History* 38: 153–83.

Hanna, Stephen, and Vincent Del Casino Jr., eds. 2003. *Mapping Tourism*. Minneapolis: University of Minnesota Press.

Hart, A., and R. Kent. 1948. *Letters from the Bahama Islands, written in 1823–4*. London: J. Culmer.

Hedrick, Basil C., and Cezarija Abartis Letson. 1975. *Once Was a Time, a Wery Good Time: An Inquiry into the Folklore of the Bahamas.* Greely: University of Northern Colorado, Museum of Anthropology, Miscellaneous Series, No. 38.

Hedrick, Basil C., and Jeanette E. Stephens. 1976. *In the Days of Yesterday and in the Days of Today: An Overview of Bahamian Folkmusic.* University Museum Studies, No. 8. Carbondale: University Museum, Southern Illinois University.

———. 1977. *It's a Natural Fact: Obeah in the Bahamas.* Museum of Anthropology Miscellaneous Series, No. 39. University of Northern Colorado Museum of Anthropology.

Hernandez, Deborah Pacini. 1995. *Bachata: A Social History of Dominican Popular Music.* Philadelphia: Temple University Press.

Herzfeld, Michael. 1997. *Cultural Intimacy: Social Poetics in the Nation-State.* New York: Routledge.

Hill, Donald. 1993. *Calypso Calaloo: Early Carnival Music in Trinidad.* Gainesville: University of Florida Press.

Hobsbawm, Eric, and Terence Ranger, eds. 1992. *The Invention of Tradition.* New York: Cambridge University Press.

Horne, Gerald C. 2007. *Cold War in a Hot Zone: The United States Confronts Labor and Independence Struggles in the British West Indies.* Philadelphia: Temple University Press.

Howard, Rosalyn. 2002. *Black Seminoles in the Bahamas.* Gainesville: University Press of Florida.

Howe, Elias. 1858. *Howe's Complete Ball-Room Hand Book.* Boston, New York, and Philadephia: Ditson and Co.

Hughes, Colin A. 1981. *Race and Politics in the Bahamas.* New York: St. Martin's Press.

Hurston, Zora Neale. 1930. "Dance Songs and Tales From the Bahamas." *Journal of American Folklore* 43/169 (July–September): 294–312.

Ives, Charles. 1880. *Isles of Summer: Or Nassau and the Bahamas.* New Haven, CT: Self-published.

Johnson, Charles [Daniel Defoe]. 1724. *A General History of the Pyrates.* London. Reprint, Nabu Press, 2010.

Johnson, Howard. 1988. "Bahamian Labor Migration to Florida in the Late Nineteenth and Early Twentieth Centuries." *International Migration Review* 22/1: 84–103.

———. 1991. *The Bahamas in Slavery and Freedom.* Kingston, Jamaica: Ian Randle.

———. 1996. *The Bahamas from Slavery to Servitude, 1783–1933.* Gainesville: University Press of Florida.

Johnson, Sara E. 2005. "Cinquillo Consciousness: The Formation of a Pan-Caribbean Musical Aesthetic." In *Music, Writing, and Cultural Unity in the Caribbean.* Edited by Timothy Reiss. Trenton, NJ: Africa World Press.

Johnson, Whittington B. 2000. *Race Relations in the Bahamas, 1784–1843: The Nonviolent Transformation from a Slave to a Free Society.* Fayetteville: University of Arkansas Press.

Junkanoo Symposium. 2003. *Junkanoo and Religion: Christianity and Cultural Identity in the Bahamas.* Papers presented at the Junkanoo Symposium, March 2002. Nassau, Bahamas: Media Enterprises.

Justilien, Christian. 2003. "Junkanoo Music," 111–14. In *Junkanoo and Religion: Christianity and Cultured Identity in the Bahamas*. Papers presented at the Junkanoo Symposium, March 2002. Nassau, Bahamas: Media Enterprises.

———. 2004. "Musicians and Entertainers of the Bahamas: An Interactive Anthology." M.M. ed. thesis, VanderCook College of Music, Chicago.

Justilien, Yonell. 2004. "Bahamas Junkanoo Music: Its History, Instruments, and Notation." M.M. ed. thesis, VanderCook College of Music, Chicago.

Keegan, William F. 1992. *The People Who Discovered Columbus: The Prehistory of the Bahamas*. Gainesville: University Press of Florida.

Kincaid, Jamaica. 2000. *A Small Place*. New York: Farrar, Straus and Giroux.

Kirshenblatt-Gimblett, Barbara. 1998. *Destination Culture: Tourism, Museums, and Heritage*. Berkeley and Los Angeles: University of California Press.

Klak, Thomas, ed. 1997. *Globalization and Neoliberalism: The Caribbean Context*. Lanham, MD: Rowman and Littlefield.

Krims, Adam. 2007. *Music and Urban Geography*. New York: Routledge.

LaFlamme, Alan G. 1985. *Green Turtle Cay: An Island in the Bahamas*. Prospect Heights, IL: Waveland Press.

Lane, Kris. 1998. *Pillaging the Empire: Piracy in the Americas, 1500–1750*. New York: M. E. Sharpe.

Leaf, Earl. 1948. *Isles of Rhythm*. New York: A. S. Barnes.

Lewin, Olive. 1968. "Jamaican Folk Music." *Caribbean Quarterly* 14: 49–56.

———. 2000. *Rock It Come Over: The Folk Music of Jamaica*. Mona, Jamaica: University of West Indies Press.

Liverpool, Hollis. 2001. *Rituals of Power and Rebelion: The Carnival Tradition in Trinidad and Tobago, 1763–1962*. Chicago: Research Associates School Times.

Lomer, Gordon. 2002. "Rake 'n scrape—Music for the Soul," 125–40. In *Bahamas Handbook and Businessman's Annual*. Nassau, Bahamas: Dupuch.

Long, Edward. 1774. *The History of Jamaica; or, General Survey of the Ancient and Modern State of that Island, with Reflections on its Situation, Settlement, Inhabitants, Climate, Productions, Commerce, Laws, and Government*. 3 volumes in 2. London: T Lowndes.

Manning, Frank E. 1973. *Black Clubs in Bermuda: Ethnography of a Play World*. Ithaca, NY: Cornell University Press.

Marks, Morton. 1974. "Uncovering Ritual Structures in Afro-American Music," 60–134. In *Religious Movements in Contemporary America*. Edited by Irving Zaretsky and Mark P. Leone. Princeton, NJ: Princeton University Press.

Marshall, Dawn I. 1979. *The Haitian Problem: Illegal Migration to the Bahamas*. St. Augustine: University of the West Indies Press, Institute for Social and Economic Research.

Maynard, Clement T. 2007. *Put On More Speed: A Bahamian Journey to Majority Rule and Sovereignty, Memoirs*. Volume 1. Nassau, Bahamas: I. Ease Publishack.

Mbembe, Achille. 2001. *On the Postcolony*. Berkeley and Los Angeles: University of California Press.

McAlister, Elizabeth. 2002. *Rara! Vodou, Power, and Performance in Haiti and Its Diaspora*. Berkeley and Los Angeles: University of California Press.

McCartney, Donald M. 2004. *Bahamian Culture and Factors Which Impact Upon It: A Compilation of Two Essays.* Pittsburgh: Dorrance Publishing.

McCartney, John T. 2001. "The Influences of the Black Panther Party (USA) on the Vanguard Party of the Bahamas, 1972–1987," 156–65. In *Liberation, Imagination, and the Black Panther Party: A New Look at the Panthers and Their Legacy.* Edited by Kathleen Cleaver and George Katsiaficas. New York: Routledge.

McDaniel, Lorna. 1998. "Grenada (and Carriacou)," 864–72. In *Garland Encyclopedia of World Music.* Volume 2, *South America, Mexico, Central America, and the Caribbean.* Edited by Dale Olsen and Daniel Sheehy. New York: Garland Publishing.

McGeary, Johanna, and Cathy Booth. 1993. "Cuba Alone" *Time* magazine, December 6. Available online at http://www.time.com/time/magazine/article/0,9171,979762,00.html.

McKinnen, D. 1804. *A tour through the British West Indies in the years 1802 and 1803 giving a particular account of the Bahama Islands.* London: J. White.

Michel, Claudine, and Patrick Bellegarde-Smith, eds. 2006. *Invisible Powers: Vodou in Haitian Life and Culture.* New York: Palgrave Macmillan.

Miller, Rebecca. 2000. "The People Like Melée: The Parang Festival of Carriacou, Grenada." PhD diss., Brown University.

———. 2005. "Performing Ambivalence: The Case of Quadrille Music and Dance in Carriacou, Grenada." *Ethnomusicology* 49/3: 403–40.

———. 2007. *Carriacou String Band Serenade: Performing Identity in the Eastern Caribbean.* Middletown, CT: Wesleyan University Press.

Minca, Claudio, and Tim Oakes, eds. 2006. *Travels in Paradox: Remapping Tourism.* New York: Rowman and Littlefield.

Minns, Eric. 1981. *Island Boy: A Novel.* Nassau, Bahamas: Loric Publishers.

Mintz, Sidney W. 1974. *Caribbean Transformations.* Chicago: Aldine.

Mintz, Sidney W., and Richard Price. 1992 [1976]. *The Birth of African-American Culture: An Anthropological Perspective.* Boston: Beacon Press.

Morison, Samuel Eliot, ed. 1963. *Journals and Other Documents on the Life and Voyages of Christopher Columbus.* Translated by Samuel Eliot Morison. New York: Heritage Press.

Moxey, Edmund. 1964. "Munnings Is Musician of the Year." *Nassau Guardian,* January 17, p. 3.

———. 2007. Interview with the author, August 11.

Muir, Elspeth. 1955. "Nassau's Jungle Queen Is Dancing Sprite." *Nassau Guardian,* January 9, p. 2.

Munnings, H. W. 1981. "Dr. Offff." *Junkanoo* August/September/October: 15–16.

Nash-Ferguson, Arlene. 2000. *I Come to Get Me.* Nassau, Bahamas: Doongalik Studios.

Nettleford, Rex. 1993. *Inward Stretch, Outward Reach: A Voice from the Caribbean.* London: Macmillan Press.

Nurse, Keith. 1999. "Globalization and Trinidad Carnival: Diaspora, Hybridity, and Identity in Global Culture." *Cultural Studies* 13/4: 661–90.

Olaniyan, Tejumola. 2001. "The Cosmopolitan Nativist: Fela Anikulapo-Kuti and the Antinomies of Postcolonial Modernity." *Research in African Literatures* 32/2: 76–89.

Oldmixon, John. 1949. *The History of the Isle of Providence*. Nassau: Providence Press. Excerpted from John Oldmixon, *The British Empire in America*, 2 vols. (London: Botherton and Clarke, 1741).

Olmos, Margarite Fernandez, and Lizabeth Paravisini-Gerbert, eds. 1997. *Sacred Possessions: Voodoo, Obeah, Santería, and the Caribbean*. New Brunswick, NJ: Rutgers University Press.

Parsons, Alan. 1926. *A Winter in Paradise*. London : A.M. Philpot.

Parsons, Elsie Clews. 1918. *Folk-Tales of Andros Island, Bahamas*. New York: American Folk-lore Society.

Pascoe, C.F. 1901. *Two Hundred Years of the S.P.G.: An Historical Account of the Society for the Propagation of the Gospel in Foreign Parts, 1701–1900*. London: Society's Office.

Patterson, Orlando. 1969. *The Sociology of Slavery: An Analysis of the Origins, Development, and Structure of Negro Slave Society in Jamaica*. Madison, NJ: Fairleigh Dickinson University Press.

Patullo, Polly. 2005. *Last Resorts: The Cost of Tourism in the Caribbean*. 2nd edition. New York: Monthly Review Press.

Pennell, C.R., ed. 2001. *Bandits at Sea: A Pirates Reader*. New York: New York University Press.

Perpall, Viraj. 2006. "Our Music Needs a Wider Audience." *Nassau Guardian*, March 15, p. 1.

Pindling, Lynden. 2000. "I am a Junkanoo." *Nassau Guardian*, September 1, p. 1.

Pintard, Michael C. 1995. *Still Standing*. Nassau, Bahamas: Guanima Press.

Powles, L.D. 1888. *The Land of the Pink Pearl, or Recollections of Life in the Bahamas*. London: Sampson, Low, Marston, Searle, and Rivington.

Prokopow, Michael J. 1996. *"To the Torrid Zones": The Fortunes and Misfortunes of American Loyalists in the Anglo-Caribbean Basin, 1774–1801*. PhD diss., Harvard University.

Rabinow, Paul. 2008. *Marking Time: On the Anthropology of the Contemporary*. Princeton, NJ: Princeton University Press.

Rahming. Patrick. 1992. *The Naïve Agenda: Social and Political Issues for the Bahamas*. Nassau, Bahamas: Patrick Rahming.

Randall, Stephen J., and Graeme S. Mount. 1998. *The Caribbean Basin: An International History*. New York: Routledge.

Rediker, Marcus. 1987. *Between the Devil and the Deep Blue Sea: Merchant Seamen, Pirates, and the Anti-American Maritime World, 1700–1750*. Cambridge: Cambridge University Press.

Reid, Ira de A. 1942. "The John Canoe Festival: A New World Africanism." *Phylon* 3/4: 349–70.

Rojek, Chris, and John Urry, eds. 1997. *Touring Cultures: Transformations of Travel and Theory*. New York: Routledge.

Rommen, Timothy. 1999. "Home Sweet Home": Junkanoo as National Discourse in the Bahamas." *Black Music Research Journal* 19/1 (Spring): 71–92.

———. 2007. *Mek Some Noise: Gospel Music and the Ethics of Style in Trinidad*. Berkeley and London: University of California Press.

———. 2009. "Come Back Home": Regional Travels, Global Encounters, and Local Nostaligas in Bahamian Popular Musics." *Latin American Music Review* 30/2: 159–83.

Rutherford, Thea. 2004. "Bringing Culture to the Tourism Market." *Nassau Guardian*, October 14, p. 1.

Sands, Rosita. 1989. "Conversation with Maureen 'Bahama Mama' DuValier and Ronald Simms: Junkanoo Past, Present, and Future." *Black Perspective in Music* 17 (1/2): 93–108.

Sands, Stafford. 1960. "Tourism, the Tide that Washes in Prosperity," 177–96. *Bahamas Handbook and Businessman's Annual*. Nassau, Bahamas: Dupuch.

Saunders, Gail. 1983. *Bahamian Loyalists and Their Slaves*. London: Macmillan Caribbean.

———. 1985. *Slavery in the Bahamas, 1648–1838*. Nassau, Bahamas: Nassau Guardian.

———. 1994. *Bahamian Society After Emancipation*. Kingston, Jamaica: Ian Randle Publishers.

———. 1997. "The Changing Face of Nassau: The Impact of Tourism on Bahamian Society in the 1920s and 1930s." *New West Indian Guide/Nieuwe West-Indische Gids* 71,1/2: 21–42.

———. 2003a. *Bahamian Society after Emancipation*. Revised edition. Princeton, NJ: M. Wiener.

———. 2003b. Foreword to *Junkanoo and Religion: Christianity and Cultural Identity in the Bahamas*. Papers presented at the Junkanoo Symposium, March 2002. Nassau, Bahamas: Media Enterprises.

———. 2006. "Entertainment and Entertainers in the 1930s" *Nassau Guardian*, Lifestyles. June 9, n.p.

Saunders, Inderia. 2007. "'The Reef' Officially Opens." *Nassau Guardian*, December 20, p. 1.

Savishinsky, Joel. 1978. *Strangers No More: Anthropological Studies of Cat Island, the Bahamas*. Ithaca, NY: Ithaca College Anthropology Department.

Schoepf, Johann David. 1911 [1788]. *Travels in the Confederation, 1783–84*. Volume 2. Translated by Alfred J. Morrison. Philadelphia: William J. Campbell.

Sheehy, Daniel E. 1998. "The Virgin Islands," 968–74. In *Garland Encyclopedia of World Music*. Volume 2, *South America, Mexico, Central America, and the Caribbean*. Edited by Dale Olsen and Daniel Sheehy. New York: Garland Publishing.

Sheller, Mimi. 2003. *Consuming the Caribbean: From Arawaks to Zombies*. New York: Routledge.

Sheller, Mimi, and John Urry. 2004. *Tourism Mobilities: Places to Play, Places in Play*. New York: Routledge.

Shepherd, Verene A. 2005. "The Ranking Game in Jamaica during Slavery." *Arts Journal* (Guyana) 1/2: 3–15.

Simpson, George Eaton. 1940. "Peasant Songs of Northern Haiti." *Journal of Negro History* 25/2: 203–15.

Sloane, Hans. 1707. *A Voyage to the Islands, Madera, Barbados, Nieves, St Christophers and Jamaica with the Natural History of the Herbs and Trees, Four-footed Beasts, Fishes, Birds, Insects, Reptiles, etc, Of the Last of Those Islands, to which is prefix'd an introduction, wherein is an account of the inhabitants, air, waters, diseases, trade, Etc, of that place, with some relations concerning the neighbouring continent, and islands of America. Illustrated with figures of the things described, which have not been heretofore engraved; in large copper-plates as big as the life*. 2 volumes. London: Printed by BM for the author.

Smith, Melanie K. 2003. *Issues in Cultural Tourism Studies*. New York: Routledge.

Stark, James H. 1891. *Stark's History and Guide to the Bahama Islands*. London: J. H. Stark.

Stewart, John. 1808. *An Account of Jamaica, and Its Inhabitants*. London: Printed for Longman, Hurst, Rees and Orme.

———. 1823. *View of the Island of Jamaica*. Edinburgh: Oliver and Boyd.

Storr, Juliette. 2000. "Changes and Challenges: A History of the Development of Broadcasting in the Commonwealth of the Bahamas, 1930–1980." PhD diss., Ohio University.

Strachan, Ian Gregory. 2002. *Paradise and Plantation: Tourism and Culture in the Anglophone Caribbean*. Charlottesville: University of Virginia Press.

Stuckey, Sterling. 1987. *Slave Culture: Nationalist Theory and the Foundations of Black America*. New York: Oxford University Press.

Stuempfle, Stephen. 1996. *The Steelband Movement: The Forging of a National Art in Trinidad and Tobago*. Philadelphia: University of Pennsylvania Press.

Szwed, John, and Morton Marks. 1988. "The African American Transformation of European Set Dances and Dance Suites." *Dance Research Journal* 20/1: 29–36.

Taussig, Michael. 1993. *Mimesis and Alterity*. New York: Routledge.

Taylor, Charles. 2004. *Modern Social Imaginaries*. Durham, NC: Duke University Press.

Taylor, Naomi. 1969. "Occupation: Fire Dancer," 40–47. *Bahamas Handbook and Businessman's Annual*. Nassau, Bahamas: Dupuch.

Taylor, Patrick. 2001. *Nation Dance: Religion, Identity, and Cultural Difference in the Caribbean*. Bloomington: Indiana University Press.

Thomas, Deborah A. 2002. "Democratizing Dance: Institutional Transformation and Hegemonic Re-Ordering in Postcolonial Jamaica." *Cultural Anthropology* 17/4: 512–50.

———. 2004. *Modern Blackness: Nationalism, Globalization, and the Politics of Culture in Jamaica*. Durham, NC: Duke University Press.

Thompson, Cordell. 1967a. "Another UNICOLL Discussion: Goombay and Calypso—Our Only True Sounds." *Nassau Guardian*, August 5, Section B, p. 3.

———. 1967b. "Bahamian Music—What It Was—What It Is Now—Where It Is Headed." *Nassau Guardian*, August 5, Section B, p. 1.

Tinker, Keith L. 1998. "Perspectives on West Indian Migration to the Bahamas: Pre-Columbian to Bahamian Independence in 1973." PhD diss., Florida State University.

Torres, Arlene, and Norman E. Whitten Jr., eds. 1998. *Blackness in Latin America and the Caribbean: Social Dynamics and Cultural Transformations*. Bloomington: Indiana University Press.

Townsend, P. S. [1823–24] 1968. *The Diary of a Physician from the United States Visiting the Island of New Providence: Nassau, Bahamas, 1823-4*. Nassau: Bahamas Historical Society.

Trouillot, Michel-Rolph. 1995. *Silencing the Past: Power and the Production of History*. Boston: Beacon Press.

———. 2002. "Culture on the Edges: Caribbean Creolization in Historical Context." In *From the Margins: Historical Anthropology and Its Futures*. Edited by Brian Keith Axel. Durham and London: Duke University Press.

———. 2003. *Global Transformations: Anthropology in the Modern World*. New York: Palgrave Macmillan.

Wagner, Christoph, ed. 2001. *Das Akkordeon oder die Erfindung der populären Music.* New York: Schott.

Walcott, Derek. 1992. *The Antilles: Fragments of Epic Memory: The Nobel Lecture.* New York: Farrar, Straus and Giroux.

Warren, Edward. 1885. *A Doctor's Experience in Three Continents.* Baltimore: Cashings and Bailey.

Wegner, Phillip E. 2002. *Imaginary Communities: Utopia, the Nation, and the Spatial Histories of Modernity.* Berkeley and Los Angeles: University of California Press.

Wells, Michelle. 2004. "Face to Face with Visage." *Nassau Guardian Weekender,* July 30, p. 1.

Wilkinson, Henry Campbell. 1958. *The Adventurers of Bermuda: A History of the Island from Its Discovery until the Dissolution of the Somers Island Company in 1684.* New York: Oxford University Press.

Williams, Colbert. 1982. *The Methodist Contribution to Education in the Bahamas, 1790–1975.* Gloucester, UK: Alan Sutton.

Wilson, Peter J. 1973. *Crab Antics: The Social Anthropology of English-Speaking Negro Societies of the Caribbean.* New Haven, CT: Yale University Press.

Wilson, T. 1816. *The Treasures of Terpsichore, or A Collection of the Most Popular English Country Dances.* 2nd edition. London: Sherwood, Neely and Jones.

Wisdom, Keith Gordon. 1985. "Bahamian Junkanoo: An Act in a Modern Social Drama." PhD diss., University of Georgia.

Wood, Vivian Nina Michelle. 1995. "Rushin' Hard and Runnin' Hot: Experiencing the Music of the Junkanoo Parade in Nassau, Bahamas." PhD diss., Indiana University.

———. 1998. "The Bahamas," 801–12. In *Garland Encyclopedia of World Music.* Volume 2, *South America, Mexico, Central America, and the Caribbean.* Edited by Dale Olsen and Daniel Sheehy. New York: Garland Publishing.

———. 2004. "Ecstasy in Junkanoo: A Public Celebration of Freedom, 76–78. In *1994 Festival of American Folklife.* Washington, DC: Smithsonian Institution.

———. 2007. "Bahamas Junkanoo Revue: Junkanoo Costumes." Historical Museum of Southern Florida. http://www.historical-museum.org/folklife/flafolk/junkanoo.htm.

Wright, James Martin. 1905. *History of the Bahamas, with a Special Study of the Abolition of Slavery in the Colony.* Baltimore: Geographical Society of Baltimore.

Wright, Richardson. 1937. *Revels in Jamaica, 1682–1838.* New York: Dodd, Mead.

Young, Thomas. 1842. *Narrative of a Residence on the Mosquito Shore, During the Years 1839, 1840, and 1841.* London: Smith, Elder and Co.

Young, William. 1801. "A Tour Through the Several Islands of Barbados, St. Vincent, Antigua, Tobago, and Grenada in the Years 1791 and 1792," 241–84. In *History, Civil, and Commercial, of the British Colonies in the West Indies,* volume 3. By Bryan Edwards. 3rd edition. London: John Stockdale.

TEXT
10/12.5 Minion Pro

DISPLAY
Minion Pro

COMPOSITOR
Westchester Book Group

PRINTER AND BINDER
IBT Global